BLUE EXORCIST

6

KAZUE KATO

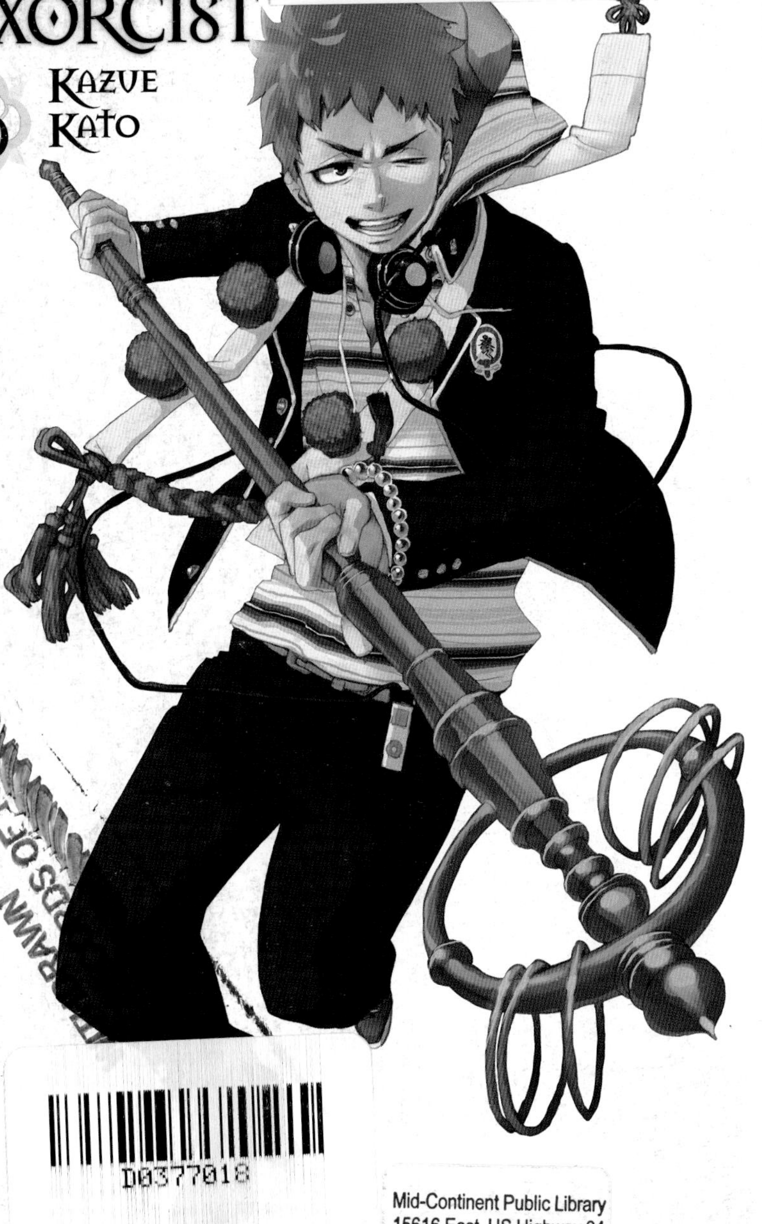

Blue Exorcist

Affliction & Ommisciono

Contents 6

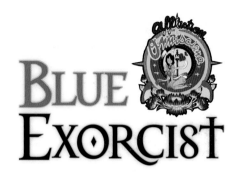

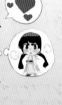

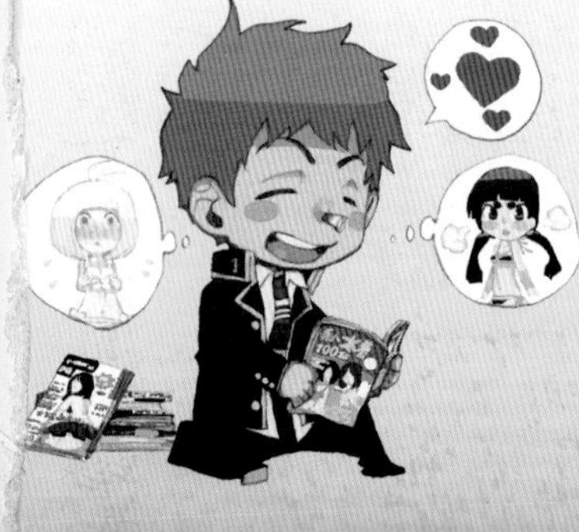

CAST OF CHARACTERS

KNIGHTS OF THE TRUE CROSS

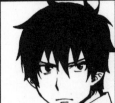

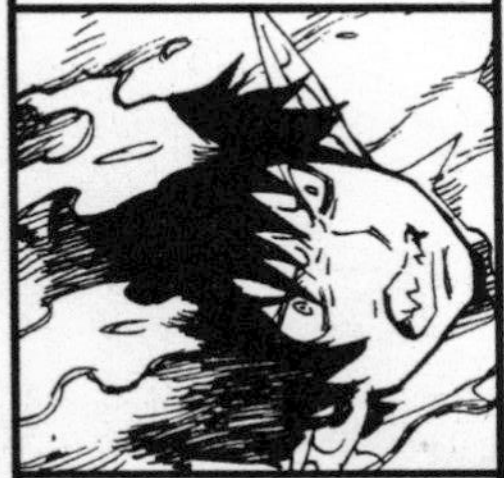

RIN OKUMURA

Born of a human mother and Satan, the God of Demons, Rin Okumura has powers he can barely control. After Satan kills Father Shiro Fujimoto, Rin's foster father, Rin decides to become an Exorcist so he can someday defeat Satan. Now a first-year student at True Cross Academy and an Exwire at the Exorcism Cram School, he hopes to someday become a Knight. When he draws the Koma Sword that Shiro gave him, he manifests his infernal power in the form of blue flames. He is currently training for the Exorcist Certification Exam, which he must pass in six months.

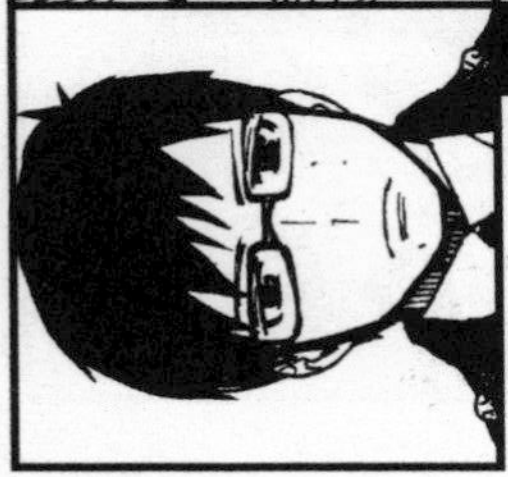

YUKIO OKUMURA

Rin's brother. He wants to become a doctor. He's a genius who is the youngest student ever to become an instructor at the Exorcism Cram School. The subject he teaches is Demon Pharmaceuticals. He possesses the titles of Doctor and Dragoon.

SHIEMI MORIYAMA

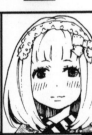

Daughter of the owner of Futsumaya, an Exorcist supply shop. Inspired by Rin and Yukio, she became an Exwire and hopes to someday become an Exorcist. She possesses the ability to become a Tamer and can summon a baby Greenman.

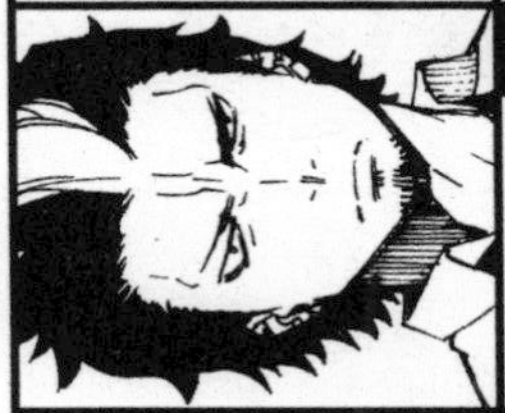

RYUJI SUGURO

Heir to the venerable Buddhist sect known as Myodha in Kyoto. He is an Exwire who hopes to become an Exorcist someday so he can reestablish his family's temple, which fell on hard times after the Blue Night. He wants to achieve the titles of Dragoon and Aria.

RENZO SHIMA

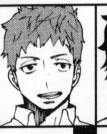

Once a pupil of Suguro's father and now Suguro's friend. He's an Exwire who wants to become an Aria. He has an easygoing personality and is totally girl-crazy.

KONEKOMARU MIWA

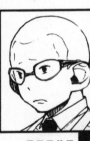

Like Shima, he was once a pupil of Suguro's father and is now Suguro's friend. He's an Exwire who hopes to become an Exorcist someday. He is small in size and has a quiet and composed personality.

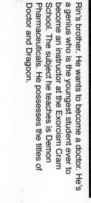

IZUMO KAMIKI

An Exwire with the blood of shrine maidens. She has the ability to become a Tamer and can summon two white foxes. Her friend Paku quit school, but she has continued attending.

SHURA KIRIGAKURE

An upper-rank special investigator dispatched by Vatican Headquarters to True Cross Academy. She's a Senior Exorcist First Class who holds the titles of Knight, Tamer, Doctor and Aria. She watches Rin to make sure he doesn't use his flame.

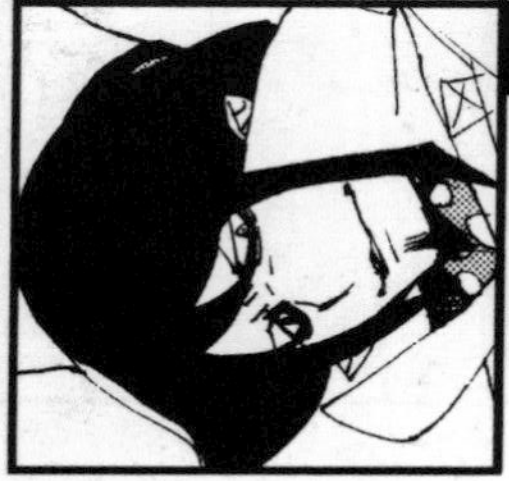

MEPHISTO PHELES

President of True Cross Academy and head of the Exorcism Cram School. He was Father Fujimoto's friend, and now he is Rin and Yukio's guardian. He plans to turn Rin into a weapon for use in the fight against Satan.

SHIRO FUJIMOTO

The man who raised Rin and Yukio. He held the rank of Paladin and once taught Demon Pharmaceuticals. Satan possessed him and he gave his life defending Rin.

KURO

A Cat Sidhe who was once Shiro's familiar. After Shiro's death, he began turning back into a demon. Rin saved him, and now the two are practically inseparable. His favorite drink is the catnip wine Shiro used to make.

TATSUMA SUGURO

Ryuji's father and the leader of the Myodha sect. He doesn't appear to be doing anything to rebuild his temple. People consider him to be an immoral monk, and Ryuji is disgusted with him.

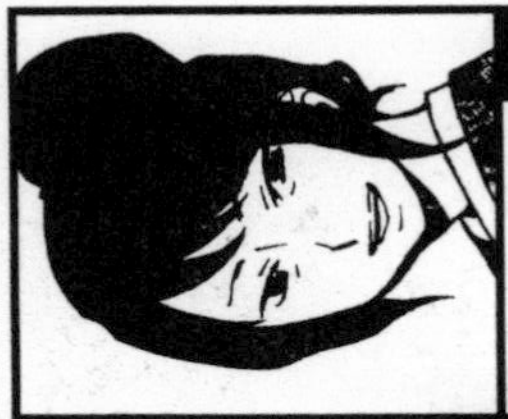

TORAKO SUGURO

Ryuji's mother. She runs the Toraya Inn and secretly uses the proceeds from it to prop up the family temple.

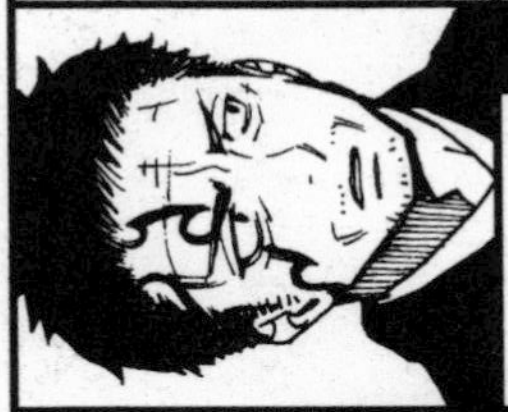

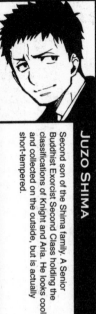

YAOZO SHIMA

Renzo's father. A Senior Buddhist Exorcist First Class holding the classifications of Knight and Aria. In Myodha, he is an Archpriest, one rank beneath Tatsuma.

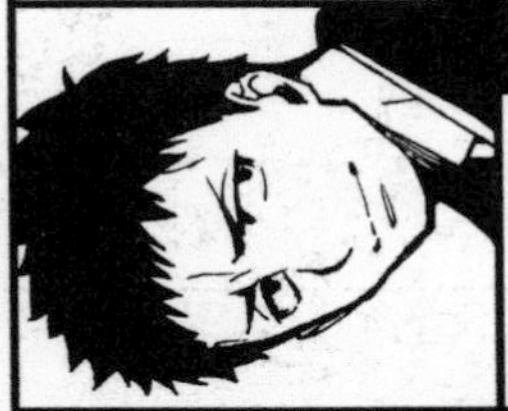

JUZO SHIMA

Second son of the Shima family. A Senior Buddhist Exorcist Second Class holding the classifications of Knight and Aria. He looks cool and collected on the outside, but is actually short-tempered.

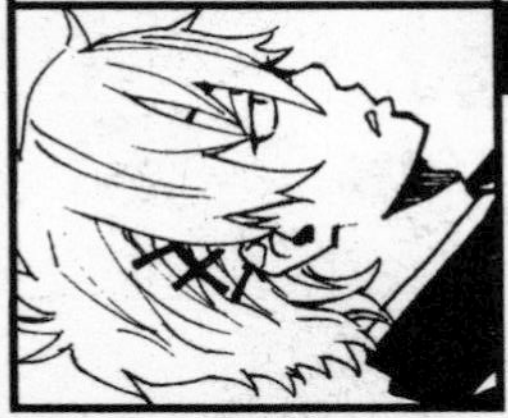

KINZO SHIMA

The fourth son of the Shima family. An Intermediate Buddhist Exorcist Second Class holding the classifications of Knight and Aria. Like Juzo, he's always ready for a fight.

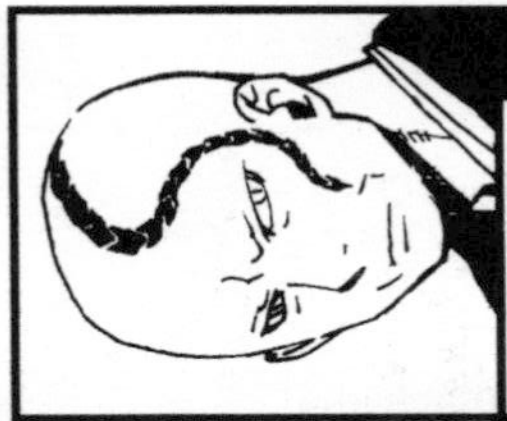

UWABAMI HOJO

A Senior Buddhist Exorcist First Class holding the classifications of Tamer and Aria. Like Yaozo, he is an Archpriest helping lead the Myodha sect.

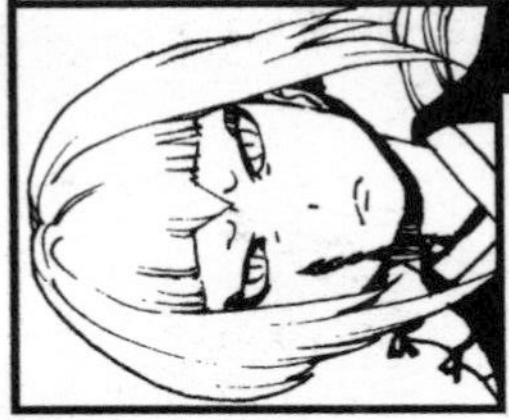

MAMUSHI HOJO

An Intermediate Buddhist Exorcist First Class holding the classifications of Tamer and Aria. She can summon Nagas into her hands. She is at odds with the Shima boys, who also come from a bloodline of archpriests.

DEMONS

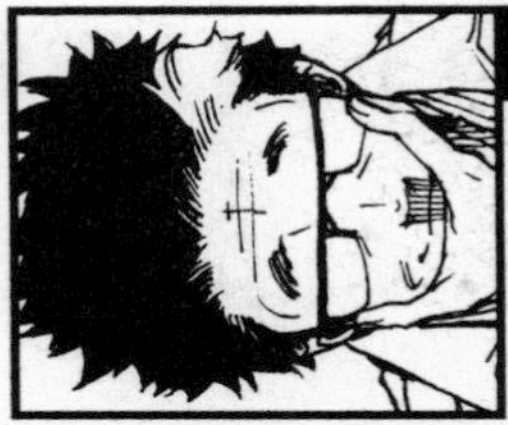

SABUROTA TODO

He comes from an honorable family that has supplied the Order with Exorcists for generations. However, he has joined the demons and stolen the Left Eye of the Impure King. The Order has revoked his Exorcist's License and issued a warrant for his arrest.

◉ THE STORY SO FAR ◉

UNKNOWN TO RIN OKUMURA, BOTH HUMAN AND DEMON BLOOD RUNS IN HIS VEINS. IN AN ARGUMENT WITH HIS FOSTER FATHER, FATHER FUJIMOTO, RIN LEARNS THAT SATAN IS HIS TRUE FATHER. SATAN SUDDENLY APPEARS AND TRIES TO DRAG RIN DOWN TO GEHENNA BECAUSE RIN HAS INHERITED HIS POWER. FATHER FUJIMOTO FIGHTS TO DEFEND RIN, BUT DIES IN THE PROCESS. RIN DECIDES TO BECOME AN EXORCIST SO HE CAN SOMEDAY DEFEAT SATAN AND BEGINS STUDYING AT THE EXORCISM CRAM SCHOOL UNDER THE INSTRUCTION OF HIS TWIN BROTHER YUKIO, WHO IS ALREADY AN EXORCIST.

IT IS NOW SUMMER VACATION, BUT THE EXORCISM CRAM SCHOOL STUDENTS MUST UNDERGO A SPECIAL TRAINING CAMP IN THE WOODS. AFTER A DIFFICULT TEST AND A FRIGHTENING ENCOUNTER WITH AMAIMON, EVERYONE LEARNS THAT RIN IS THE SON OF SATAN. RIN IS FORCED TO APPEAR AS EVIDENCE AT AN INQUIRY OF MEPHISTO BY THE KNIGHTS OF THE TRUE CROSS. THE COURT LETS RIN GO ON THE CONDITION THAT HE PASS THE EXORCIST CERTIFICATION EXAM IN SIX MONTHS. UNDER THE SUPERVISION OF SHURA AND YUKIO, HE BEGINS LEARNING TO CONTROL HIS FLAME.

ON THE FIRST DAY OF TRAINING, SOMEONE STEALS THE LEFT EYE OF THE IMPURE KING FROM THE ACADEMY'S DEEP KEEP AND YUKIO GETS A PHONE CALL INFORMING HIM OF AN EMERGENCY SUMMONS. THE CULPRIT BEHIND THE CRISIS IS SABUROTA TODO, A FORMER TEACHER WHO HAS SINCE JOINED THE DEMONS...

AFTER FAILING TO CAPTURE TODO, RIN AND YUKIO GO WITH THE OTHER STUDENTS TO THE KYOTO FIELD OFFICE TO HELP GUARD THE RIGHT EYE OF THE IMPURE KING. THIS IS RIN'S FIRST ACTIVITY WITH THE OTHER CRAM SCHOOL STUDENTS SINCE THE INQUIRY AND AN APPARENTLY UNBRIDGEABLE RIFT HAS OPENED BETWEEN THEM...

Chapter 20
Traitor

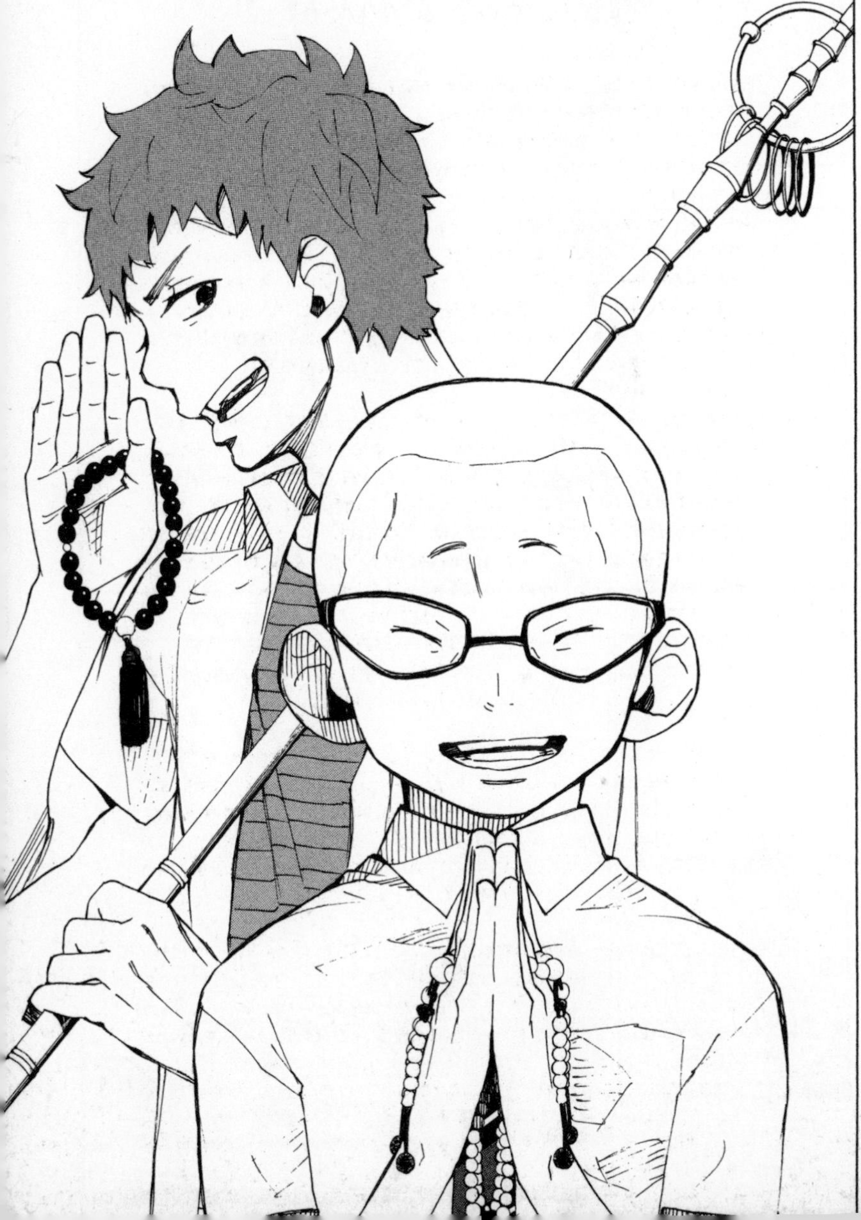

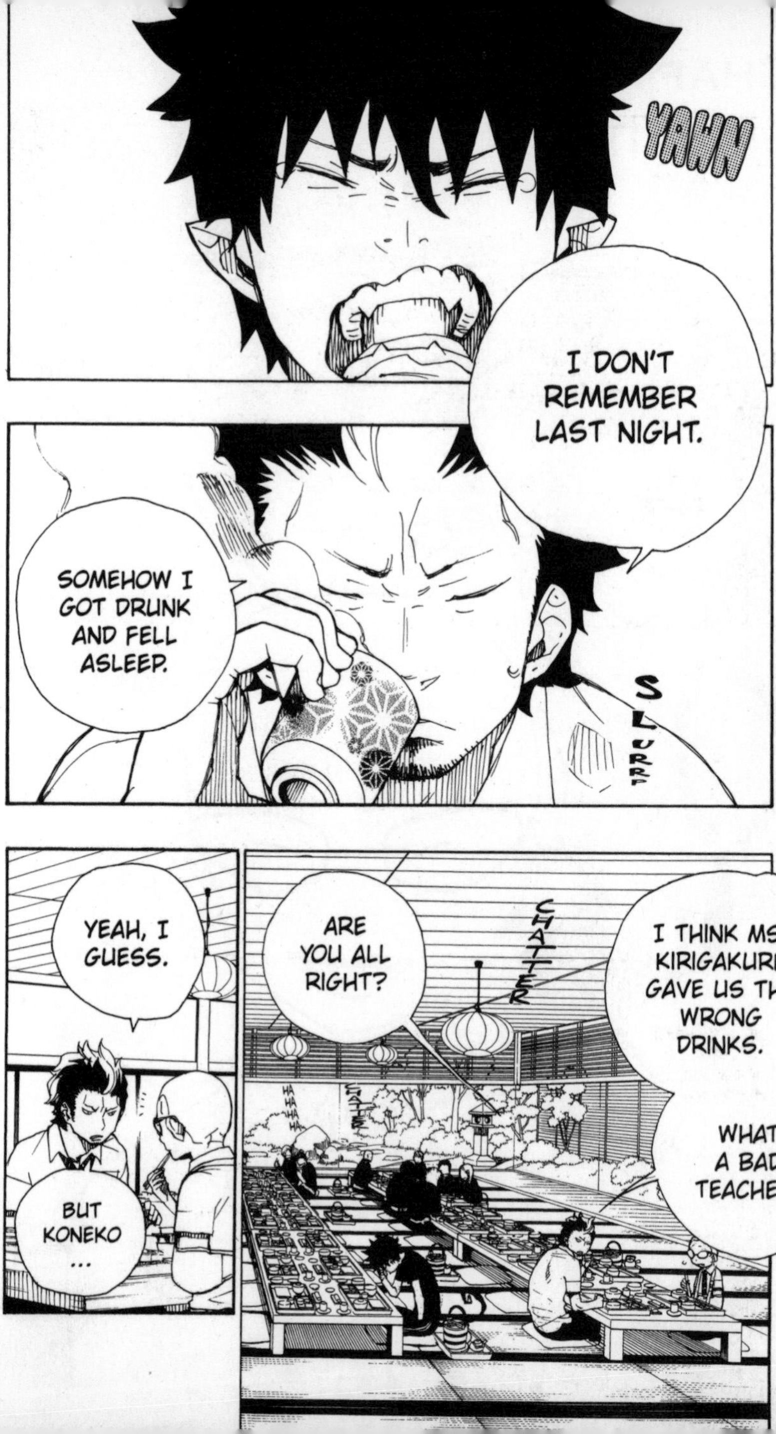
YAWN
I DON'T REMEMBER LAST NIGHT.
SOMEHOW I GOT DRUNK AND FELL ASLEEP.
SLURRP
I THINK MS. KIRIGAKURE GAVE US THE WRONG DRINKS.
CHATTER
ARE YOU ALL RIGHT?
WHAT A BAD TEACHER!
HA HA HA HA
CHATTER
YEAH, I GUESS.
BUT KONEKO ...

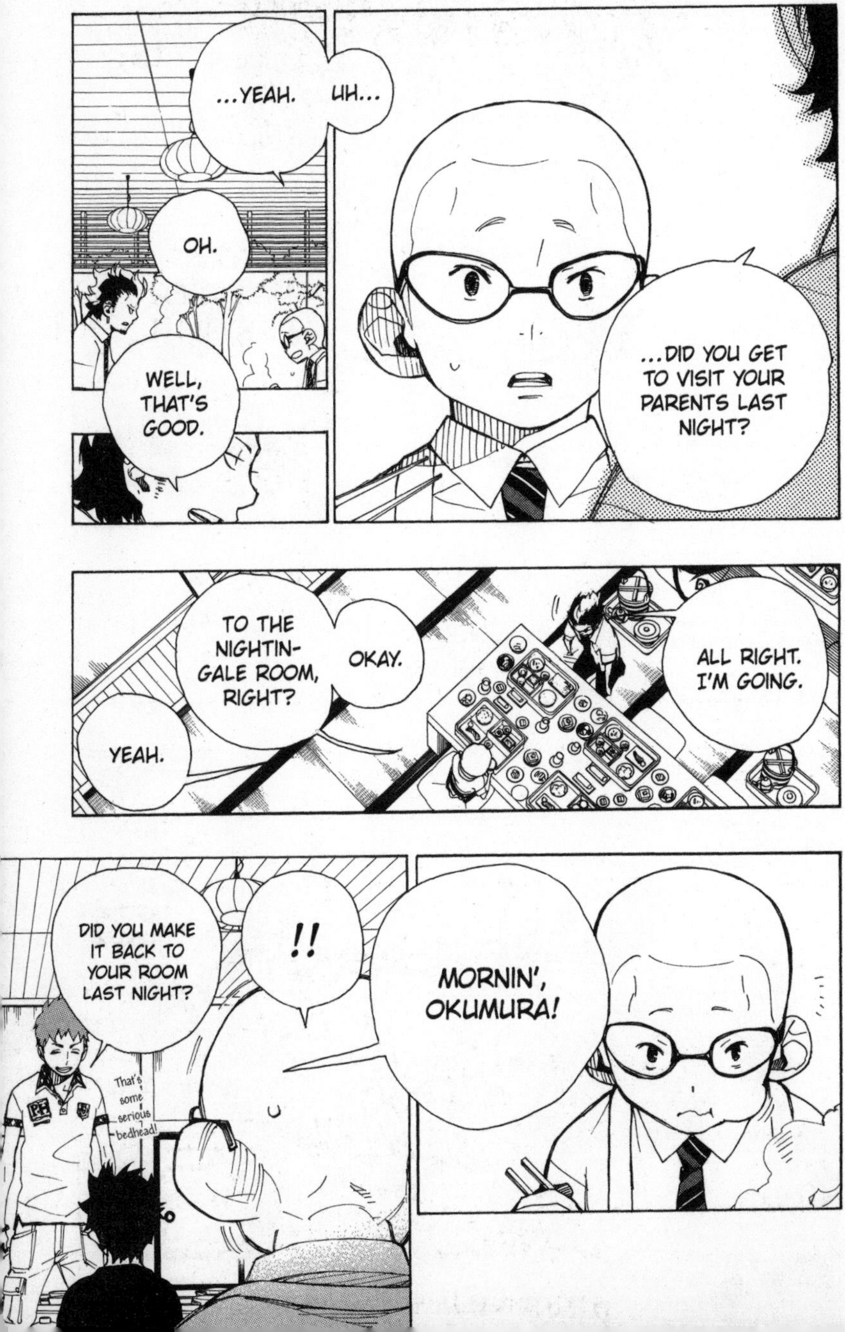
...DID YOU GET TO VISIT YOUR PARENTS LAST NIGHT?
...YEAH.
UH...
OH.
WELL, THAT'S GOOD.
ALL RIGHT. I'M GOING.
OKAY.
TO THE NIGHTIN-GALE ROOM, RIGHT?
YEAH.
MORNIN', OKUMURA!
!!
DID YOU MAKE IT BACK TO YOUR ROOM LAST NIGHT?
That's some serious bedhead!

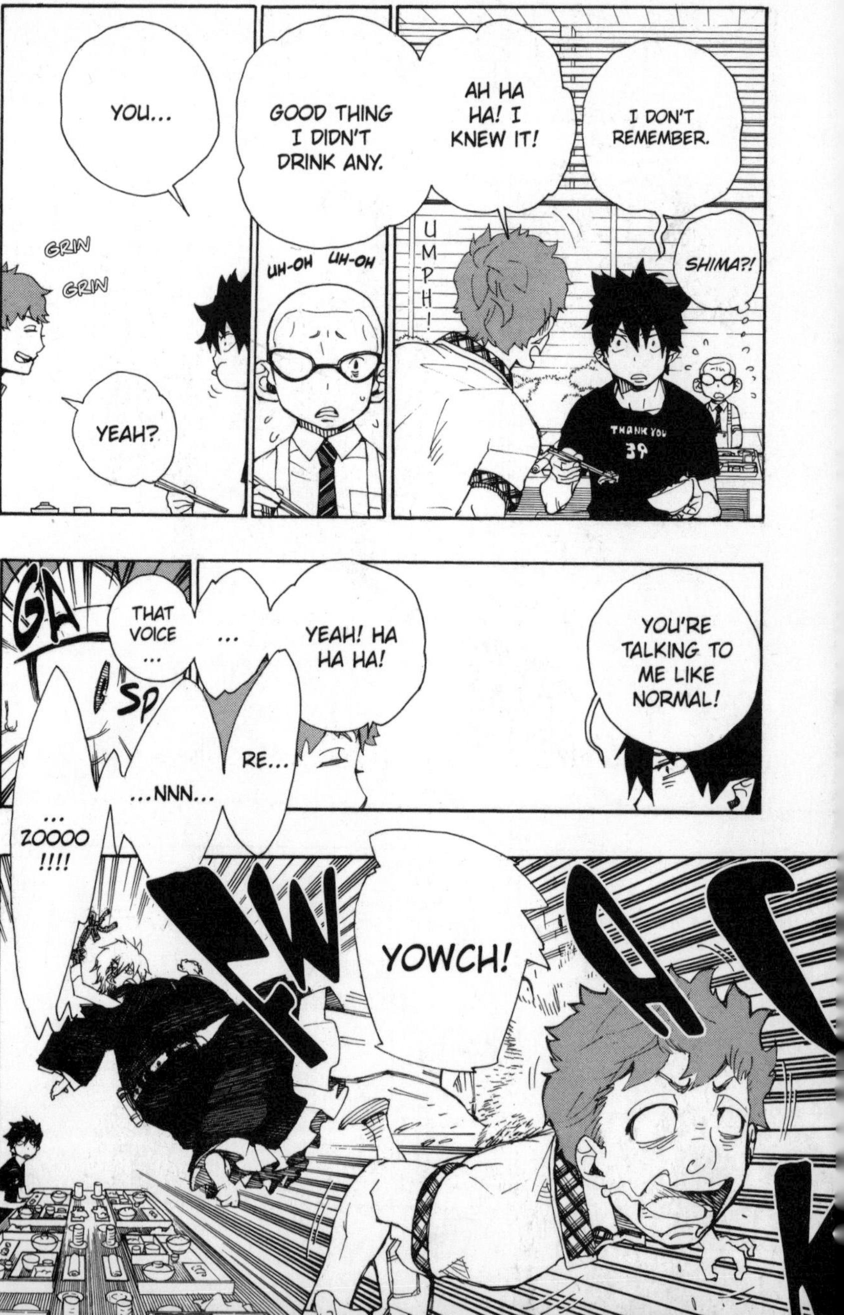
I DON'T REMEMBER.
AH HA HA! I KNEW IT!
SHIMA?!
UMPH!
THANK YOU 39
GOOD THING I DIDN'T DRINK ANY.
UH-OH UH-OH
YOU...
GRIN
GRIN
YEAH?
YOU'RE TALKING TO ME LIKE NORMAL!
YEAH! HA HA HA!
...
THAT VOICE ...
GA
RE...
...NNN...
... ZOOOO !!!!
YOWCH!

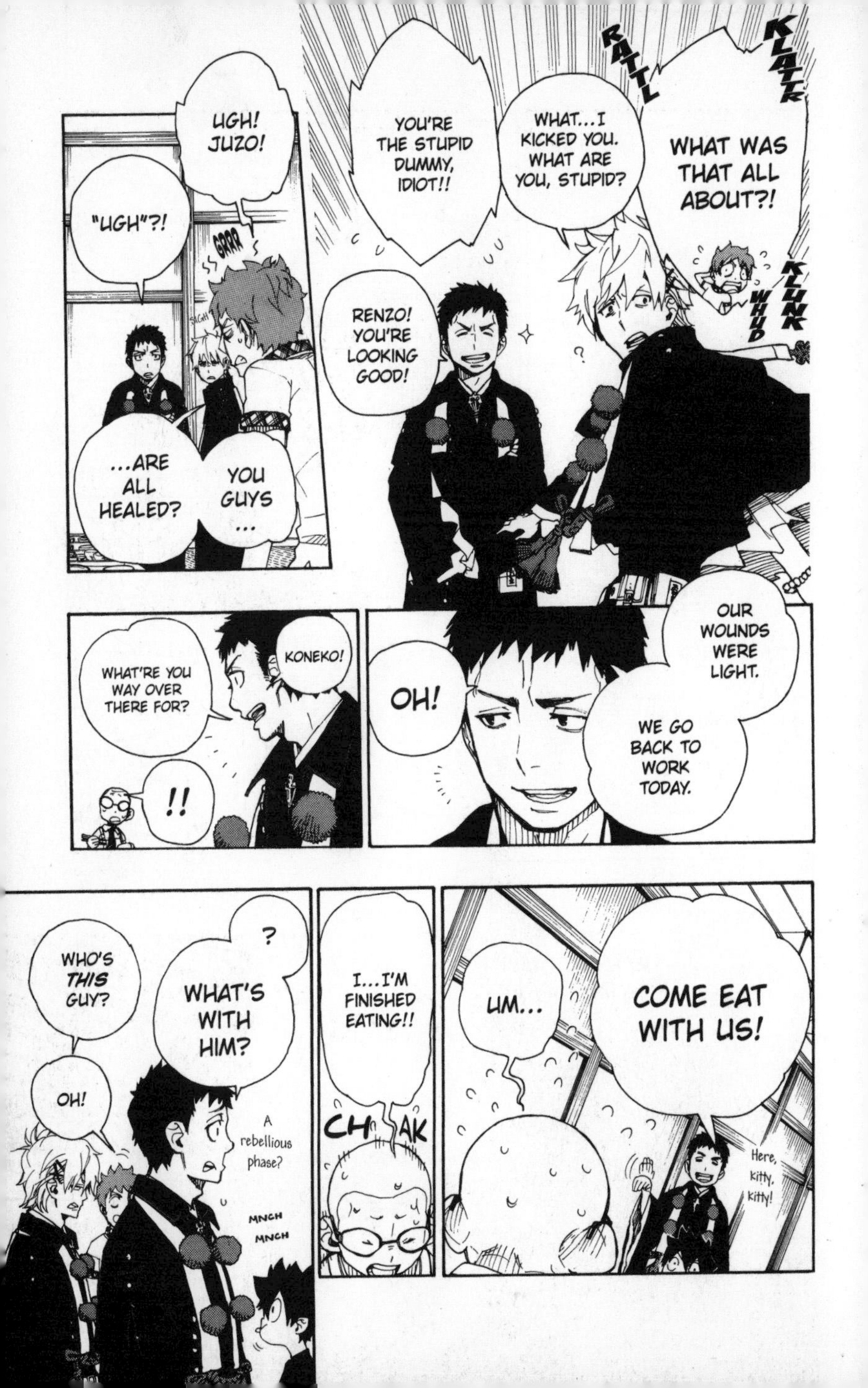
KLATTR
RATTL
WHAT WAS THAT ALL ABOUT?!
WHAT...I KICKED YOU. WHAT ARE YOU, STUPID?
YOU'RE THE STUPID DUMMY, IDIOT!!
KLUNK
WHUD
RENZO! YOU'RE LOOKING GOOD!
UGH! JUZO!
"UGH"?!
GRRR
YOU GUYS...
...ARE ALL HEALED?
OUR WOUNDS WERE LIGHT.
WE GO BACK TO WORK TODAY.
OH!
KONEKO!
WHAT'RE YOU WAY OVER THERE FOR?
!!
COME EAT WITH US!
UM...
Here, kitty, kitty!
I...I'M FINISHED EATING!!
CHAK
?
WHAT'S WITH HIM?
WHO'S *THIS* GUY?
OH!
A rebellious phase?
MNCH
MNCH

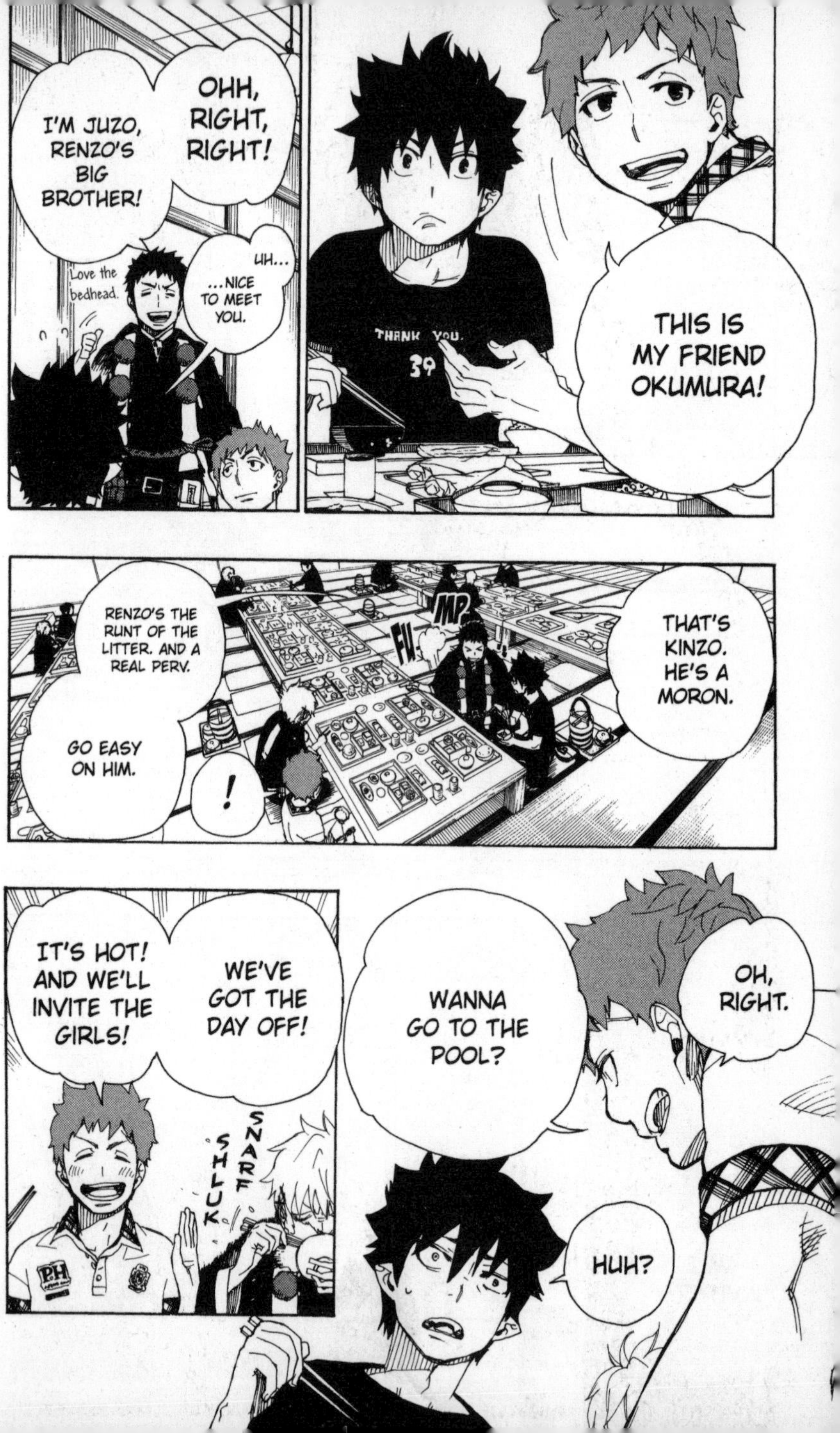
THIS IS MY FRIEND OKUMURA!
THANK YOU. 39
OHH, RIGHT, RIGHT!
I'M JUZO, RENZO'S BIG BROTHER!
UH... ...NICE TO MEET YOU.
Love the bedhead.
THAT'S KINZO. HE'S A MORON.
FUMP
!
RENZO'S THE RUNT OF THE LITTER. AND A REAL PERV.
GO EASY ON HIM.
OH, RIGHT.
HUH?
WANNA GO TO THE POOL?
WE'VE GOT THE DAY OFF!
IT'S HOT! AND WE'LL INVITE THE GIRLS!
SNARF
SHLUK

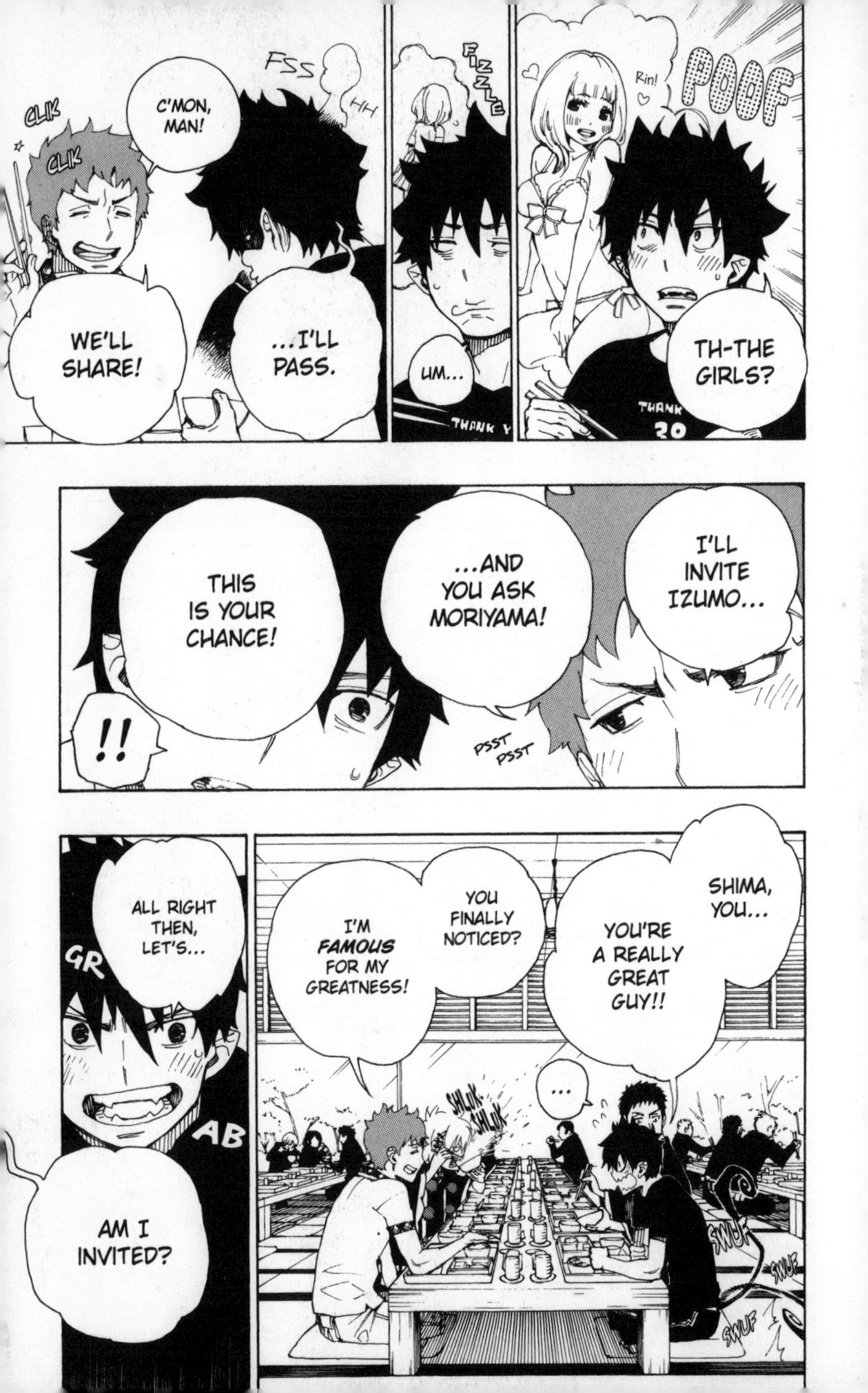
Rin!
POOF
TH-THE GIRLS?
FIZZLE
UM...
FSS
HH
C'MON, MAN!
CLIK
CLIK
...I'LL PASS.
WE'LL SHARE!
I'LL INVITE IZUMO...
...AND YOU ASK MORIYAMA!
PSST PSST
THIS IS YOUR CHANCE!
!!
SHIMA, YOU...
YOU'RE A REALLY GREAT GUY!!
YOU FINALLY NOTICED?
I'M *FAMOUS* FOR MY GREATNESS!
...
SHLUK SHLUK
SWUF
SWUF
SWUF
ALL RIGHT THEN, LET'S...
GR
AB
AM I INVITED?

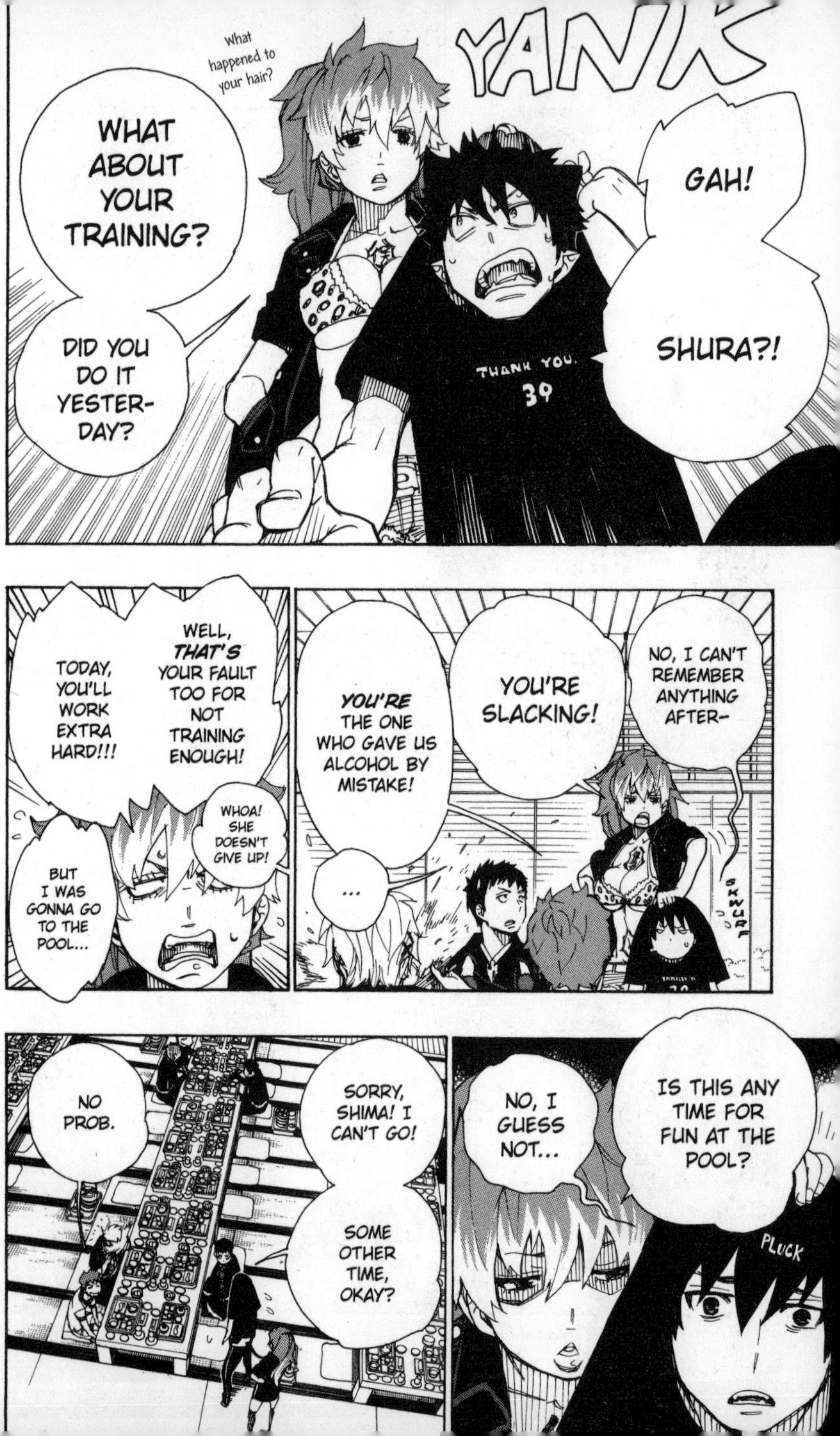
YANK
GAH!
SHURA?!
What happened to your hair?
WHAT ABOUT YOUR TRAINING?
DID YOU DO IT YESTER-DAY?
THANK YOU. 39
NO, I CAN'T REMEMBER ANYTHING AFTER-
YOU'RE SLACKING!
YOU'RE THE ONE WHO GAVE US ALCOHOL BY MISTAKE!
SKWURF
...
WELL, THAT'S YOUR FAULT TOO FOR NOT TRAINING ENOUGH!
TODAY, YOU'LL WORK EXTRA HARD!!!
WHOA! SHE DOESN'T GIVE UP!
BUT I WAS GONNA GO TO THE POOL...
IS THIS ANY TIME FOR FUN AT THE POOL?
NO, I GUESS NOT...
PLUCK
SORRY, SHIMA! I CAN'T GO!
SOME OTHER TIME, OKAY?
NO PROB.

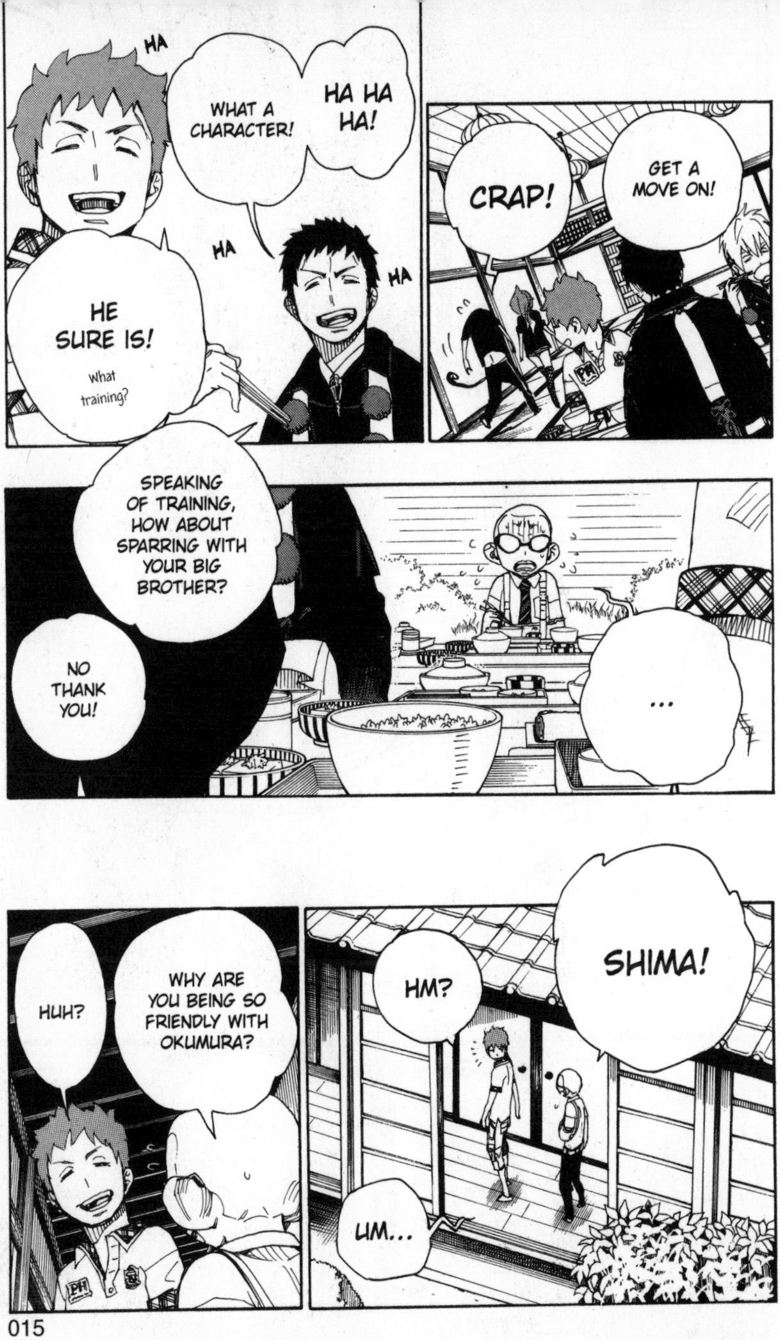
GET A MOVE ON!
CRAP!
HA
HA HA HA!
WHAT A CHARACTER!
HA
HA
HE SURE IS!
What training?
...
SPEAKING OF TRAINING, HOW ABOUT SPARRING WITH YOUR BIG BROTHER?
NO THANK YOU!
SHIMA!
HM?
UM...
WHY ARE YOU BEING SO FRIENDLY WITH OKUMURA?
HUH?

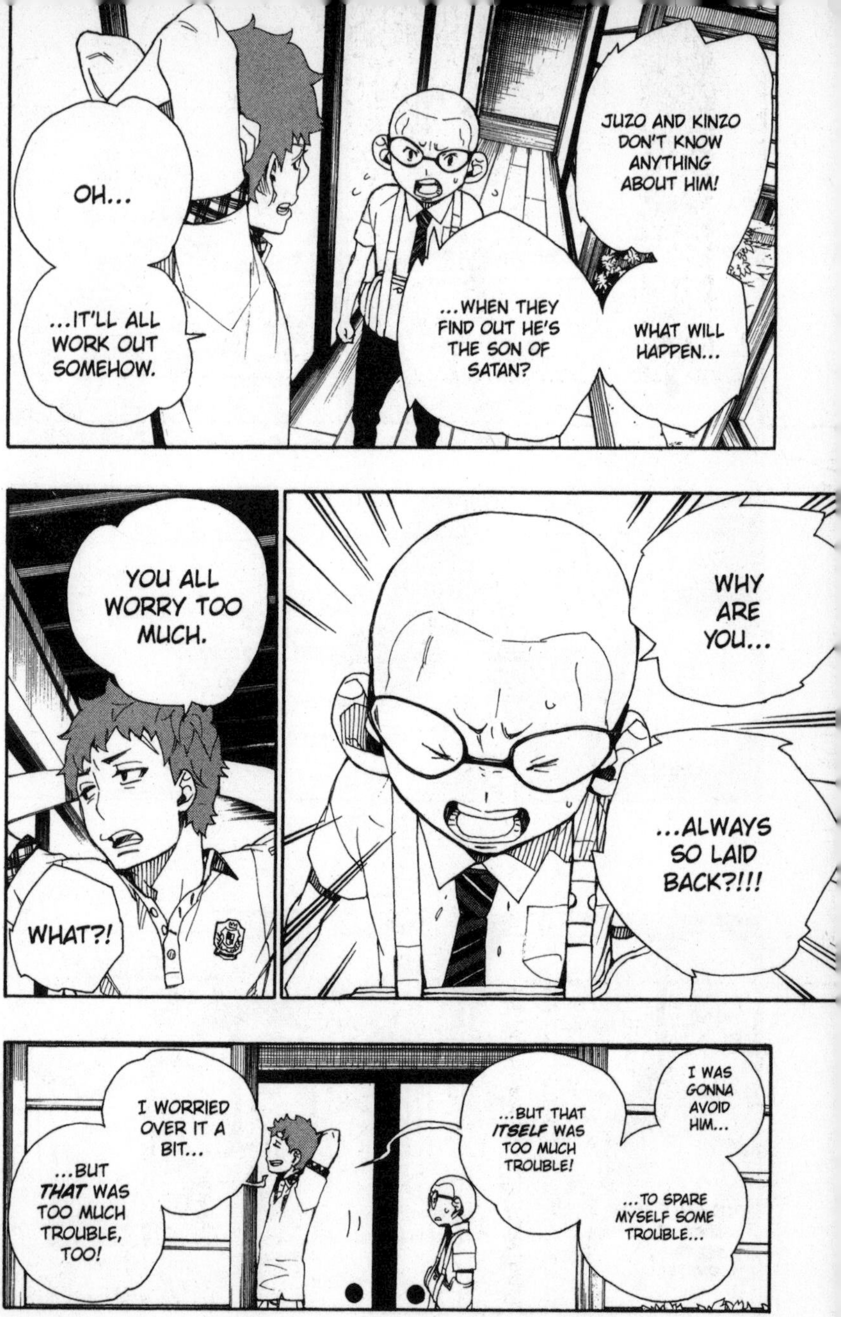
JUZO AND KINZO DON'T KNOW ANYTHING ABOUT HIM!
WHAT WILL HAPPEN...
...WHEN THEY FIND OUT HE'S THE SON OF SATAN?
OH...
...IT'LL ALL WORK OUT SOMEHOW.
WHY ARE YOU...
...ALWAYS SO LAID BACK?!!!
YOU ALL WORRY TOO MUCH.
WHAT?!
I WAS GONNA AVOID HIM...
...TO SPARE MYSELF SOME TROUBLE...
...BUT THAT *ITSELF* WAS TOO MUCH TROUBLE!
I WORRIED OVER IT A BIT...
...BUT *THAT* WAS TOO MUCH TROUBLE, TOO!

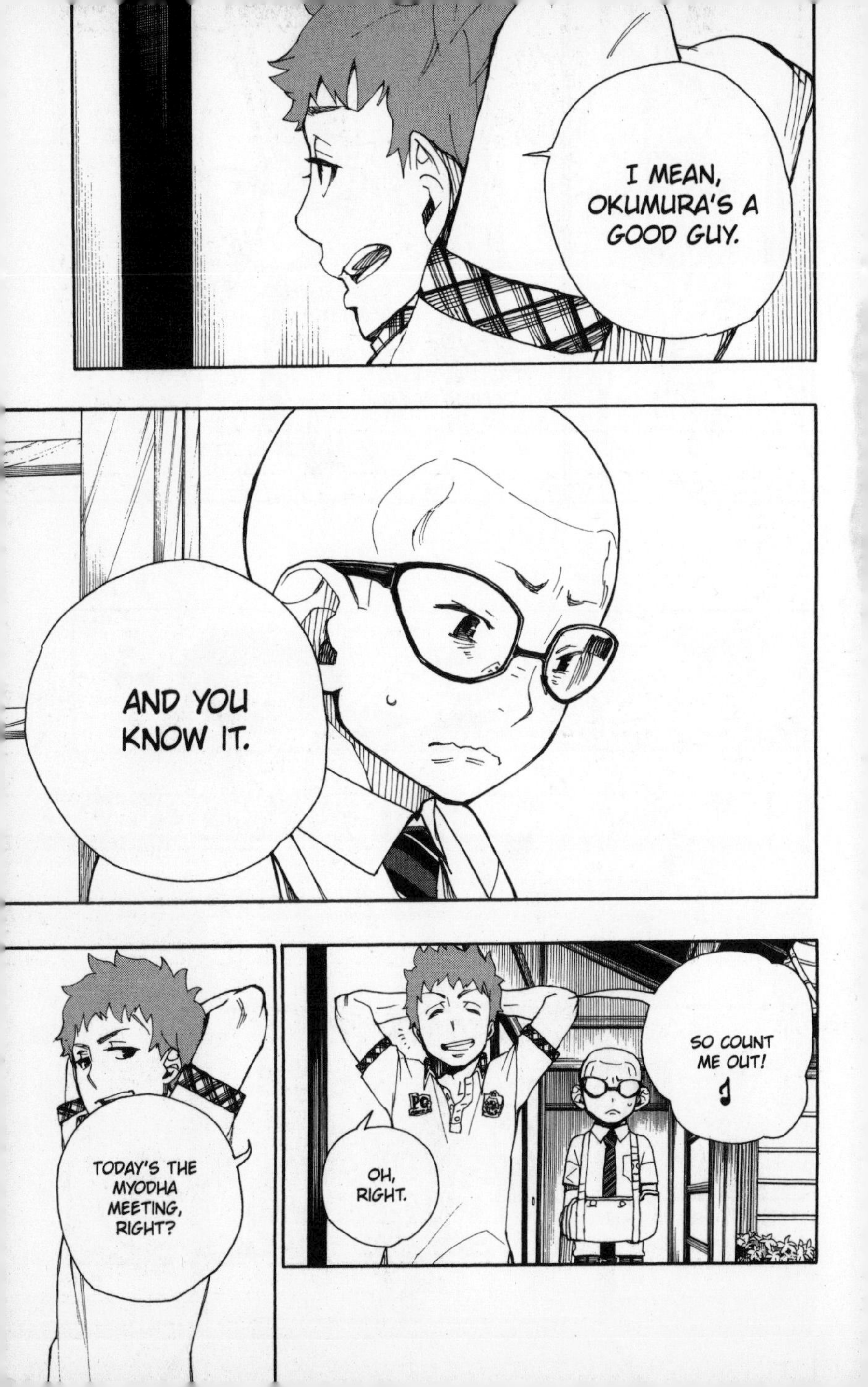
I MEAN, OKUMURA'S A GOOD GUY.
AND YOU KNOW IT.
SO COUNT ME OUT! ♪
OH, RIGHT.
TODAY'S THE MYODHA MEETING, RIGHT?

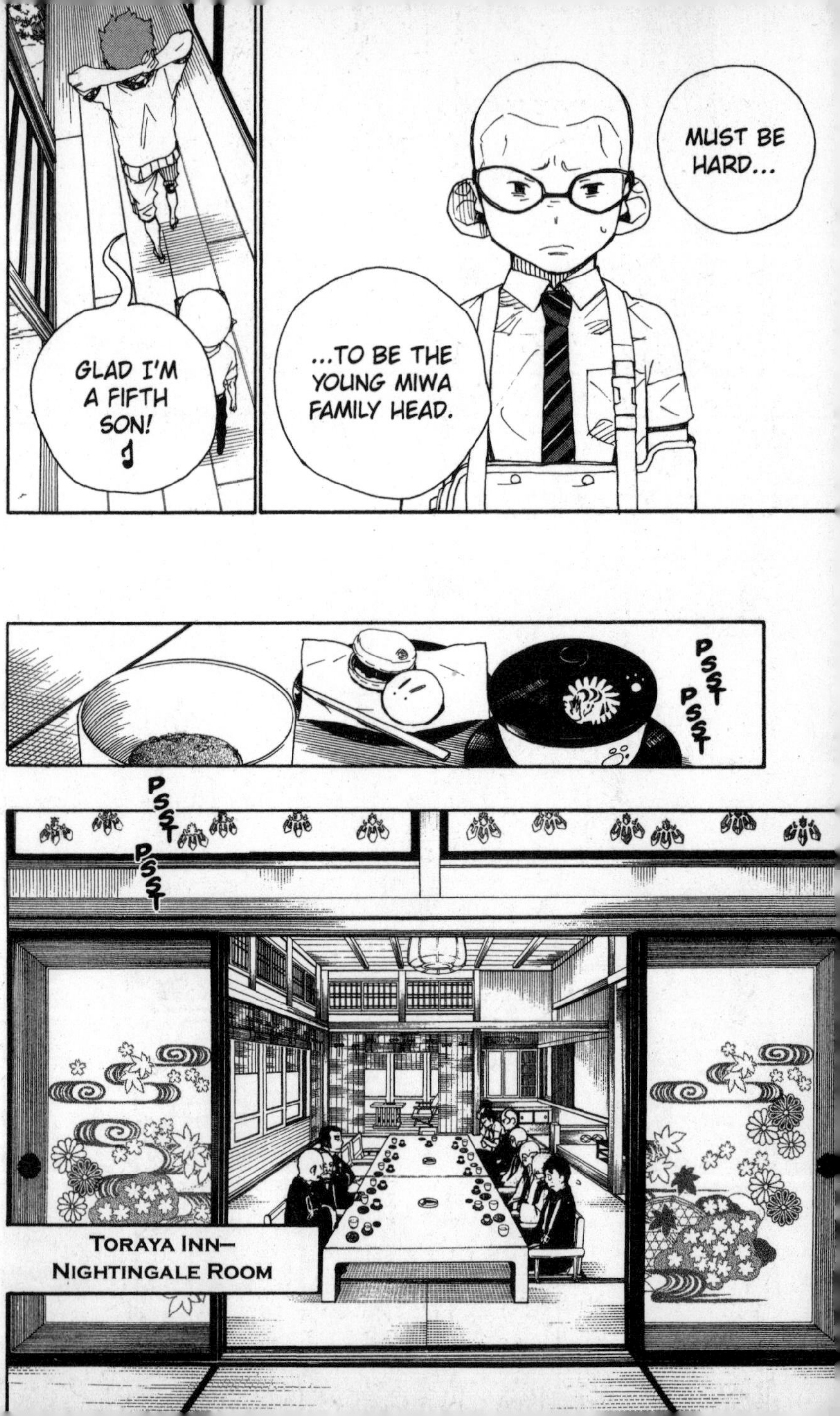
MUST BE HARD...
...TO BE THE YOUNG MIWA FAMILY HEAD.
GLAD I'M A FIFTH SON! ♪
PSST PSST
PSST PSST
TORAYA INN— NIGHTINGALE ROOM

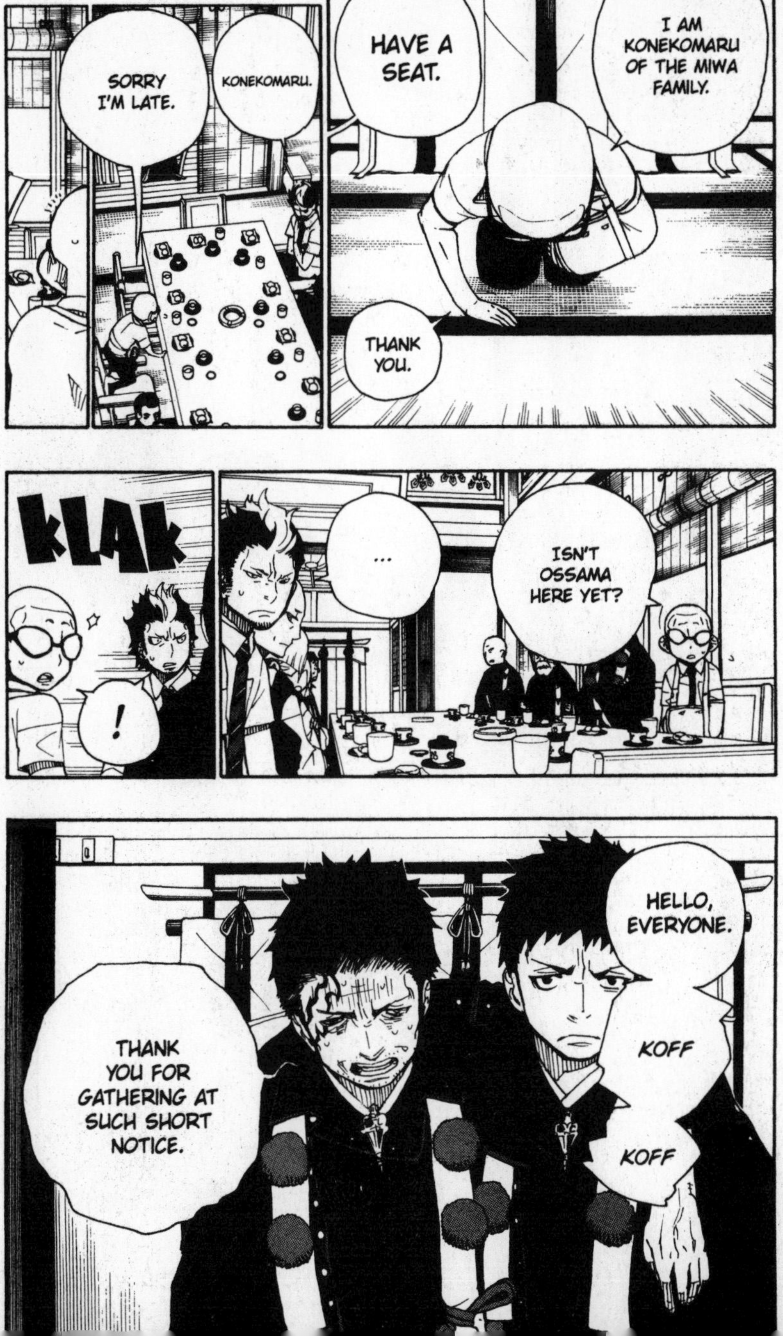
I AM KONEKOMARU OF THE MIWA FAMILY.
HAVE A SEAT.
THANK YOU.
KONEKOMARU.
SORRY I'M LATE.
ISN'T OSSAMA HERE YET?
...
KLAK
!
HELLO, EVERYONE.
KOFF
KOFF
THANK YOU FOR GATHERING AT SUCH SHORT NOTICE.

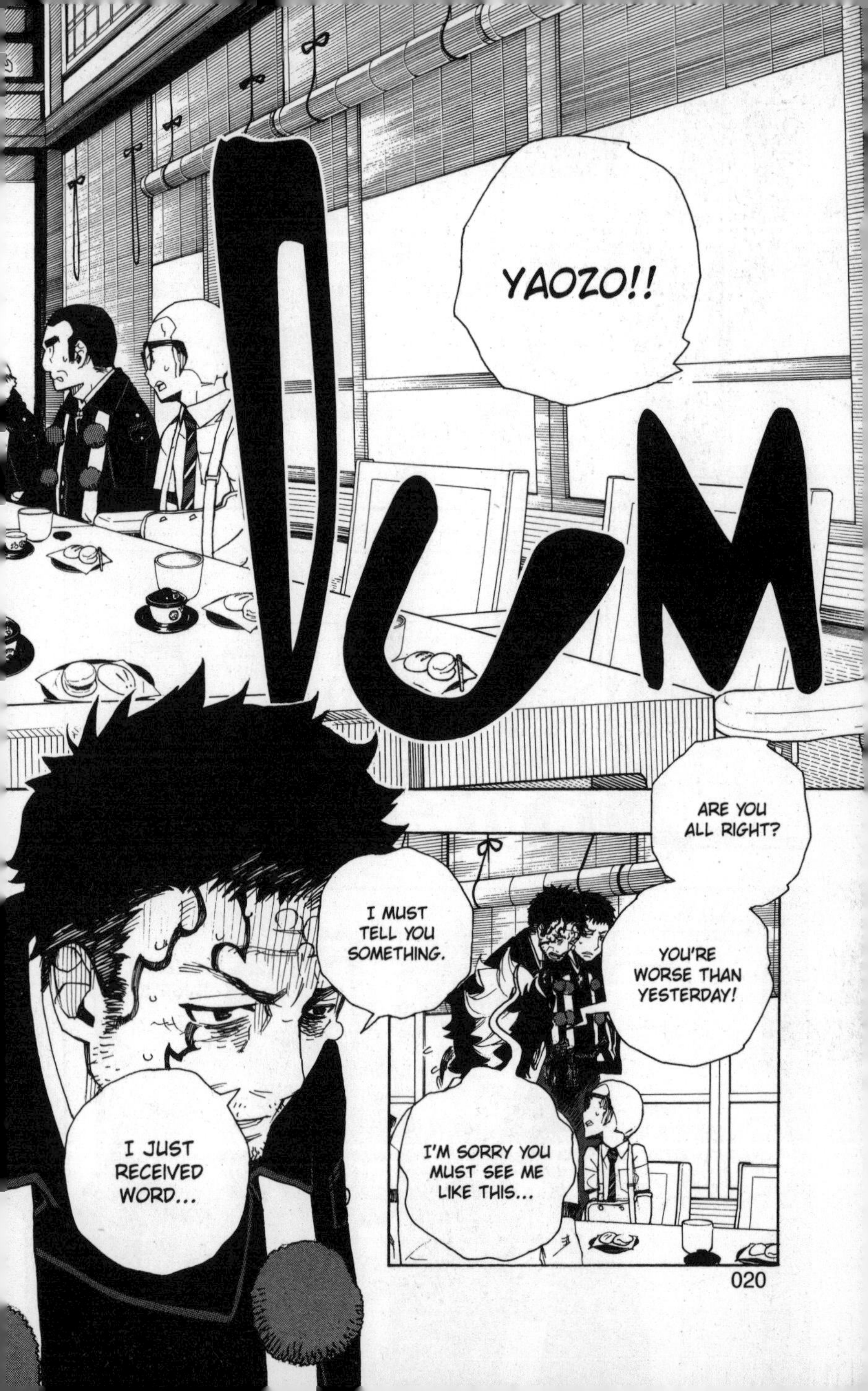
YAOZO!!
DUM
ARE YOU ALL RIGHT?
YOU'RE WORSE THAN YESTERDAY!
I'M SORRY YOU MUST SEE ME LIKE THIS...
I MUST TELL YOU SOMETHING.
I JUST RECEIVED WORD...

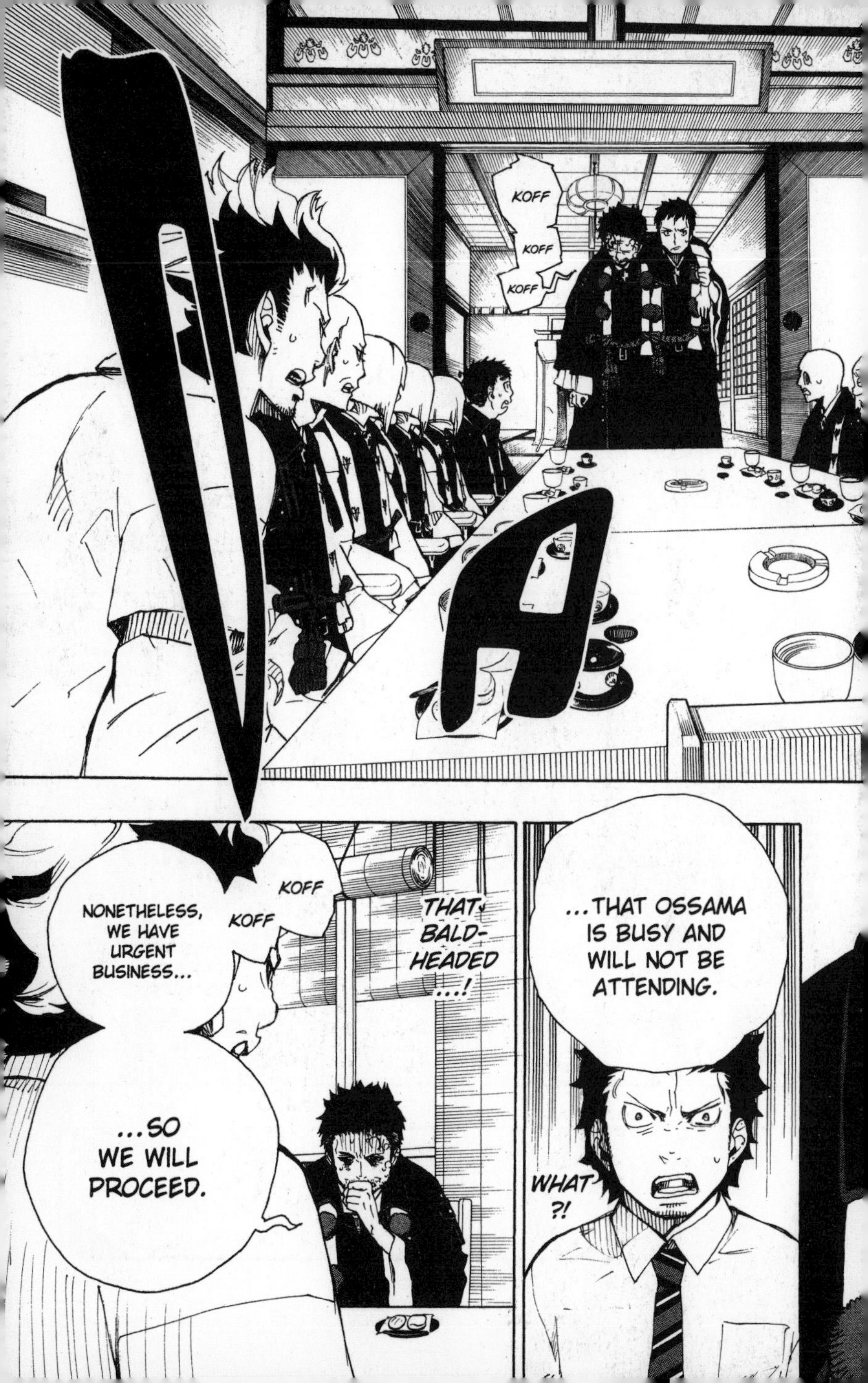
KOFF
KOFF
KOFF
...THAT OSSAMA IS BUSY AND WILL NOT BE ATTENDING.
WHAT ?!
KOFF
KOFF
NONETHELESS, WE HAVE URGENT BUSINESS...
...SO WE WILL PROCEED.
THAT BALD-HEADED ...!

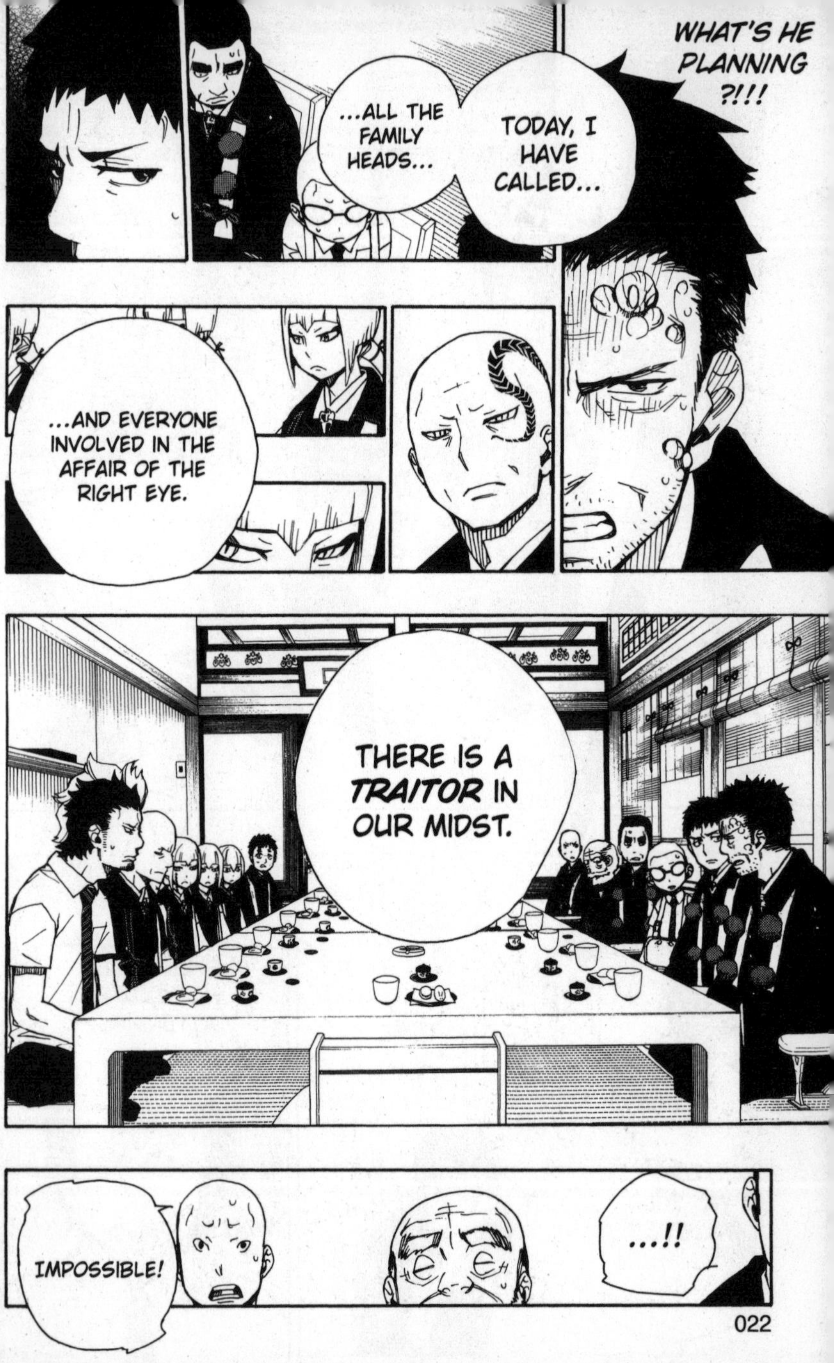
WHAT'S HE PLANNING ?!!!
TODAY, I HAVE CALLED...
...ALL THE FAMILY HEADS...
...AND EVERYONE INVOLVED IN THE AFFAIR OF THE RIGHT EYE.
THERE IS A *TRAITOR* IN OUR MIDST.
...!!
IMPOSSIBLE!

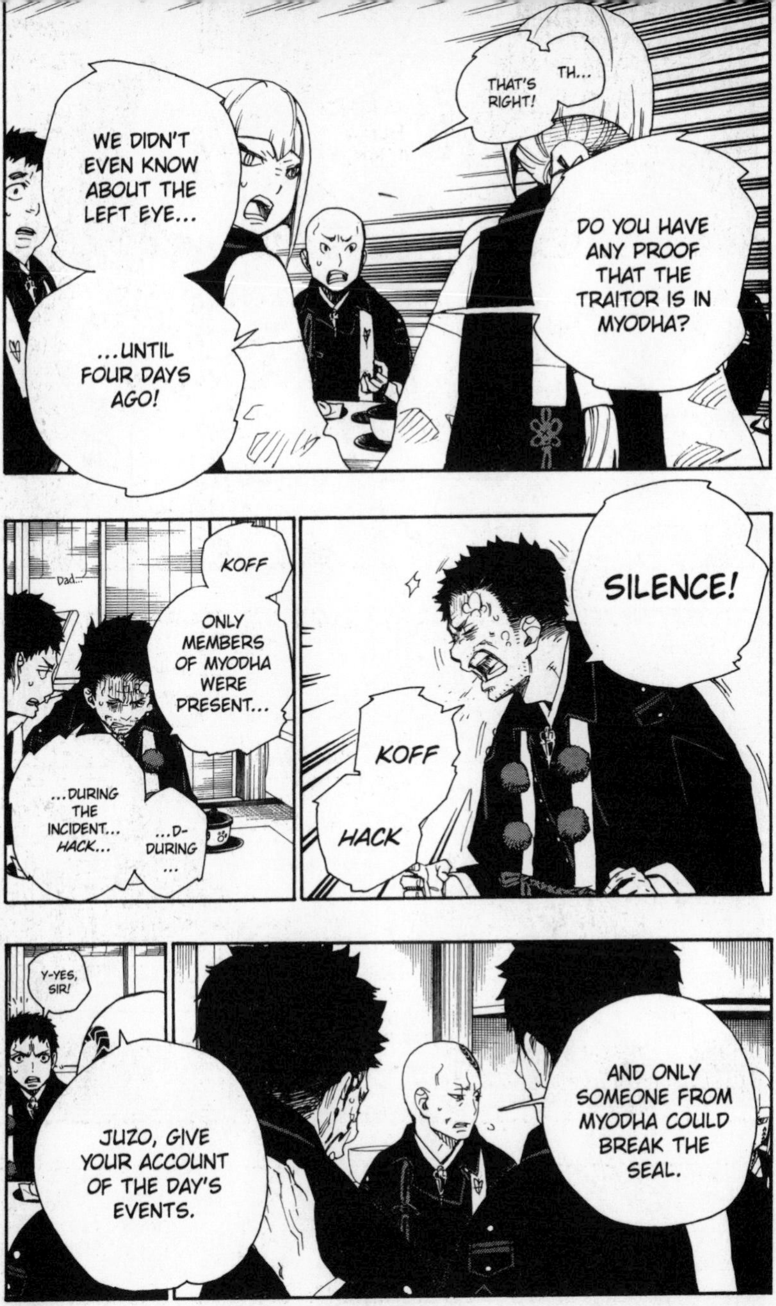
TH... THAT'S RIGHT!
DO YOU HAVE ANY PROOF THAT THE TRAITOR IS IN MYODHA?
WE DIDN'T EVEN KNOW ABOUT THE LEFT EYE...
...UNTIL FOUR DAYS AGO!
SILENCE!
KOFF
HACK
KOFF
ONLY MEMBERS OF MYODHA WERE PRESENT...
Dad...
...D-DURING...
...DURING THE INCIDENT... HACK...
AND ONLY SOMEONE FROM MYODHA COULD BREAK THE SEAL.
JUZO, GIVE YOUR ACCOUNT OF THE DAY'S EVENTS.
Y-YES, SIR!

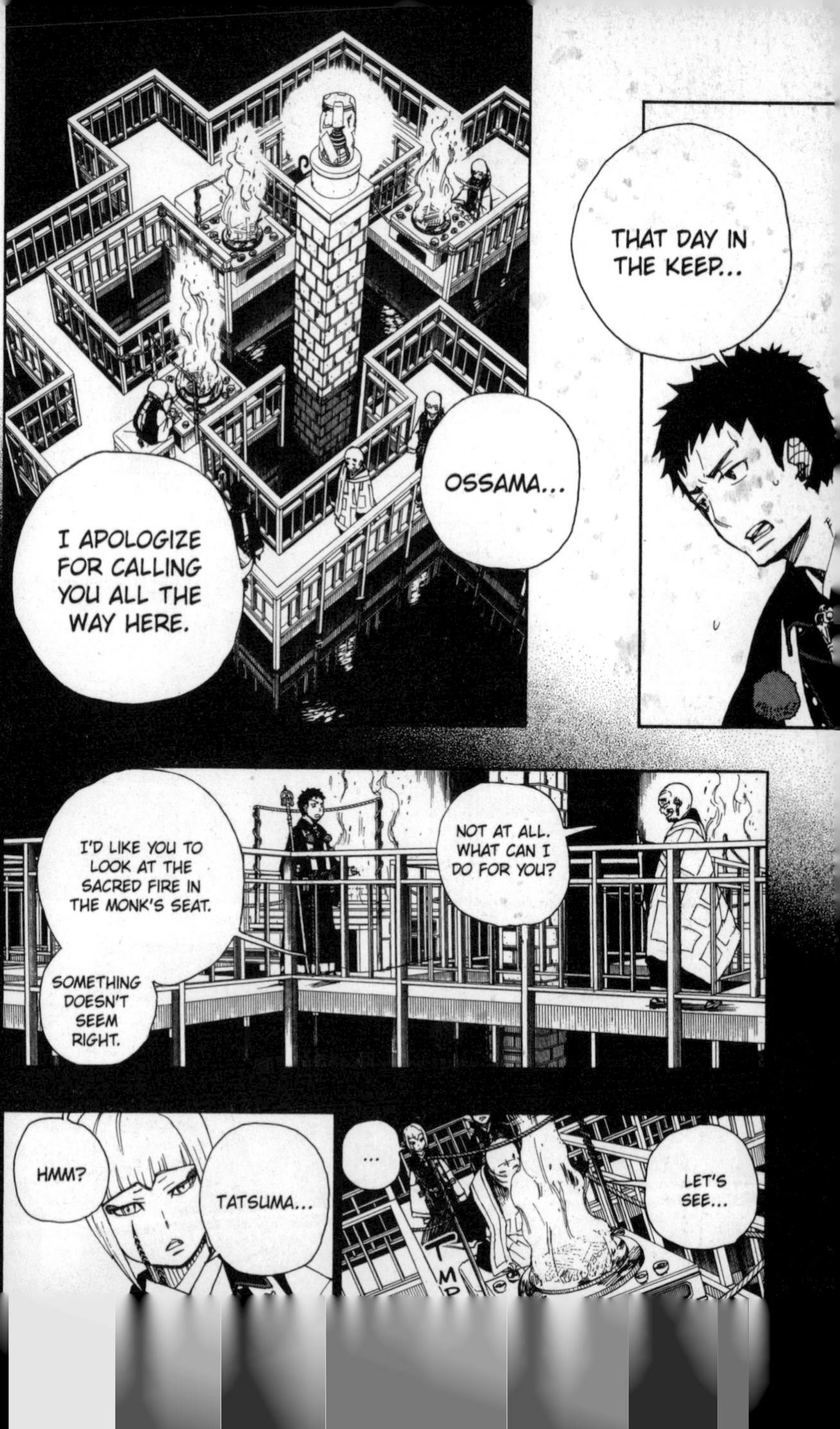
THAT DAY IN THE KEEP...
OSSAMA...
I APOLOGIZE FOR CALLING YOU ALL THE WAY HERE.
NOT AT ALL. WHAT CAN I DO FOR YOU?
I'D LIKE YOU TO LOOK AT THE SACRED FIRE IN THE MONK'S SEAT.
SOMETHING DOESN'T SEEM RIGHT.
LET'S SEE...
...
TMP
TATSUMA...
HMM?

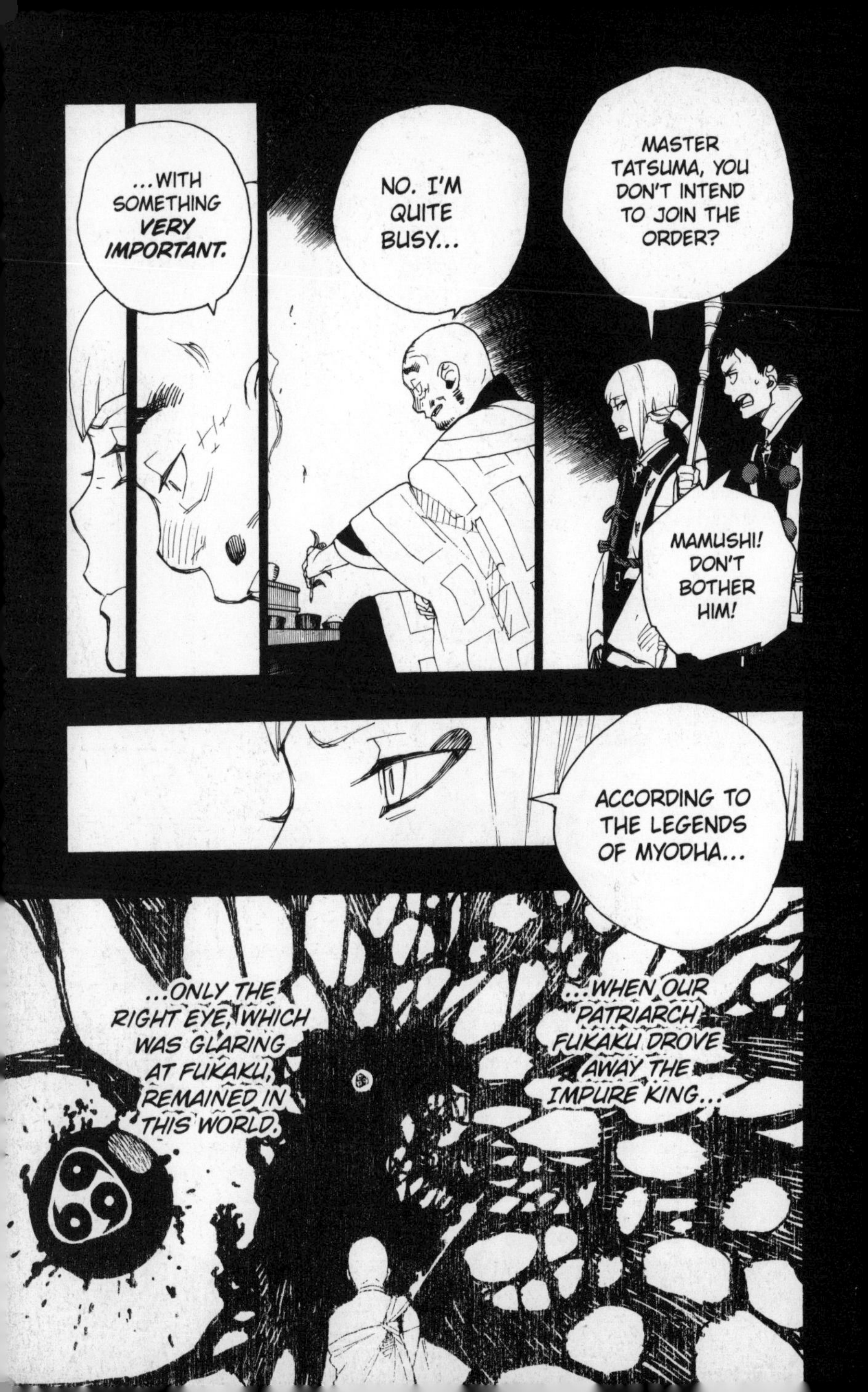
MASTER TATSUMA, YOU DON'T INTEND TO JOIN THE ORDER?
MAMUSHI! DON'T BOTHER HIM!
NO. I'M QUITE BUSY...
...WITH SOMETHING *VERY IMPORTANT.*
ACCORDING TO THE LEGENDS OF MYODHA...
...WHEN OUR PATRIARCH FUKAKU DROVE AWAY THE IMPURE KING...
...ONLY THE RIGHT EYE, WHICH WAS GLARING AT FUKAKU, REMAINED IN THIS WORLD.

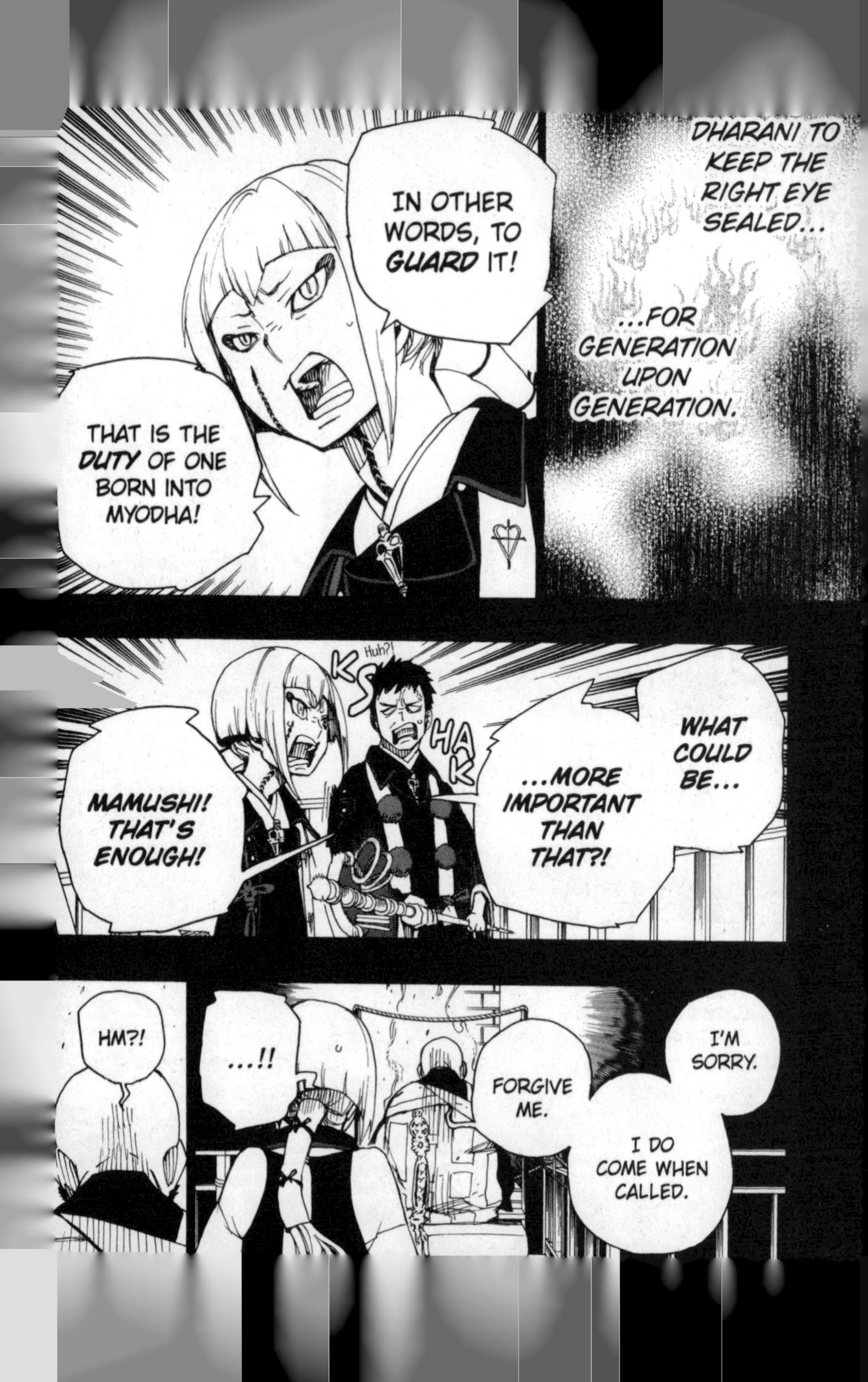
DHARANI TO KEEP THE RIGHT EYE SEALED...
...FOR GENERATION UPON GENERATION.
IN OTHER WORDS, TO GUARD IT!
THAT IS THE DUTY OF ONE BORN INTO MYODHA!
WHAT COULD BE...
...MORE IMPORTANT THAN THAT?!
KSHAK
Huh?!
MAMUSHI! THAT'S ENOUGH!
I'M SORRY.
FORGIVE ME.
I DO COME WHEN CALLED.
...!!
HM?!

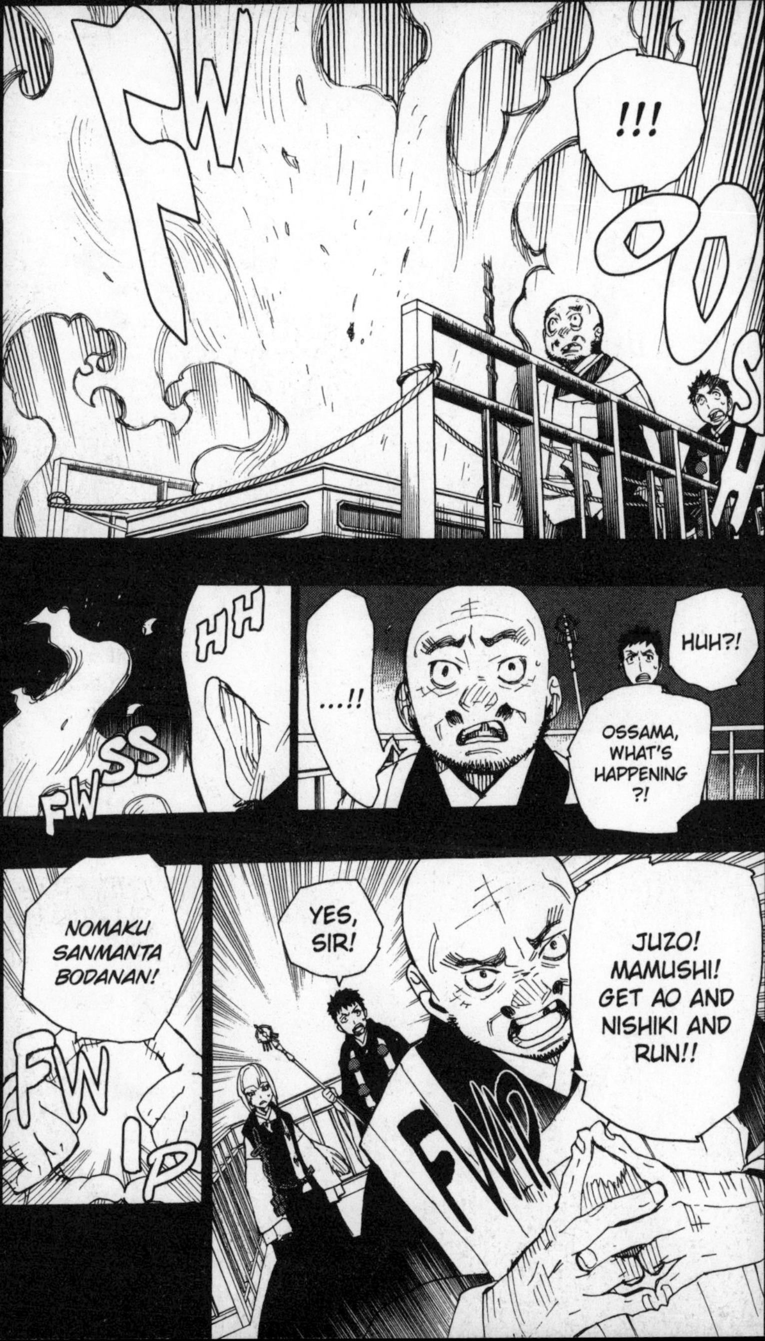
!!!
OOOSH
FW
HUH?!
OSSAMA, WHAT'S HAPPENING ?!
...!!
HH
FWSS
JUZO! MAMUSHI! GET AO AND NISHIKI AND RUN!!
YES, SIR!
FWP
NOMAKU SANMANTA BODANAN!
FWIP

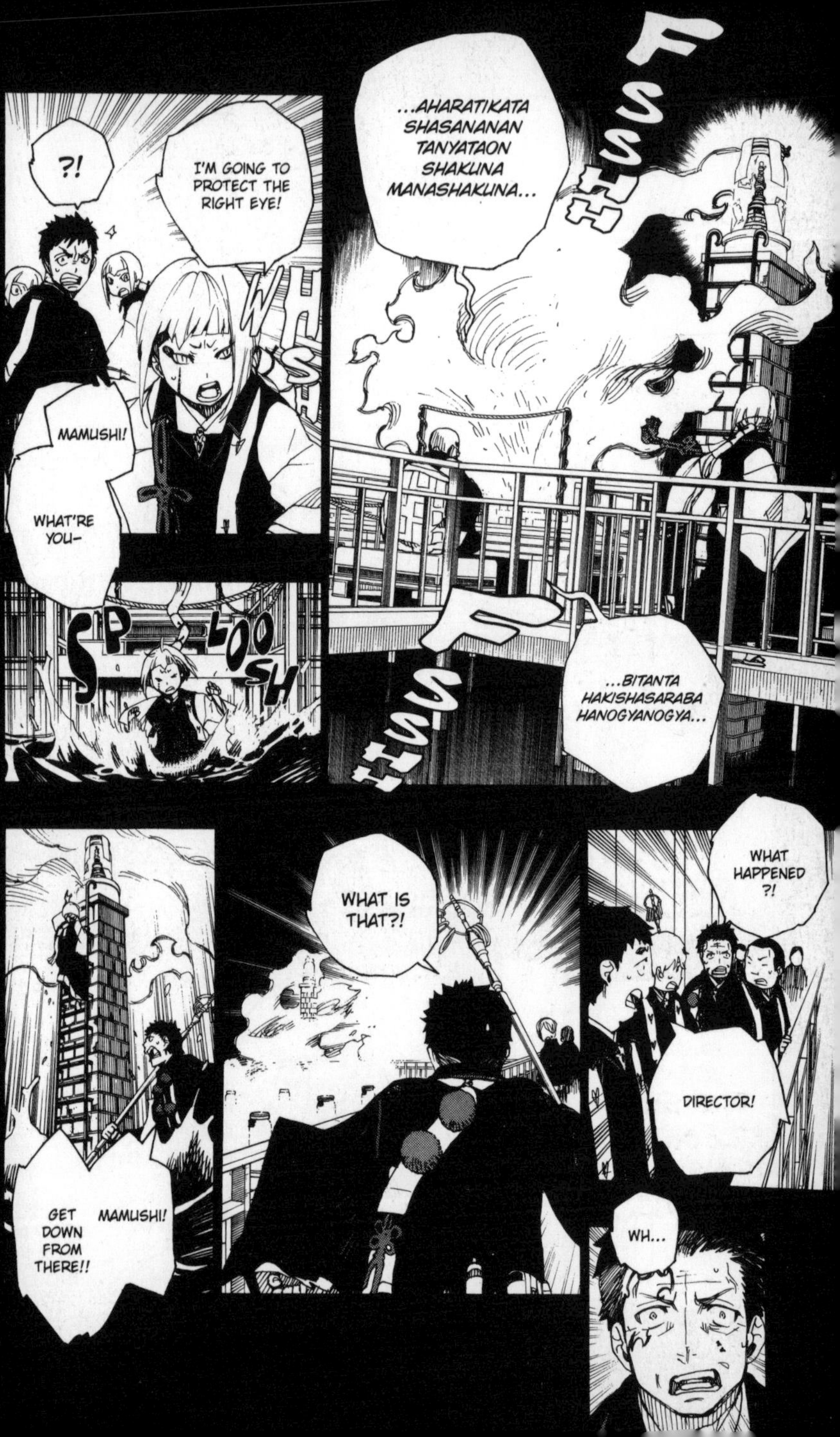
FSSHH
...AHARATIKATA SHASANANAN TANYATAON SHAKUNA MANASHAKUNA...
...BITANTA HAKISHASARABA HANOGYANOGYA...
FSSHH
I'M GOING TO PROTECT THE RIGHT EYE!
?!
MAMUSHI!
WHAT'RE YOU-
SPLOOSH
WHAT HAPPENED?!
DIRECTOR!
WH...
WHAT IS THAT?!
MAMUSHI!
GET DOWN FROM THERE!!

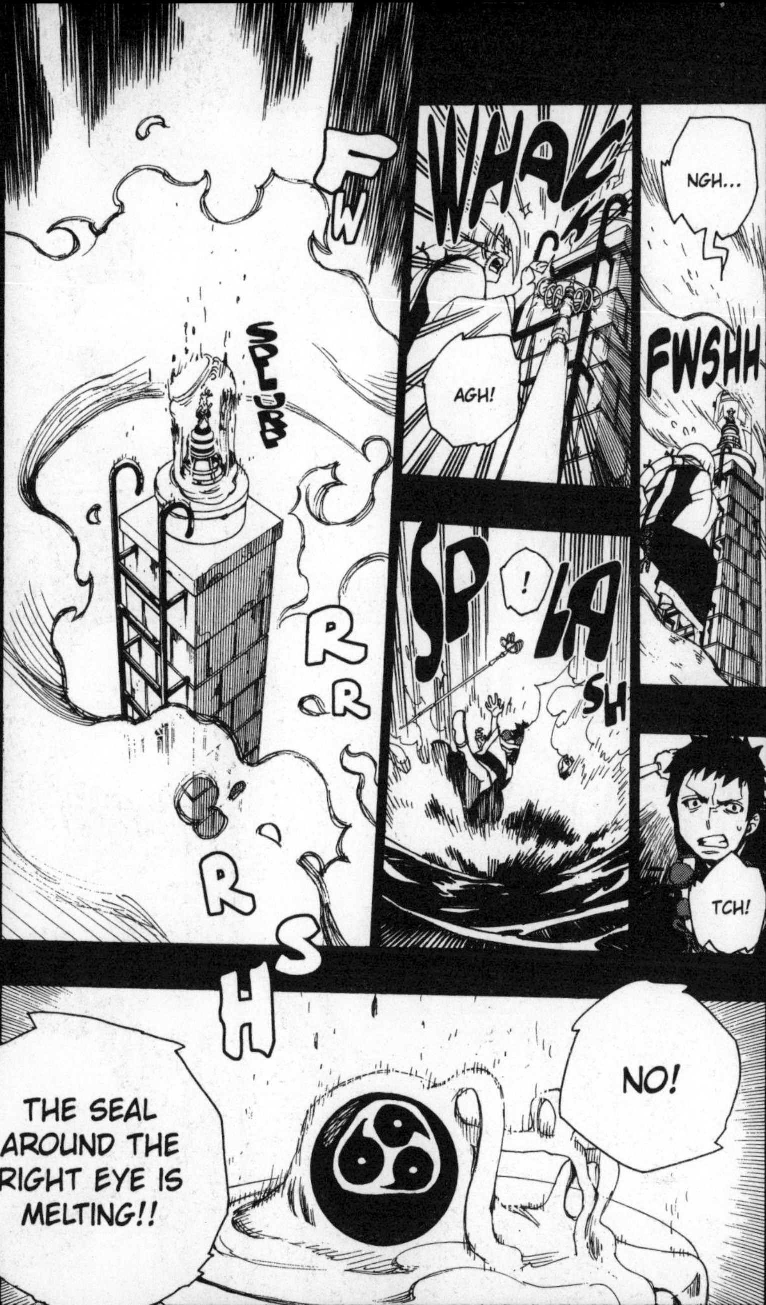
NGH...
FWSHH
TCH!
WHACK
AGH!
SPLASH
!
FW
SPLUBB
RRRRSH
NO!
THE SEAL AROUND THE RIGHT EYE IS MELTING!!

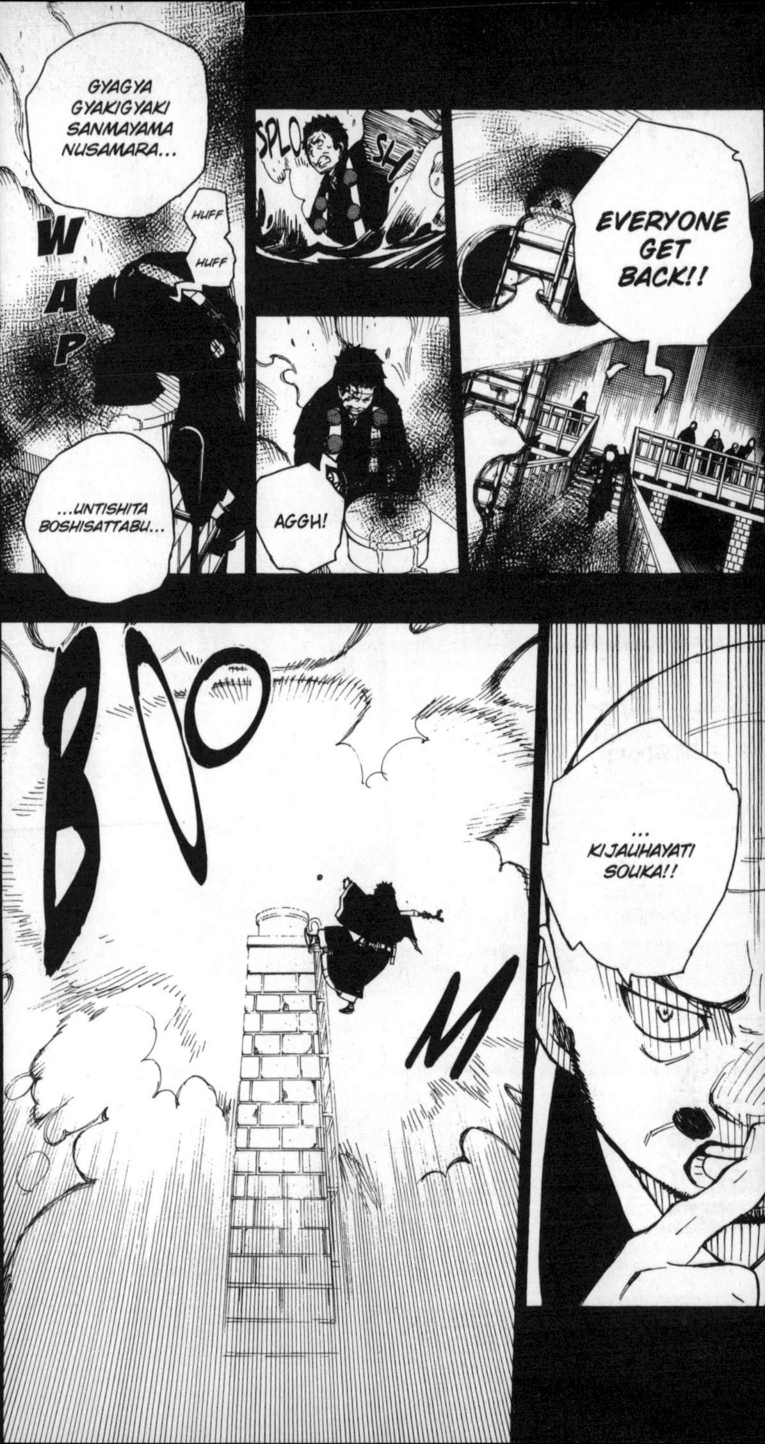
EVERYONE GET BACK!!
SPLOSH
AGGH!
GYAGYA GYAKIGYAKI SANMAYAMA NUSAMARA...
HUFF
HUFF
WAP
...UNTISHITA BOSHISATTABU...
... KIJAUHAYATI SOUKA!!
BOOM

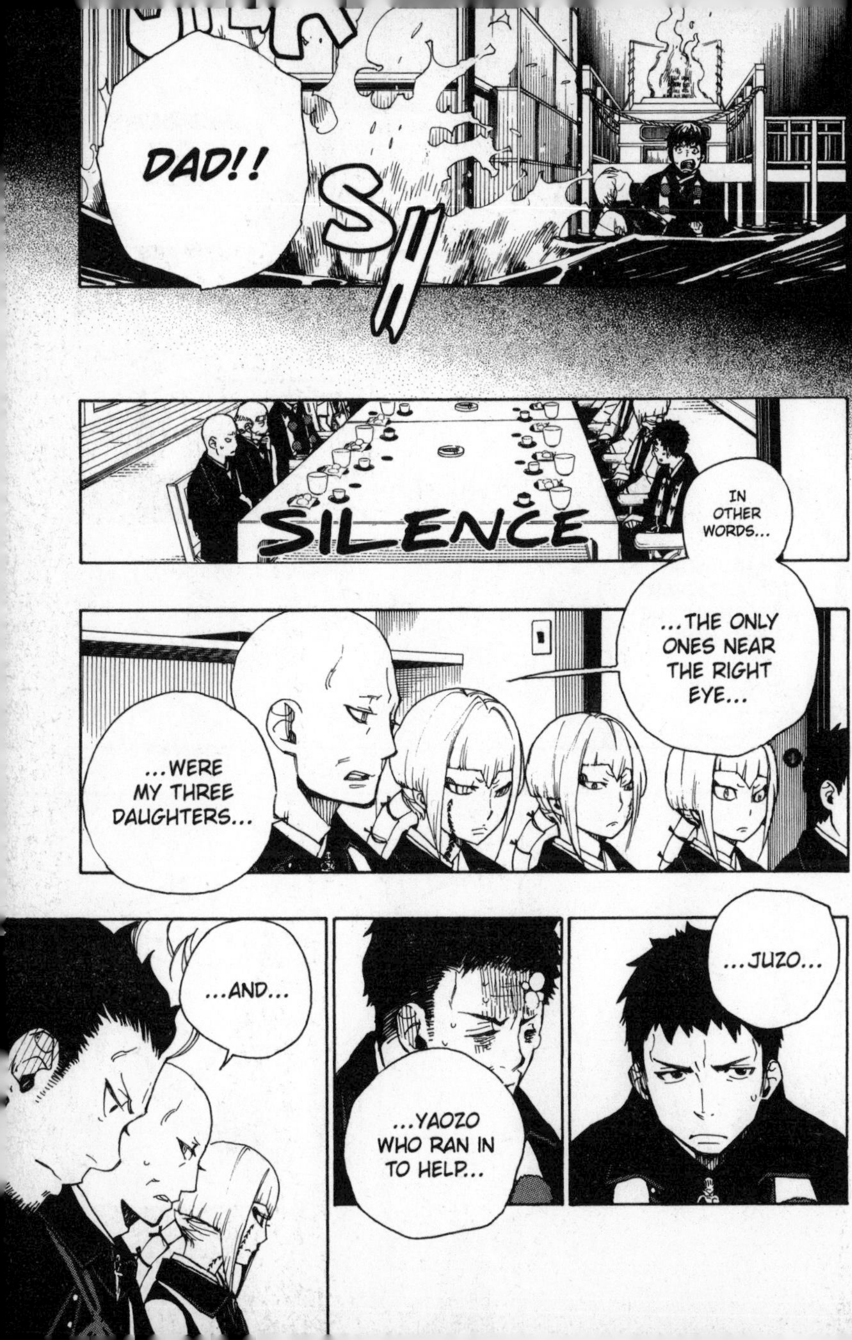
DAD!!
SH
SILENCE
IN OTHER WORDS...
...THE ONLY ONES NEAR THE RIGHT EYE...
...WERE MY THREE DAUGHTERS...
...JUZO...
...YAOZO WHO RAN IN TO HELP...
...AND...

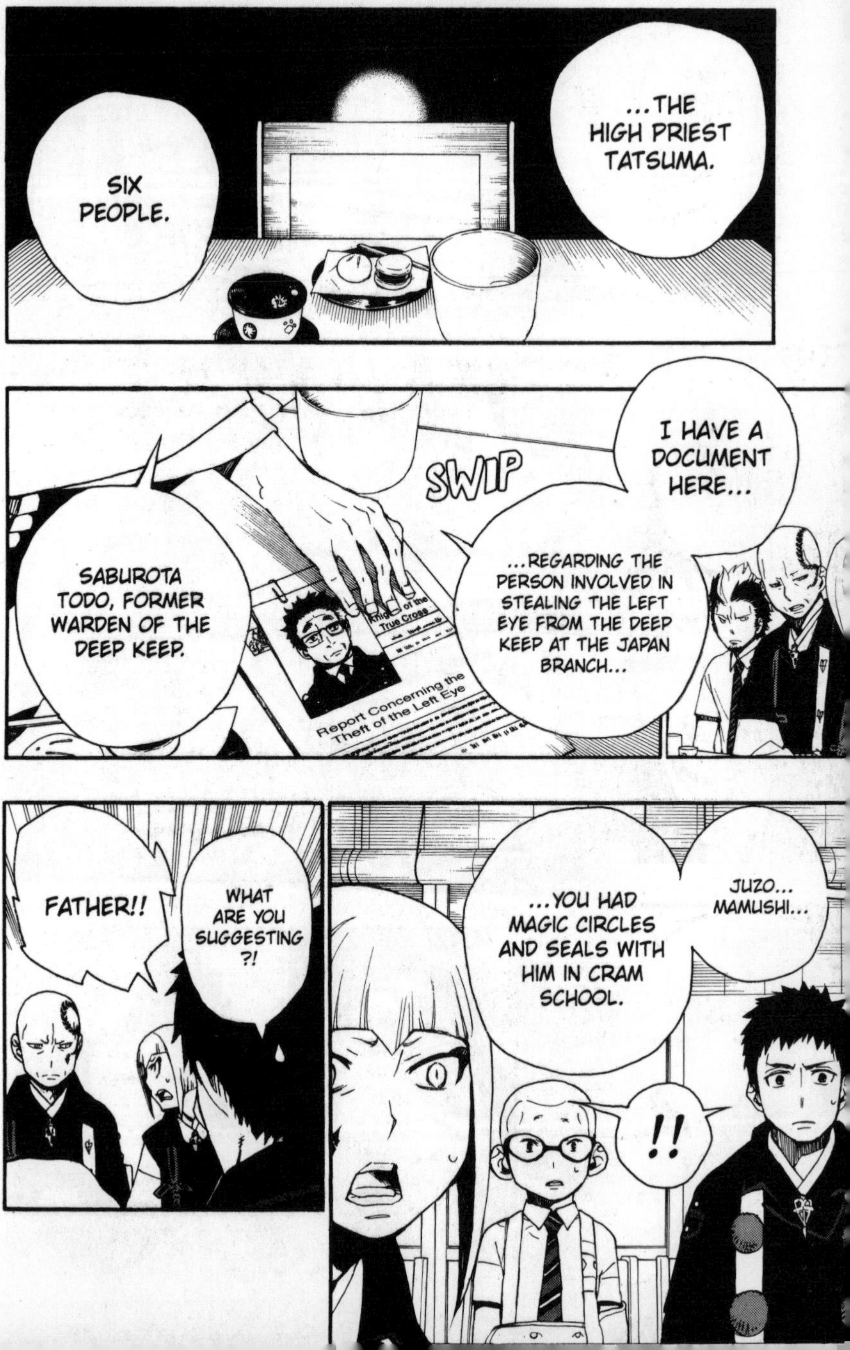
...THE HIGH PRIEST TATSUMA.
SIX PEOPLE.
I HAVE A DOCUMENT HERE...
...REGARDING THE PERSON INVOLVED IN STEALING THE LEFT EYE FROM THE DEEP KEEP AT THE JAPAN BRANCH...
SWIP
Report Concerning the Theft of the Left Eye
SABUROTA TODO, FORMER WARDEN OF THE DEEP KEEP.
JUZO... MAMUSHI...
...YOU HAD MAGIC CIRCLES AND SEALS WITH HIM IN CRAM SCHOOL.
!!
WHAT ARE YOU SUGGESTING?!
FATHER!!

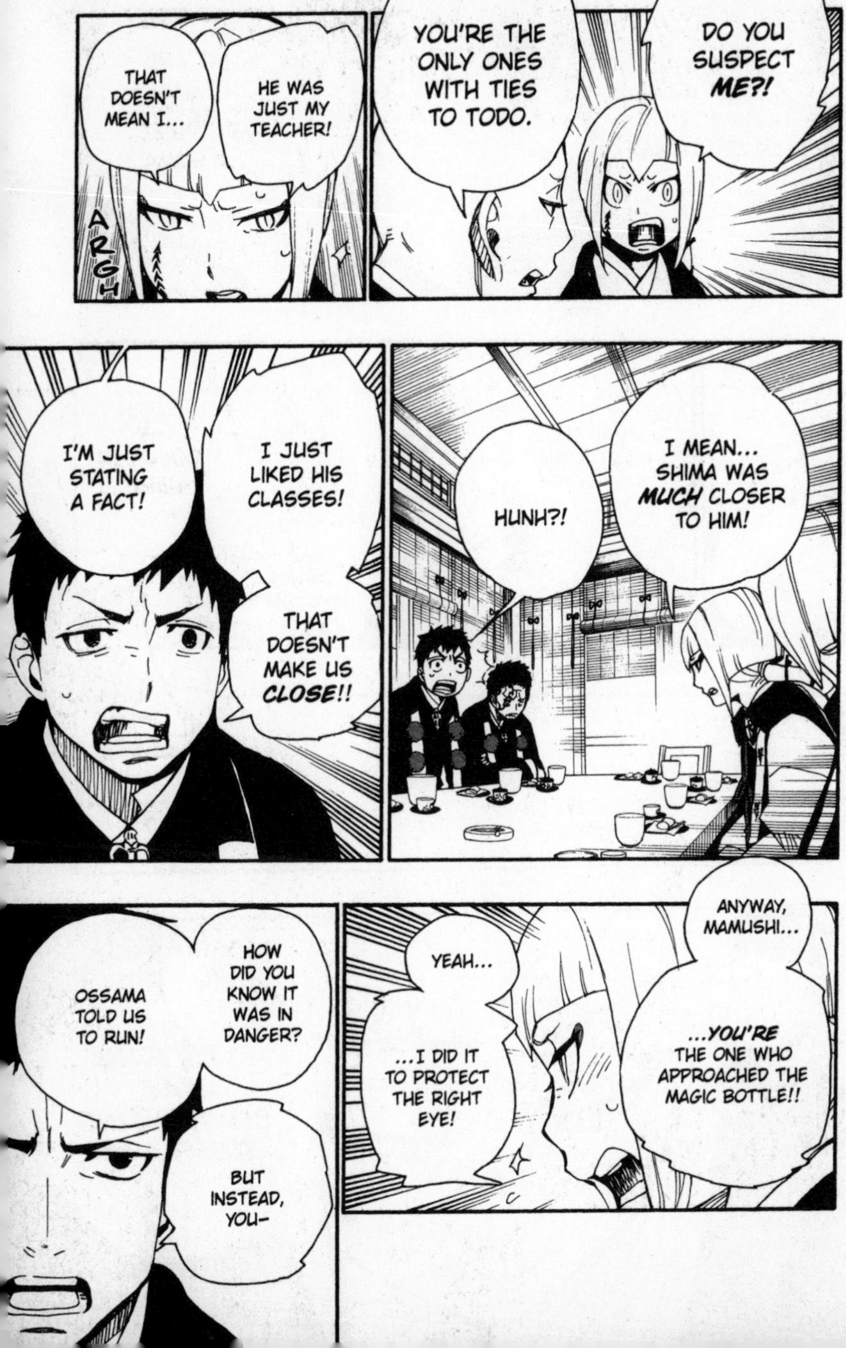
DO YOU SUSPECT ME?!
YOU'RE THE ONLY ONES WITH TIES TO TODO.
HE WAS JUST MY TEACHER!
THAT DOESN'T MEAN I...
ARGH
I MEAN... SHIMA WAS MUCH CLOSER TO HIM!
HUNH?!
I JUST LIKED HIS CLASSES!
THAT DOESN'T MAKE US CLOSE!!
I'M JUST STATING A FACT!
ANYWAY, MAMUSHI...
...YOU'RE THE ONE WHO APPROACHED THE MAGIC BOTTLE!!
YEAH...
...I DID IT TO PROTECT THE RIGHT EYE!
HOW DID YOU KNOW IT WAS IN DANGER?
OSSAMA TOLD US TO RUN!
BUT INSTEAD, YOU-

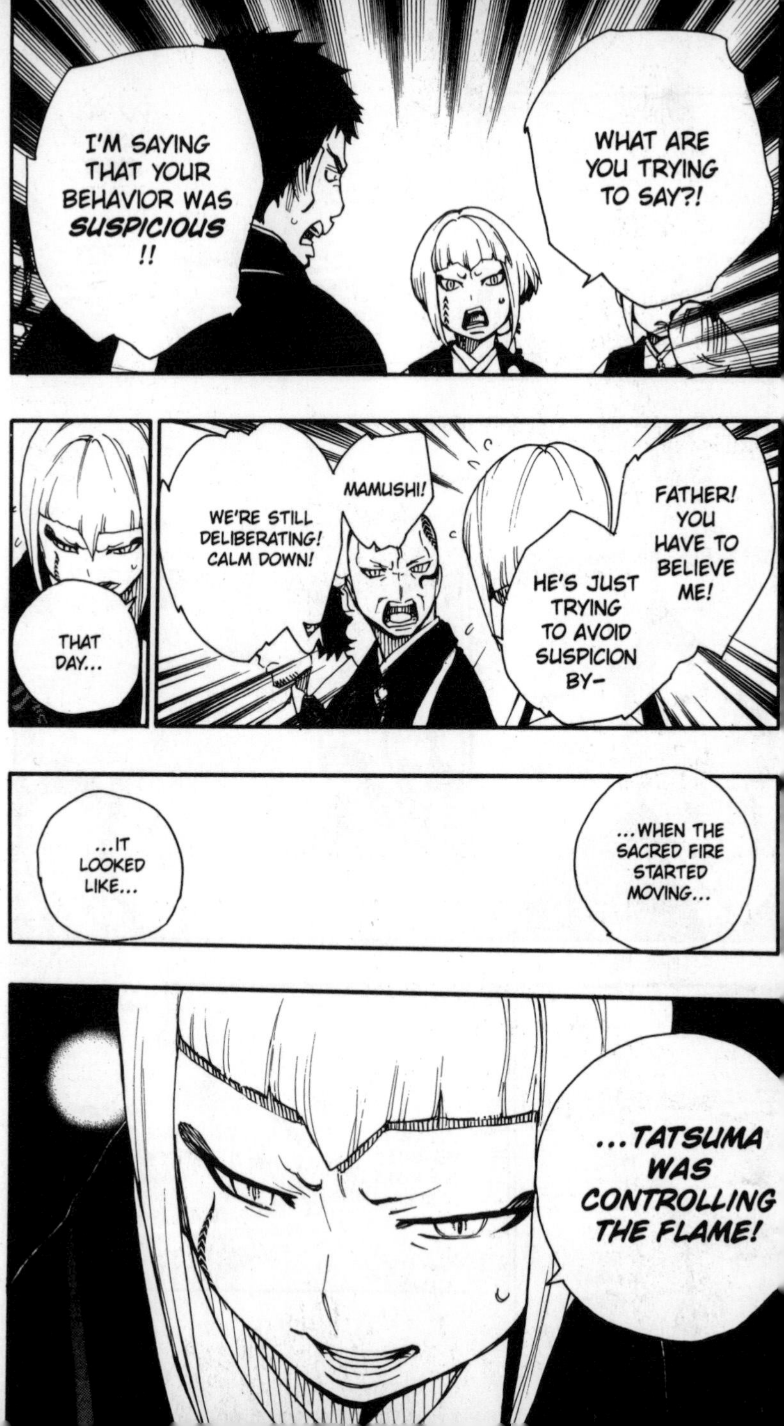
WHAT ARE YOU TRYING TO SAY?!
I'M SAYING THAT YOUR BEHAVIOR WAS SUSPICIOUS!!
FATHER! YOU HAVE TO BELIEVE ME!
HE'S JUST TRYING TO AVOID SUSPICION BY–
MAMUSHI!
WE'RE STILL DELIBERATING! CALM DOWN!
THAT DAY...
...WHEN THE SACRED FIRE STARTED MOVING...
...IT LOOKED LIKE...
...TATSUMA WAS CONTROLLING THE FLAME!

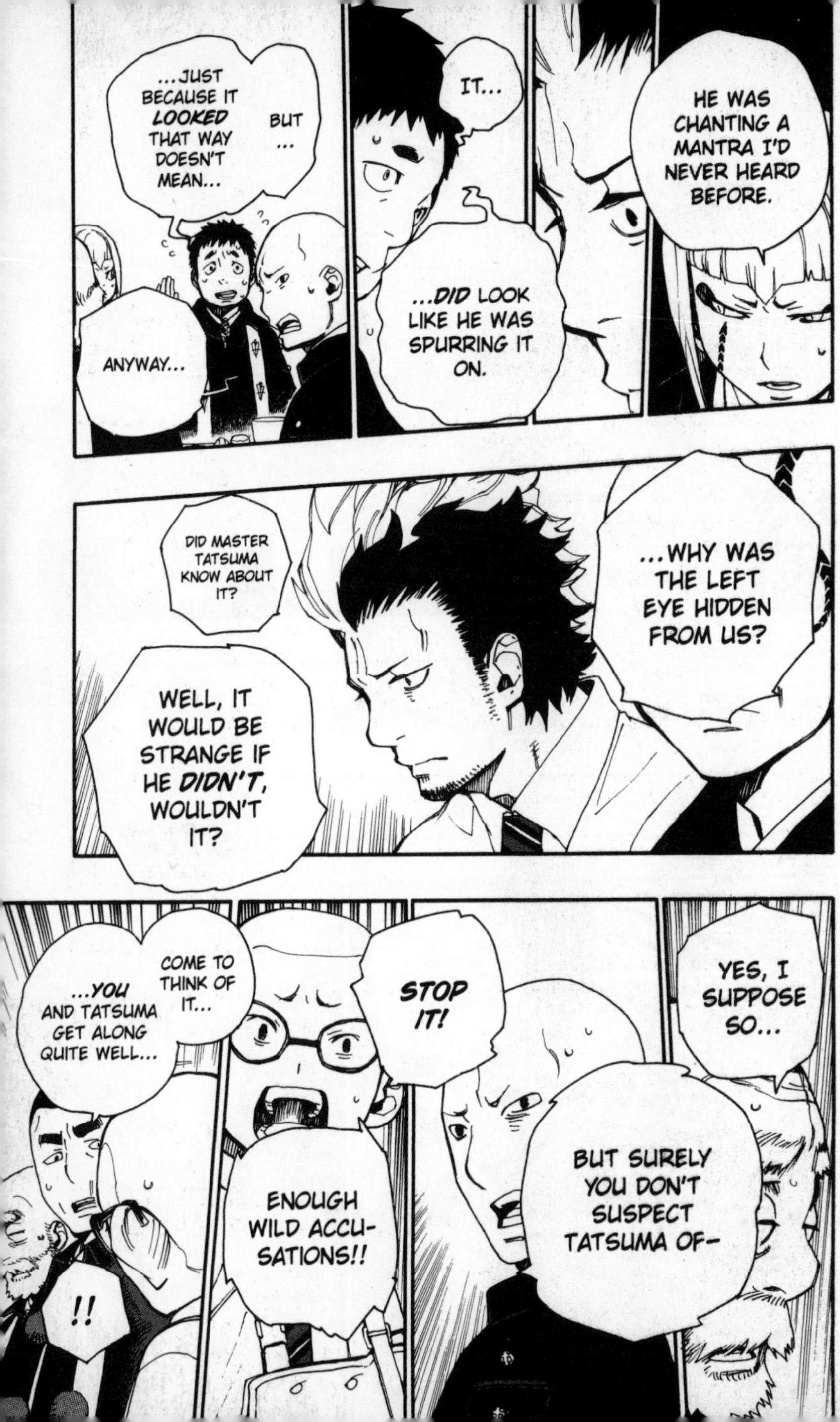
HE WAS CHANTING A MANTRA I'D NEVER HEARD BEFORE.
IT...
...*DID* LOOK LIKE HE WAS SPURRING IT ON.
BUT ...
...JUST BECAUSE IT *LOOKED* THAT WAY DOESN'T MEAN...
ANYWAY...
...WHY WAS THE LEFT EYE HIDDEN FROM US?
DID MASTER TATSUMA KNOW ABOUT IT?
WELL, IT WOULD BE STRANGE IF HE *DIDN'T*, WOULDN'T IT?
YES, I SUPPOSE SO...
BUT SURELY YOU DON'T SUSPECT TATSUMA OF-
STOP IT!
ENOUGH WILD ACCU-SATIONS!!
COME TO THINK OF IT...
...*YOU* AND TATSUMA GET ALONG QUITE WELL...
!!

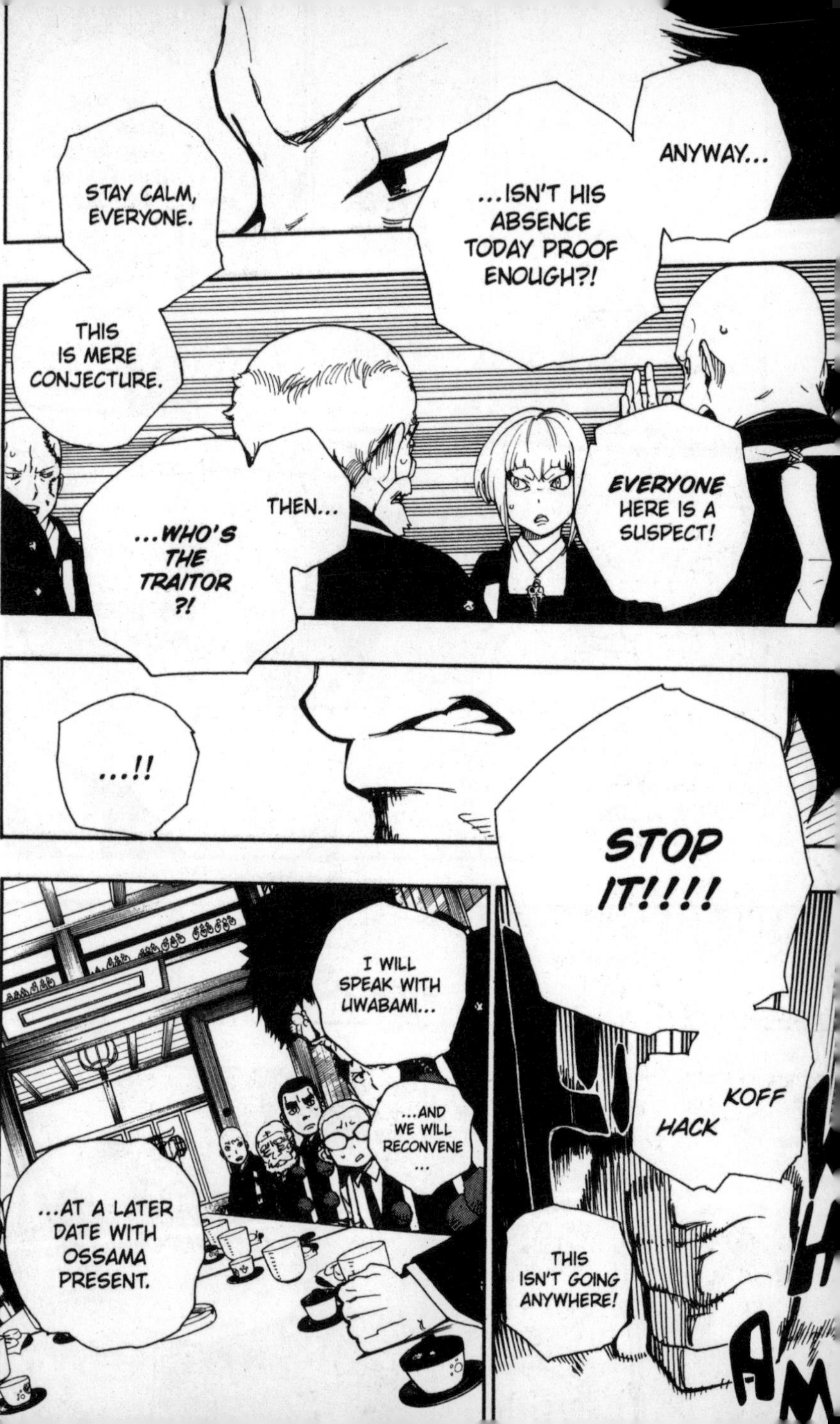
ANYWAY...
...ISN'T HIS ABSENCE TODAY PROOF ENOUGH?!
STAY CALM, EVERYONE.
EVERYONE HERE IS A SUSPECT!
THIS IS MERE CONJECTURE.
THEN...
...WHO'S THE TRAITOR?!
...!!
STOP IT!!!!
KOFF
HACK
THIS ISN'T GOING ANYWHERE!
I WILL SPEAK WITH UWABAMI...
...AND WE WILL RECONVENE...
...AT A LATER DATE WITH OSSAMA PRESENT.

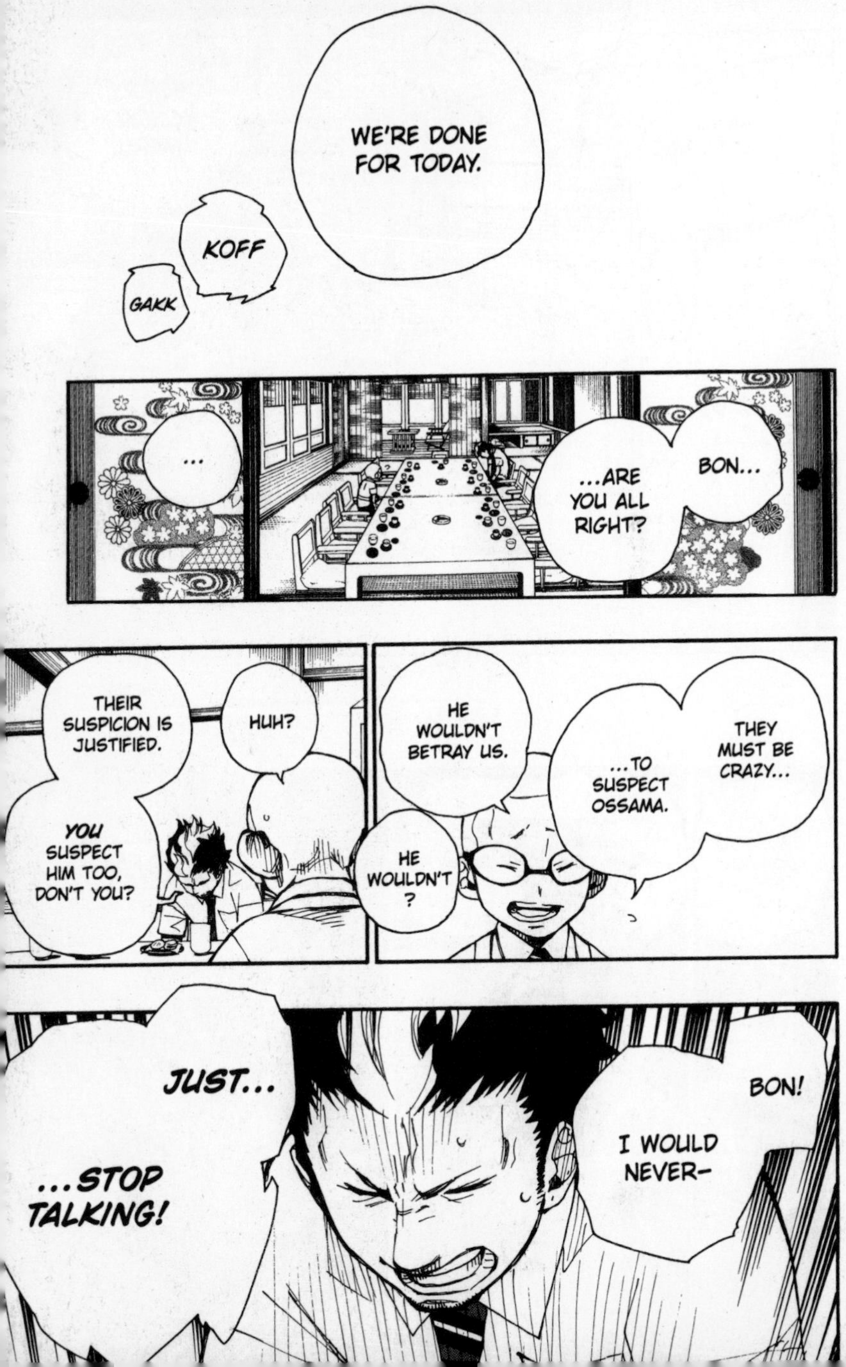
WE'RE DONE FOR TODAY.
KOFF
GAKK
BON...
...ARE YOU ALL RIGHT?
...
THEY MUST BE CRAZY...
...TO SUSPECT OSSAMA.
HE WOULDN'T BETRAY US.
HE WOULDN'T ?
HUH?
THEIR SUSPICION IS JUSTIFIED.
YOU SUSPECT HIM TOO, DON'T YOU?
BON!
I WOULD NEVER-
JUST...
...STOP TALKING!

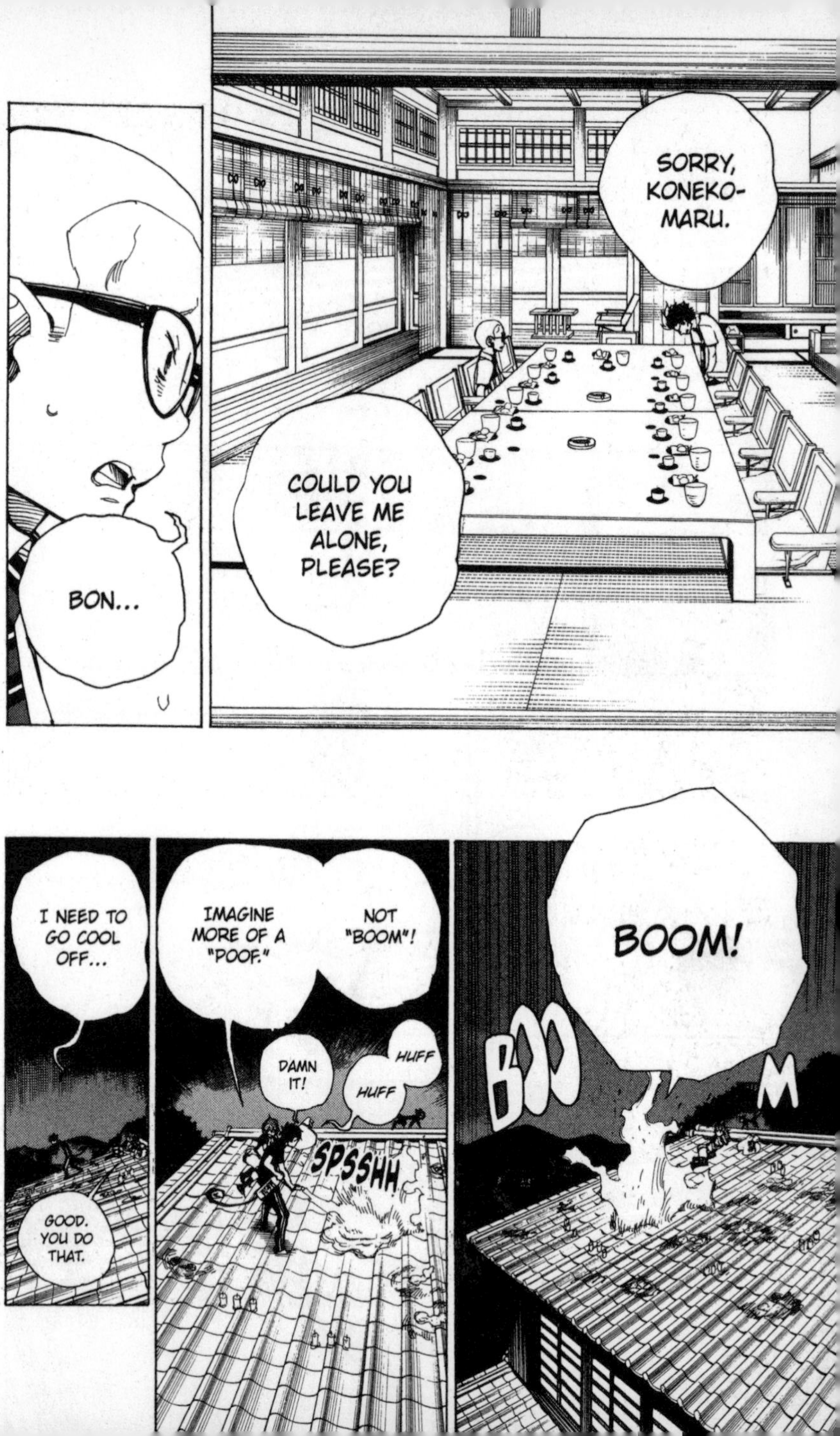
SORRY, KONEKO-MARU.
COULD YOU LEAVE ME ALONE, PLEASE?
BON...
BOOM!
BOOM
NOT "BOOM"!
IMAGINE MORE OF A "POOF."
HUFF
HUFF
DAMN IT!
SPSSHH
I NEED TO GO COOL OFF...
GOOD. YOU DO THAT.

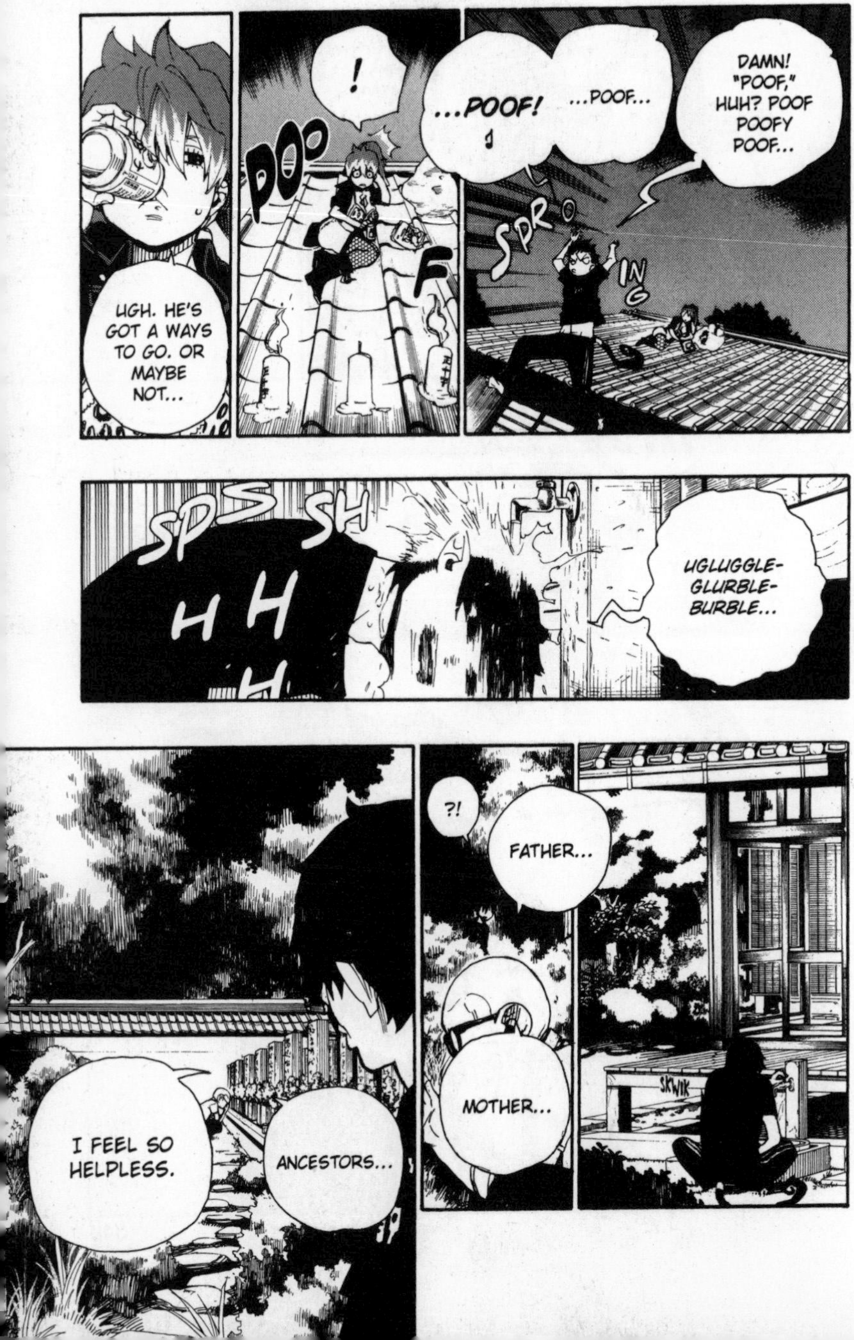
DAMN! "POOF," HUH? POOF POOFY POOF...
...POOF...
...POOF!
SPRO ING
!
DOO
F
UGH. HE'S GOT A WAYS TO GO. OR MAYBE NOT...
UGLUGGLE-GLURBLE-BURBLE...
SPSSH
HHH
SKWIK
?!
FATHER...
MOTHER...
ANCESTORS...
I FEEL SO HELPLESS.

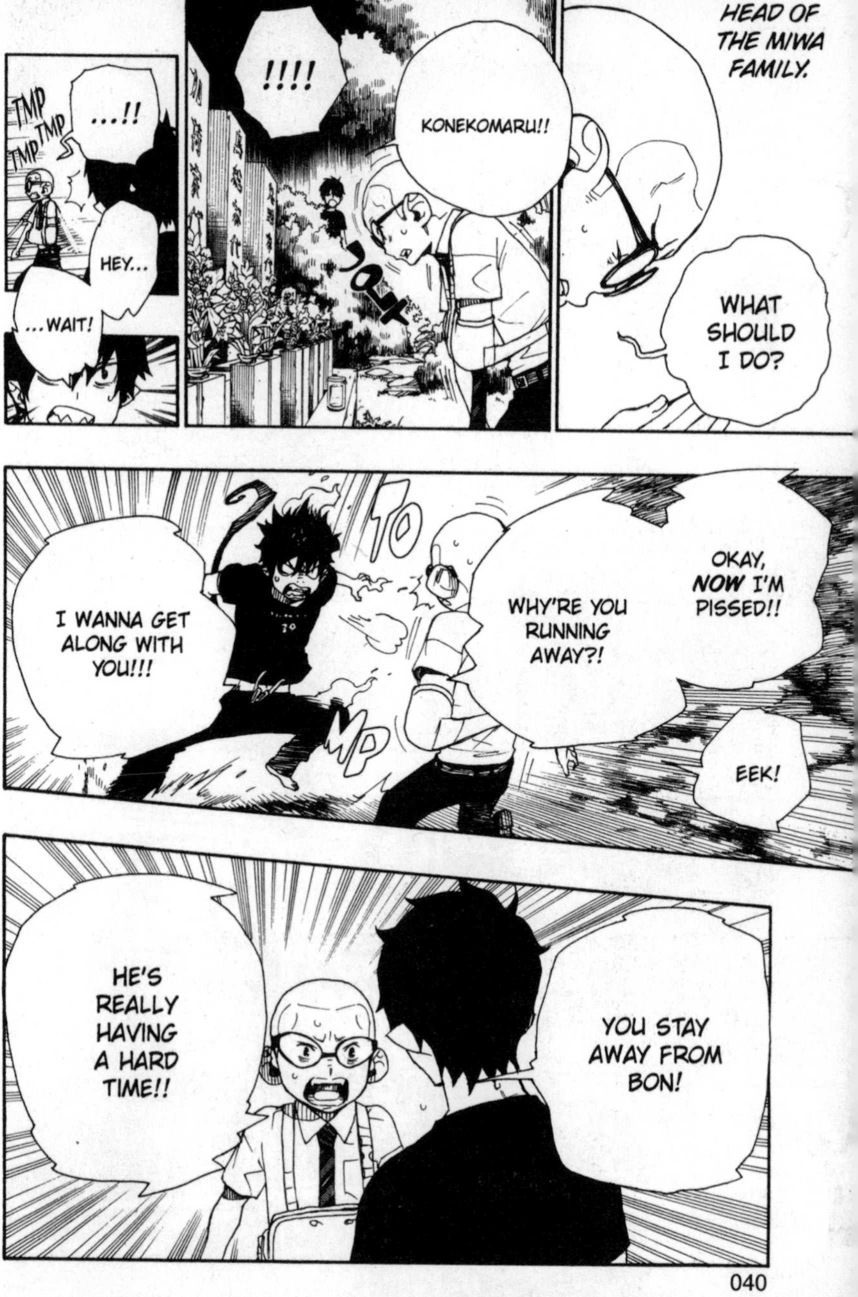
HEAD OF THE MIWA FAMILY.
WHAT SHOULD I DO?
KONEKOMARU!!
!!!!
TMP TMP TMP
...!!
HEY...
...WAIT!
OKAY, **NOW** I'M PISSED!!
WHY'RE YOU RUNNING AWAY?!
TO
EEK!
I WANNA GET ALONG WITH YOU!!!
MP
YOU STAY AWAY FROM BON!
HE'S REALLY HAVING A HARD TIME!!

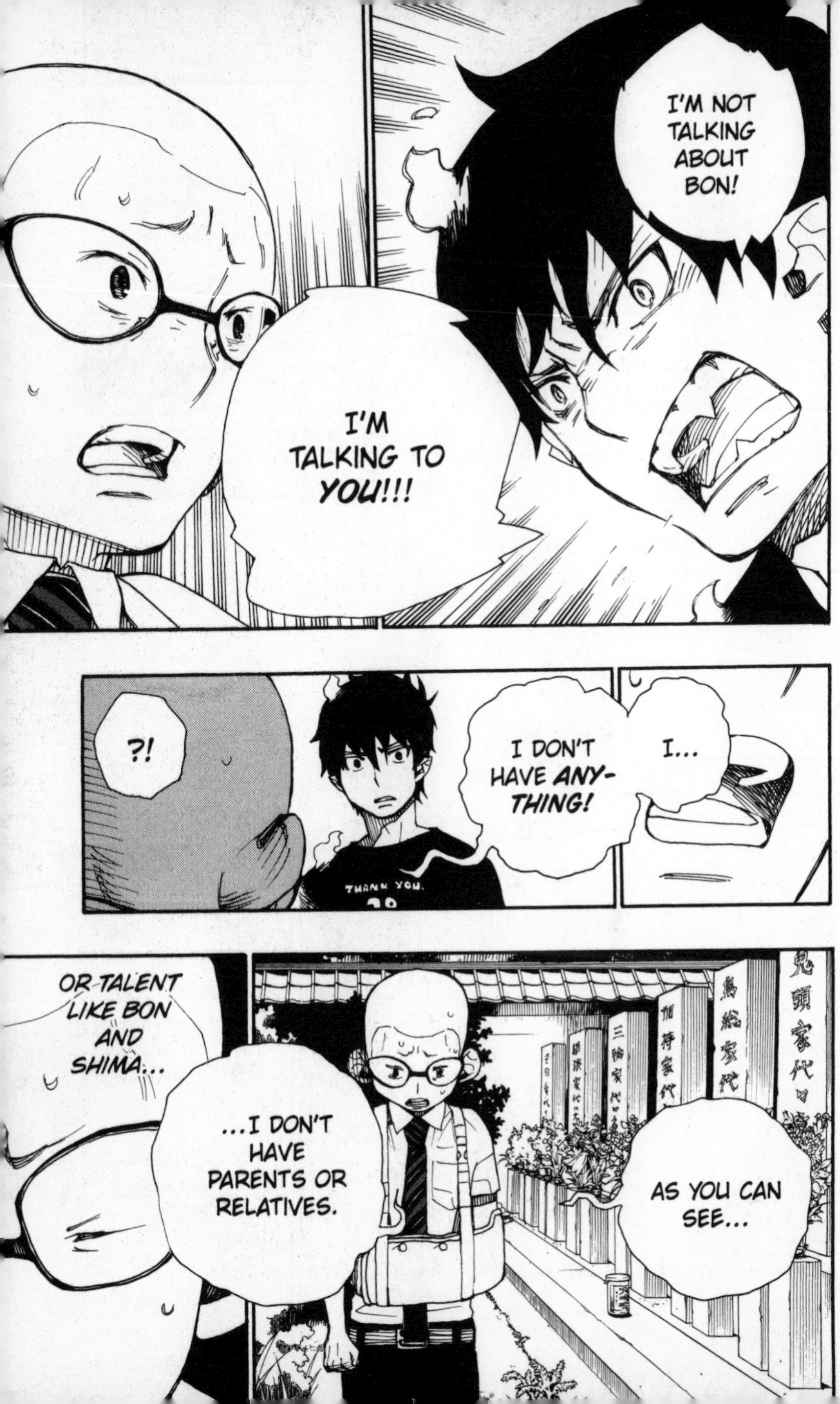
I'M NOT TALKING ABOUT BON!
I'M TALKING TO *YOU*!!!
I...
I DON'T HAVE *ANYTHING!*
?!
AS YOU CAN SEE...
...I DON'T HAVE PARENTS OR RELATIVES.
OR TALENT LIKE BON AND SHIMA...

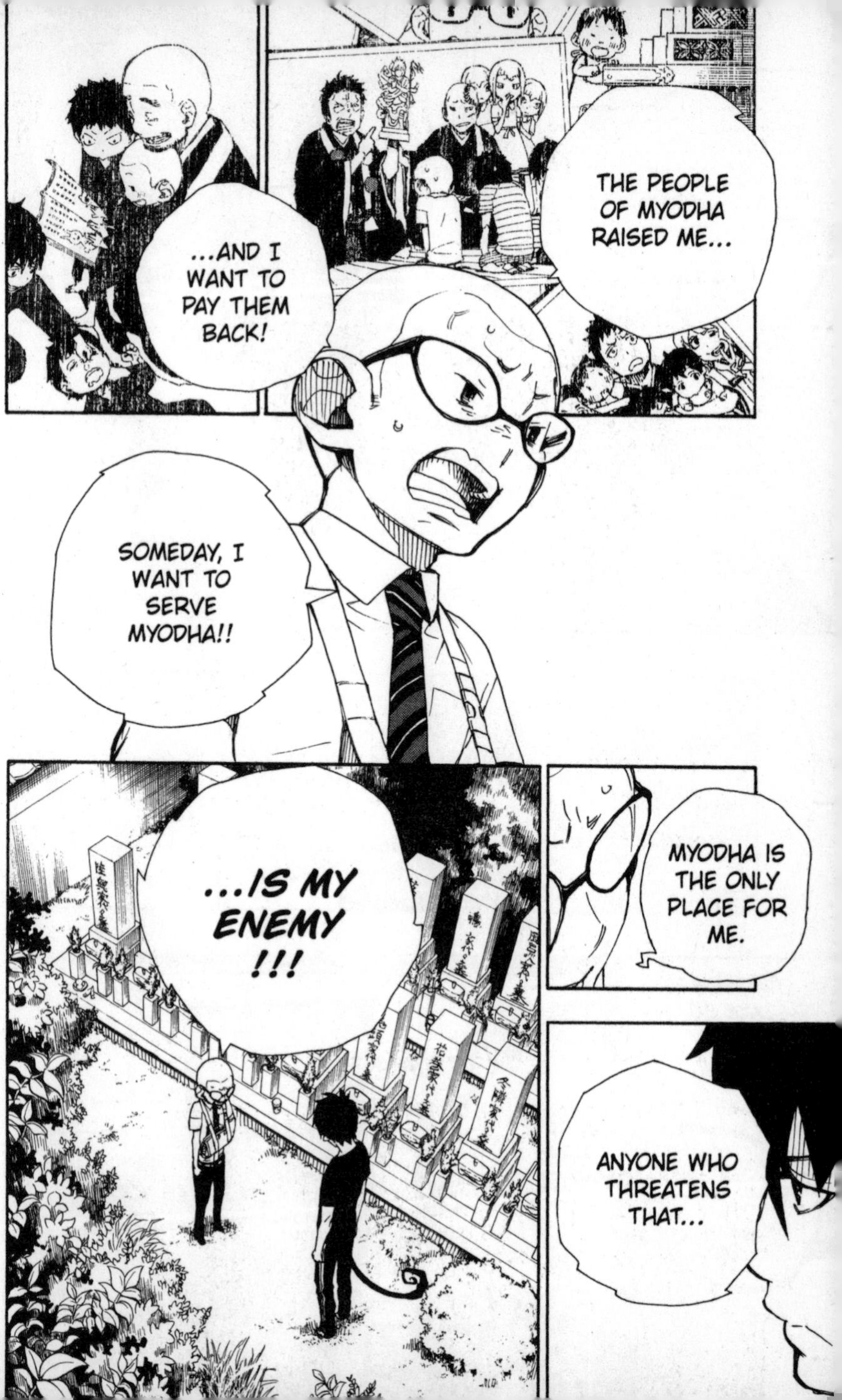
THE PEOPLE OF MYODHA RAISED ME...
...AND I WANT TO PAY THEM BACK!
SOMEDAY, I WANT TO SERVE MYODHA!!
MYODHA IS THE ONLY PLACE FOR ME.
ANYONE WHO THREATENS THAT...
...IS MY ENEMY !!!

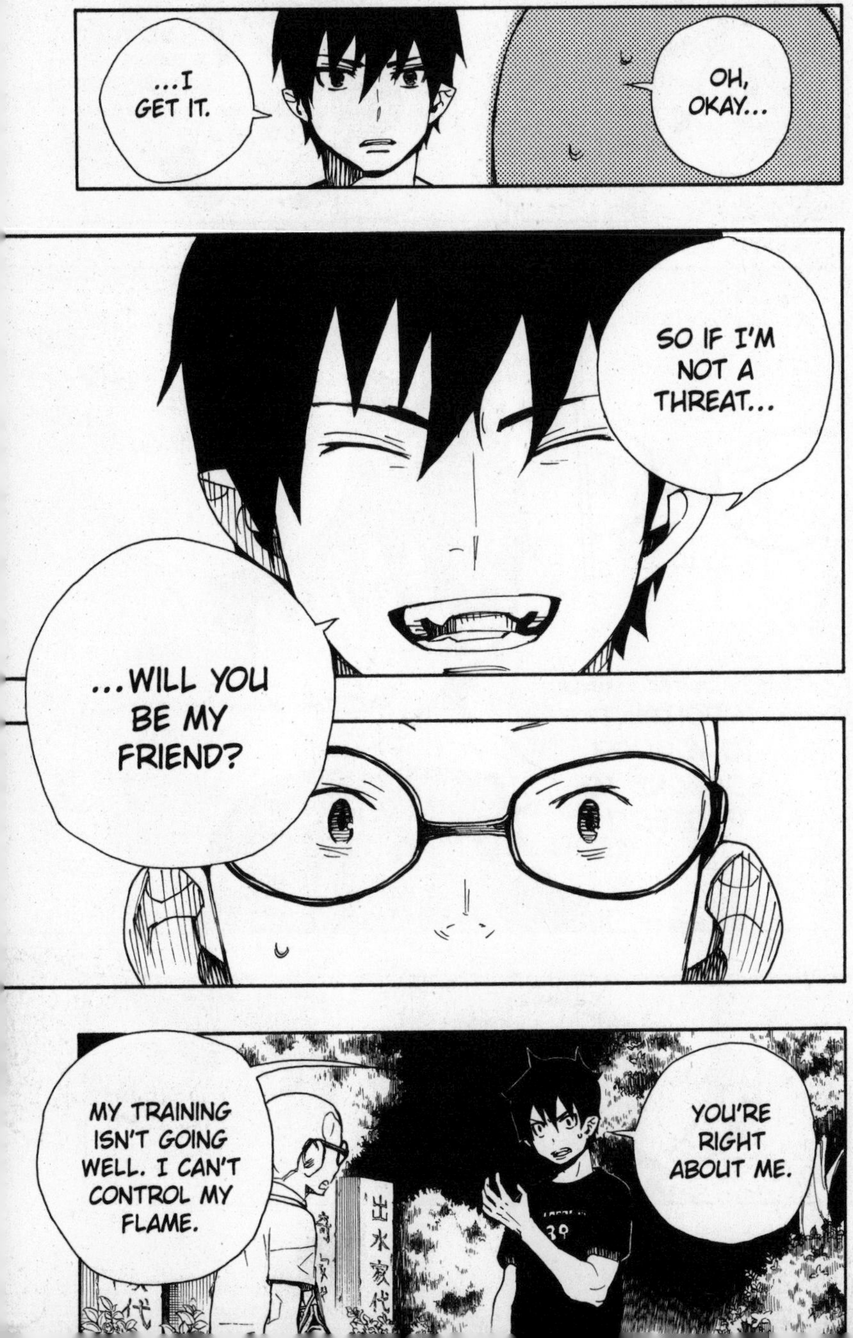
OH, OKAY...
...I GET IT.
SO IF I'M NOT A THREAT...
...WILL YOU BE MY FRIEND?
YOU'RE RIGHT ABOUT ME.
MY TRAINING ISN'T GOING WELL. I CAN'T CONTROL MY FLAME.

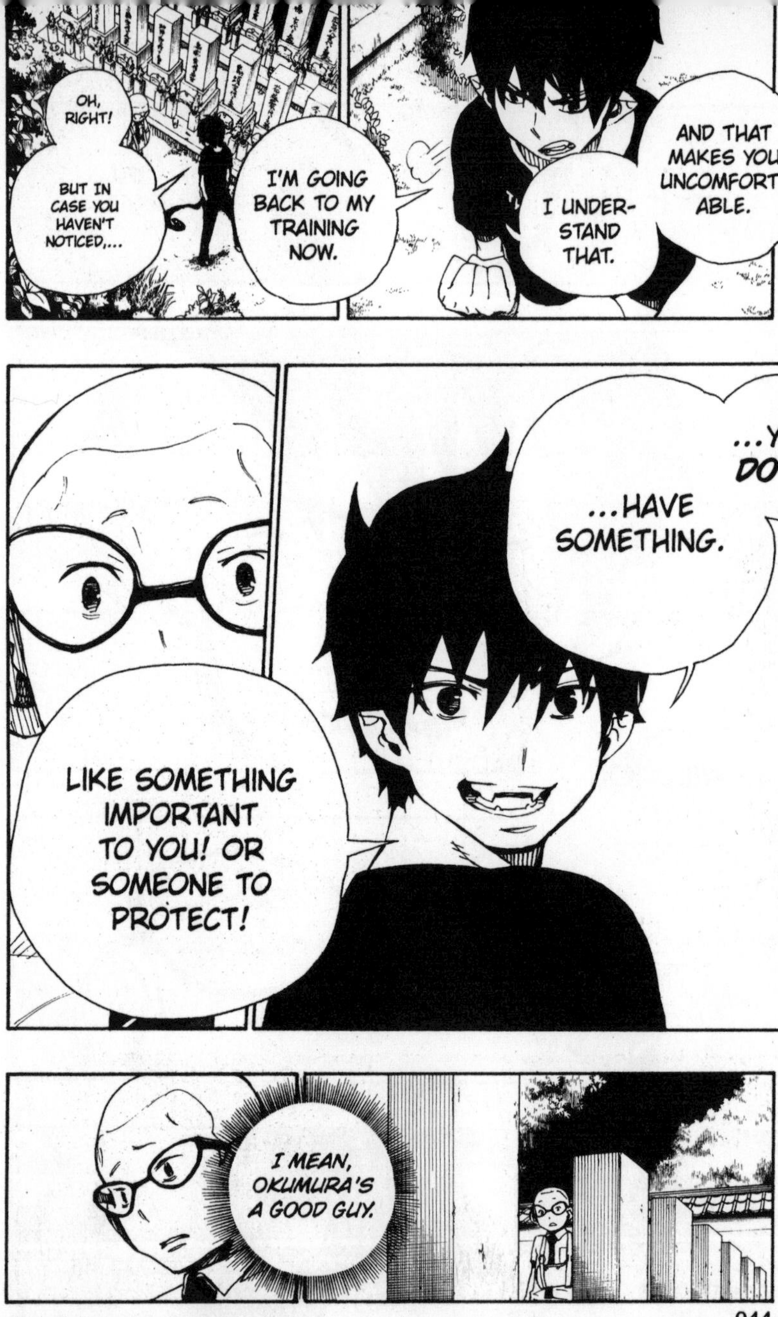
AND THAT MAKES YOU UNCOMFORTABLE.
I UNDERSTAND THAT.
I'M GOING BACK TO MY TRAINING NOW.
OH, RIGHT!
BUT IN CASE YOU HAVEN'T NOTICED,...
...YOU DO...
...HAVE SOMETHING.
LIKE SOMETHING IMPORTANT TO YOU! OR SOMEONE TO PROTECT!
I MEAN, OKUMURA'S A GOOD GUY.

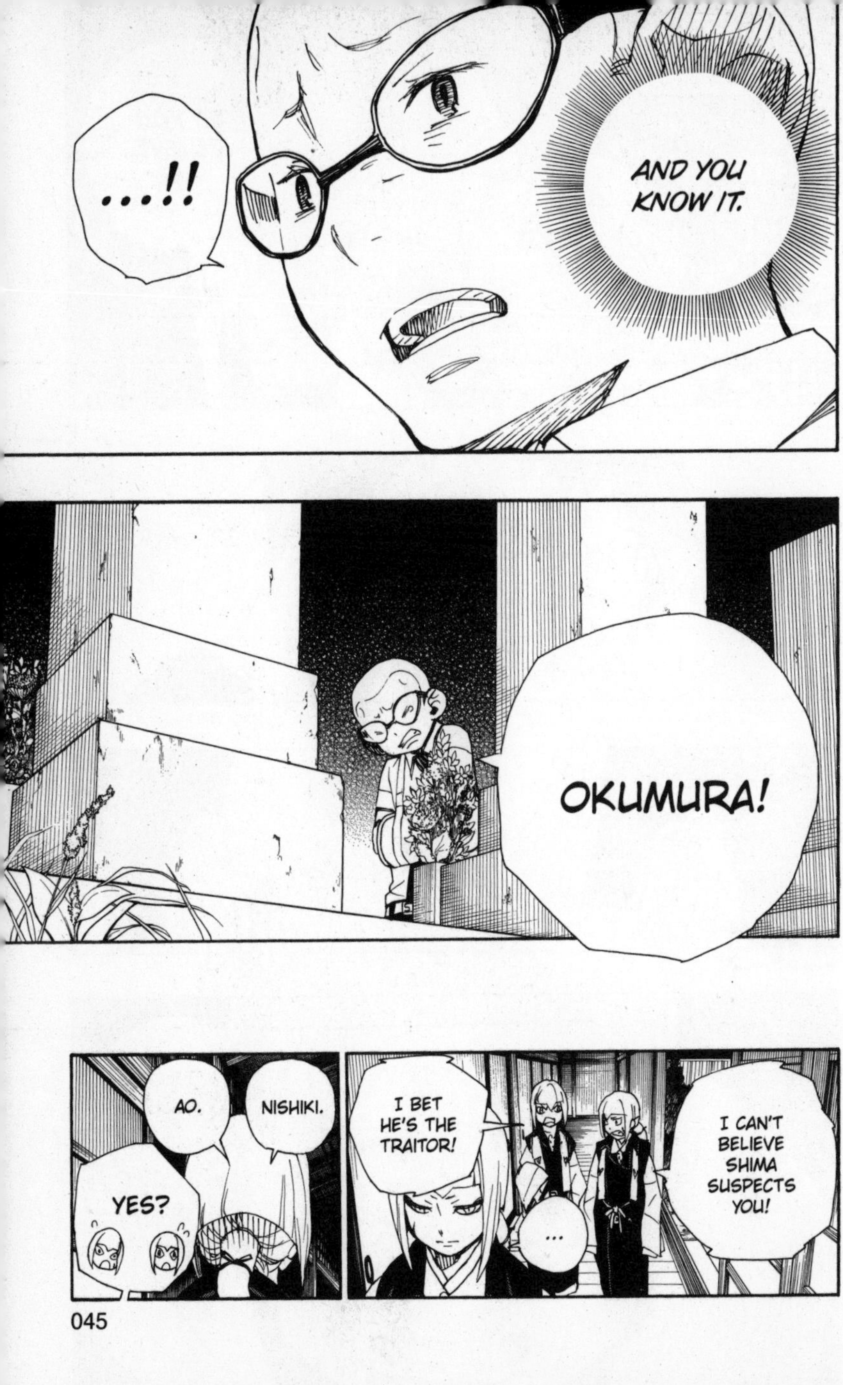
AND YOU KNOW IT.
...!!
OKUMURA!
I CAN'T BELIEVE SHIMA SUSPECTS YOU!
I BET HE'S THE TRAITOR!
...
NISHIKI.
AO.
YES?

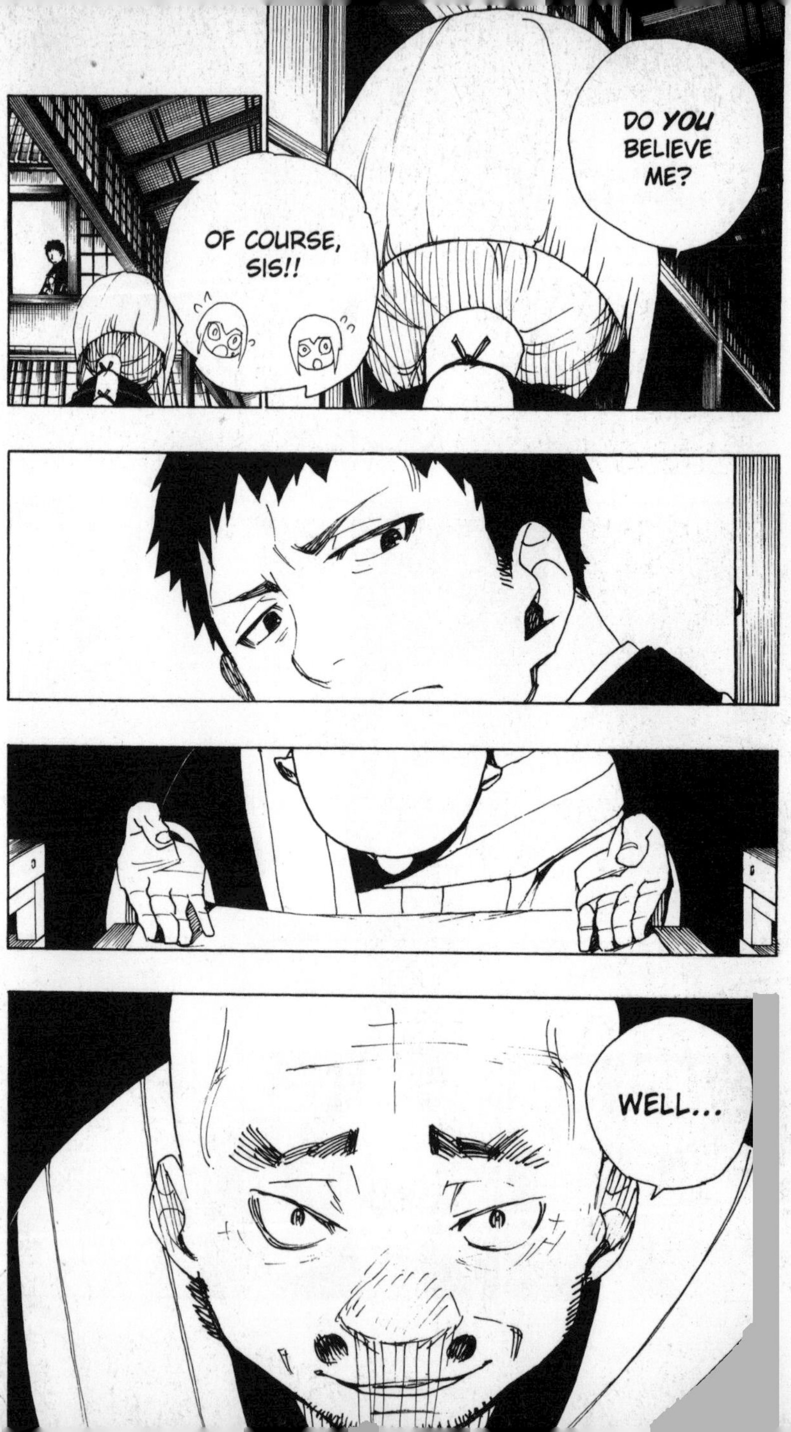
DO YOU BELIEVE ME?
OF COURSE, SIS!!
WELL...

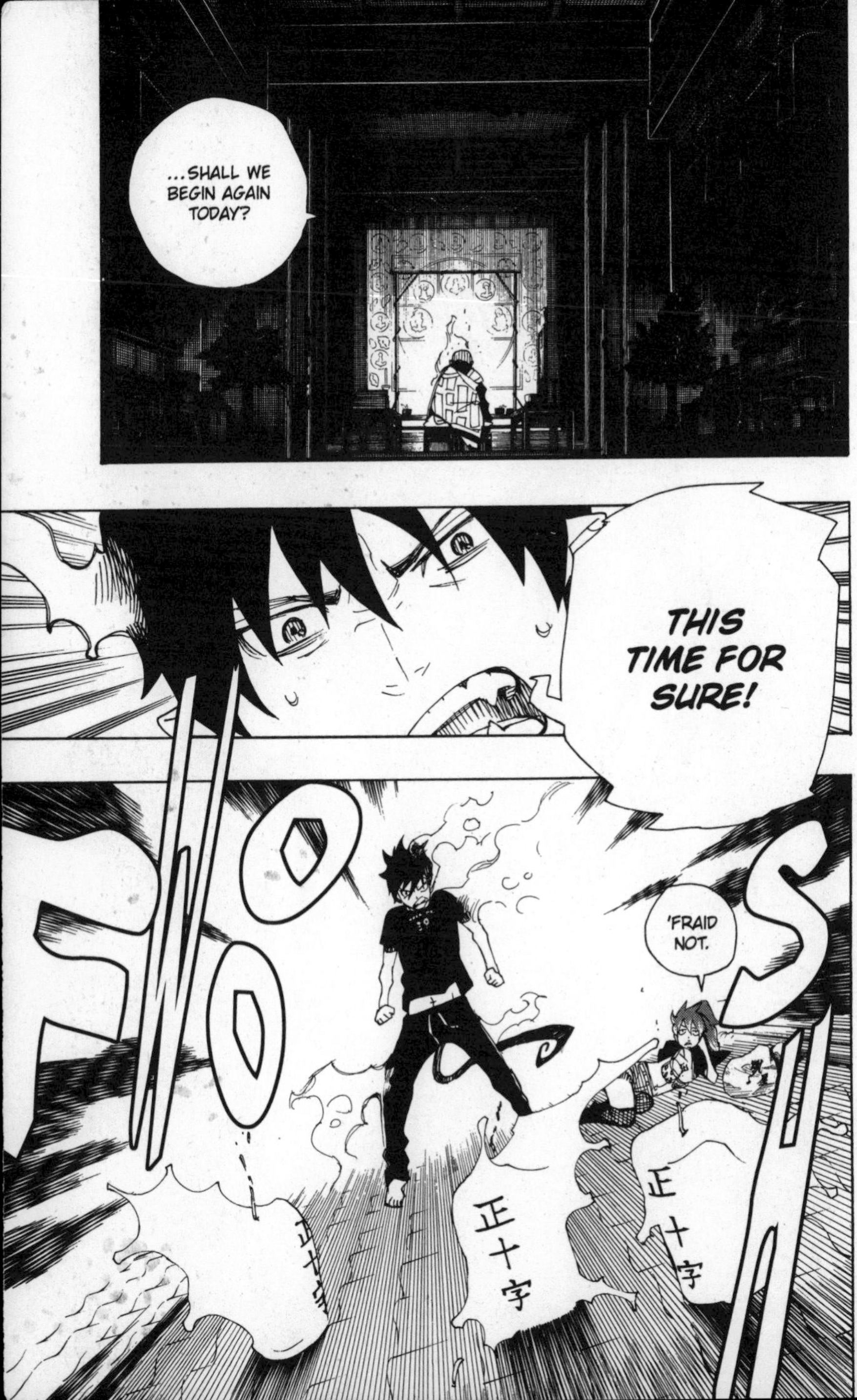
...SHALL WE BEGIN AGAIN TODAY?
THIS TIME FOR SURE!
'FRAID NOT.
正十字
正十字
正十字

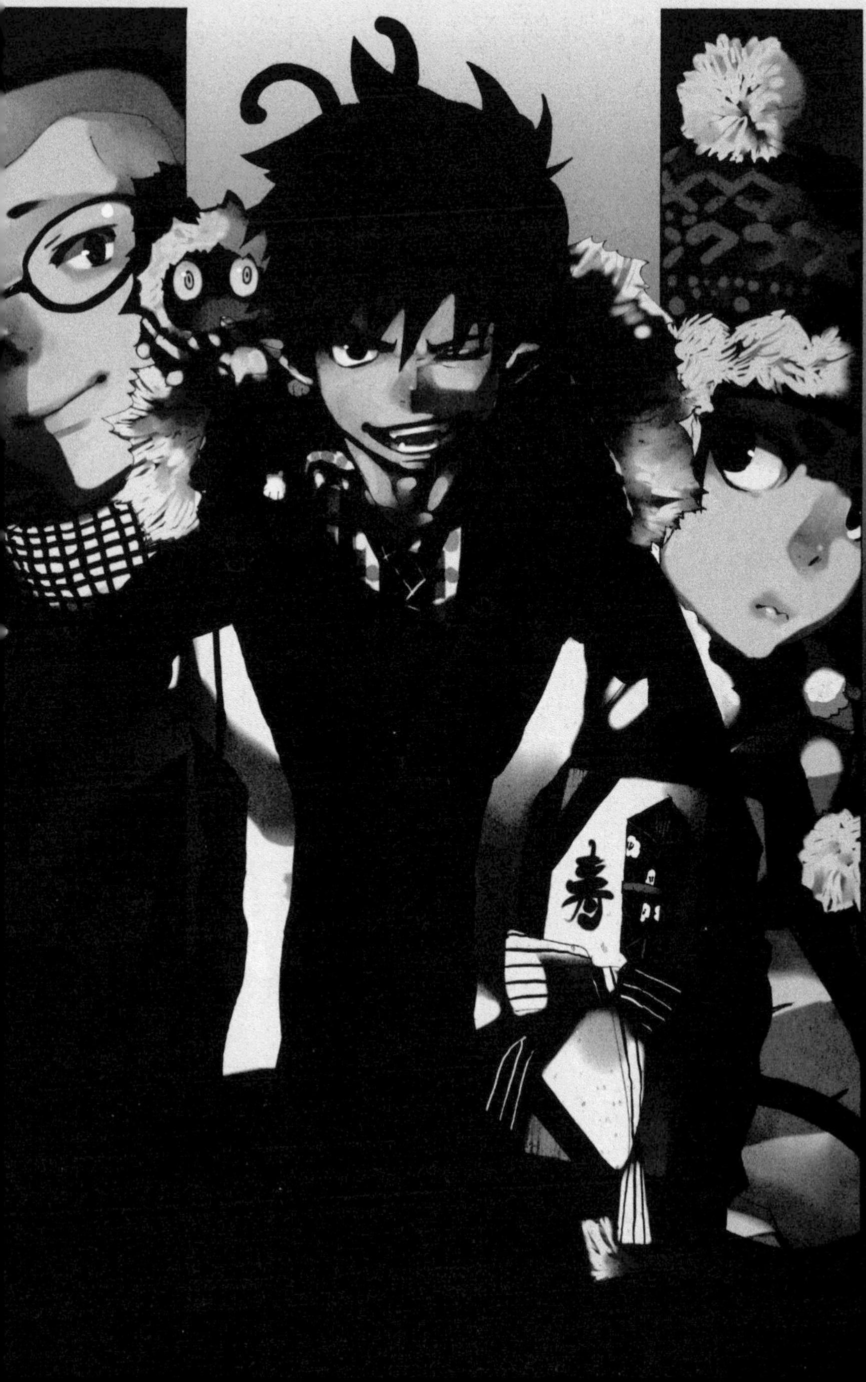
寿

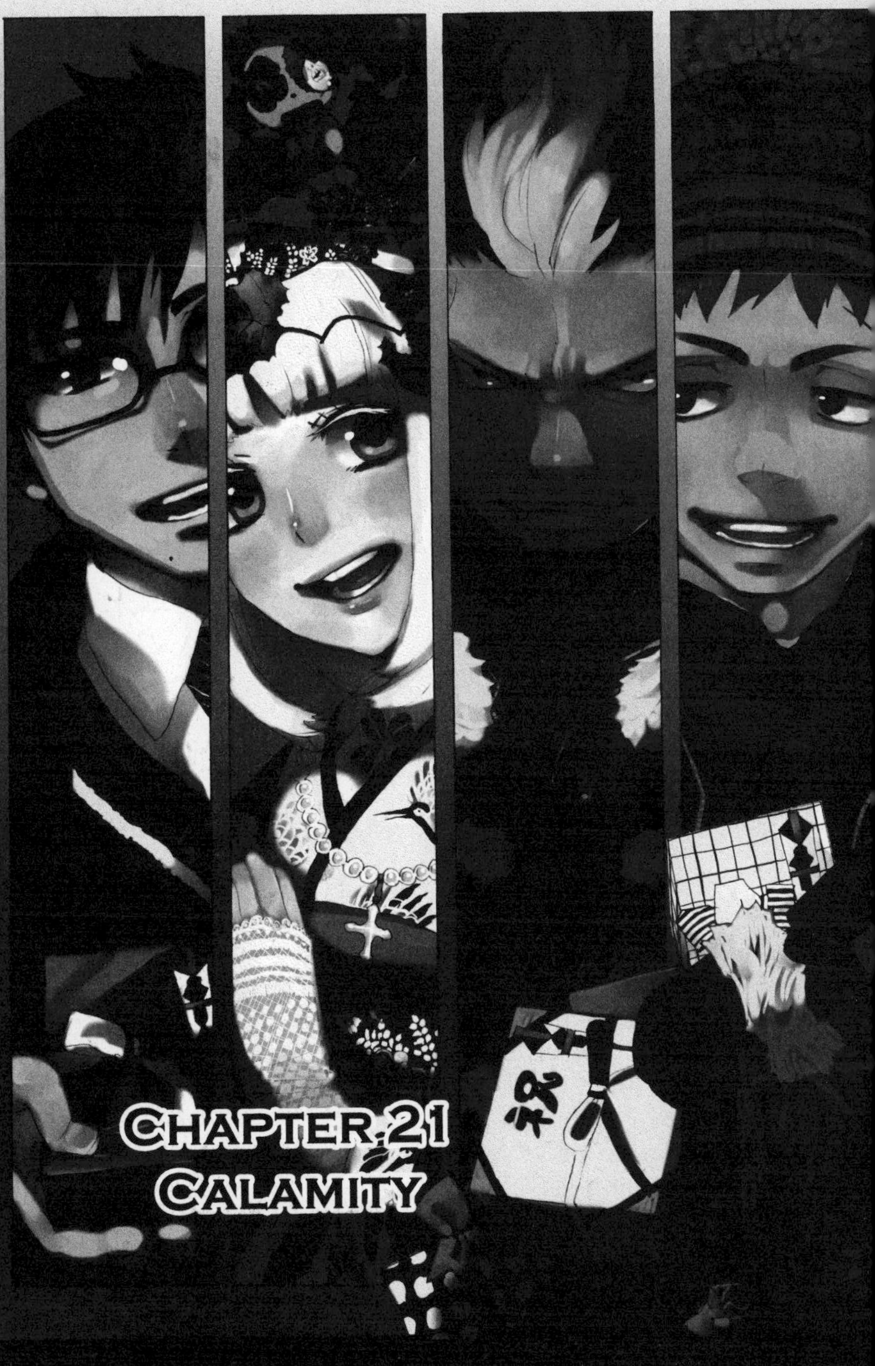
CHAPTER 21
CALAMITY

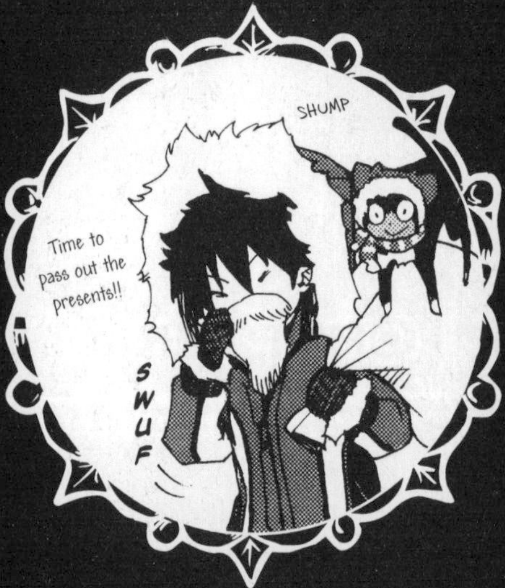
SHUMP
Time to pass out the presents!!
SWUF

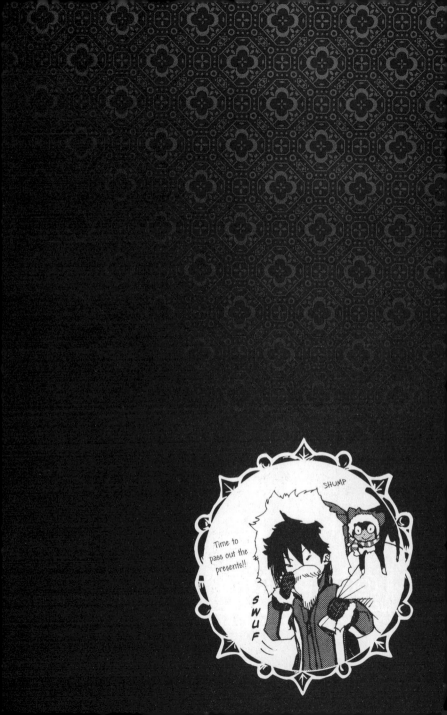

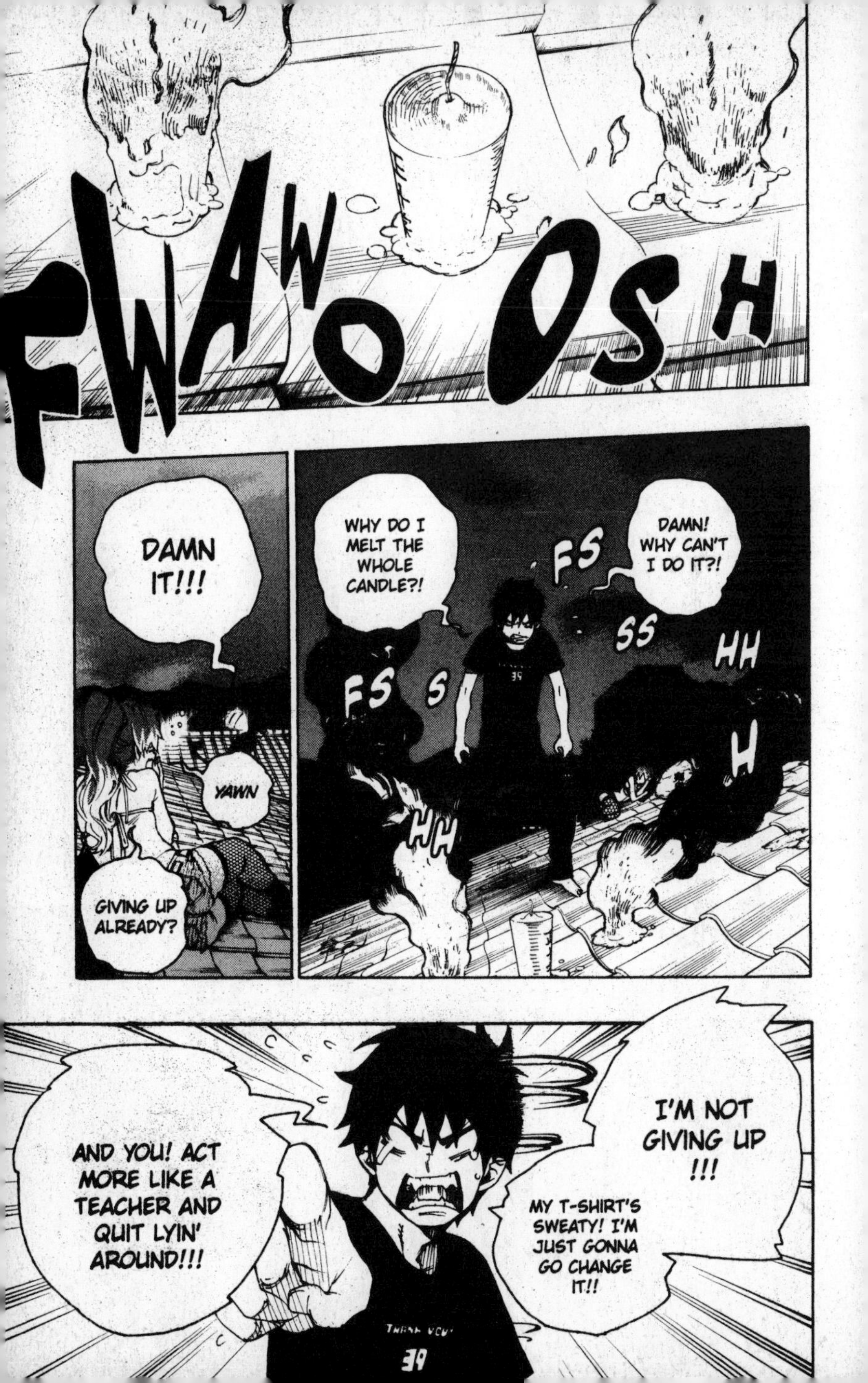
FWAWOOSH
DAMN! WHY CAN'T I DO IT?!
FS
SS
HH
H
WHY DO I MELT THE WHOLE CANDLE?!
FS
S
HH
DAMN IT!!!
YAWN
GIVING UP ALREADY?
I'M NOT GIVING UP !!!
MY T-SHIRT'S SWEATY! I'M JUST GONNA GO CHANGE IT!!
AND YOU! ACT MORE LIKE A TEACHER AND QUIT LYIN' AROUND!!!

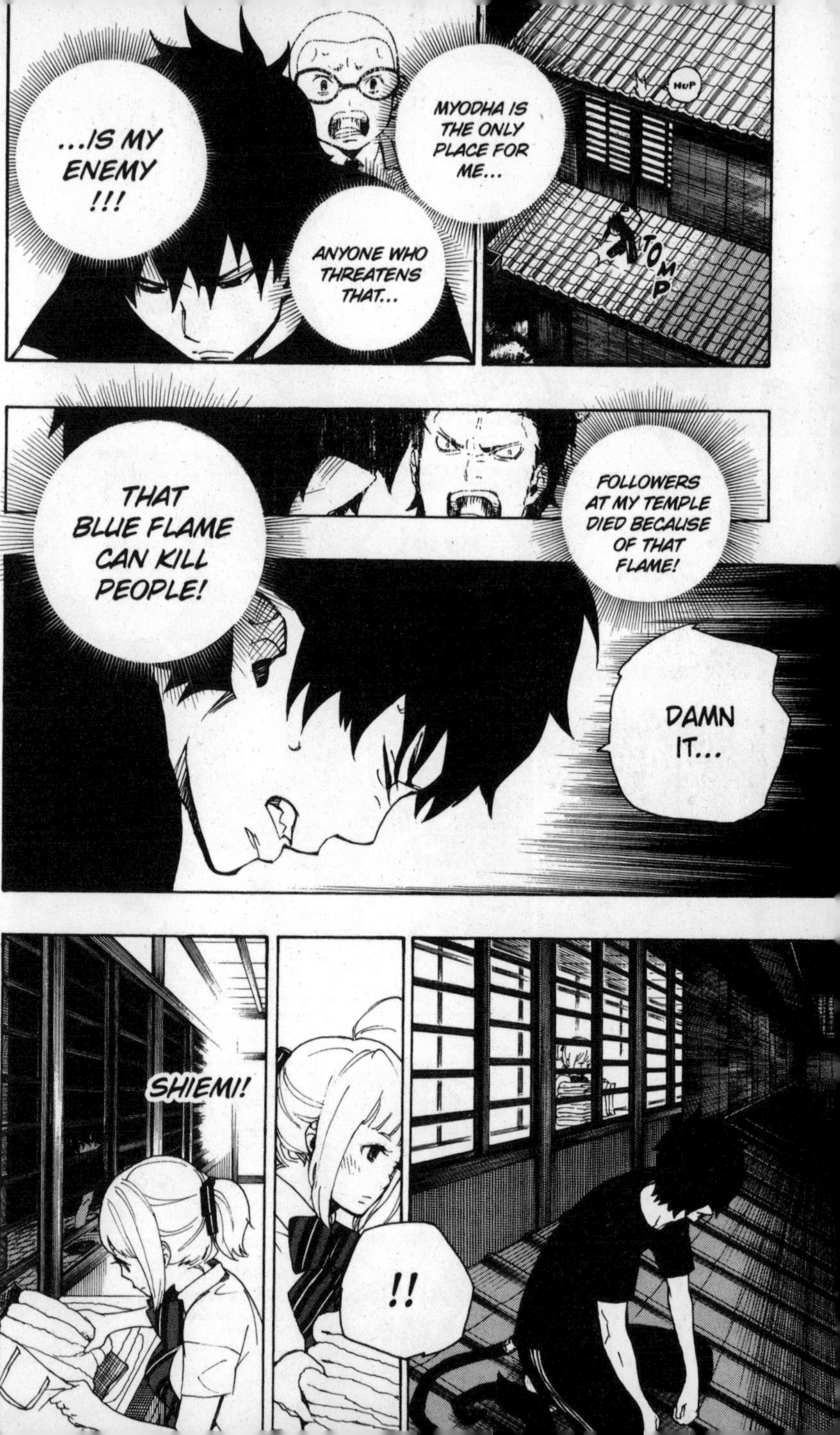
HUP
TOMP
MYODHA IS THE ONLY PLACE FOR ME...
ANYONE WHO THREATENS THAT...
...IS MY ENEMY !!!
FOLLOWERS AT MY TEMPLE DIED BECAUSE OF THAT FLAME!
THAT BLUE FLAME CAN KILL PEOPLE!
DAMN IT...
!!
SHIEMI!

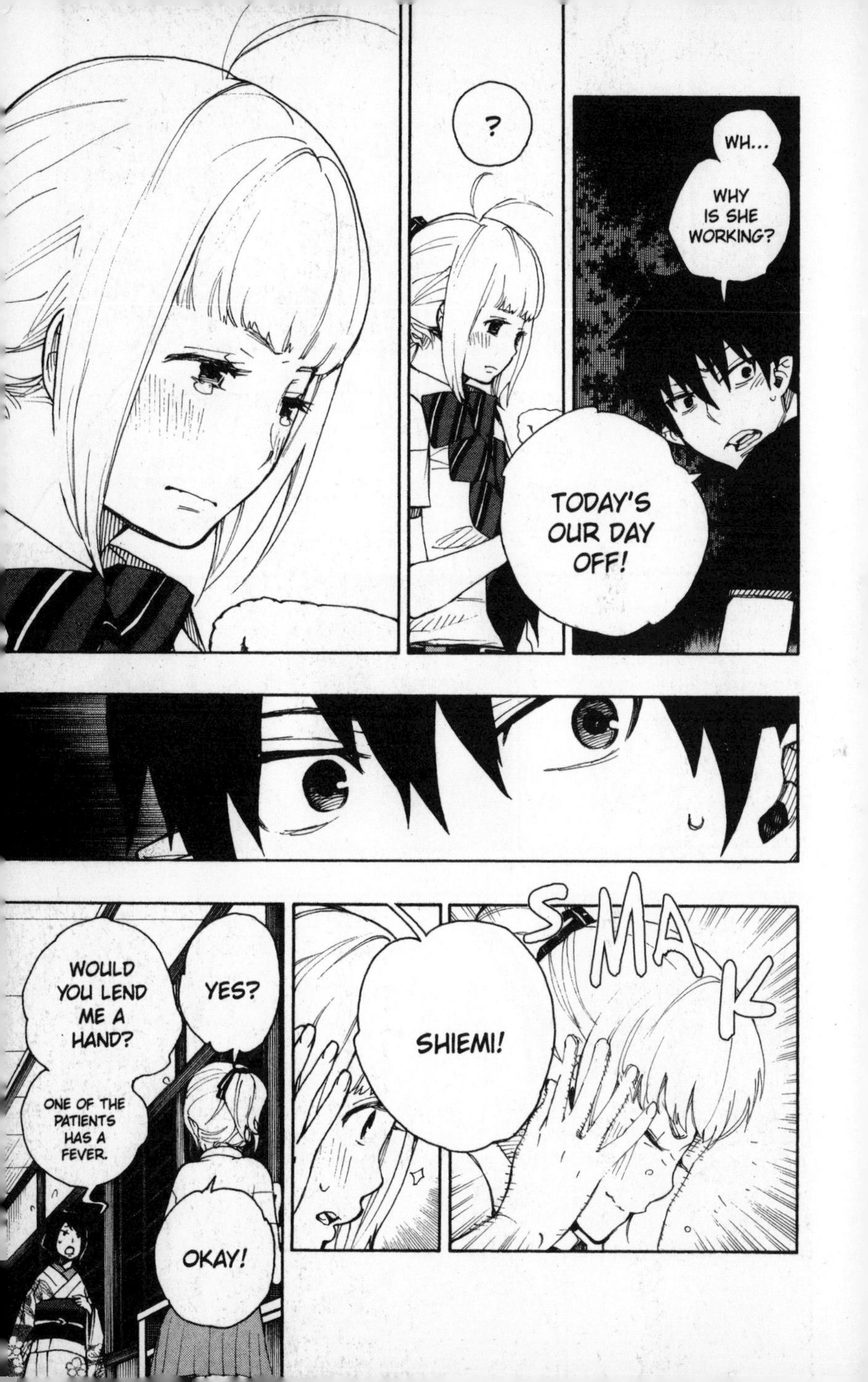
WH...
WHY IS SHE WORKING?
TODAY'S OUR DAY OFF!
?
SMAK
SHIEMI!
YES?
WOULD YOU LEND ME A HAND?
ONE OF THE PATIENTS HAS A FEVER.
OKAY!

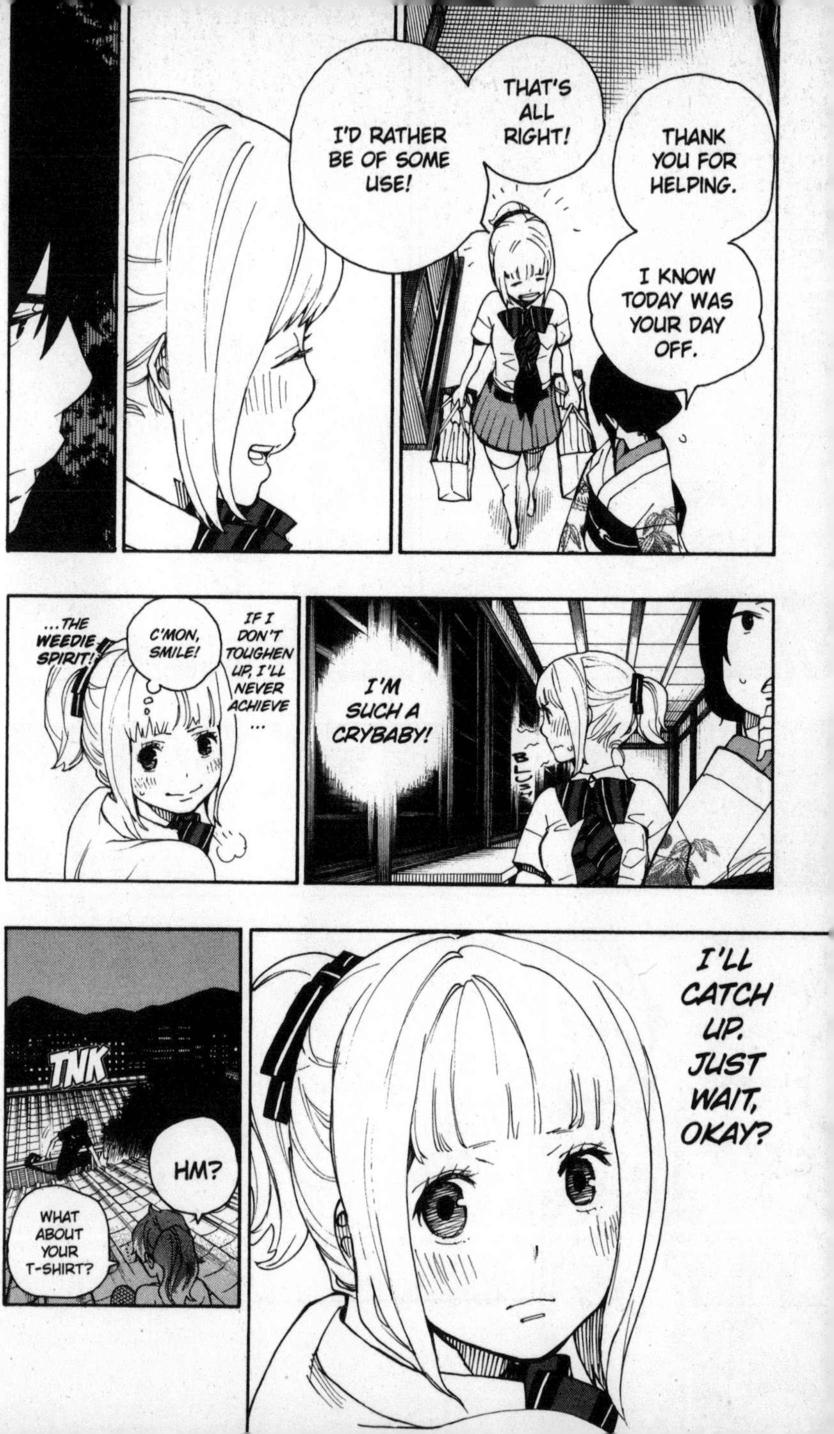
THANK YOU FOR HELPING.
I KNOW TODAY WAS YOUR DAY OFF.
THAT'S ALL RIGHT!
I'D RATHER BE OF SOME USE!
I'M SUCH A CRYBABY!
IF I DON'T TOUGHEN UP, I'LL NEVER ACHIEVE ...
C'MON, SMILE!
...THE WEEDIE SPIRIT!
I'LL CATCH UP. JUST WAIT, OKAY?
TNK
HM?
WHAT ABOUT YOUR T-SHIRT?

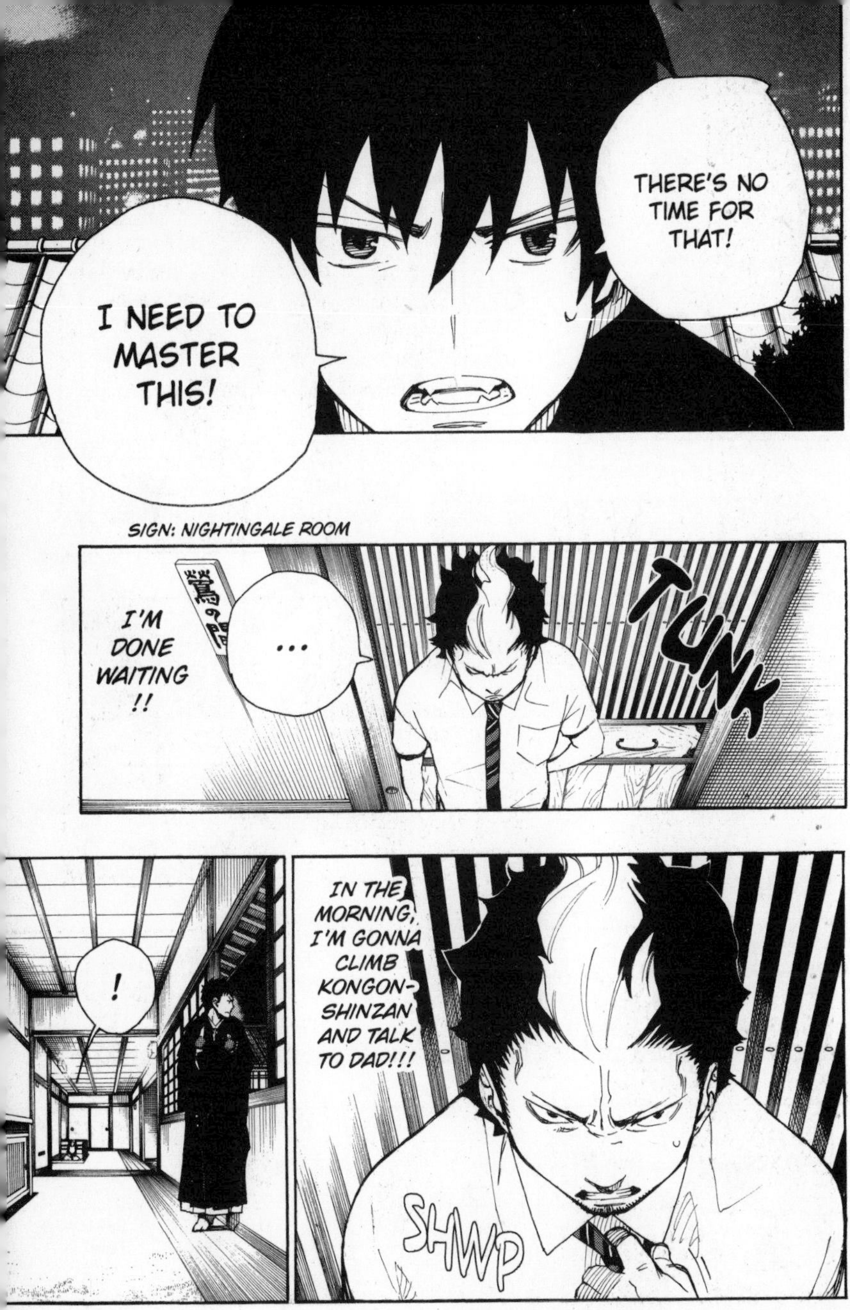
THERE'S NO TIME FOR THAT!
I NEED TO MASTER THIS!
SIGN: NIGHTINGALE ROOM
TUNK
...
I'M DONE WAITING !!
IN THE MORNING, I'M GONNA CLIMB KONGON-SHINZAN AND TALK TO DAD!!!
SHWP
!

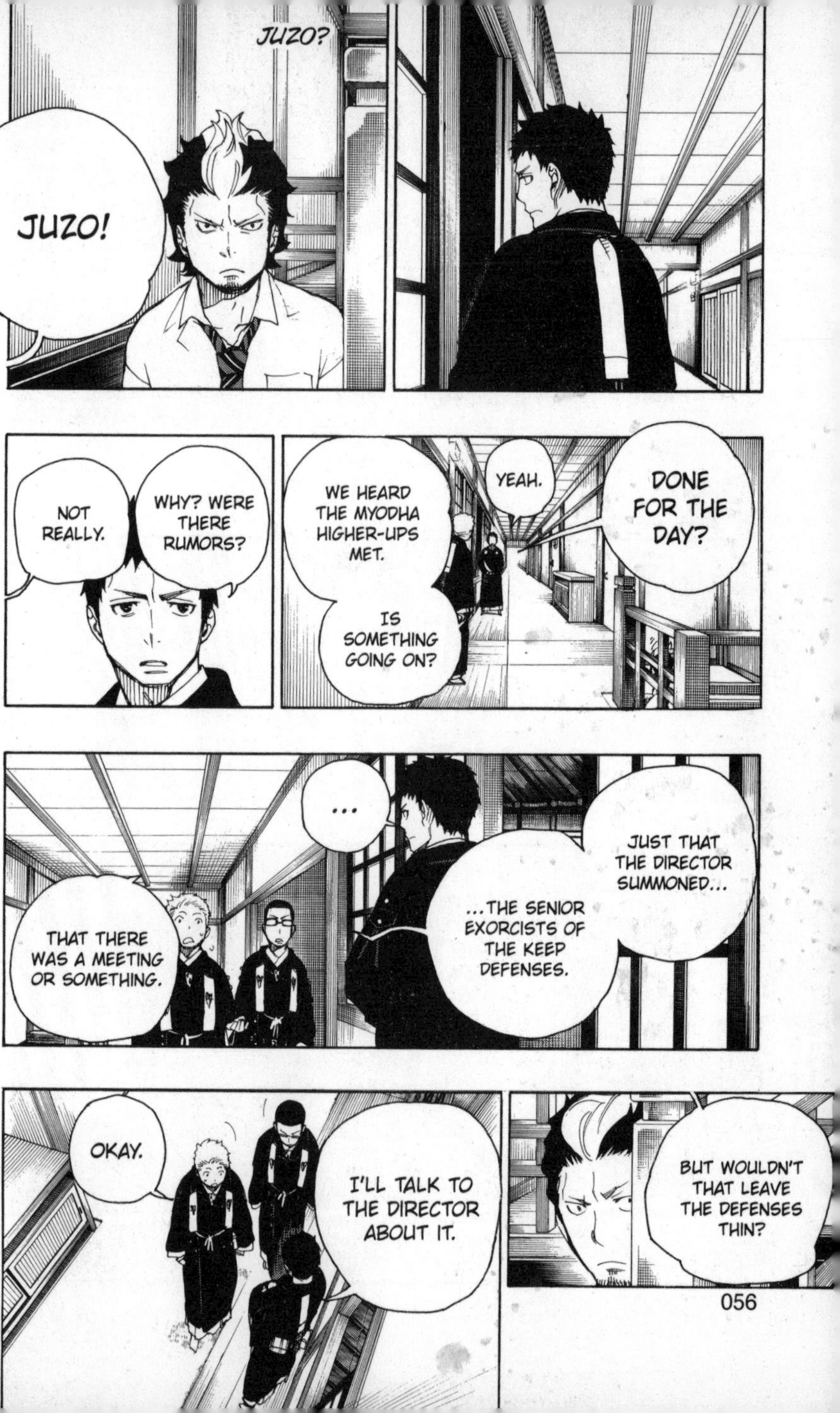
JUZO?
JUZO!
DONE FOR THE DAY?
YEAH.
WE HEARD THE MYODHA HIGHER-UPS MET.
IS SOMETHING GOING ON?
WHY? WERE THERE RUMORS?
NOT REALLY.
JUST THAT THE DIRECTOR SUMMONED...
...THE SENIOR EXORCISTS OF THE KEEP DEFENSES.
...
THAT THERE WAS A MEETING OR SOMETHING.
BUT WOULDN'T THAT LEAVE THE DEFENSES THIN?
I'LL TALK TO THE DIRECTOR ABOUT IT.
OKAY.

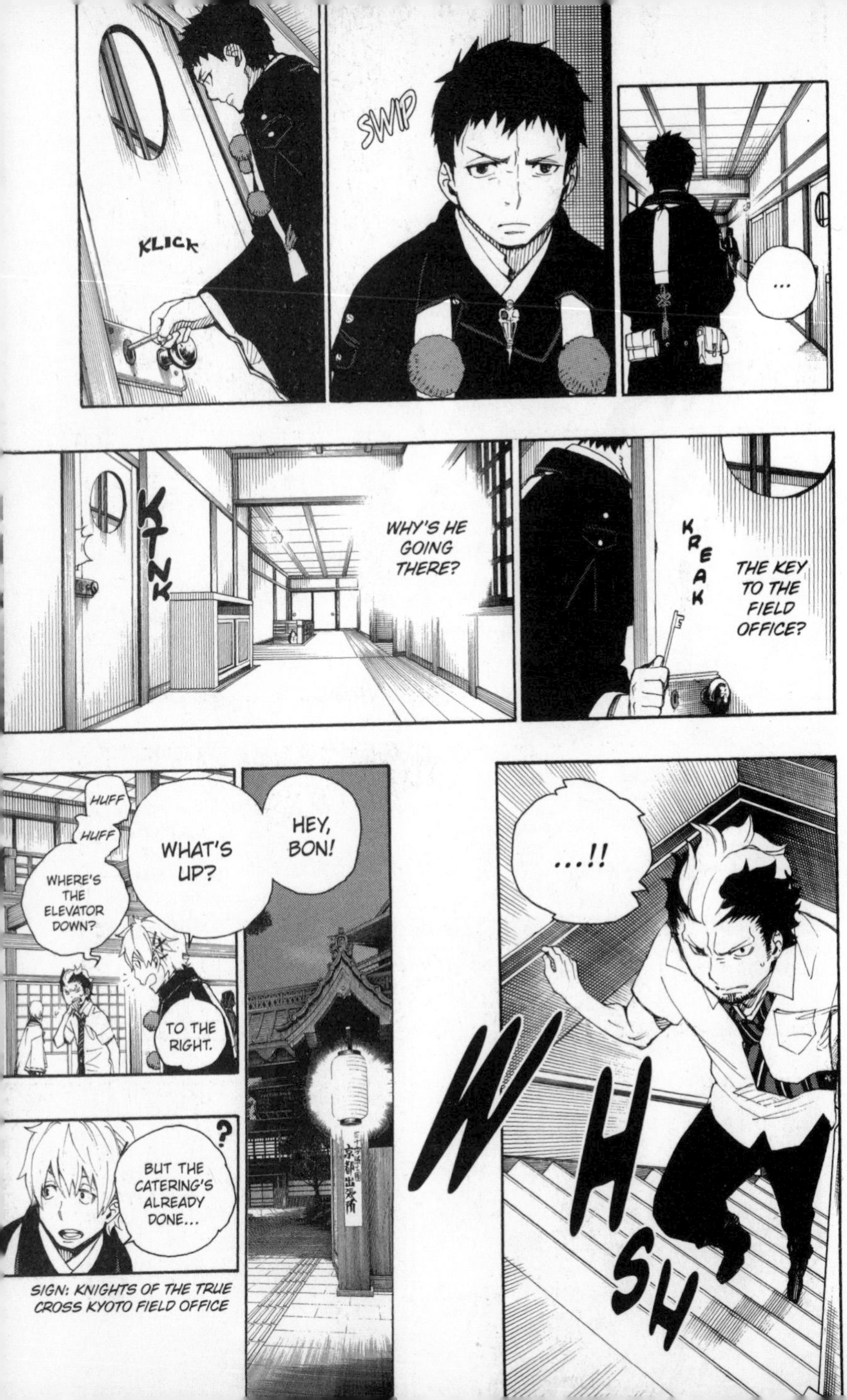
...
SWIP
KLICK
KREAK
THE KEY TO THE FIELD OFFICE?
WHY'S HE GOING THERE?
KTNK
...!!
WHSH
HEY, BON!
WHAT'S UP?
HUFF
HUFF
WHERE'S THE ELEVATOR DOWN?
TO THE RIGHT.
?
BUT THE CATERING'S ALREADY DONE...
SIGN: KNIGHTS OF THE TRUE CROSS KYOTO FIELD OFFICE

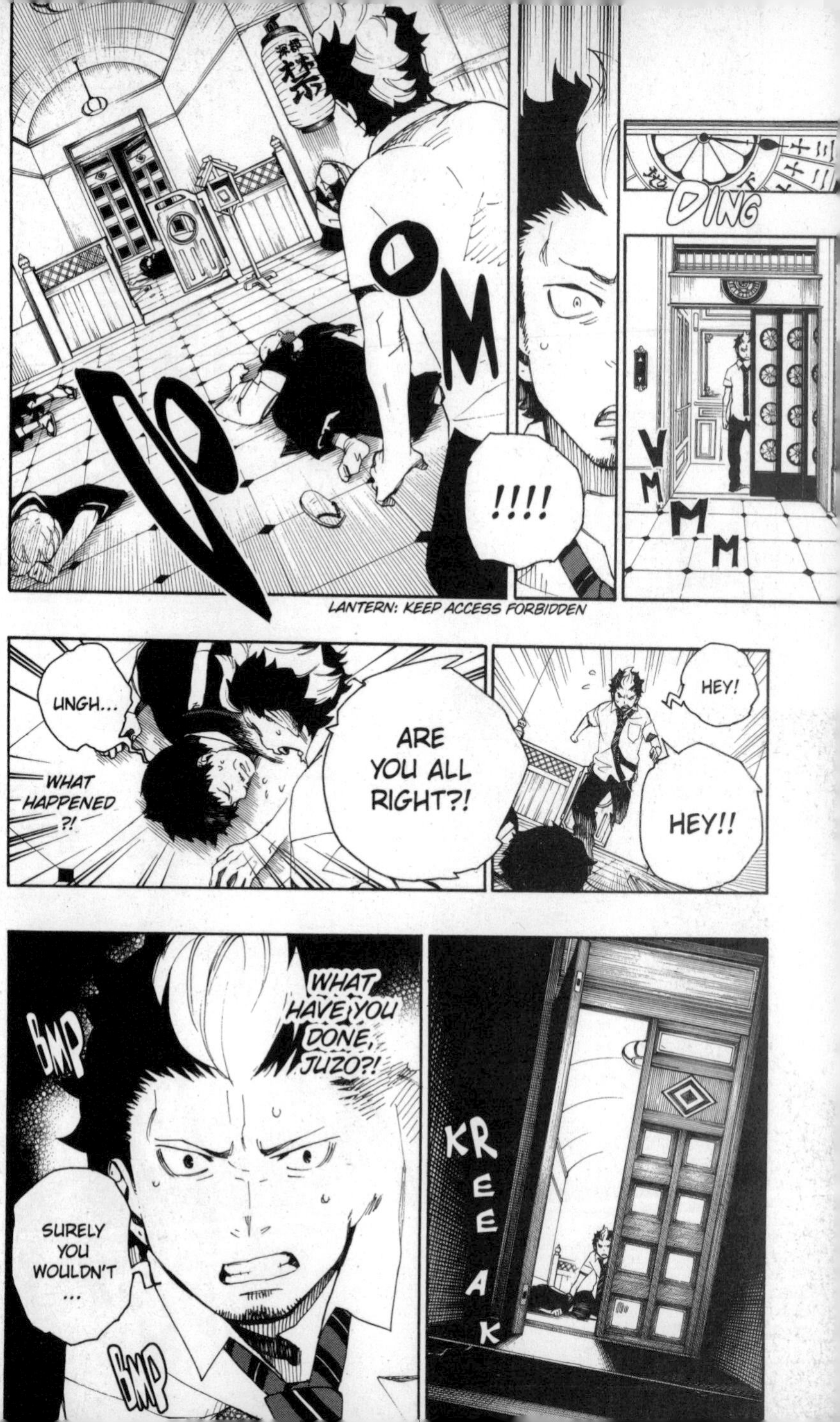
DING
VMMM
!!!!
DOOM
LANTERN: KEEP ACCESS FORBIDDEN
HEY!
HEY!!
ARE YOU ALL RIGHT?!
UNGH...
WHAT HAPPENED ?!
KREEAK
WHAT HAVE YOU DONE, JUZO?!
BMP
SURELY YOU WOULDN'T ...
BMP

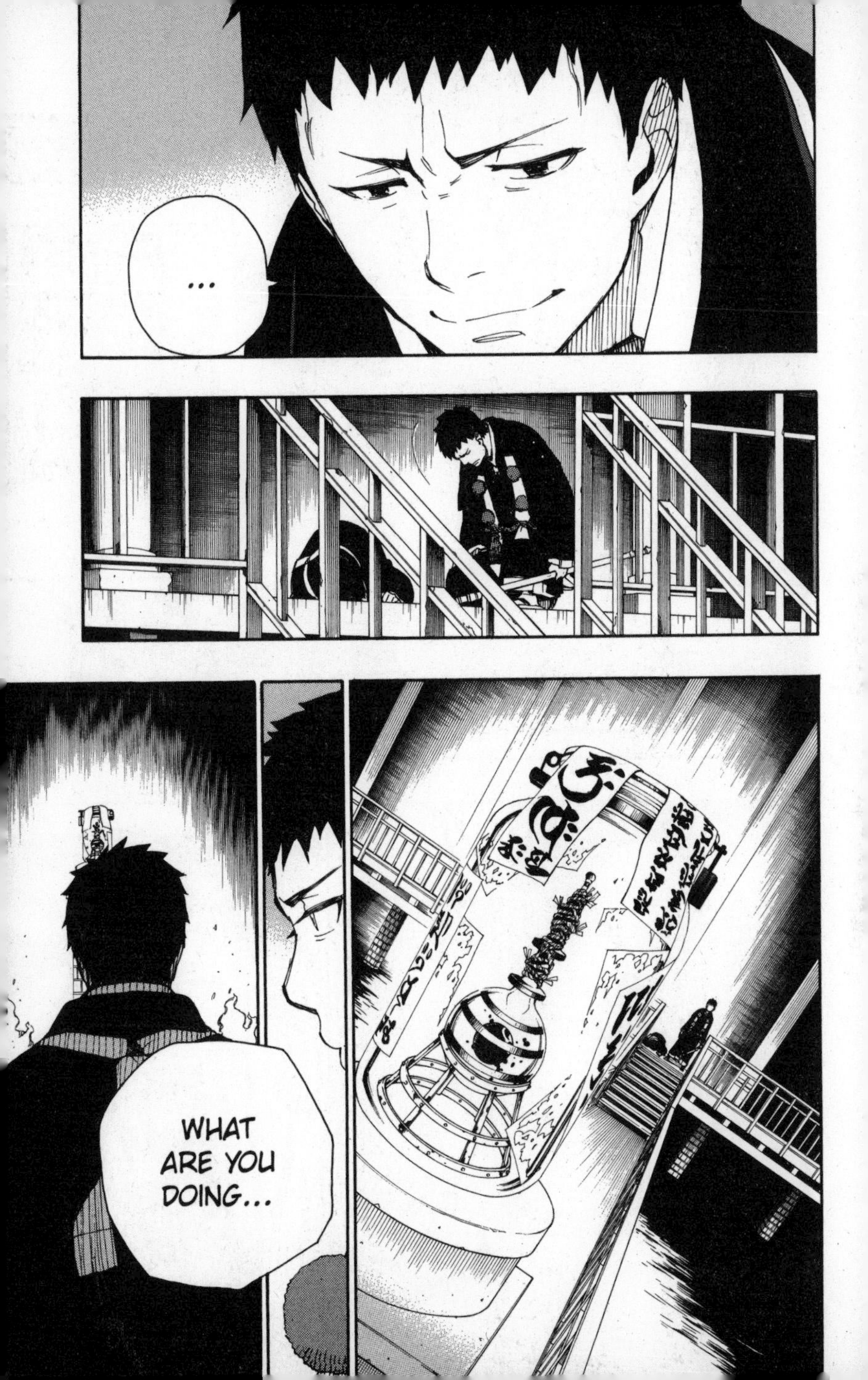
...
WHAT ARE YOU DOING...

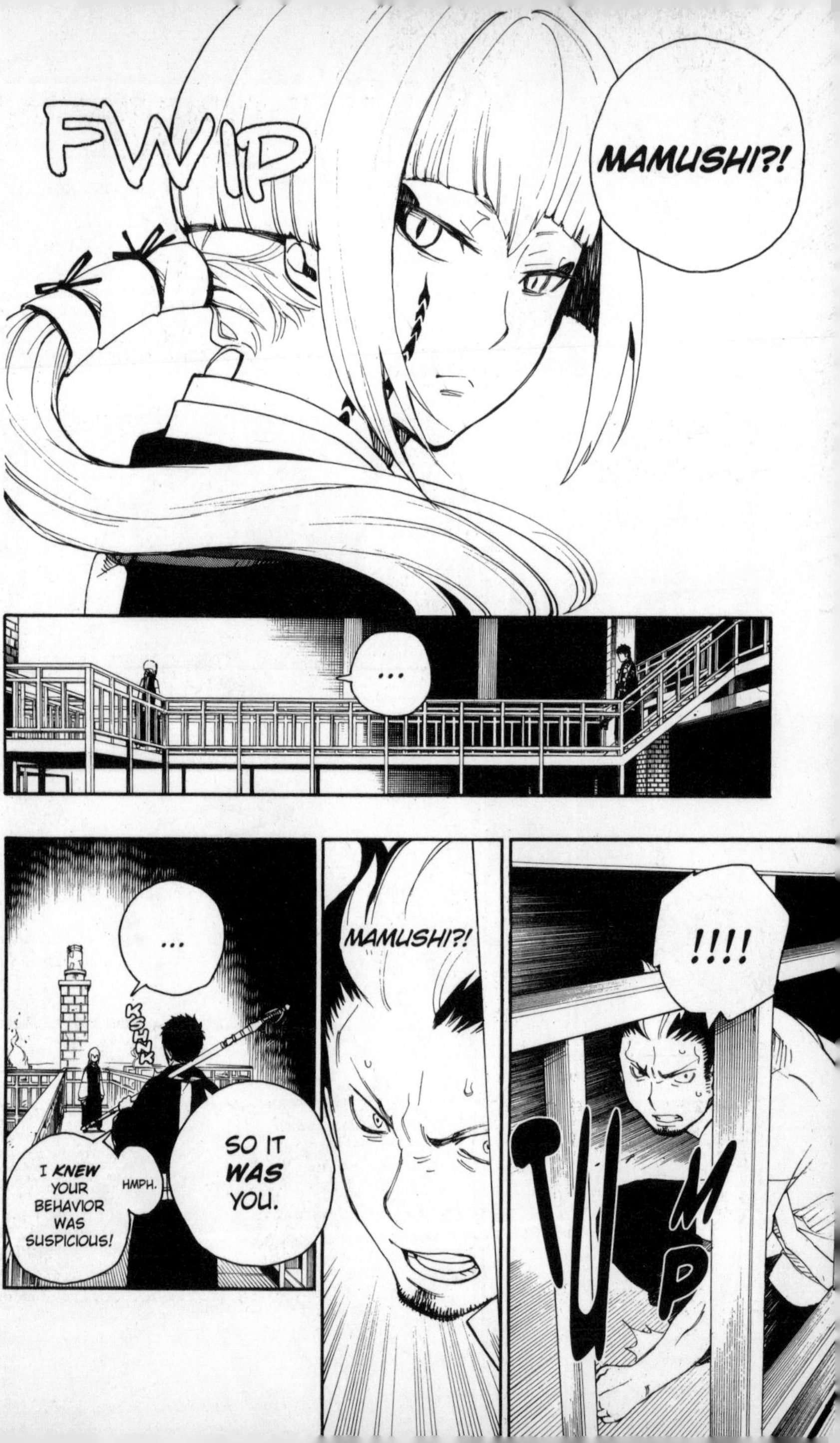
MAMUSHI?!
FWIP
...
!!!!
TUMP
MAMUSHI?!
...
KSHNK
SO IT WAS YOU.
HMPH.
I KNEW YOUR BEHAVIOR WAS SUSPICIOUS!

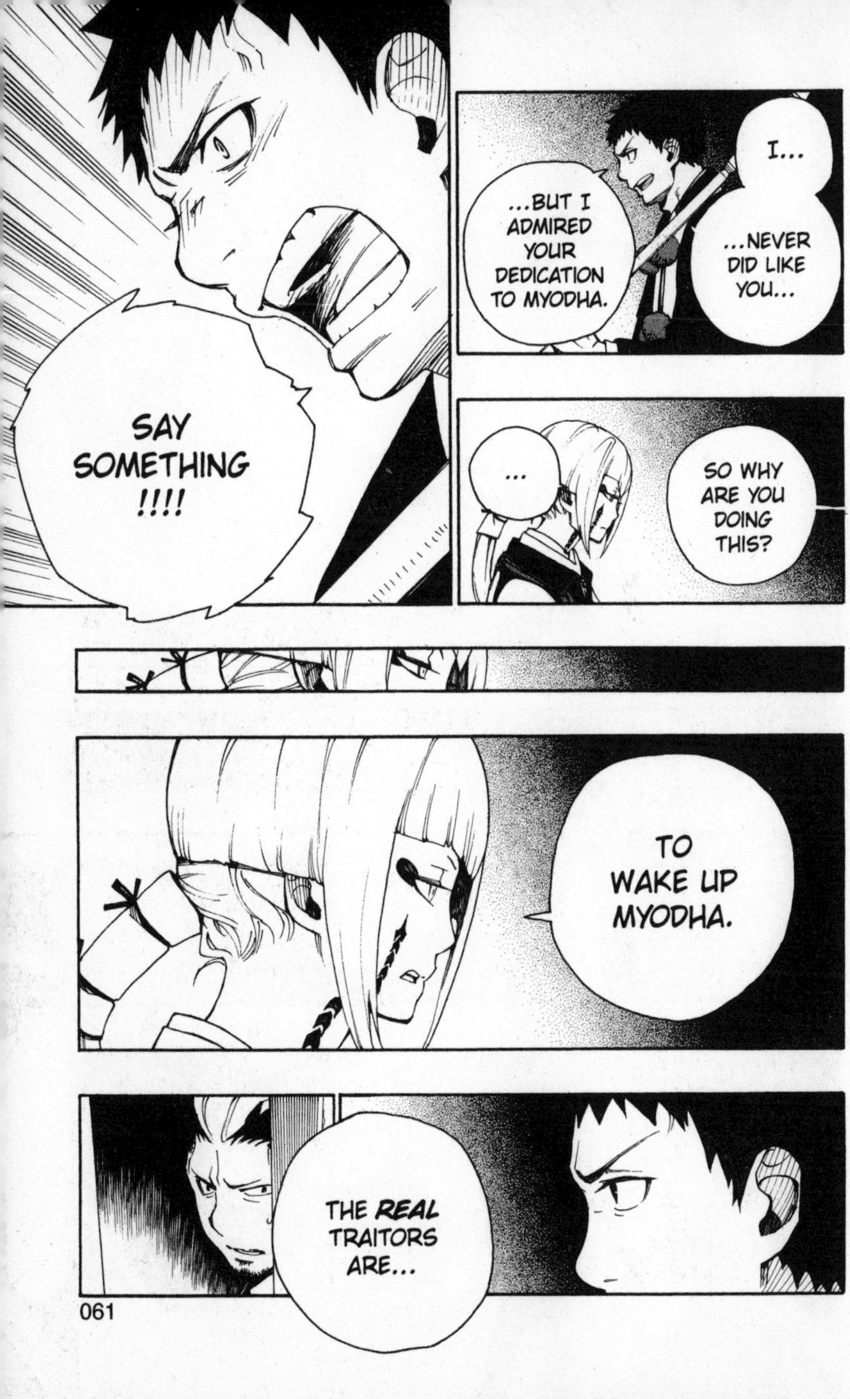
I...
...NEVER DID LIKE YOU...
...BUT I ADMIRED YOUR DEDICATION TO MYODHA.
SO WHY ARE YOU DOING THIS?
...
SAY SOMETHING !!!!
TO WAKE UP MYODHA.
THE *REAL* TRAITORS ARE...

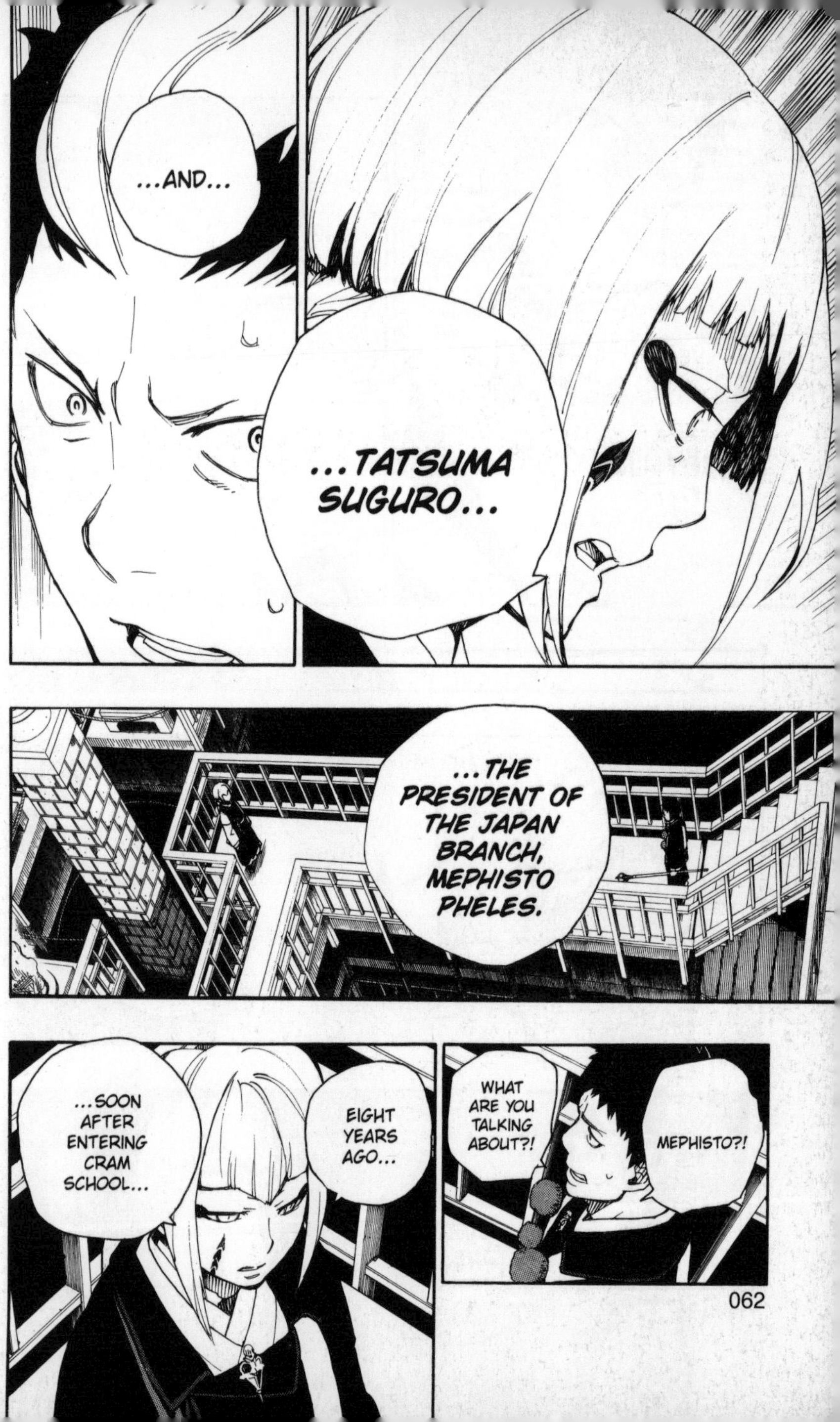
...TATSUMA SUGURO...
...AND...
...THE PRESIDENT OF THE JAPAN BRANCH, MEPHISTO PHELES.
MEPHISTO?!
WHAT ARE YOU TALKING ABOUT?!
EIGHT YEARS AGO...
...SOON AFTER ENTERING CRAM SCHOOL...

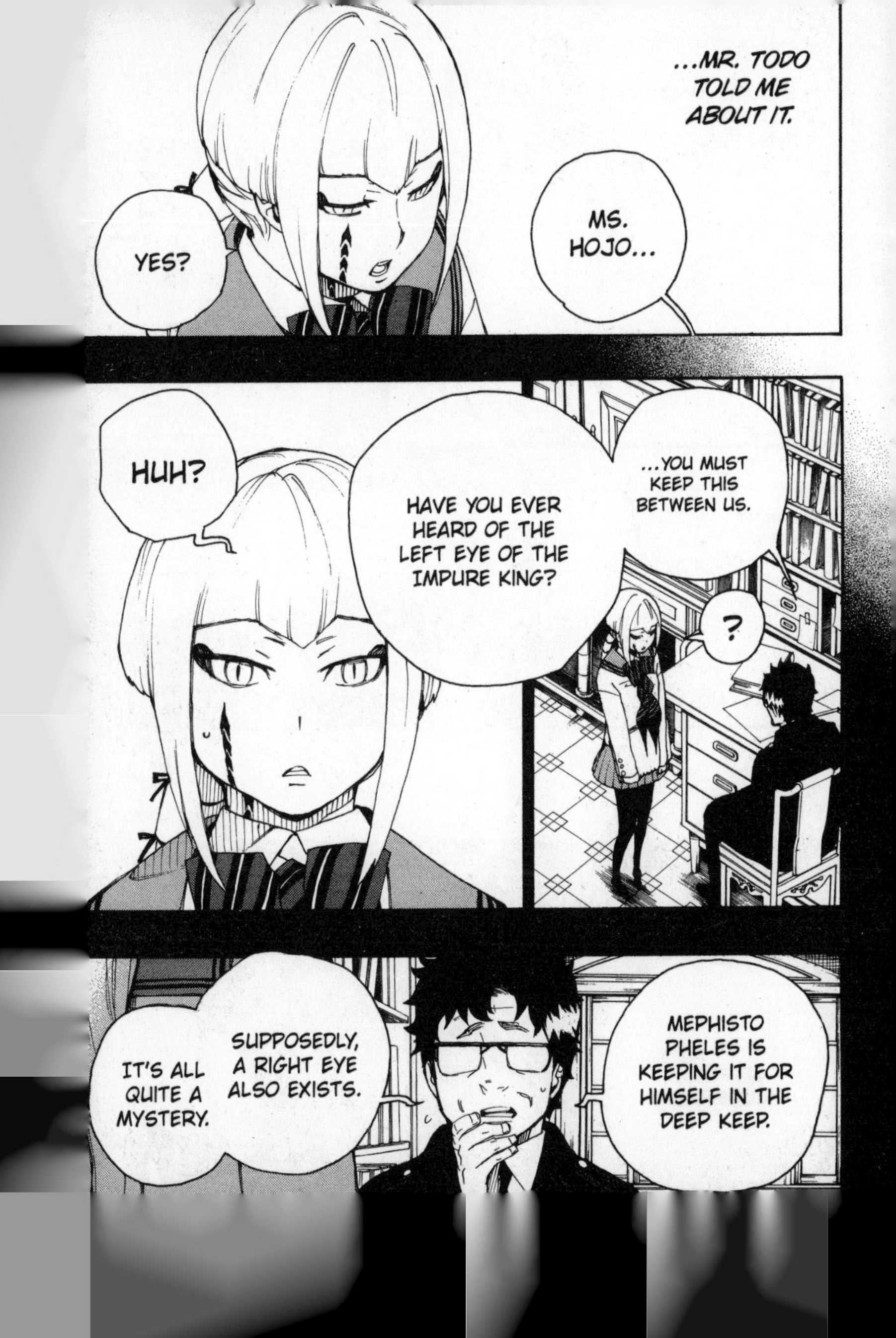
...MR. TODO TOLD ME ABOUT IT.
MS. HOJO...
YES?
...YOU MUST KEEP THIS BETWEEN US.
?
HAVE YOU EVER HEARD OF THE LEFT EYE OF THE IMPURE KING?
HUH?
MEPHISTO PHELES IS KEEPING IT FOR HIMSELF IN THE DEEP KEEP.
SUPPOSEDLY, A RIGHT EYE ALSO EXISTS.
IT'S ALL QUITE A MYSTERY.

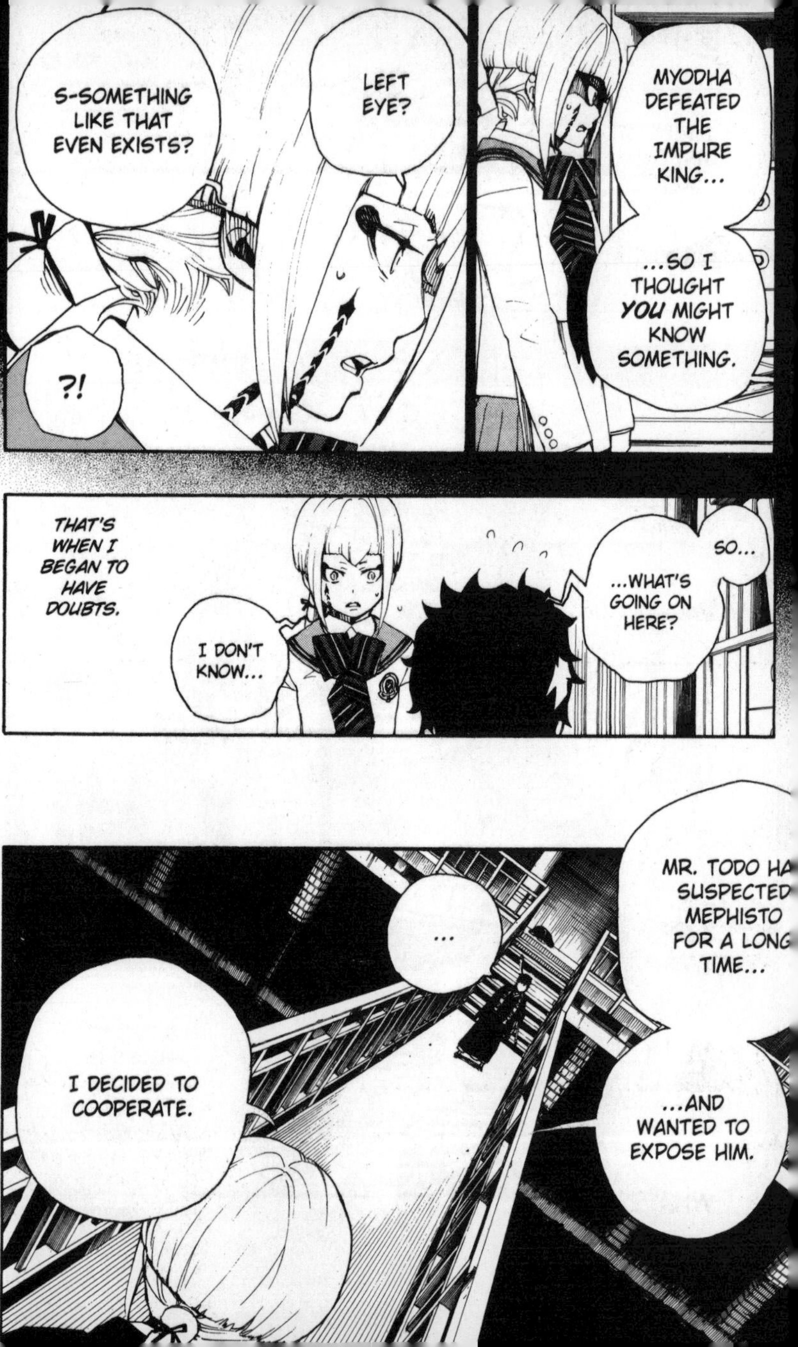
MYODHA DEFEATED THE IMPURE KING...
...SO I THOUGHT *YOU* MIGHT KNOW SOMETHING.
LEFT EYE?
S-SOMETHING LIKE THAT EVEN EXISTS?
?!
SO... ...WHAT'S GOING ON HERE?
I DON'T KNOW...
THAT'S WHEN I BEGAN TO HAVE DOUBTS.
MR. TODO HA SUSPECTED MEPHISTO FOR A LONG TIME...
...AND WANTED TO EXPOSE HIM.
...
I DECIDED TO COOPERATE.

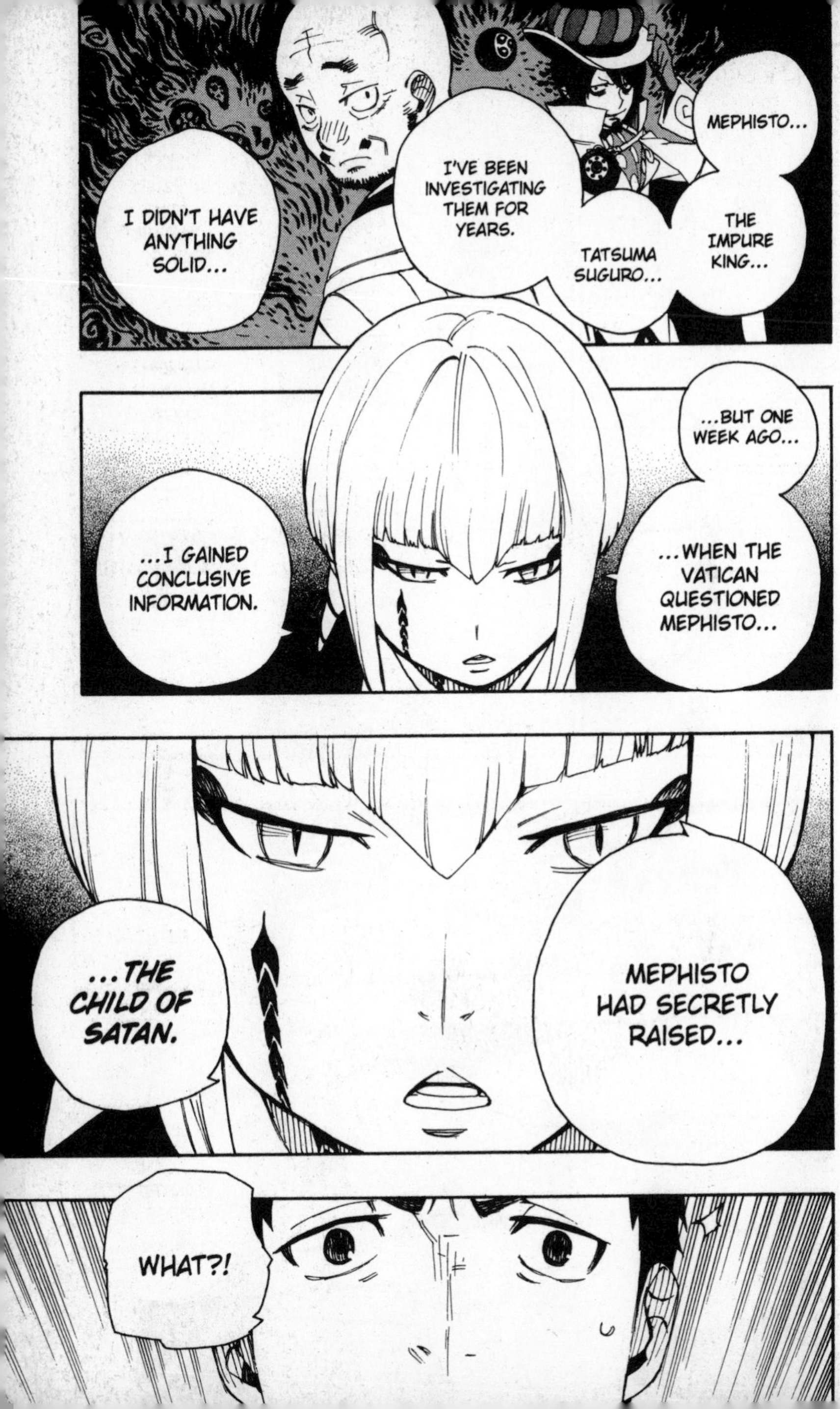
MEPHISTO...
THE IMPURE KING...
TATSUMA SUGURO...
I'VE BEEN INVESTIGATING THEM FOR YEARS.
I DIDN'T HAVE ANYTHING SOLID...
...BUT ONE WEEK AGO...
...WHEN THE VATICAN QUESTIONED MEPHISTO...
...I GAINED CONCLUSIVE INFORMATION.
MEPHISTO HAD SECRETLY RAISED...
...THE CHILD OF SATAN.
WHAT?!

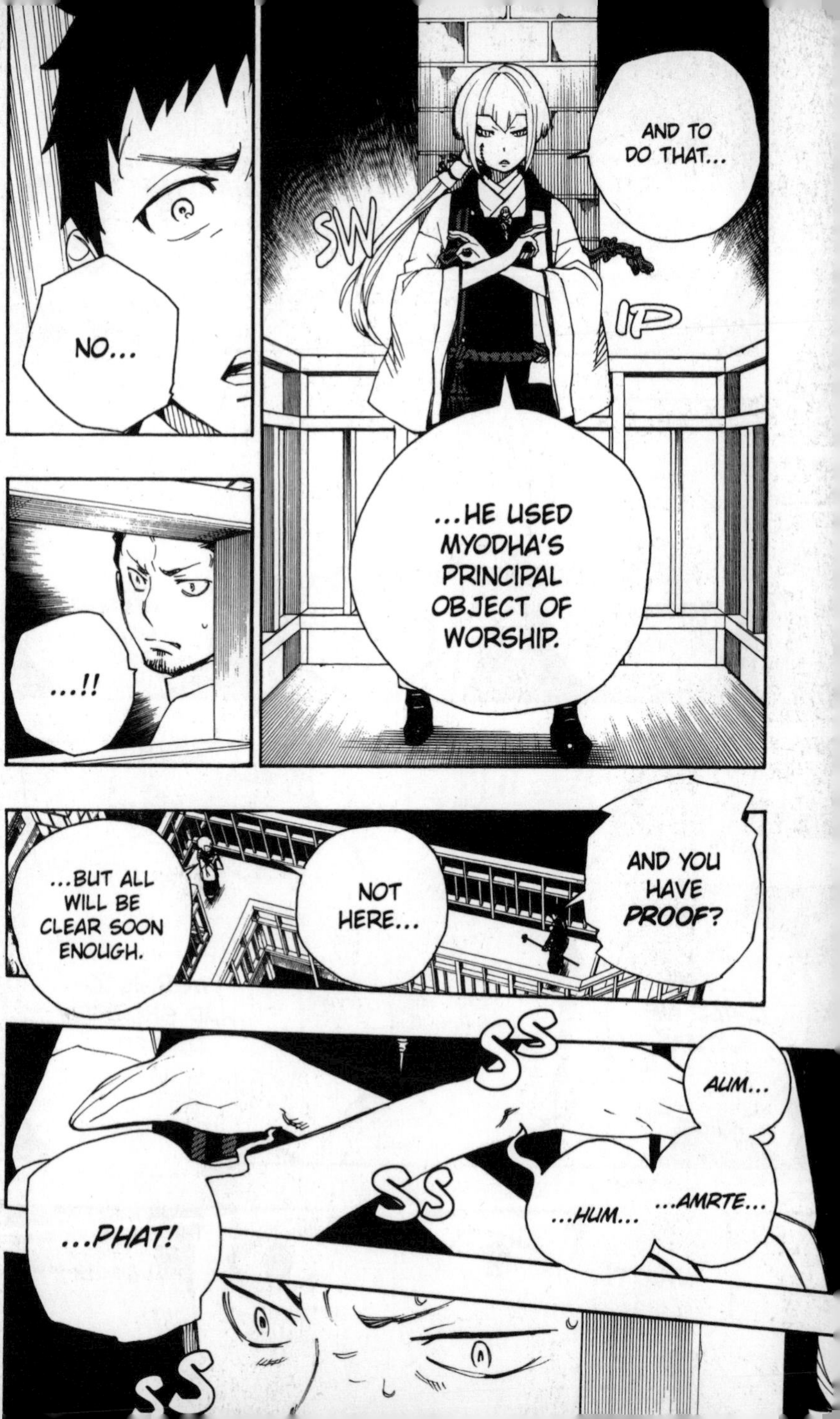
AND TO DO THAT...
SW
IP
...HE USED MYODHA'S PRINCIPAL OBJECT OF WORSHIP.
NO...
...!!
AND YOU HAVE PROOF?
NOT HERE...
...BUT ALL WILL BE CLEAR SOON ENOUGH.
SS
AUM...
...AMRTE...
...HUM...
SS
...PHAT!
SS

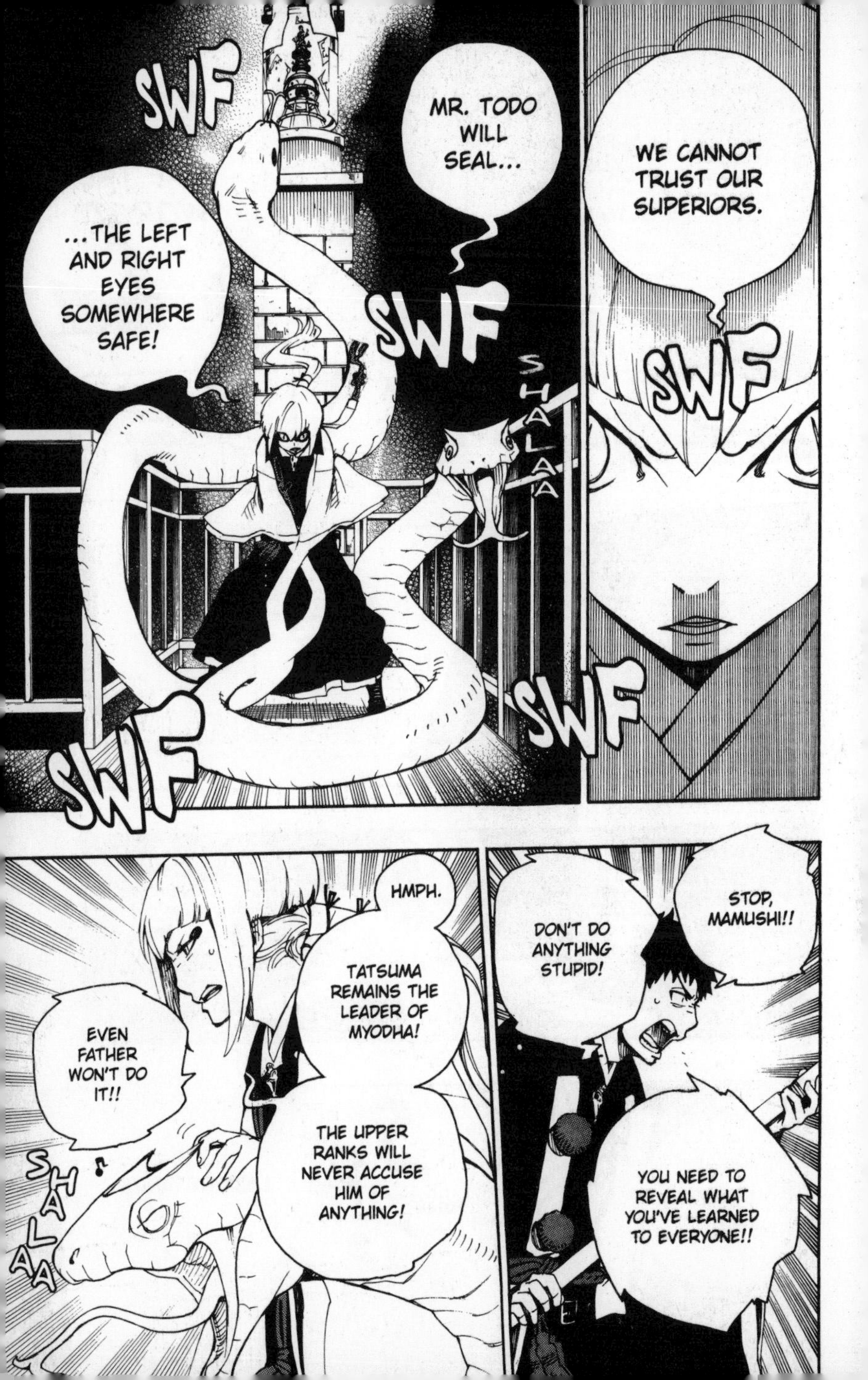
WE CANNOT TRUST OUR SUPERIORS.
SWF
SWF
MR. TODO WILL SEAL...
...THE LEFT AND RIGHT EYES SOMEWHERE SAFE!
SWF
SWF
SHALAA
SWF
STOP, MAMUSHI!!
DON'T DO ANYTHING STUPID!
YOU NEED TO REVEAL WHAT YOU'VE LEARNED TO EVERYONE!!
HMPH.
TATSUMA REMAINS THE LEADER OF MYODHA!
THE UPPER RANKS WILL NEVER ACCUSE HIM OF ANYTHING!
EVEN FATHER WON'T DO IT!!
SHALAA

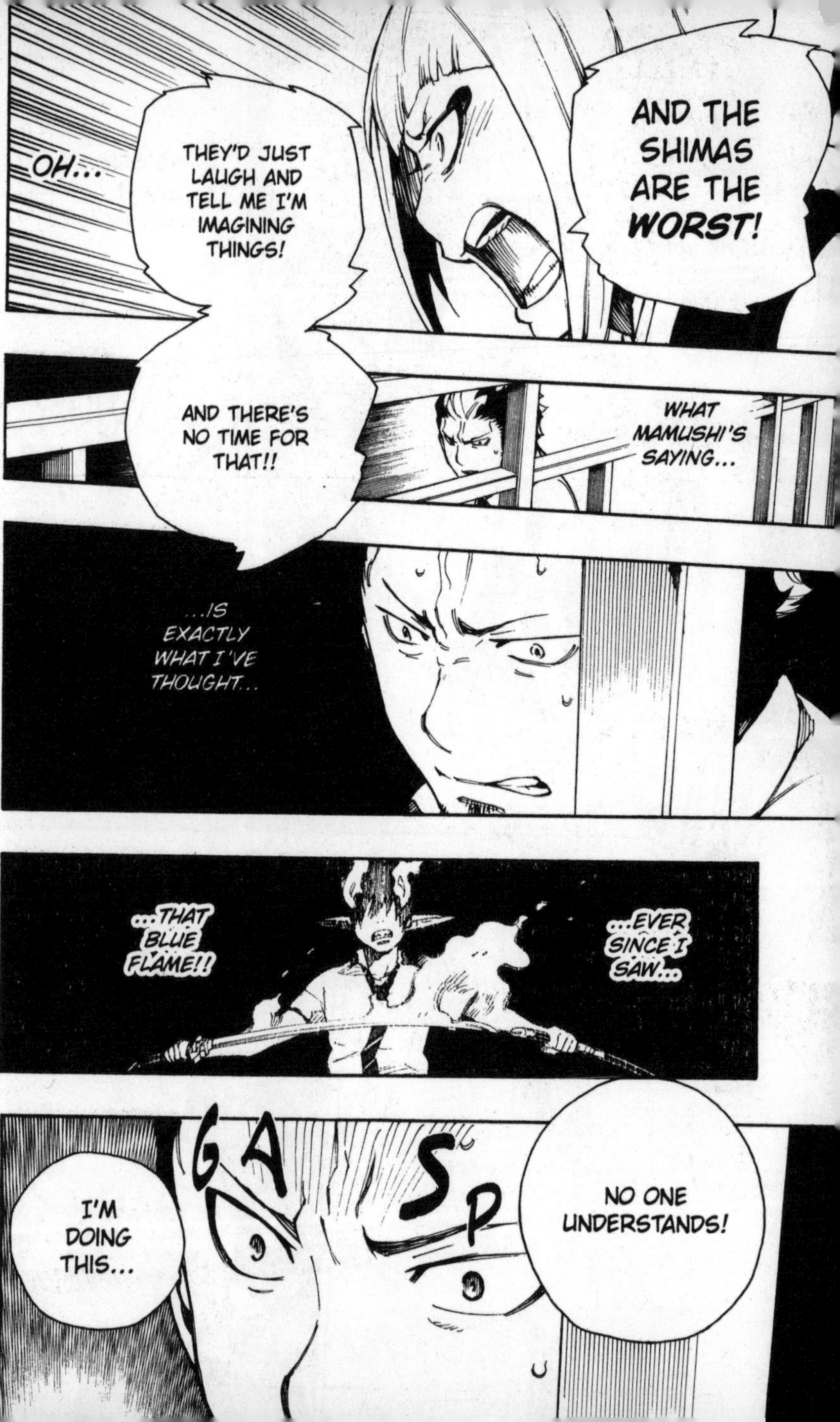
AND THE SHIMAS ARE THE WORST!
THEY'D JUST LAUGH AND TELL ME I'M IMAGINING THINGS!
OH...
AND THERE'S NO TIME FOR THAT!!
WHAT MAMUSHI'S SAYING...
...IS EXACTLY WHAT I'VE THOUGHT...
...EVER SINCE I SAW...
...THAT BLUE FLAME!!
NO ONE UNDERSTANDS!
GASP
I'M DOING THIS...

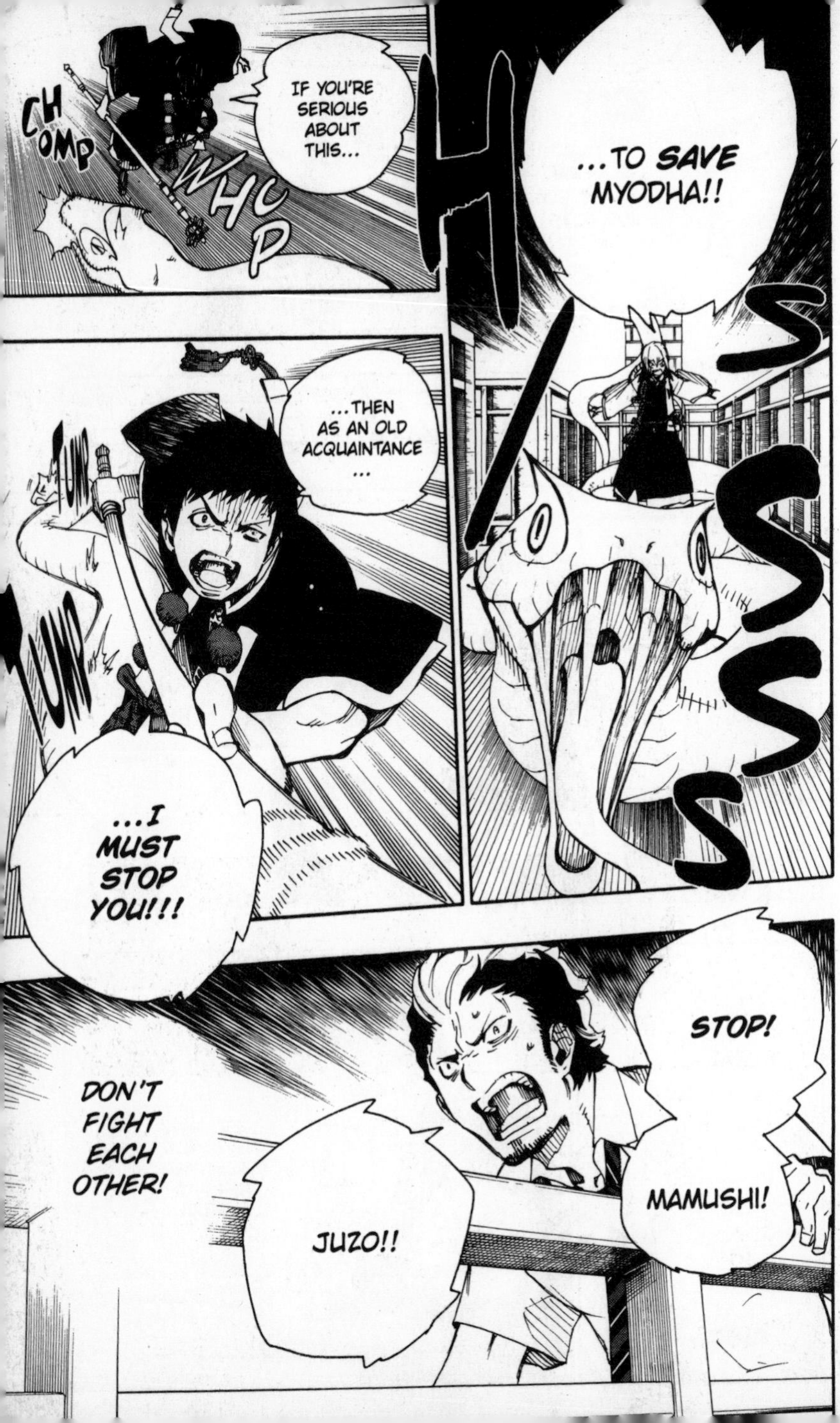
IF YOU'RE SERIOUS ABOUT THIS...
CHOMP
WHUP
...TO SAVE MYODHA!!
HISSSS
...THEN AS AN OLD ACQUAINTANCE ...
TUMP
TUMP
...I MUST STOP YOU!!!
STOP!
MAMUSHI!
JUZO!!
DON'T FIGHT EACH OTHER!

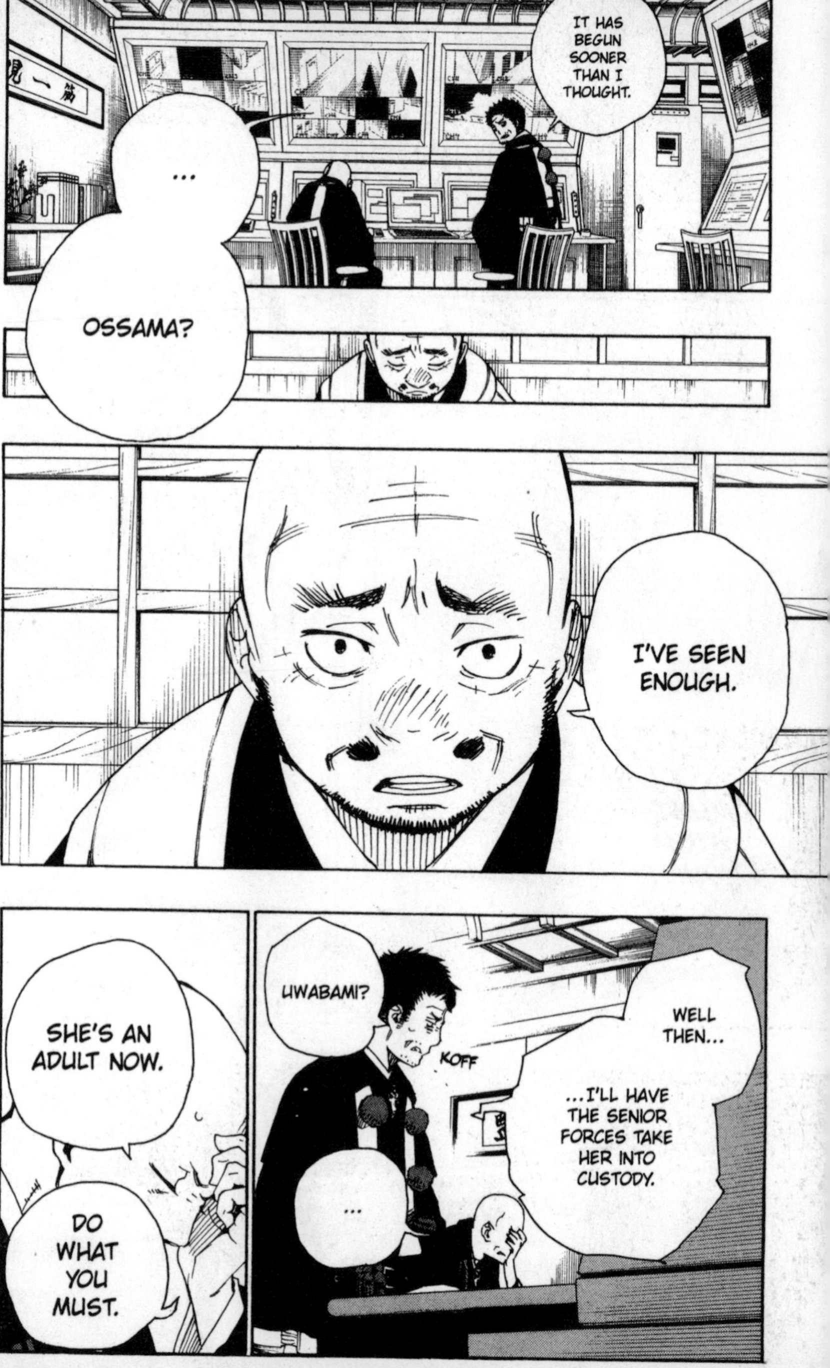
IT HAS BEGUN SOONER THAN I THOUGHT.
...
OSSAMA?
I'VE SEEN ENOUGH.
UWABAMI?
KOFF
WELL THEN...
...I'LL HAVE THE SENIOR FORCES TAKE HER INTO CUSTODY.
...
SHE'S AN ADULT NOW.
DO WHAT YOU MUST.

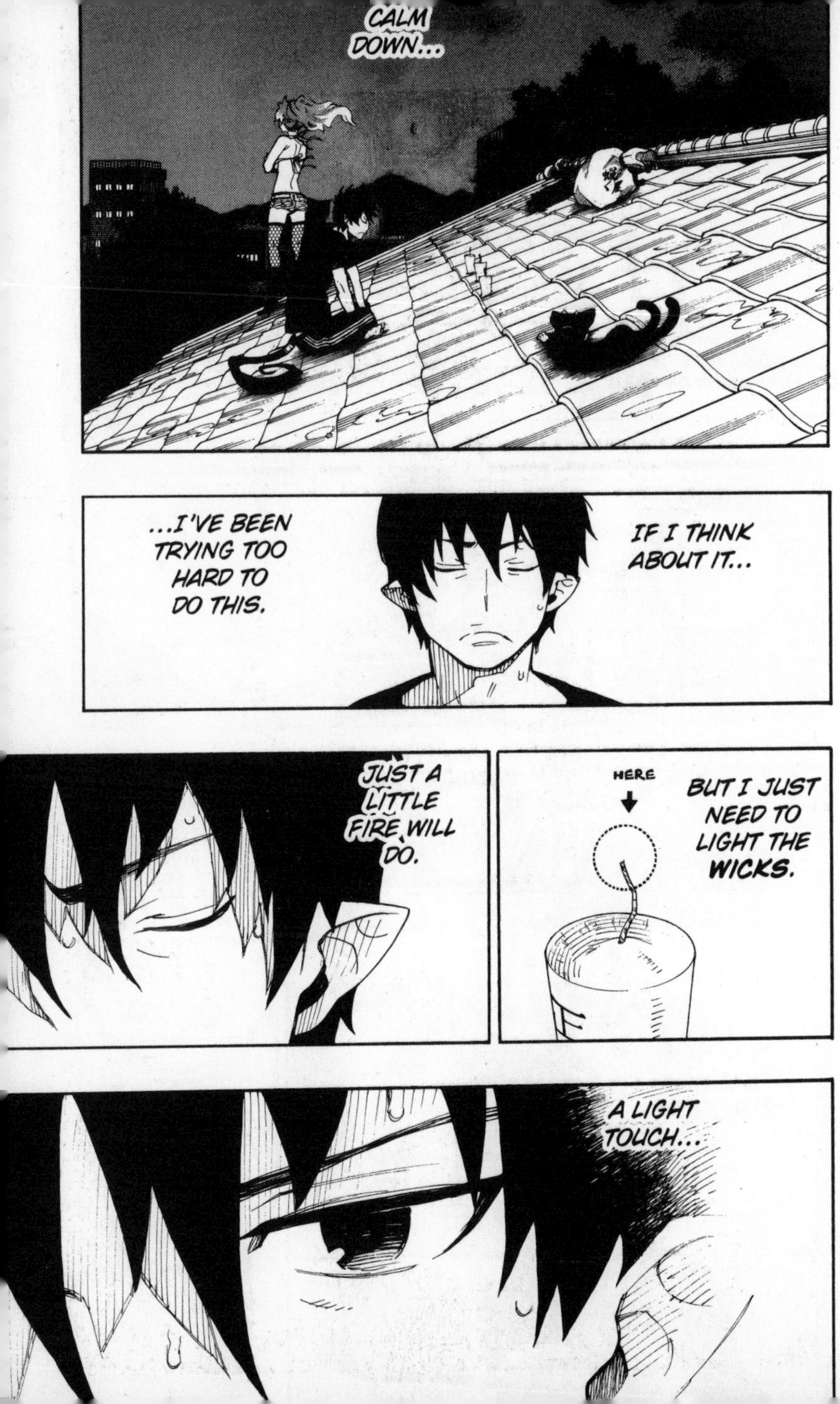
CALM DOWN...
IF I THINK ABOUT IT...
...I'VE BEEN TRYING TOO HARD TO DO THIS.
HERE
BUT I JUST NEED TO LIGHT THE **WICKS.**
JUST A LITTLE FIRE WILL DO.
A LIGHT TOUCH...

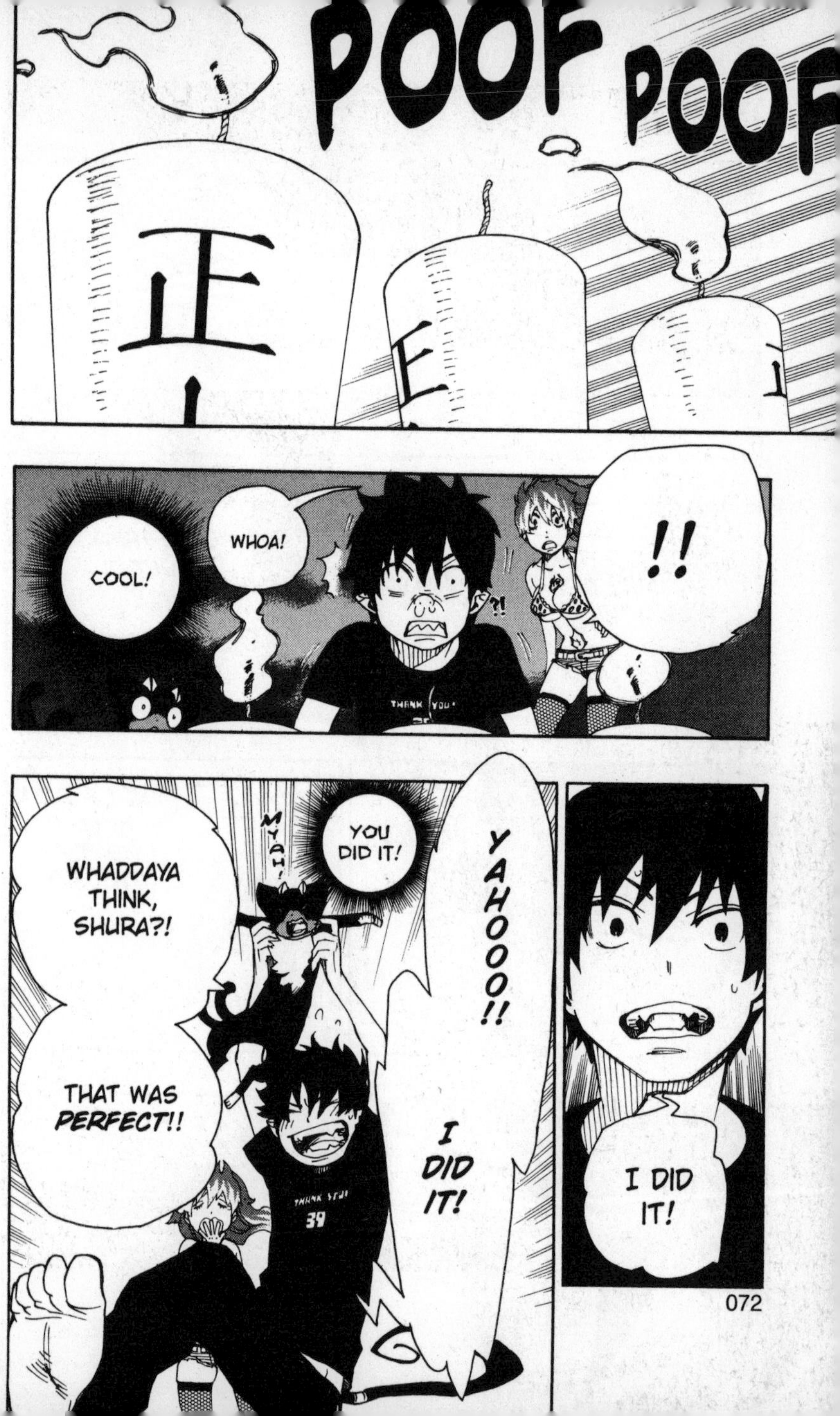
POOF
POOF
!!
?!
WHOA!
COOL!
I DID IT!
YAHOOOO!!
I DID IT!
YOU DID IT!
MYAH!
WHADDAYA THINK, SHURA?!
THAT WAS *PERFECT*!!

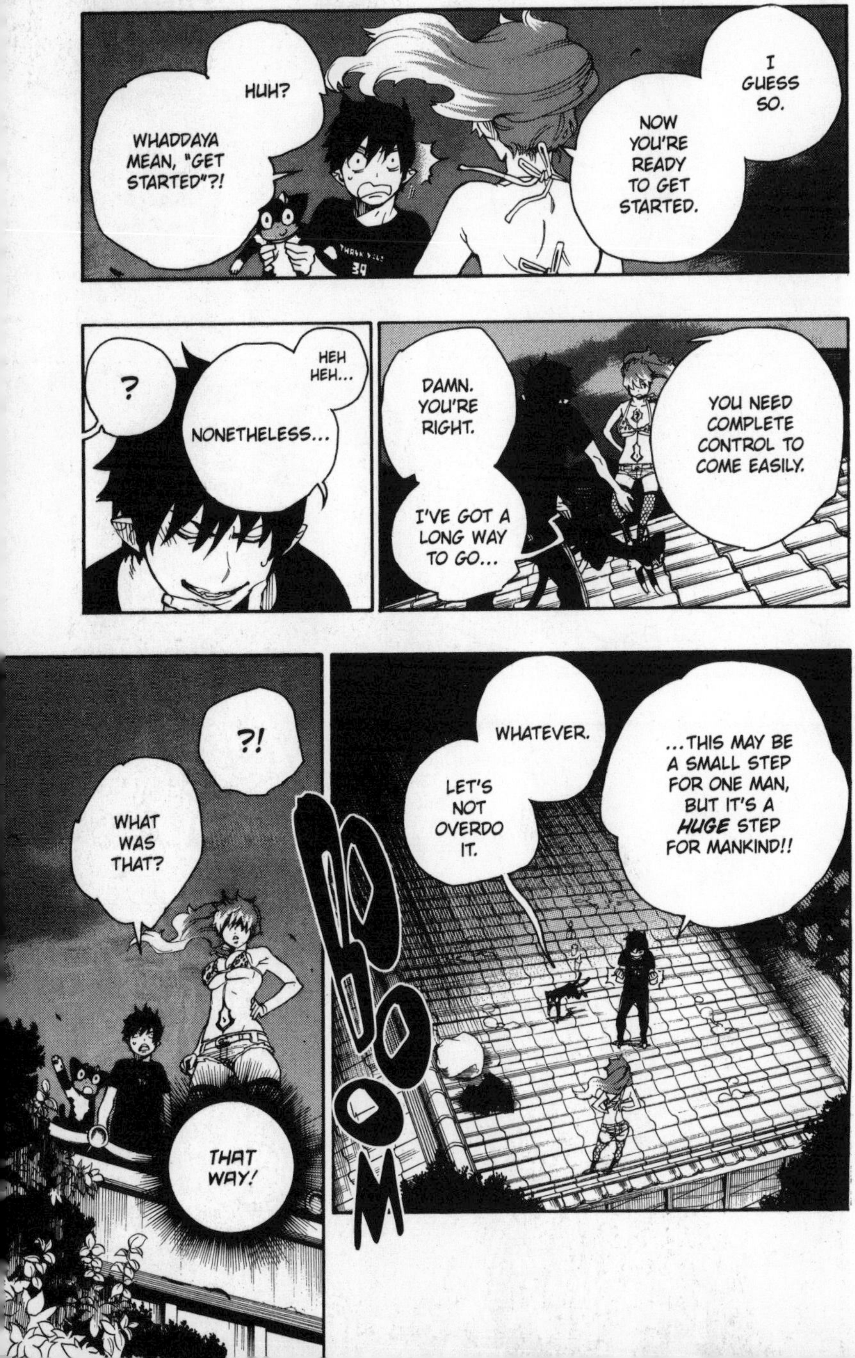
I GUESS SO.
NOW YOU'RE READY TO GET STARTED.
HUH?
WHADDAYA MEAN, "GET STARTED"?!
YOU NEED COMPLETE CONTROL TO COME EASILY.
DAMN. YOU'RE RIGHT.
I'VE GOT A LONG WAY TO GO...
HEH HEH...
NONETHELESS...
?
...THIS MAY BE A SMALL STEP FOR ONE MAN, BUT IT'S A *HUGE* STEP FOR MANKIND!!
WHATEVER.
LET'S NOT OVERDO IT.
BOOM
?!
WHAT WAS THAT?
THAT WAY!

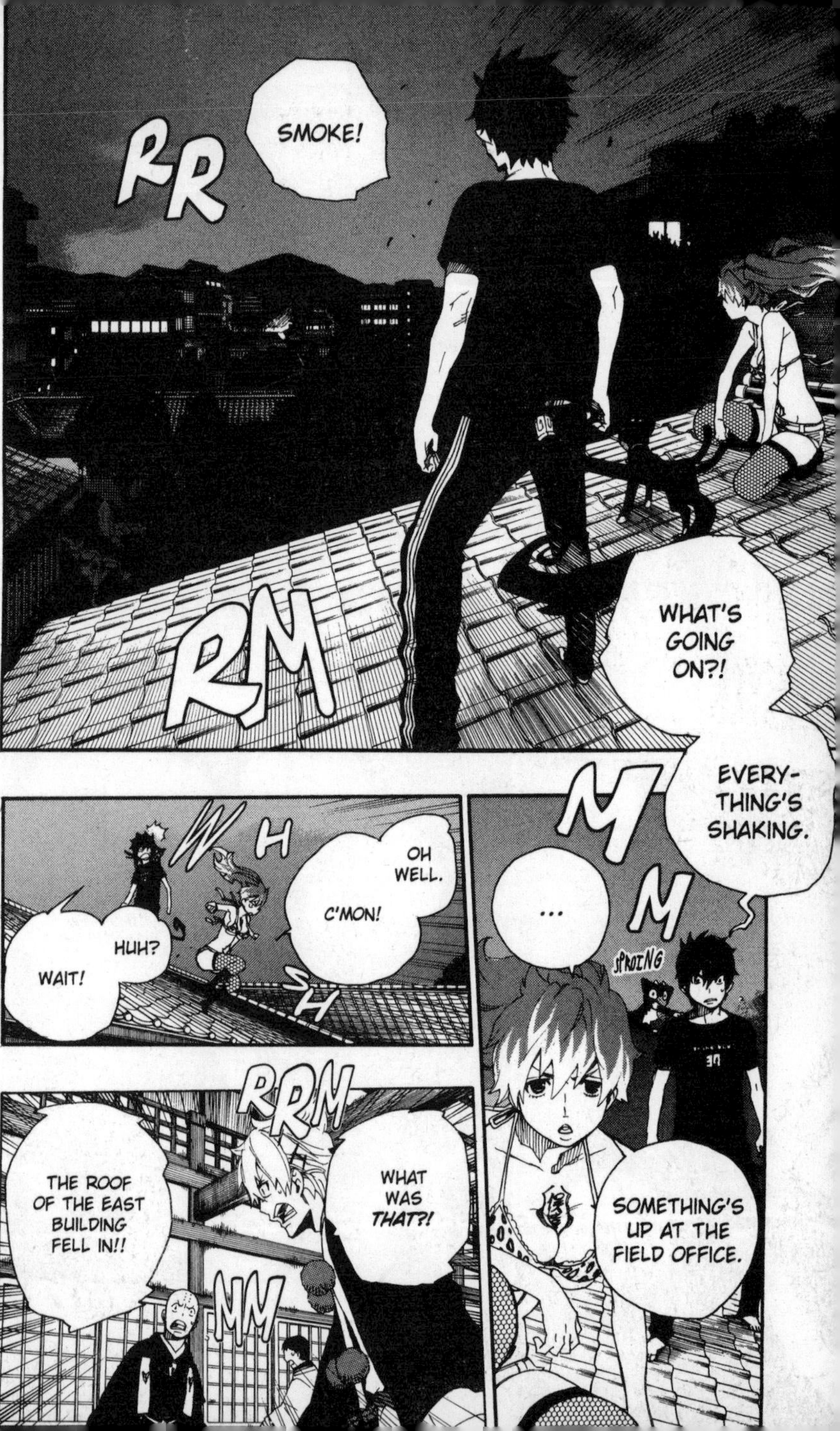
SMOKE!
RR
WHAT'S GOING ON?!
RM
EVERY-THING'S SHAKING.
M
M
...
SPROING
SOMETHING'S UP AT THE FIELD OFFICE.
OH WELL.
C'MON!
WH
SH
HUH?
WAIT!
RRM
WHAT WAS THAT?!
THE ROOF OF THE EAST BUILDING FELL IN!!
MM

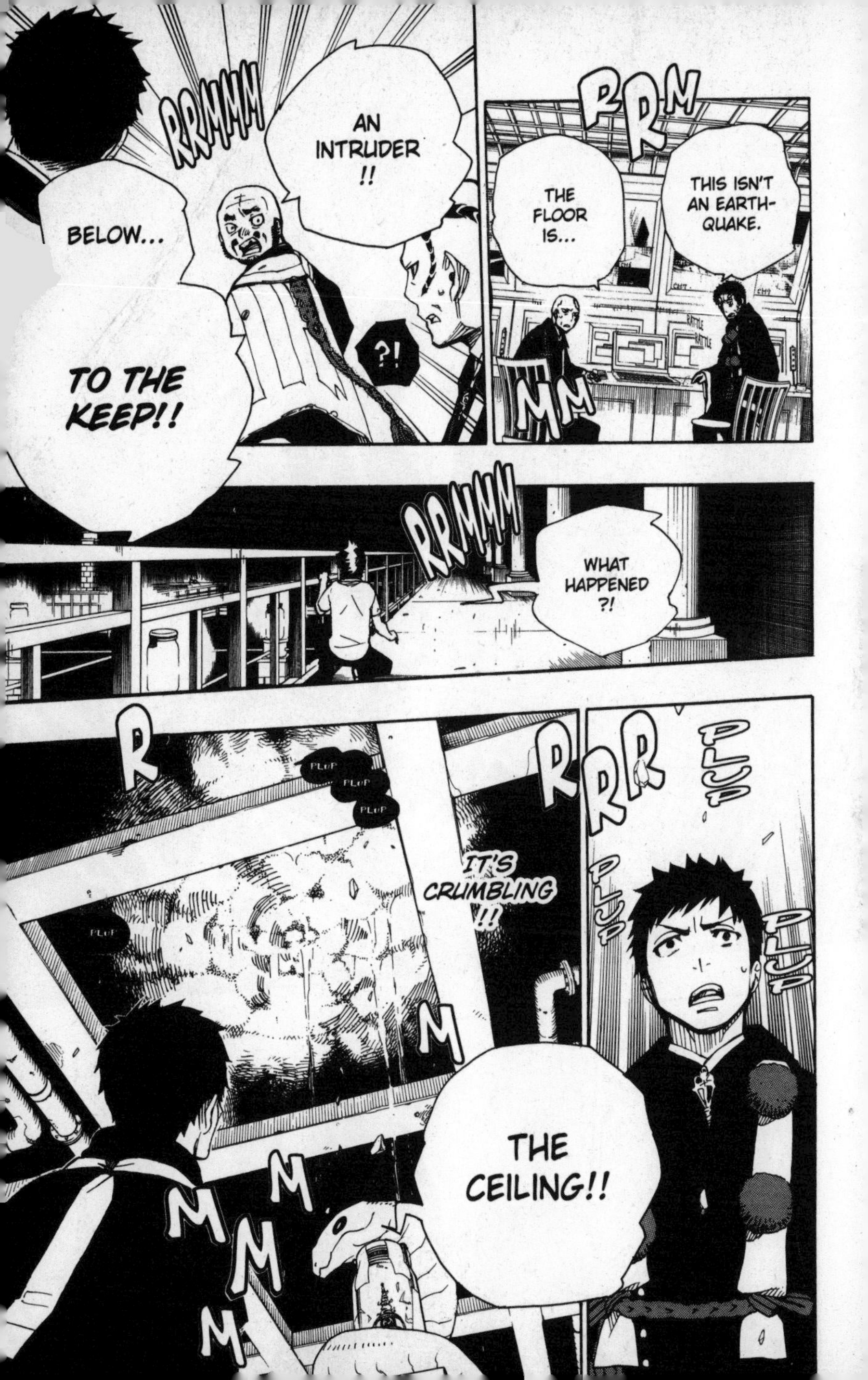
RRM
THIS ISN'T AN EARTH-QUAKE.
THE FLOOR IS...
RATTLE RATTLE
MM
AN INTRUDER !!
RRMMM
?!
BELOW...
TO THE KEEP!!
RRMMM
WHAT HAPPENED ?!
RRR
PLUP
PLUP
PLUP
THE CEILING!!
R
PLUP
PLUP
PLUP
IT'S CRUMBLING !!
PLUP
M
MMMMM

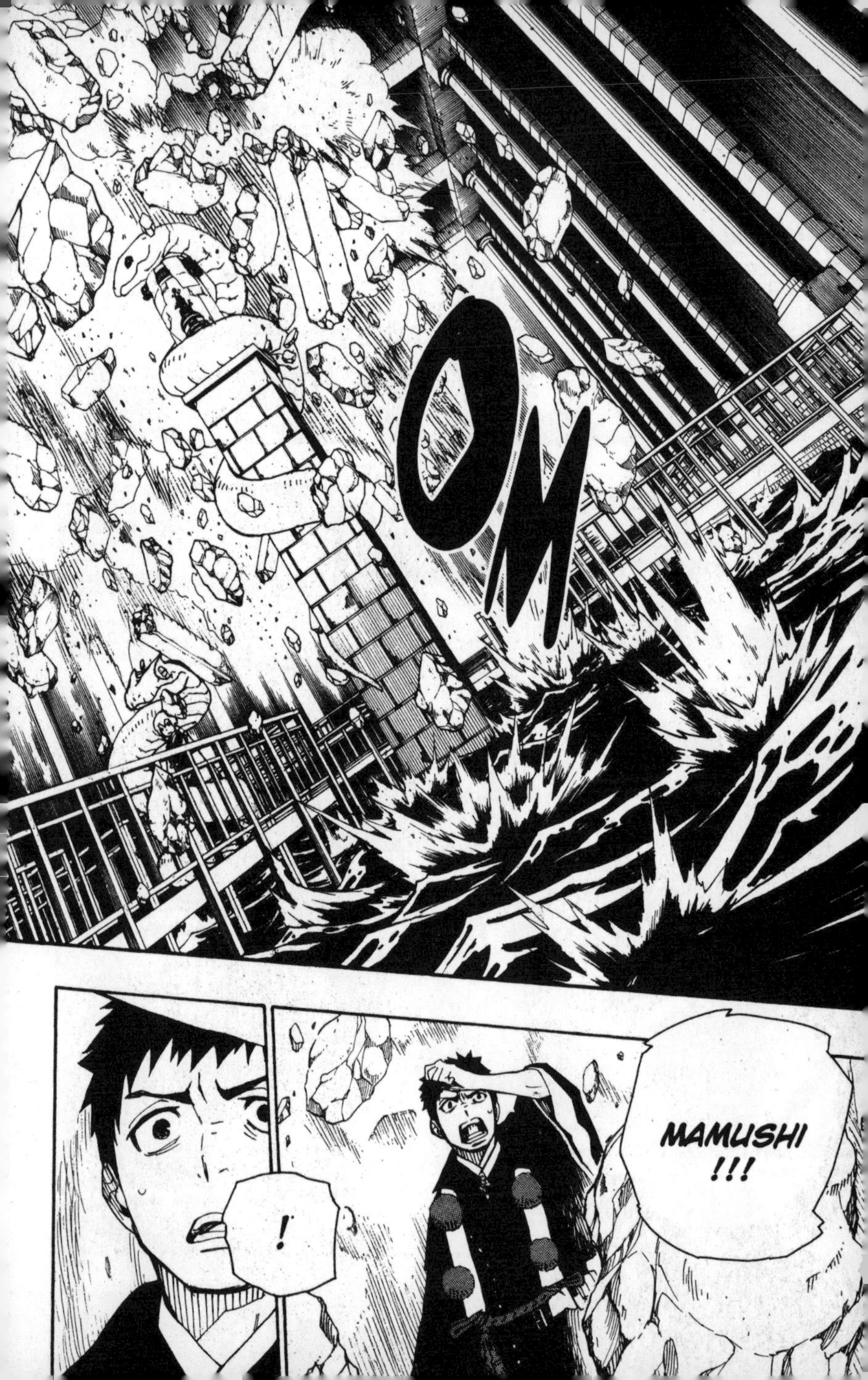
MAMUSHI !!!
!

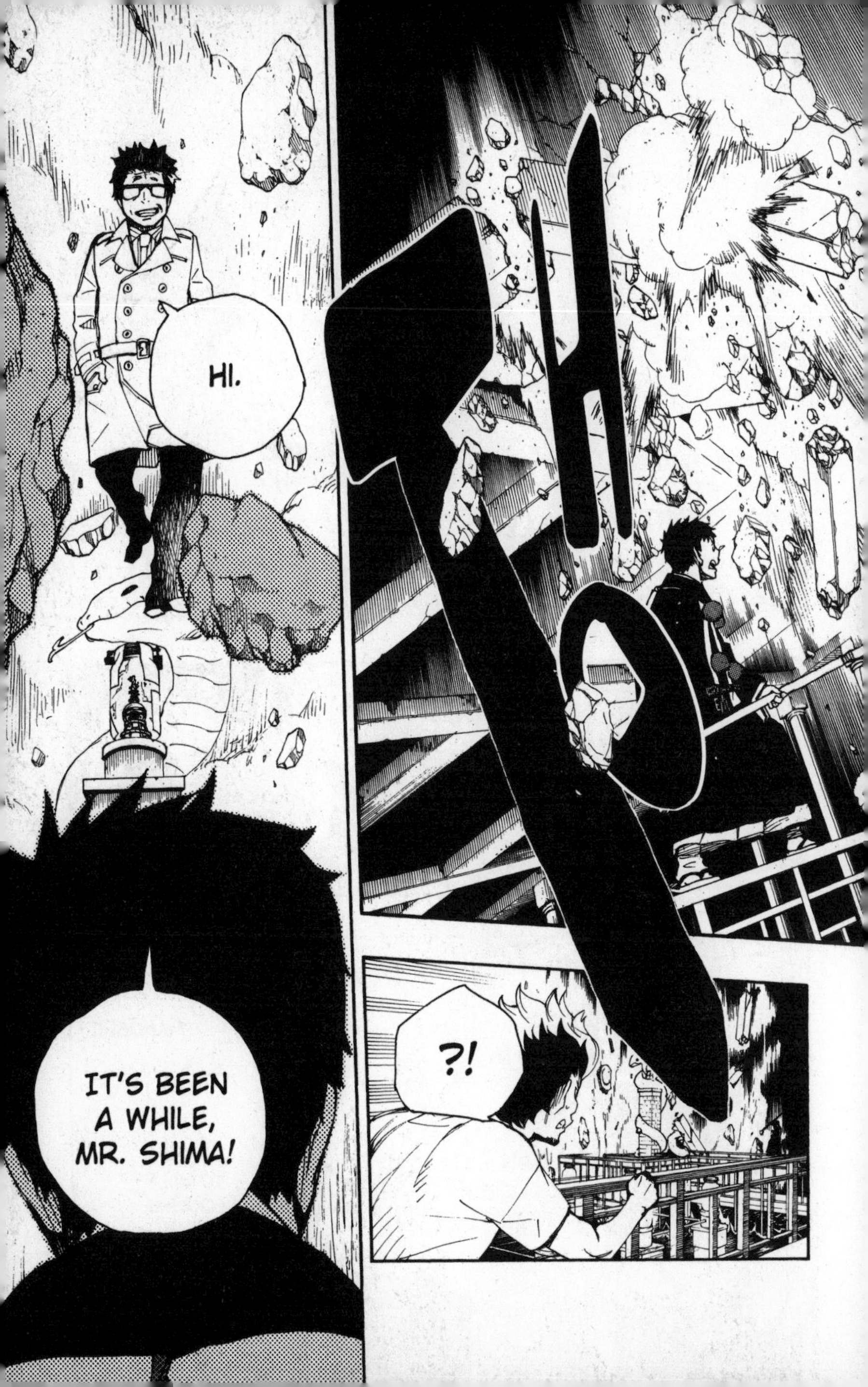
?!
HI.
IT'S BEEN A WHILE, MR. SHIMA!

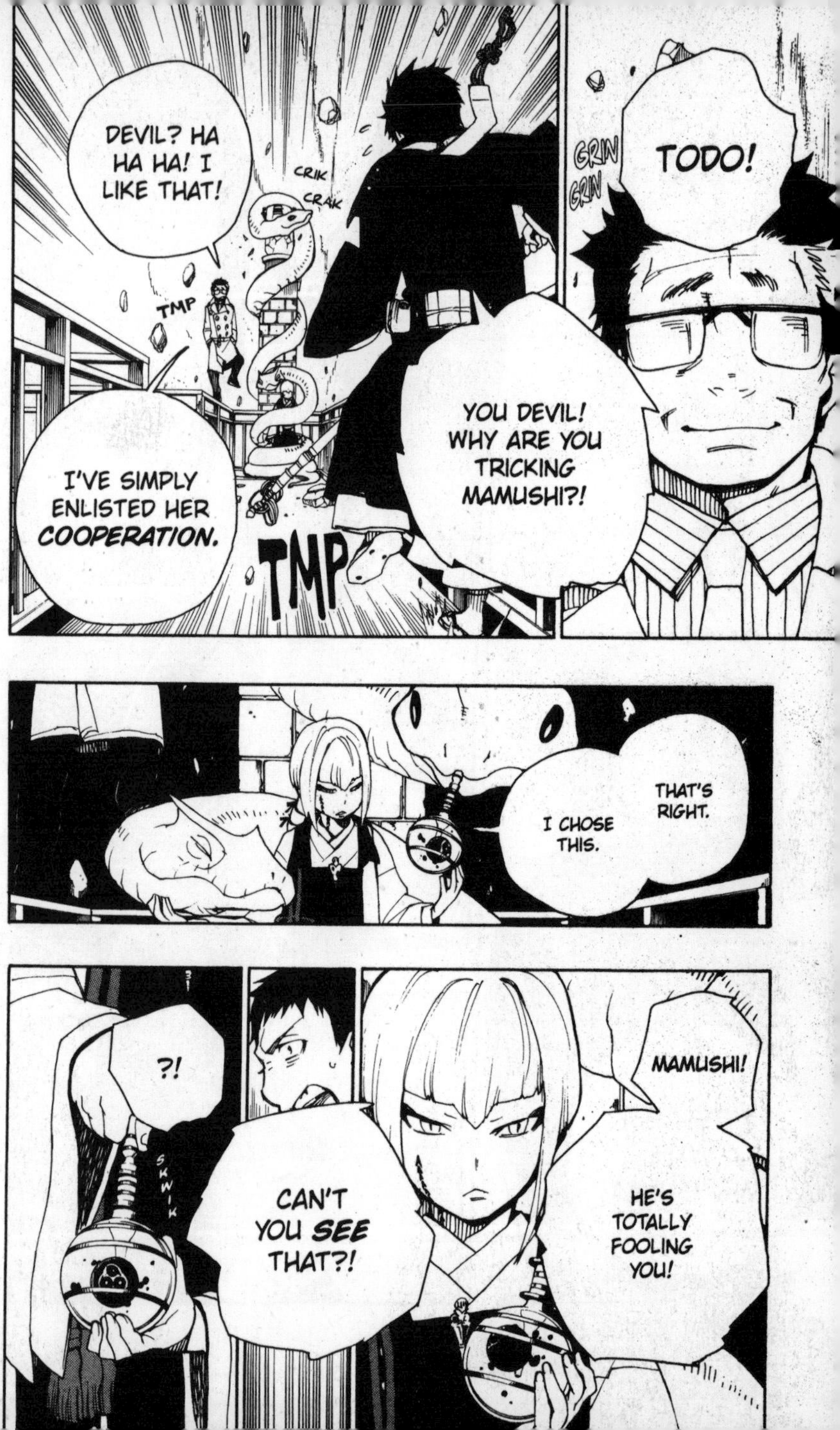
TODO!
GRIN GRIN
YOU DEVIL! WHY ARE YOU TRICKING MAMUSHI?!
DEVIL? HA HA HA! I LIKE THAT!
CRIK
CRAK
TMP
I'VE SIMPLY ENLISTED HER *COOPERATION.*
TMP
THAT'S RIGHT.
I CHOSE THIS.
MAMUSHI!
HE'S TOTALLY FOOLING YOU!
CAN'T YOU *SEE* THAT?!
?!
SKWIK

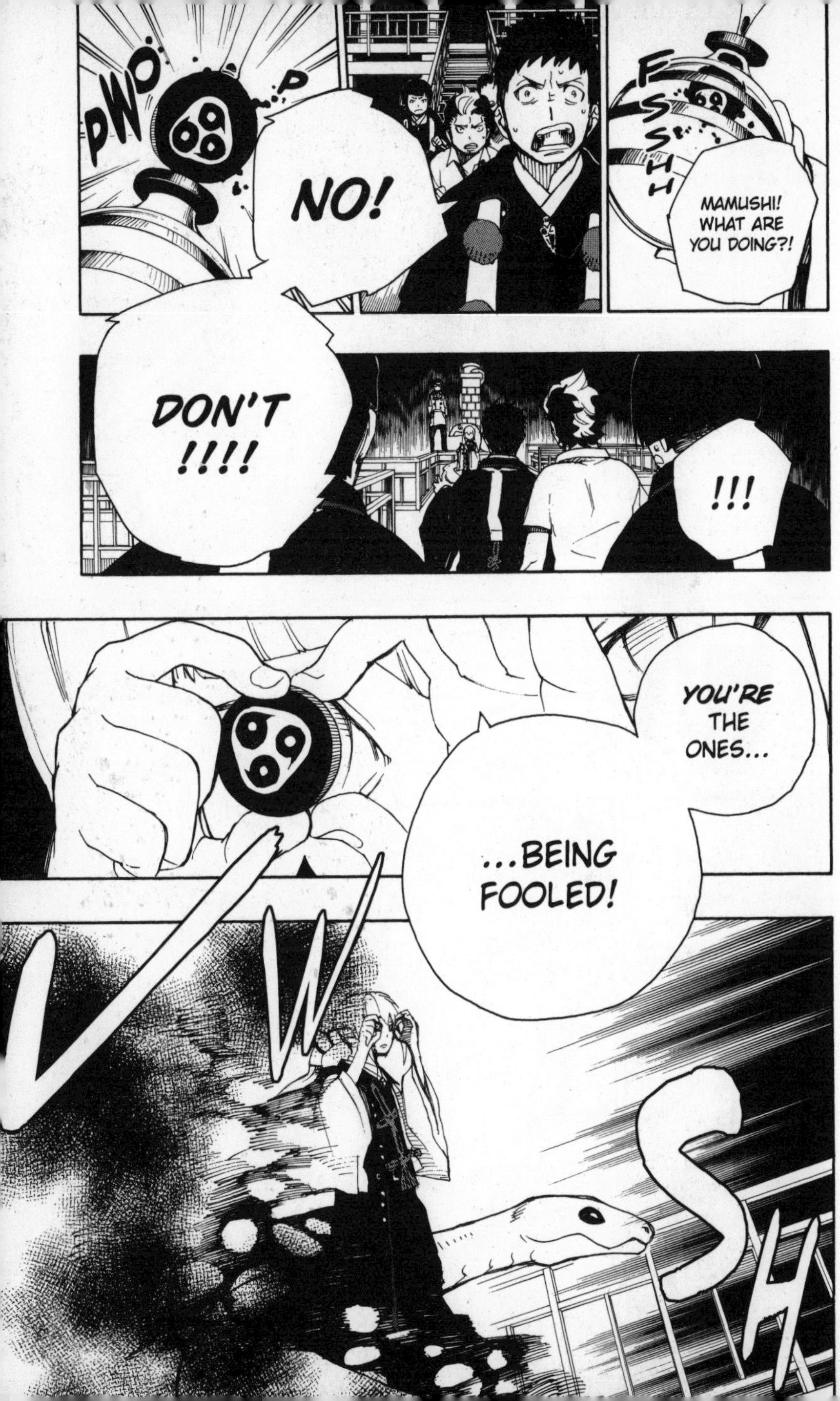
FSSHH
MAMUSHI! WHAT ARE YOU DOING?!
PWOP
NO!
DON'T !!!!
!!!
YOU'RE THE ONES...
...BEING FOOLED!
SH

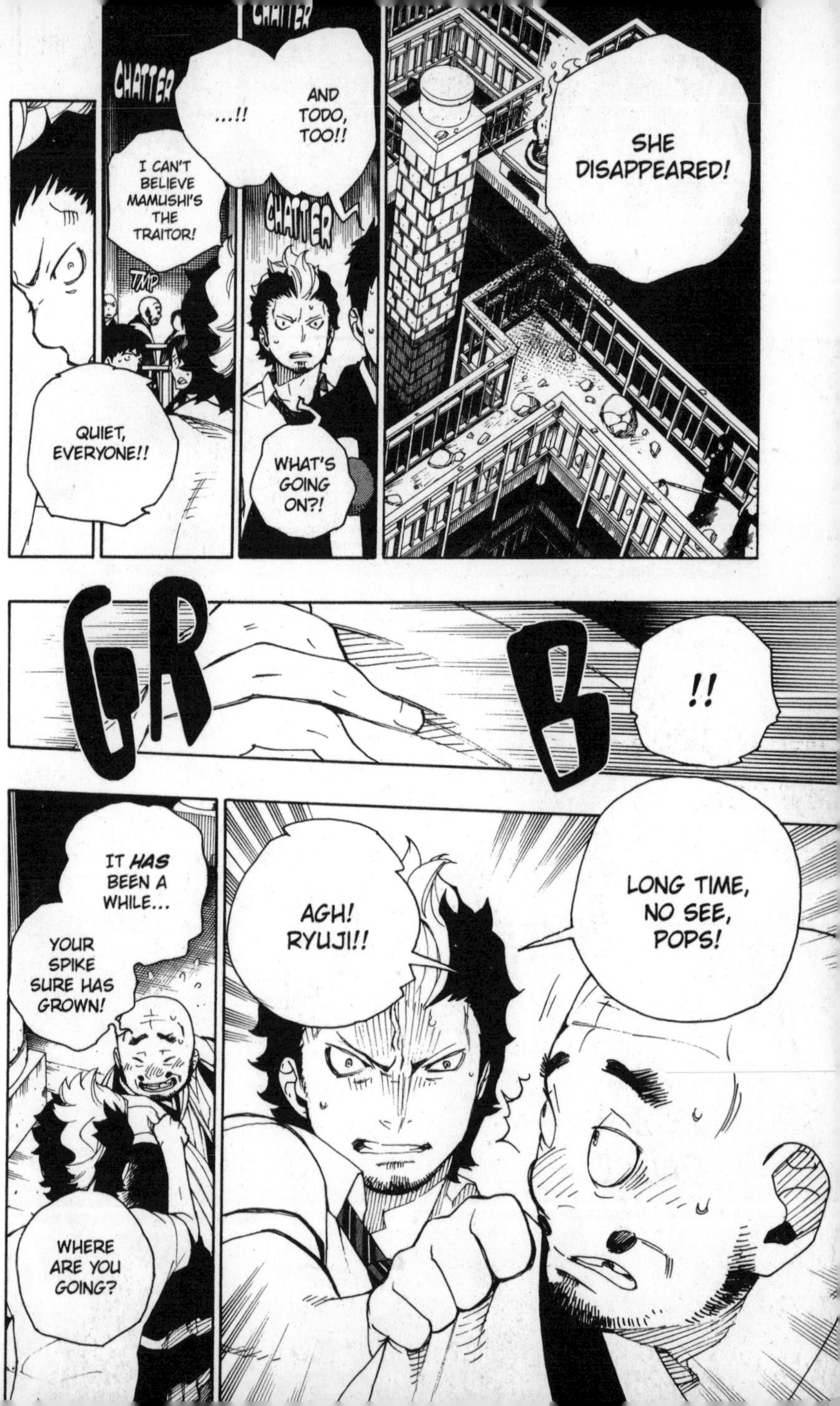
SHE DISAPPEARED!
CHATTER
AND TODO, TOO!!
...!!
CHATTER
WHAT'S GOING ON?!
CHATTER
I CAN'T BELIEVE MAMUSHI'S THE TRAITOR!
TMP
QUIET, EVERYONE!!
!!
GR B
LONG TIME, NO SEE, POPS!
AGH! RYUJI!!
IT *HAS* BEEN A WHILE...
YOUR SPIKE SURE HAS GROWN!
WHERE ARE YOU GOING?

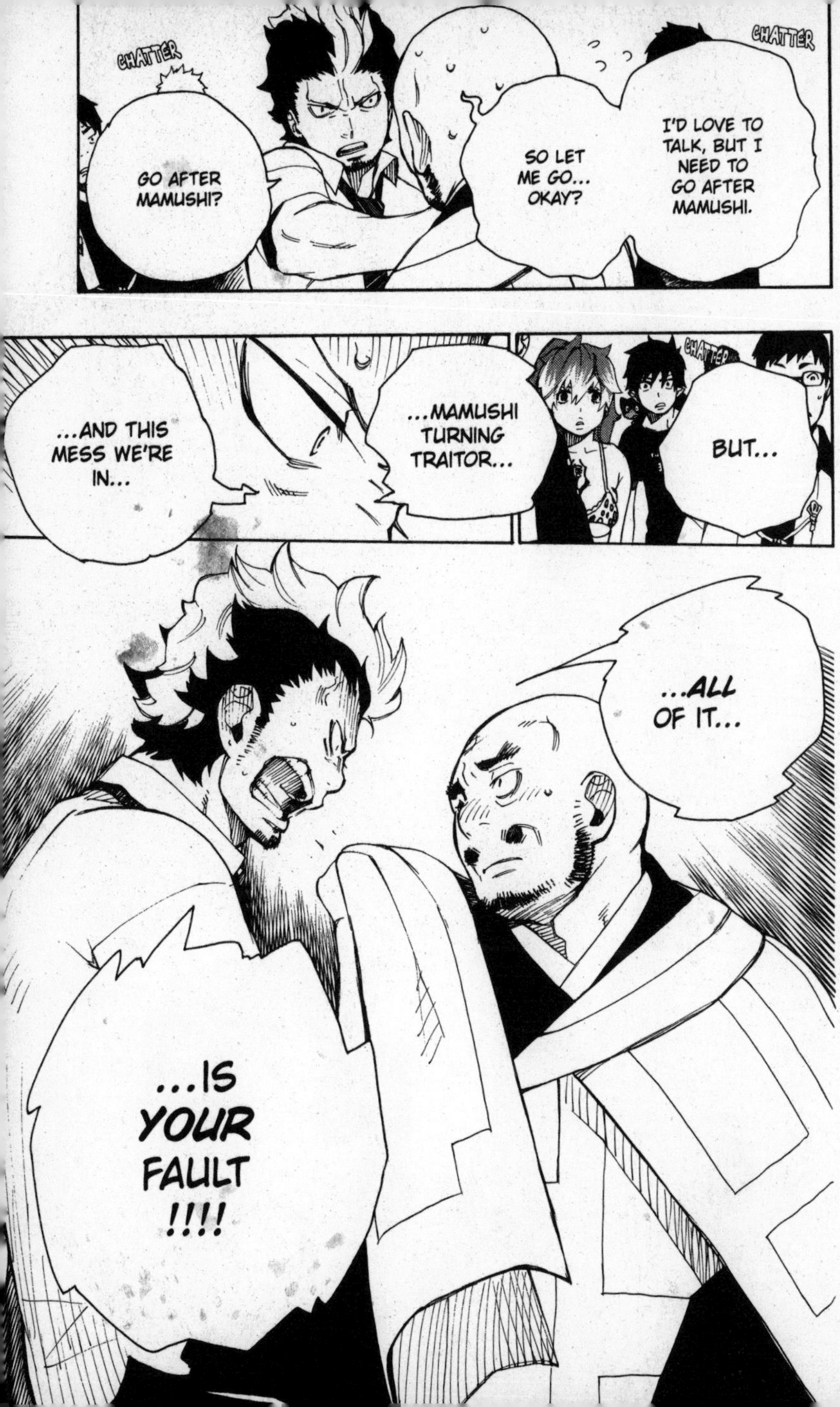
CHATTER
I'D LOVE TO TALK, BUT I NEED TO GO AFTER MAMUSHI.
SO LET ME GO... OKAY?
CHATTER
GO AFTER MAMUSHI?
CHATTER
BUT...
...MAMUSHI TURNING TRAITOR...
...AND THIS MESS WE'RE IN...
...ALL OF IT...
...IS YOUR FAULT !!!!

BLUE EXORCIST CHAPTER 21 CALAMITY

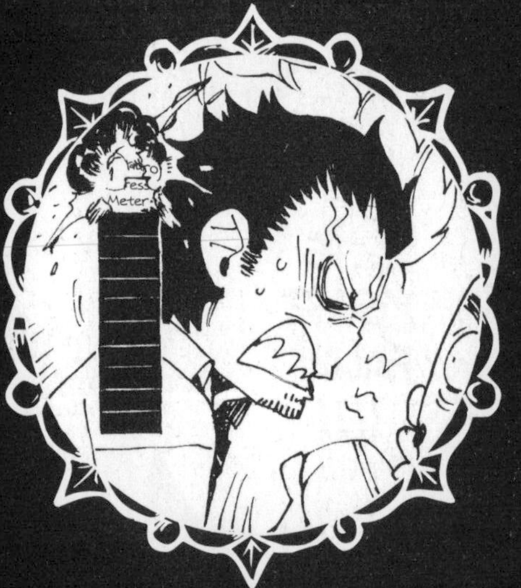
Fess
Meter

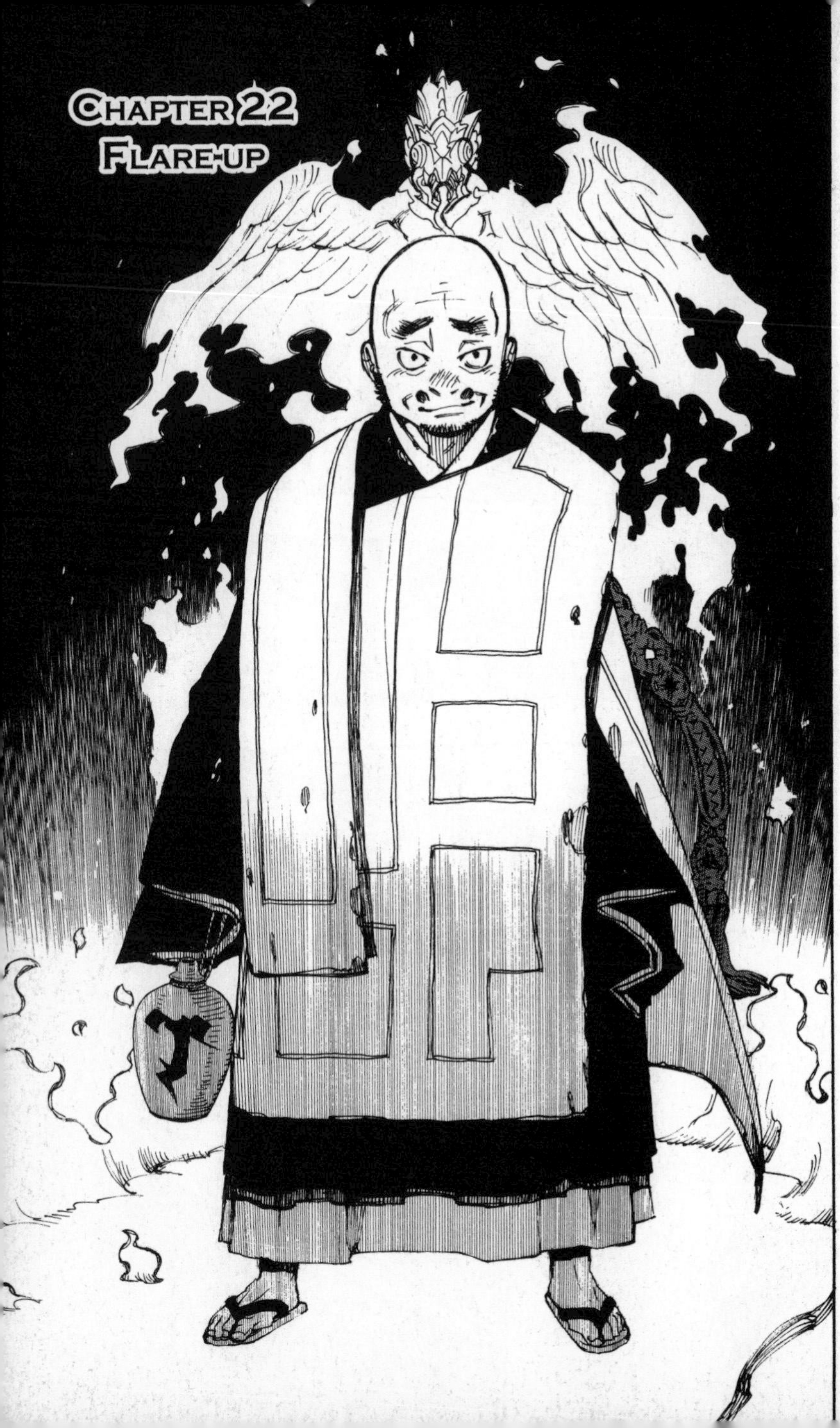
Chapter 22
Flare-up

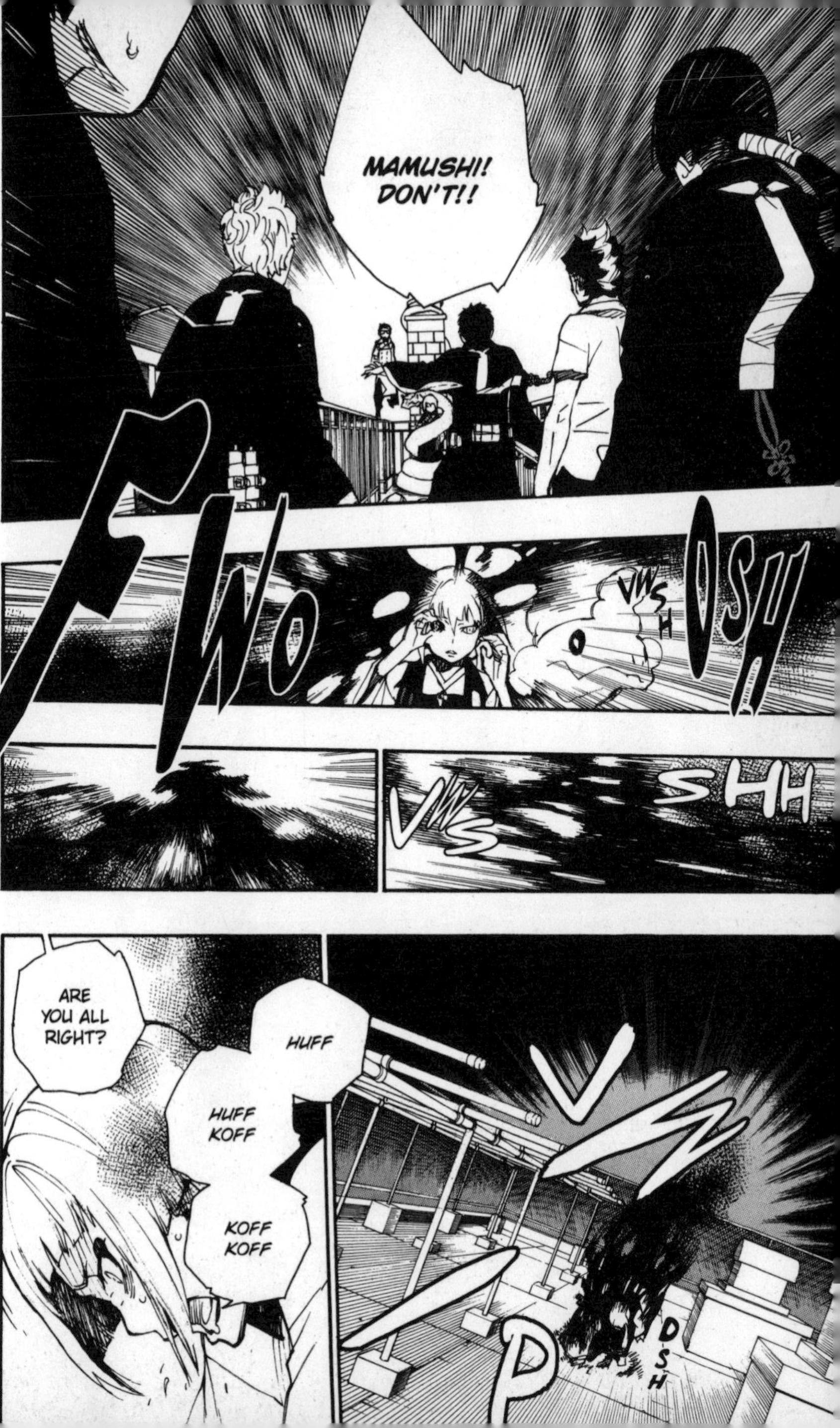
MAMUSHI! DON'T!!
FWOOSH
VWSH
VWS
SHH
DSH
ARE YOU ALL RIGHT?
HUFF
HUFF KOFF
KOFF KOFF

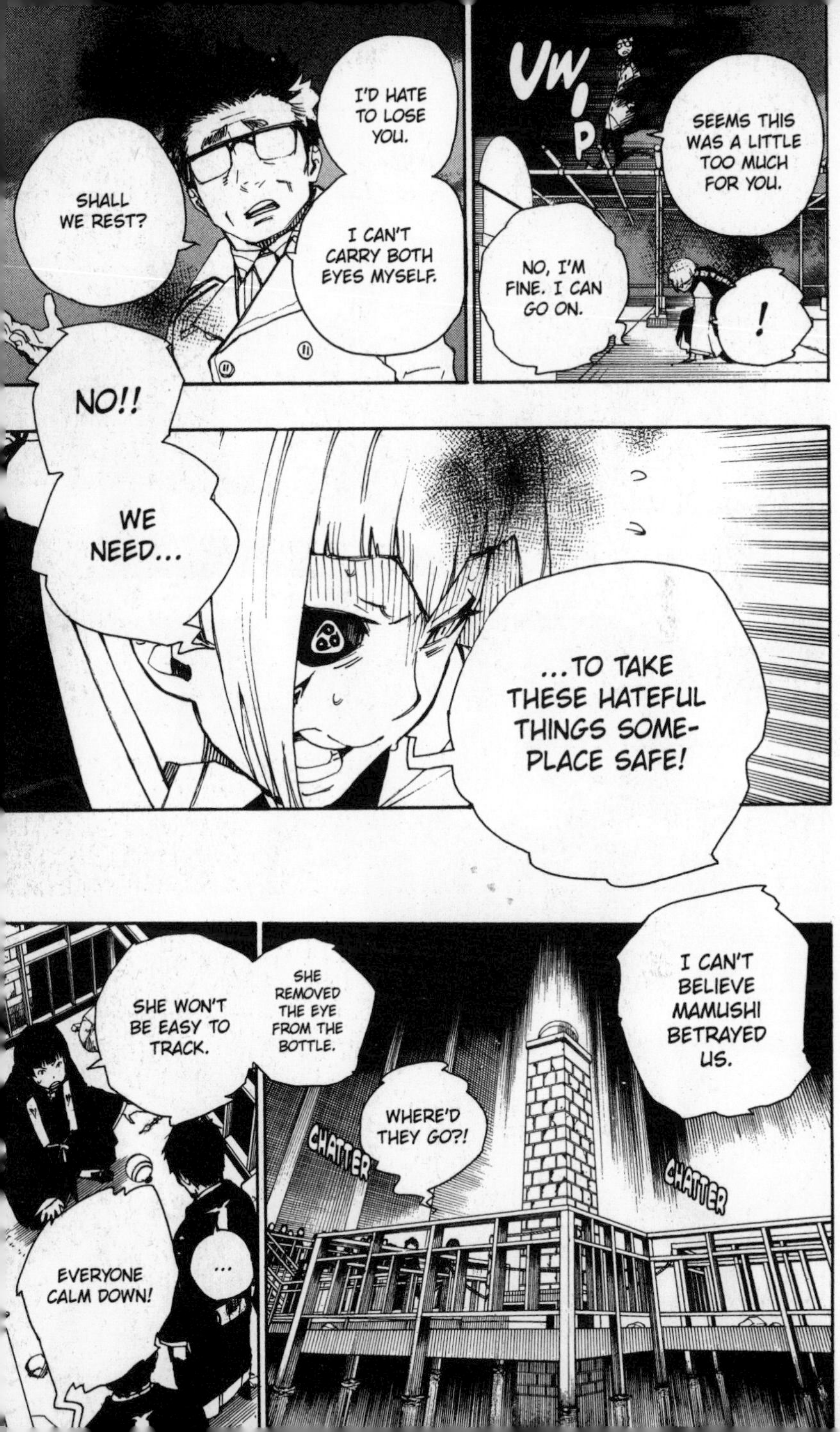
UWIP
SEEMS THIS WAS A LITTLE TOO MUCH FOR YOU.
!
NO, I'M FINE. I CAN GO ON.
I'D HATE TO LOSE YOU.
I CAN'T CARRY BOTH EYES MYSELF.
SHALL WE REST?
NO!!
WE NEED...
...TO TAKE THESE HATEFUL THINGS SOME-PLACE SAFE!
I CAN'T BELIEVE MAMUSHI BETRAYED US.
CHATTER
WHERE'D THEY GO?!
CHATTER
SHE REMOVED THE EYE FROM THE BOTTLE.
SHE WON'T BE EASY TO TRACK.
...
EVERYONE CALM DOWN!

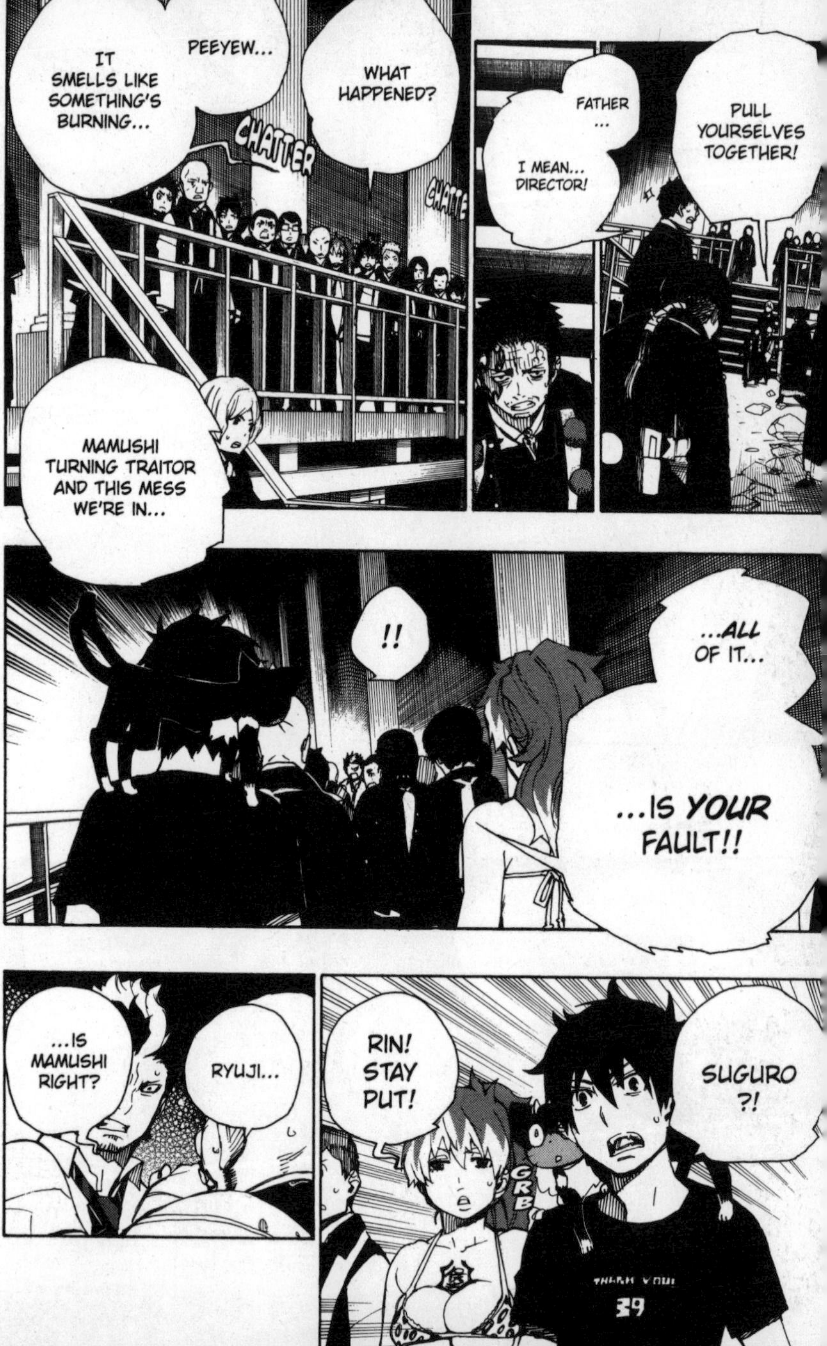
PULL YOURSELVES TOGETHER!
FATHER ...
I MEAN... DIRECTOR!
CHATTE
WHAT HAPPENED?
CHATTER
PEEYEW...
IT SMELLS LIKE SOMETHING'S BURNING...
MAMUSHI TURNING TRAITOR AND THIS MESS WE'RE IN...
...ALL OF IT...
...IS YOUR FAULT!!
!!
SUGURO ?!
GRB
RIN! STAY PUT!
RYUJI...
...IS MAMUSHI RIGHT?

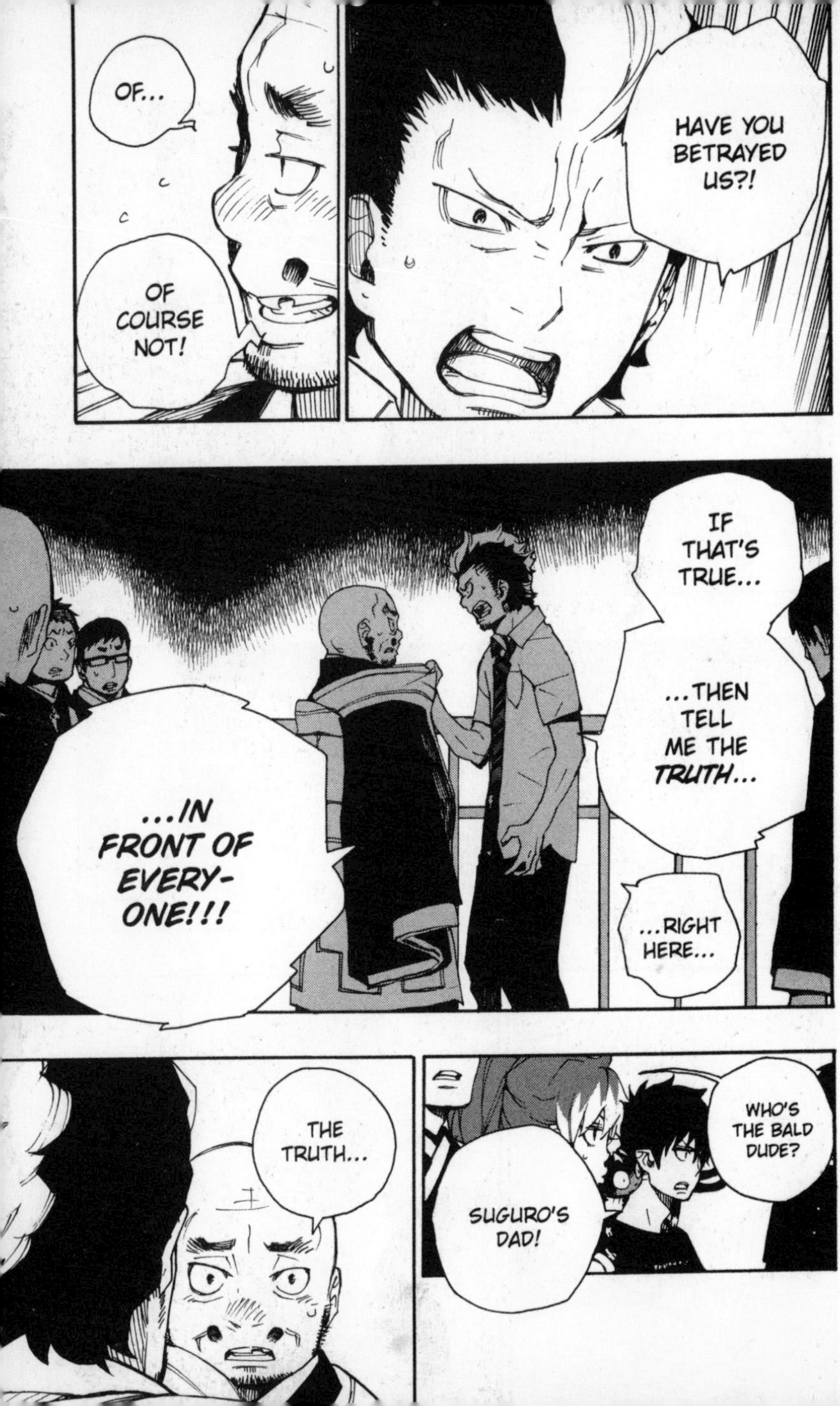
HAVE YOU BETRAYED US?!
OF...
OF COURSE NOT!
IF THAT'S TRUE...
...THEN TELL ME THE TRUTH...
...RIGHT HERE...
...IN FRONT OF EVERY-ONE!!!
WHO'S THE BALD DUDE?
SUGURO'S DAD!
THE TRUTH...

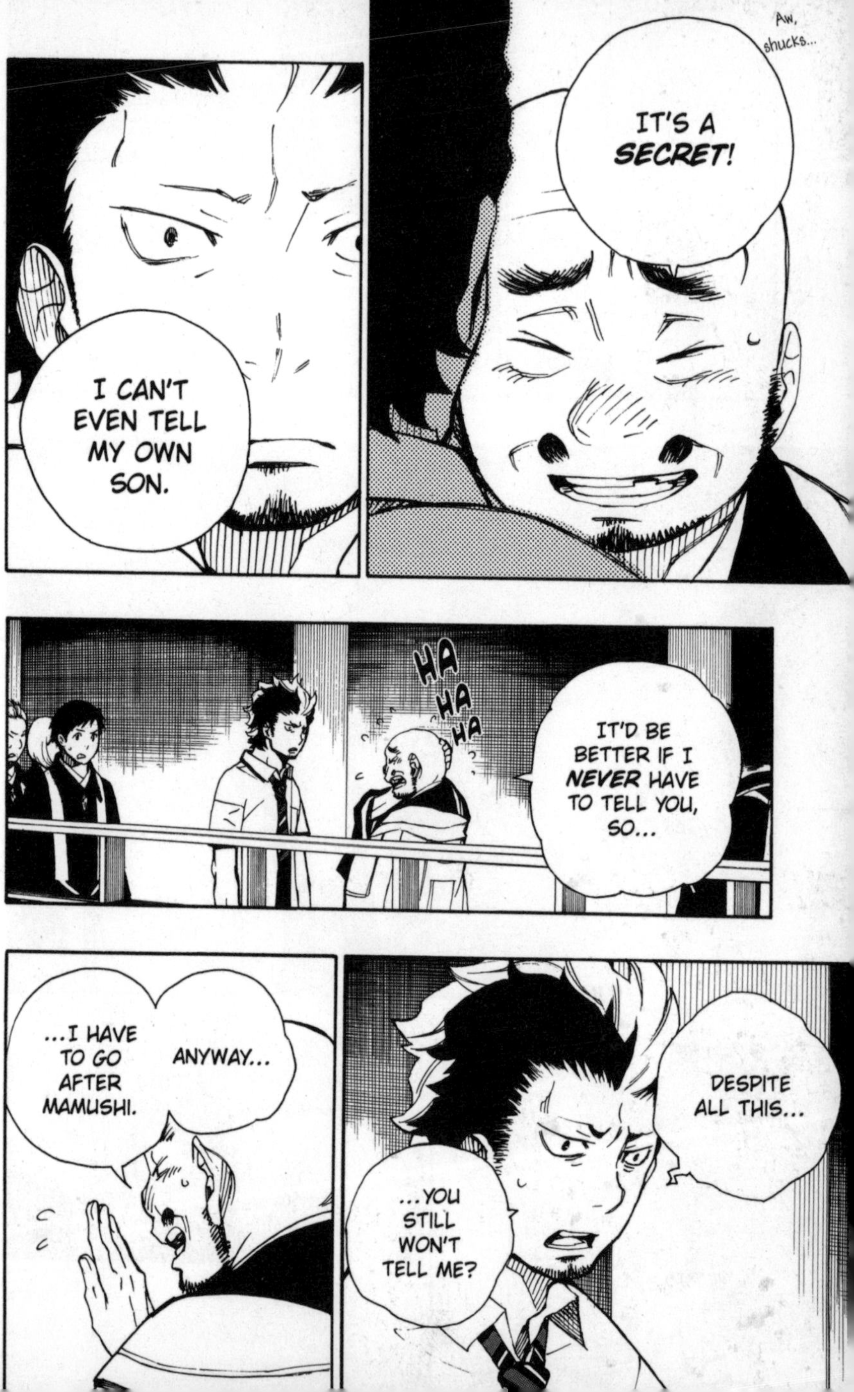
Aw, shucks...
IT'S A SECRET!
I CAN'T EVEN TELL MY OWN SON.
HA HA HA
IT'D BE BETTER IF I NEVER HAVE TO TELL YOU, SO...
DESPITE ALL THIS...
...YOU STILL WON'T TELL ME?
ANYWAY...
...I HAVE TO GO AFTER MAMUSHI.

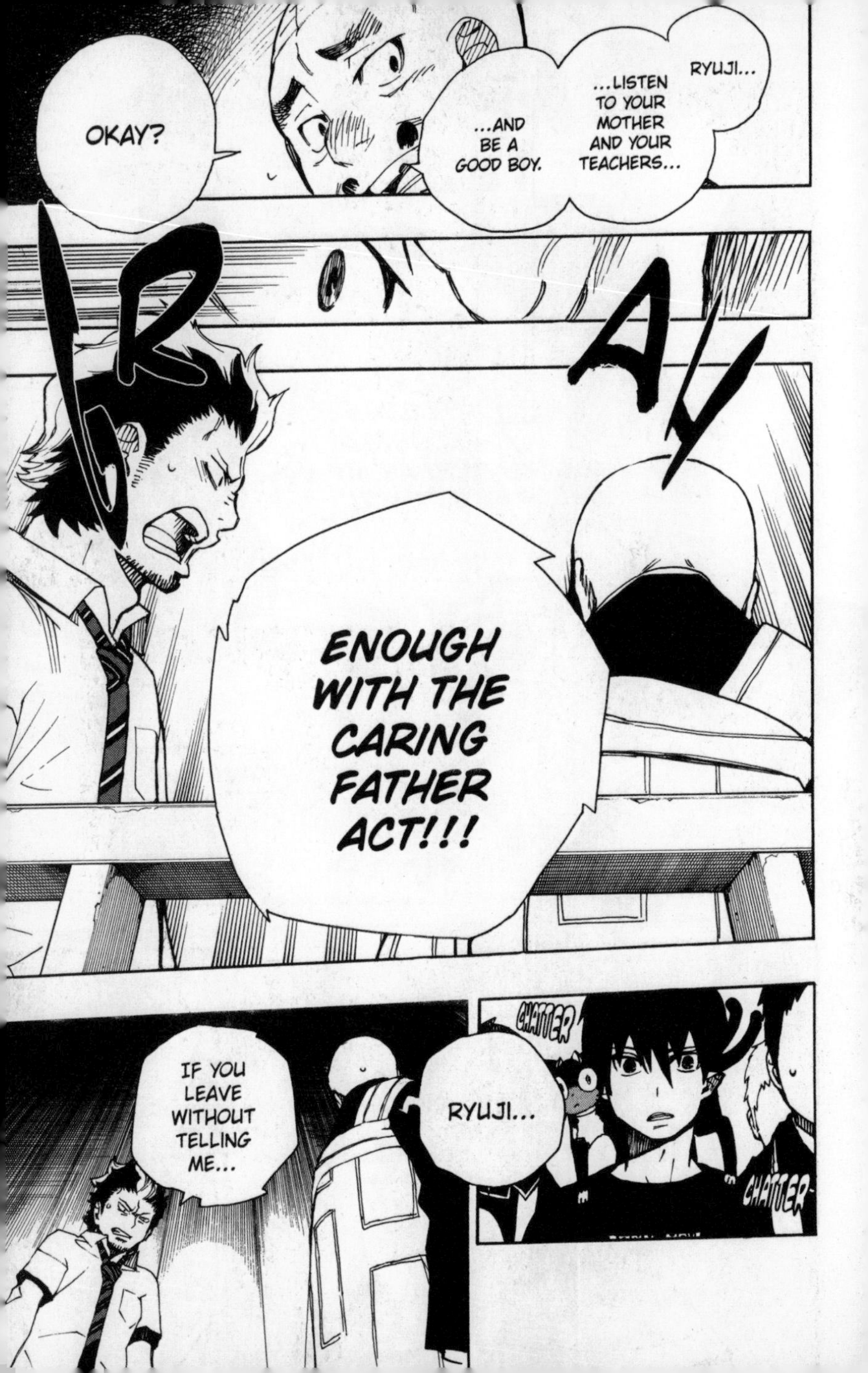
RYUJI...
...LISTEN TO YOUR MOTHER AND YOUR TEACHERS...
...AND BE A GOOD BOY.
OKAY?
ENOUGH WITH THE CARING FATHER ACT!!!
CHATTER
CHATTER
RYUJI...
IF YOU LEAVE WITHOUT TELLING ME...

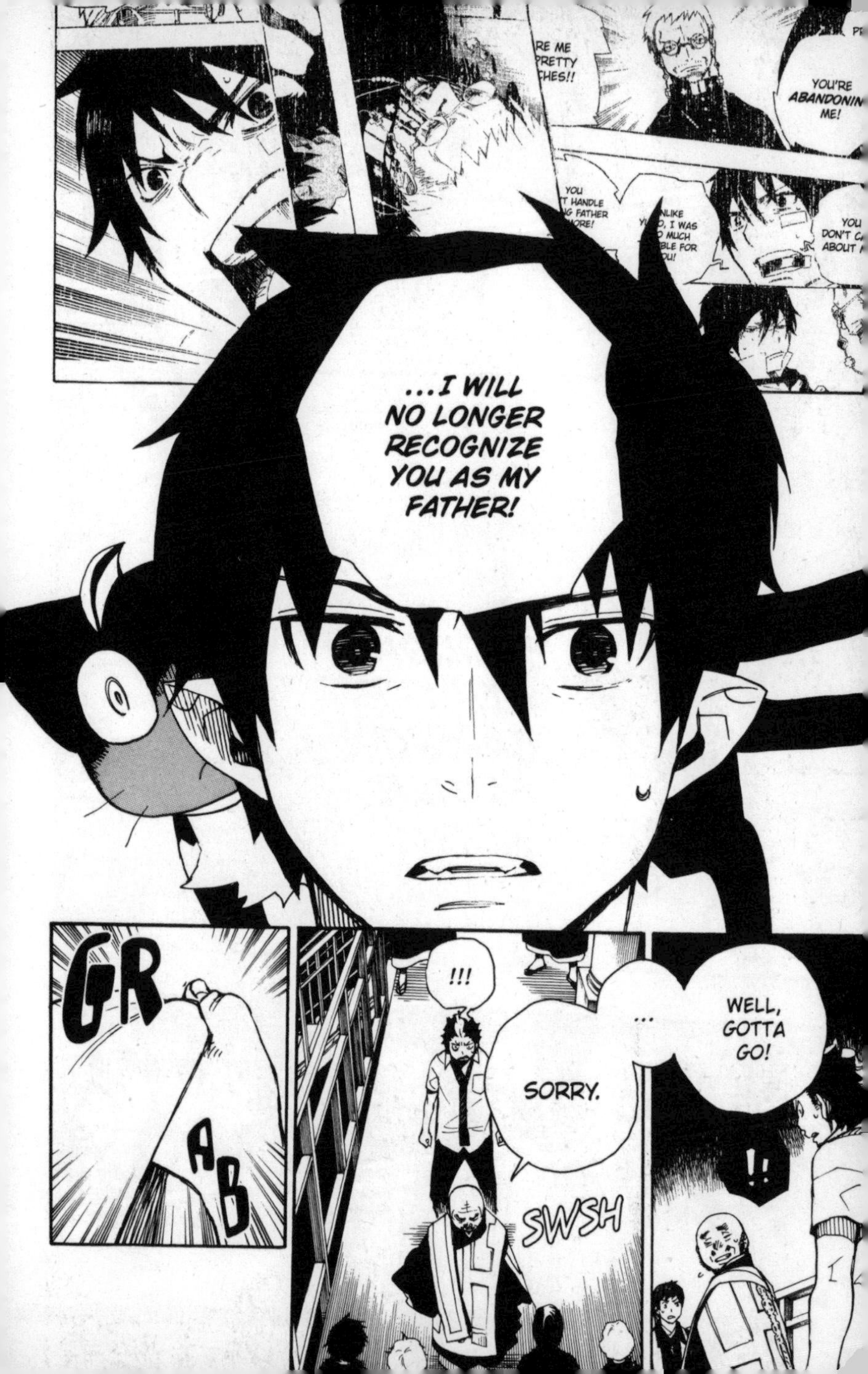

YOU'RE ABANDONIN ME!
...I WILL NO LONGER RECOGNIZE YOU AS MY FATHER!
WELL, GOTTA GO!
!!
!!!
...
SORRY.
SWSH
GRAB

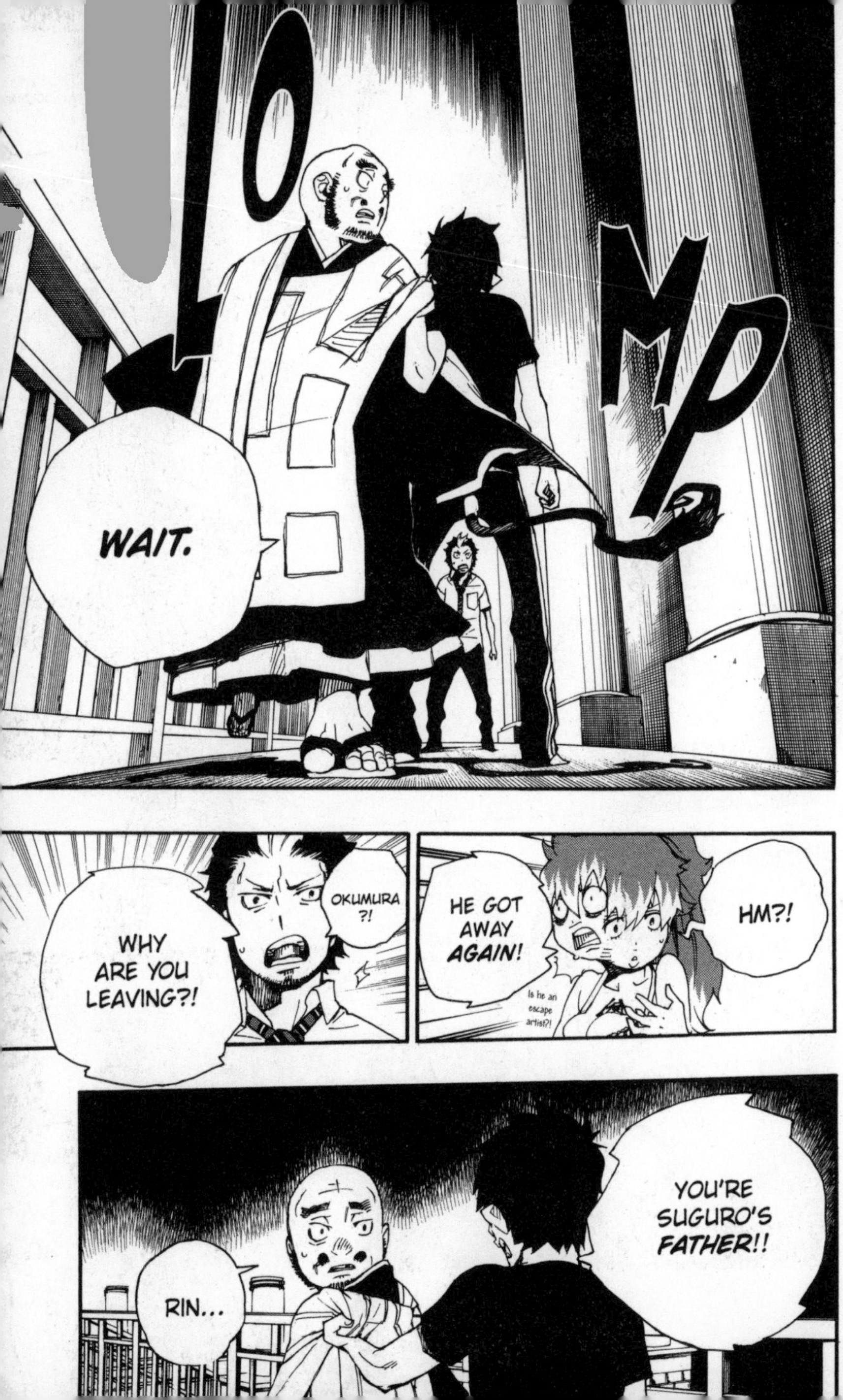
WAIT.
HM?!
HE GOT AWAY AGAIN!
Is he an escape artist?!
OKUMURA?!
WHY ARE YOU LEAVING?!
YOU'RE SUGURO'S FATHER!!
RIN...

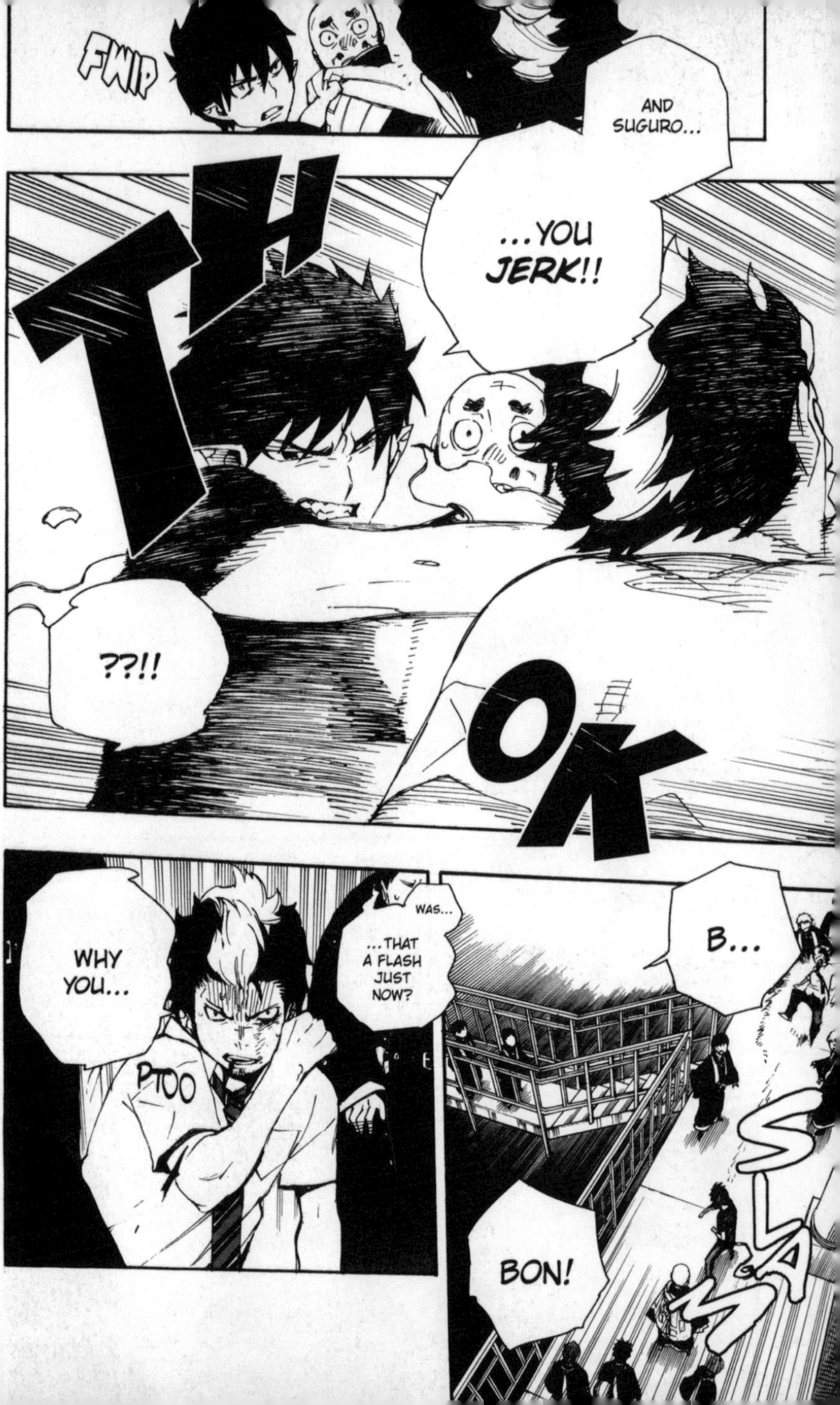
AND SUGURO...
FWIP
...YOU JERK!!
TH
OK
??!!
B...
SLAM
BON!
WAS...
...THAT A FLASH JUST NOW?
WHY YOU...
PTOO

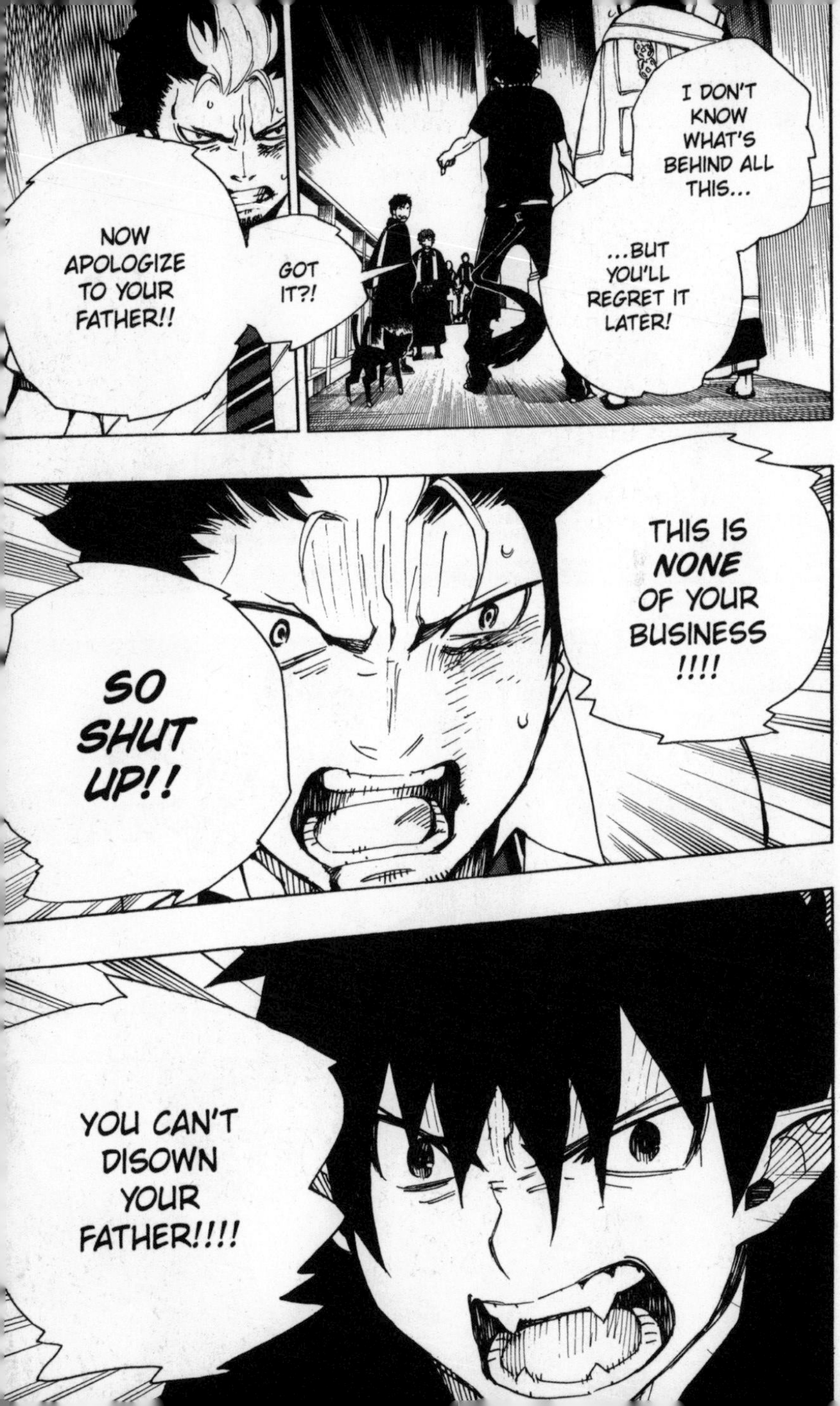
I DON'T KNOW WHAT'S BEHIND ALL THIS...
...BUT YOU'LL REGRET IT LATER!
NOW APOLOGIZE TO YOUR FATHER!!
GOT IT?!
THIS IS *NONE* OF YOUR BUSINESS !!!!
SO SHUT UP!!
YOU CAN'T DISOWN YOUR FATHER!!!!

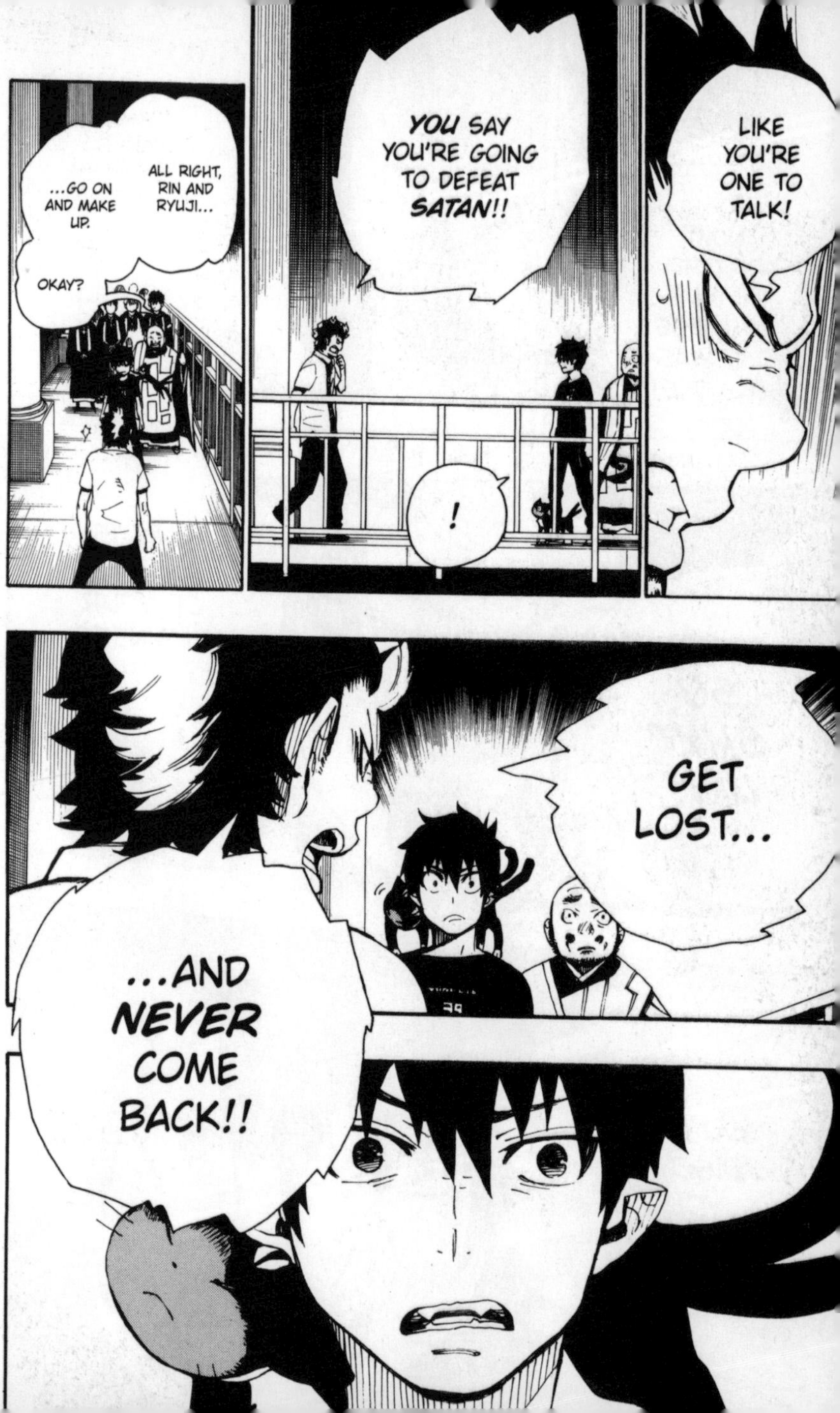
LIKE YOU'RE ONE TO TALK!
YOU SAY YOU'RE GOING TO DEFEAT SATAN!!
!
ALL RIGHT, RIN AND RYUJI...
...GO ON AND MAKE UP.
OKAY?
GET LOST...
...AND NEVER COME BACK!!

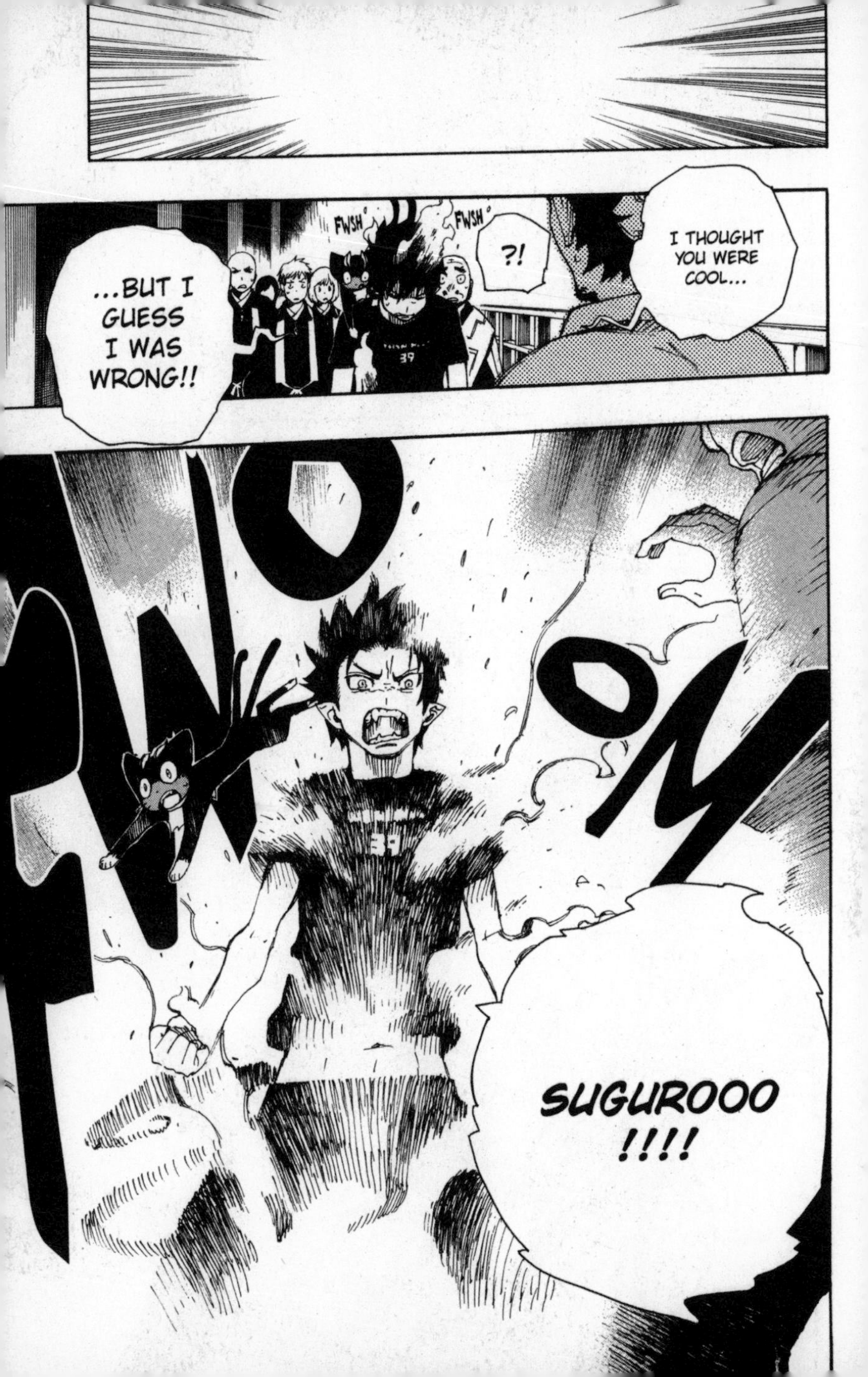
I THOUGHT YOU WERE COOL...
?!
FWSH
FWSH
...BUT I GUESS I WAS WRONG!!
SUGUROOO !!!!

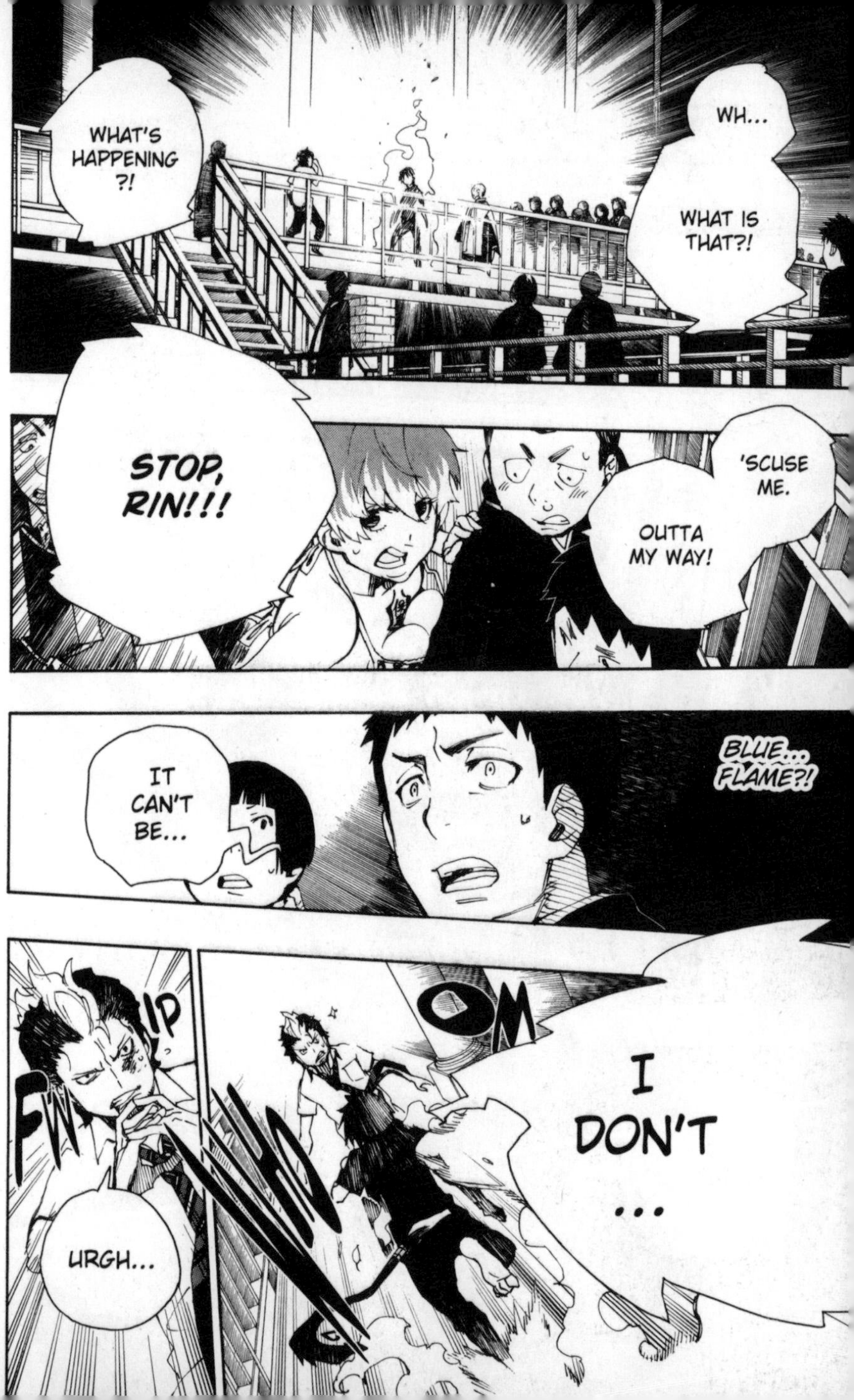
WH...
WHAT IS THAT?!
WHAT'S HAPPENING ?!
'SCUSE ME.
OUTTA MY WAY!
STOP, RIN!!!
BLUE... FLAME?!
IT CAN'T BE...
OM
I DON'T ...
IP
FW
URGH...

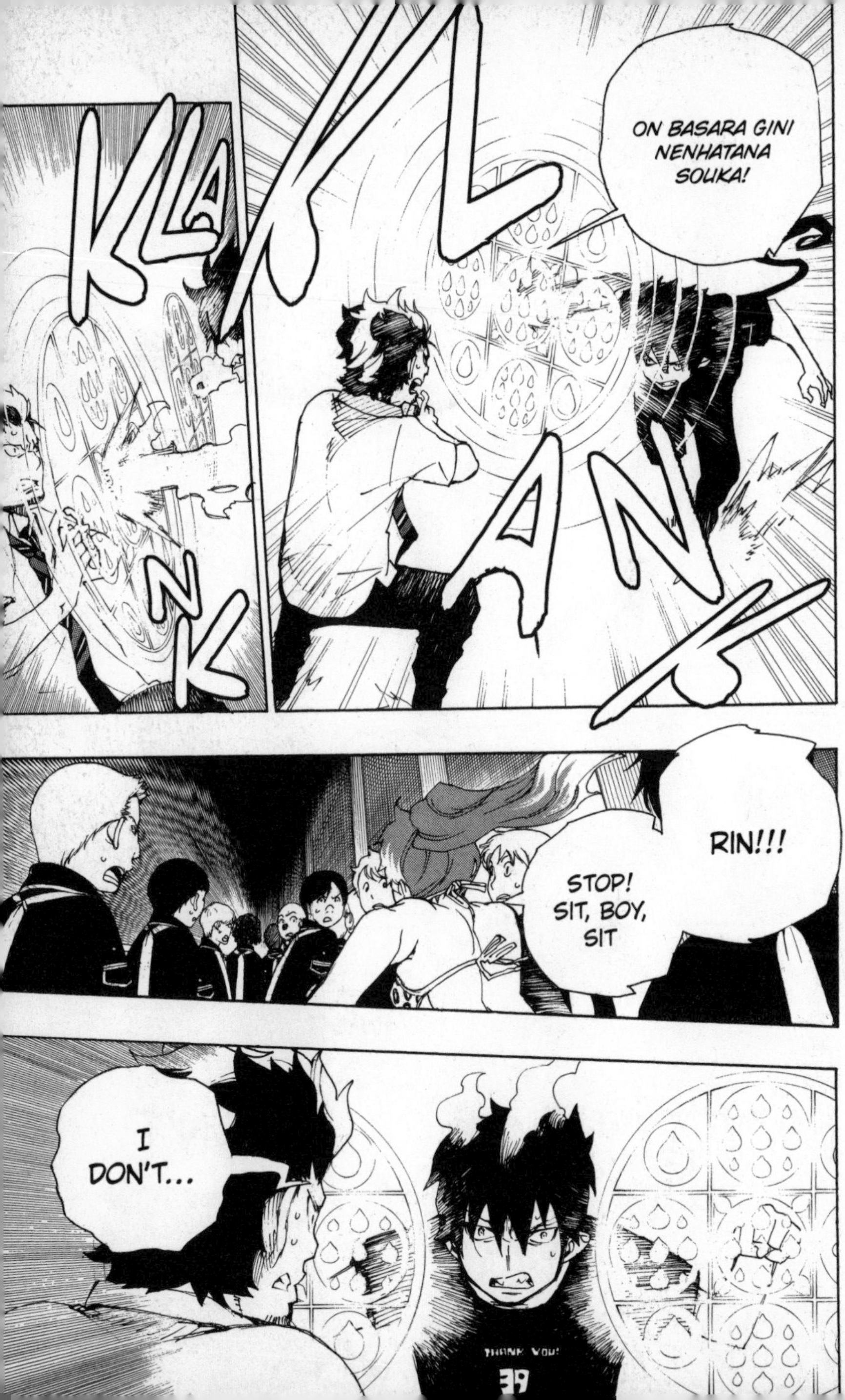
ON BASARA GINI NENHATANA SOUKA!
KLANK
KLANK
RIN!!!
STOP! SIT, BOY, SIT
I DON'T...
THANK YOU!
39

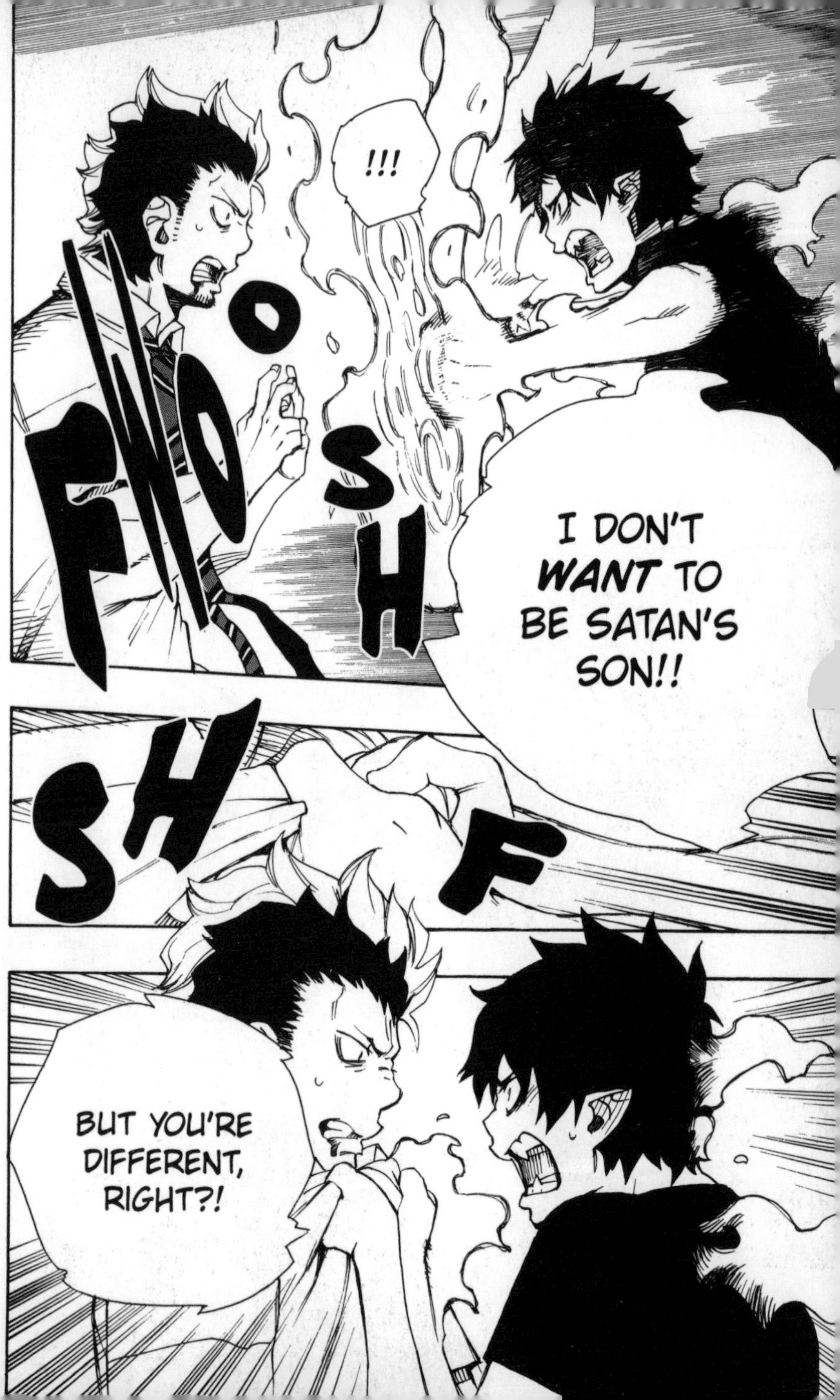
!!!
I DON'T *WANT* TO BE SATAN'S SON!!
FWOOSH
SHF
BUT YOU'RE DIFFERENT, RIGHT?!

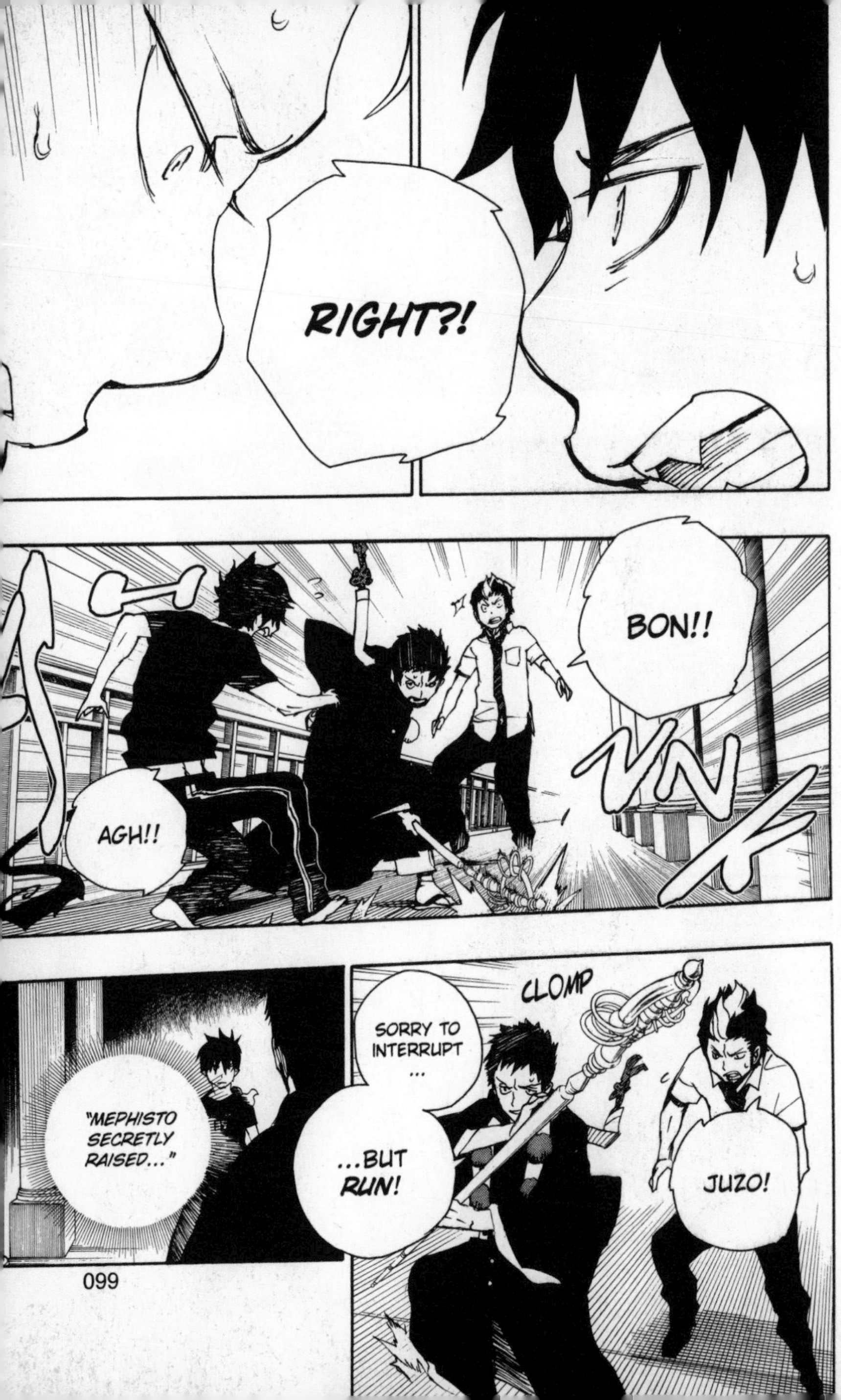
RIGHT?!
BON!!
AGH!!
CLOMP
JUZO!
SORRY TO INTERRUPT ...
...BUT RUN!
"MEPHISTO SECRETLY RAISED..."

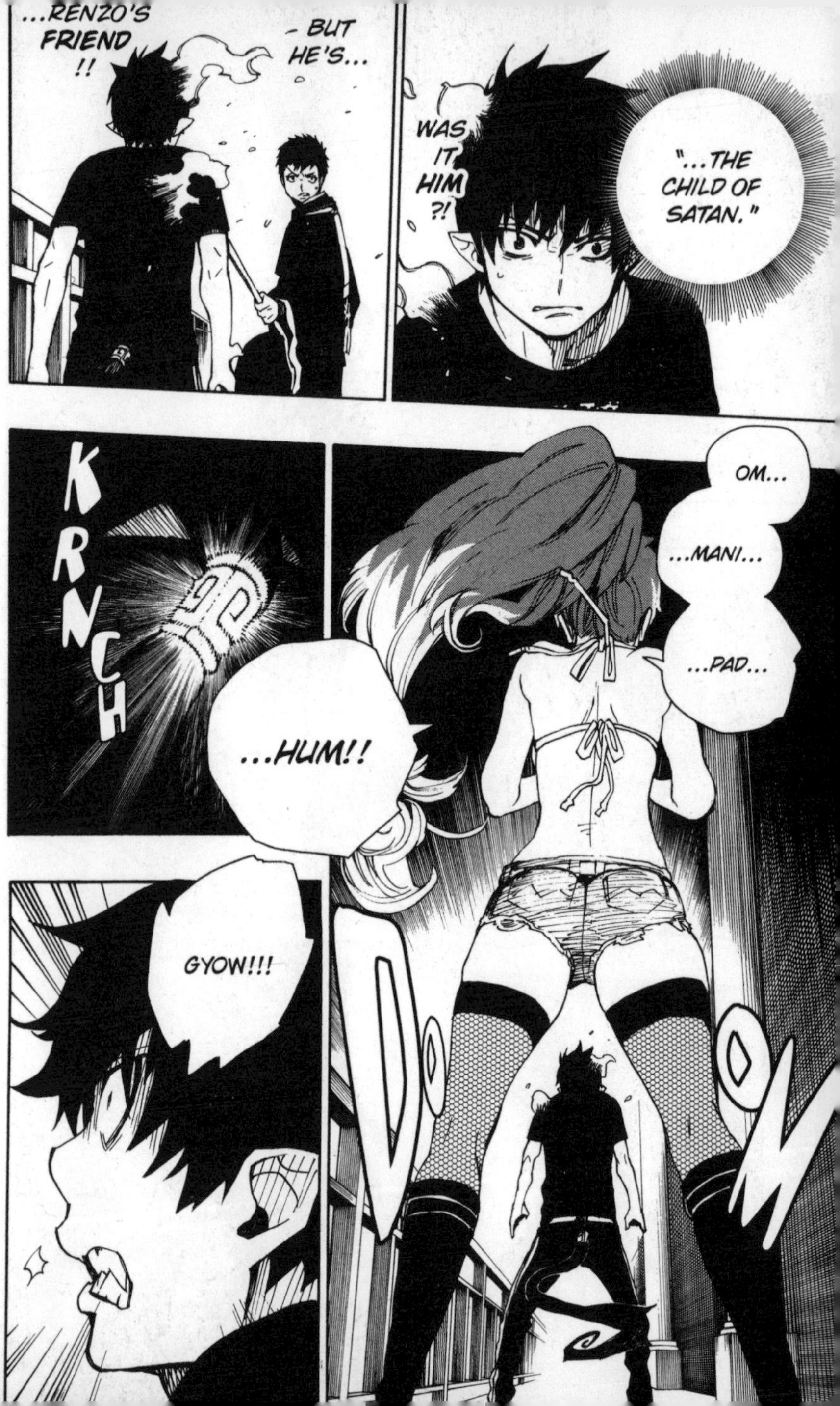

"...THE CHILD OF SATAN."
WAS IT HIM ?!
- BUT HE'S...
...RENZO'S FRIEND !!
OM...
...MANI...
...PAD...
...HUM!!
KRNCH
GYOW!!!

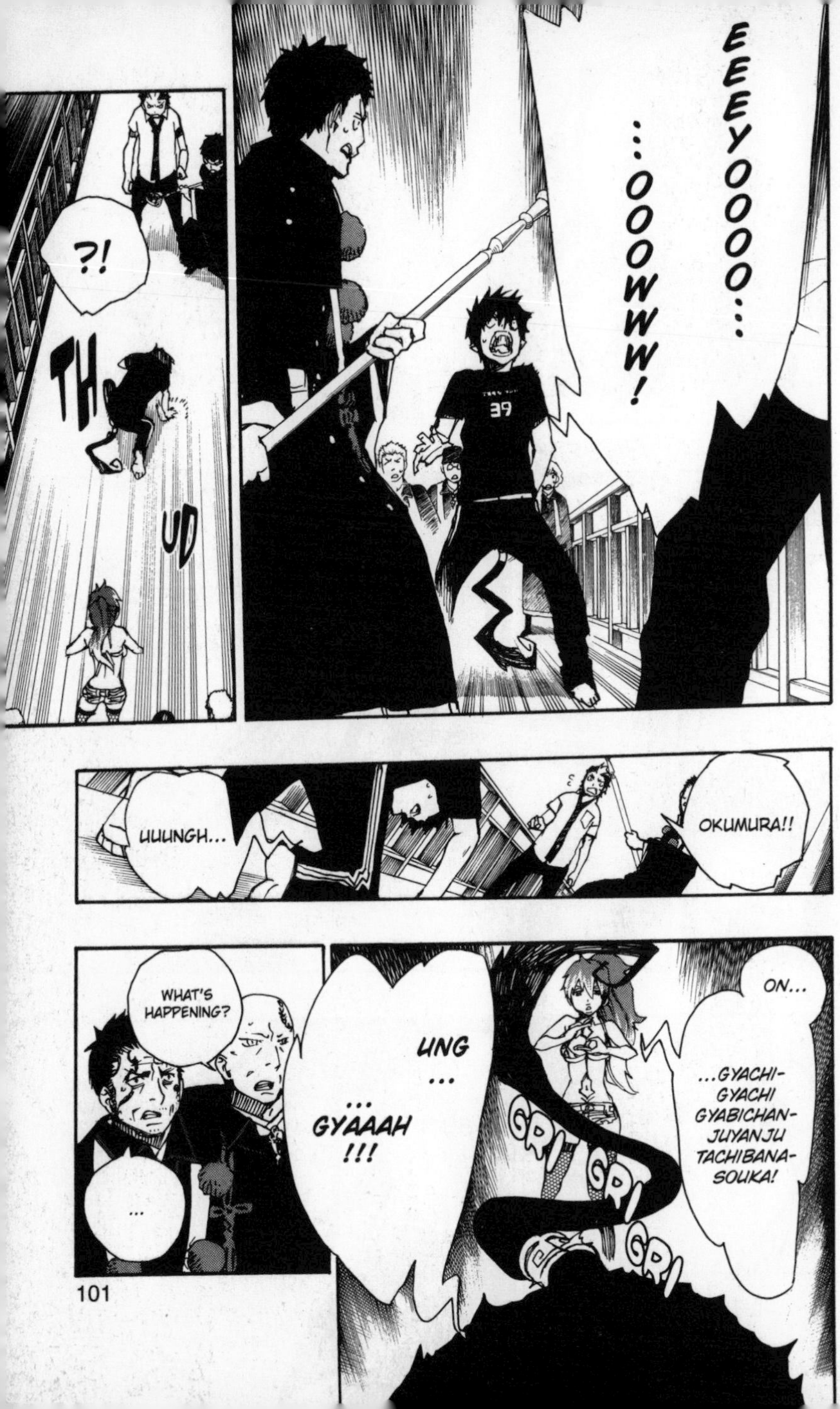
EEEYOOOO...
...OOOWWW!
?!
THUD
OKUMURA!!
UUUNGH...
ON...
...GYACHI-GYACHI GYABICHAN-JUYANJU TACHIBANA-SOUKA!
UNG...
...GYAAAH!!!
GRI GRI GRI
WHAT'S HAPPENING?
...

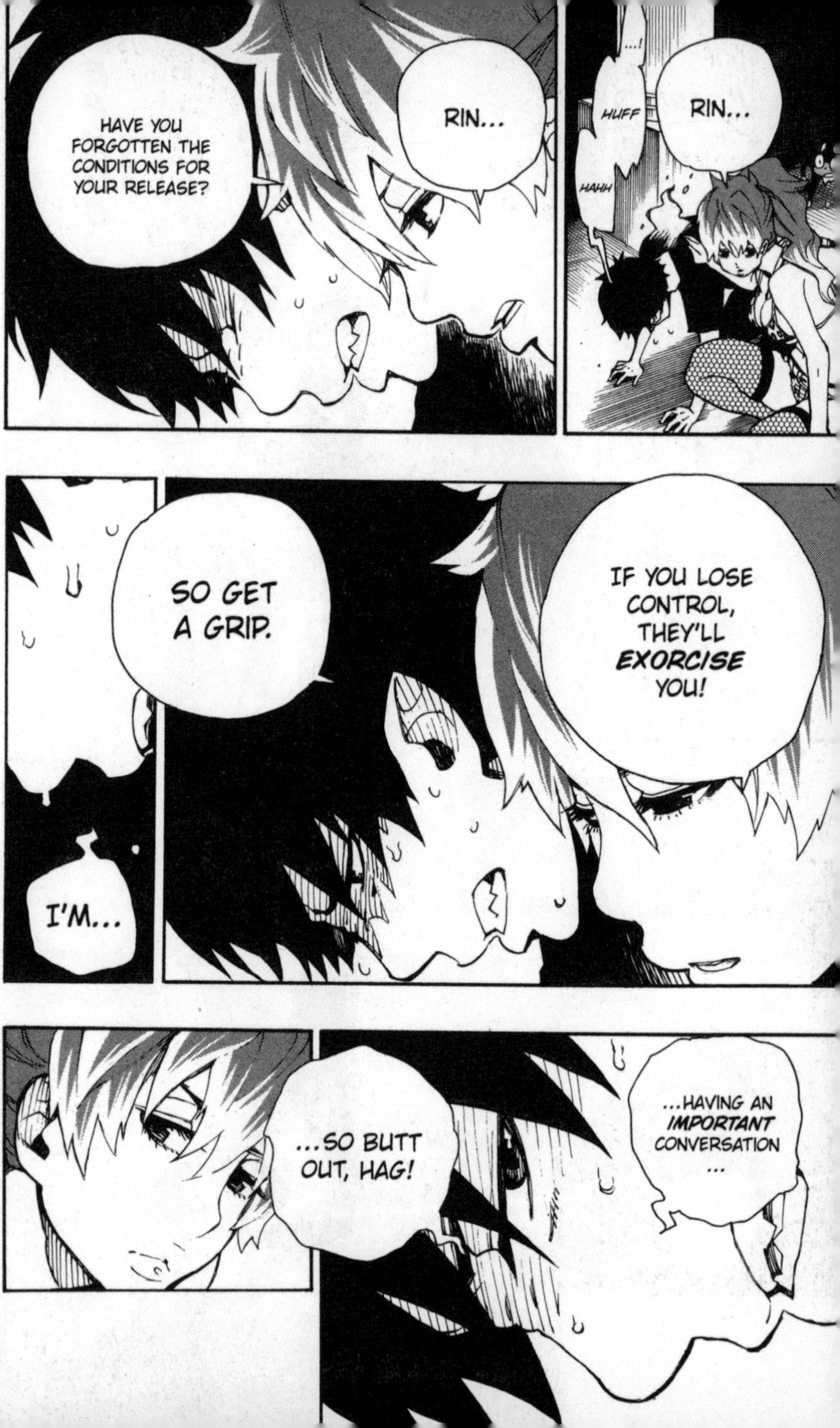
RIN...
...!
HUFF
HAHH
RIN...
HAVE YOU FORGOTTEN THE CONDITIONS FOR YOUR RELEASE?
IF YOU LOSE CONTROL, THEY'LL EXORCISE YOU!
SO GET A GRIP.
I'M...
...HAVING AN IMPORTANT CONVERSATION ...
...SO BUTT OUT, HAG!

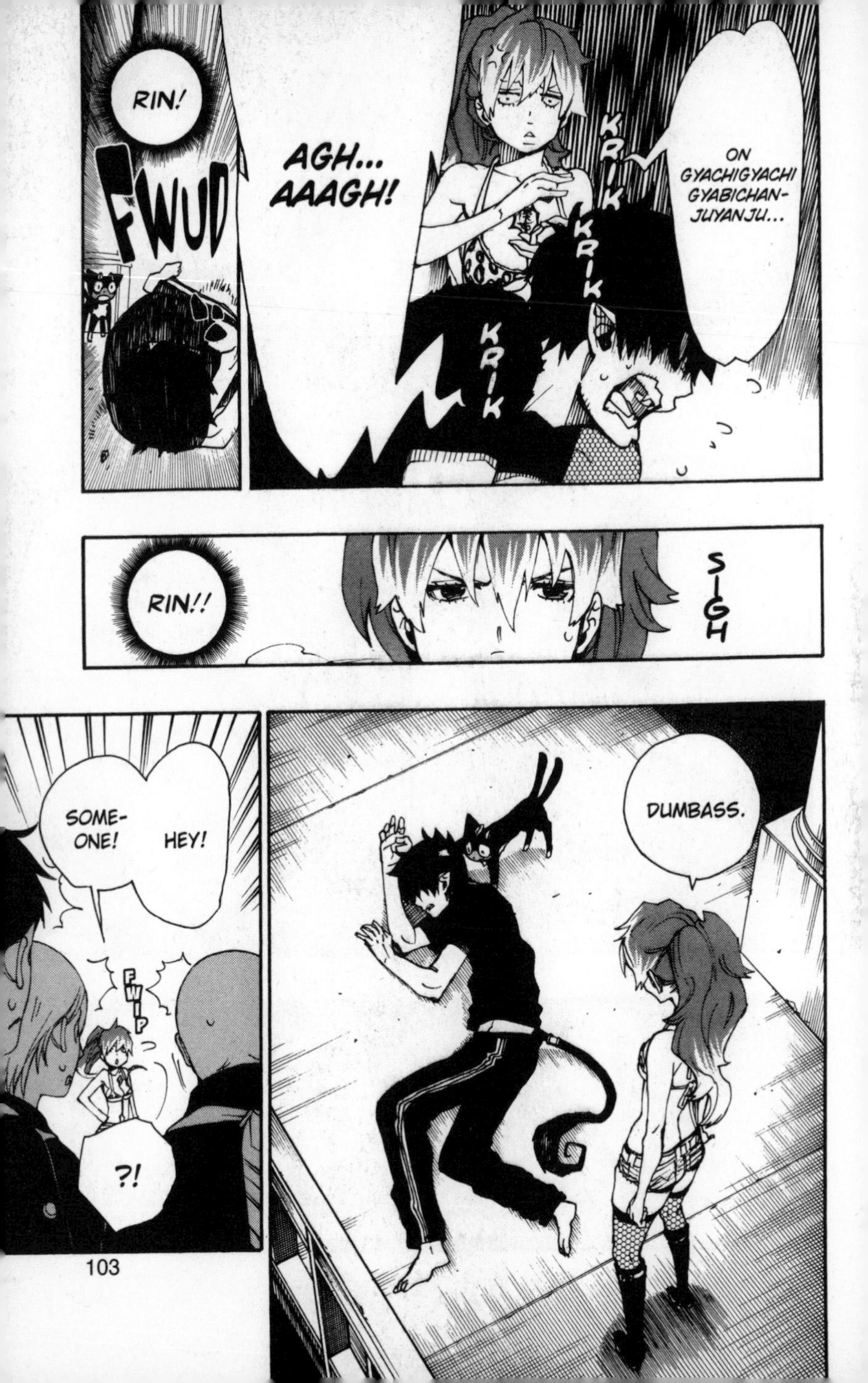

ON GYACHIGYACHI GYABICHAN-JUYANJU...
KRIK KRIK KRIK KRIK
AGH... AAAGH!
RIN!
FWUD
SIGH
RIN!!
DUMBASS.
SOME-ONE! HEY!
FWIP
?!

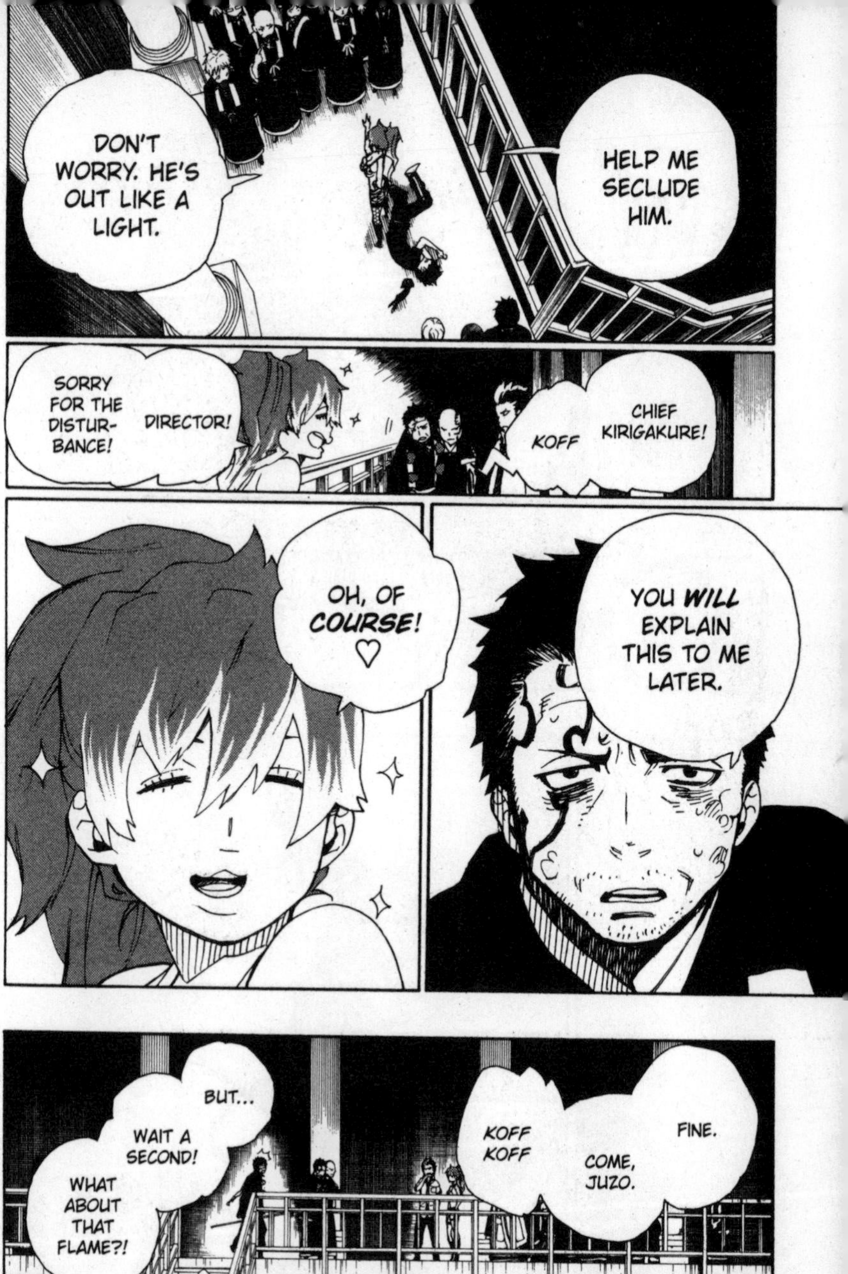
HELP ME SECLUDE HIM.
DON'T WORRY. HE'S OUT LIKE A LIGHT.
CHIEF KIRIGAKURE!
KOFF
DIRECTOR!
SORRY FOR THE DISTURBANCE!
YOU WILL EXPLAIN THIS TO ME LATER.
OH, OF COURSE! ♡
FINE.
COME, JUZO.
KOFF KOFF
BUT...
WAIT A SECOND!
WHAT ABOUT THAT FLAME?!

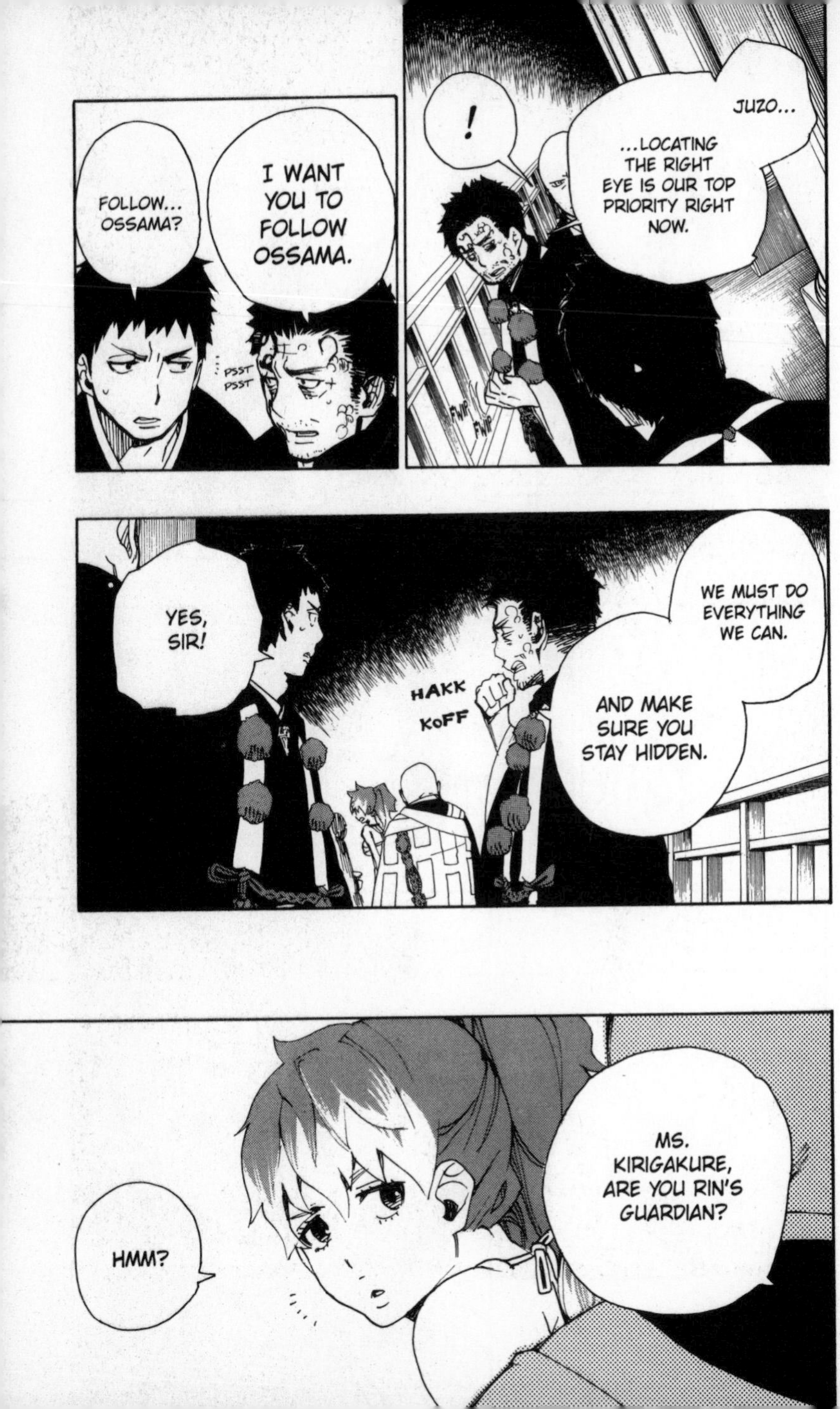
JUZO...
...LOCATING THE RIGHT EYE IS OUR TOP PRIORITY RIGHT NOW.
!
FWIP FWIP
I WANT YOU TO FOLLOW OSSAMA.
PSST PSST
FOLLOW... OSSAMA?
WE MUST DO EVERYTHING WE CAN.
AND MAKE SURE YOU STAY HIDDEN.
HAKK KOFF
YES, SIR!
MS. KIRIGAKURE, ARE YOU RIN'S GUARDIAN?
HMM?

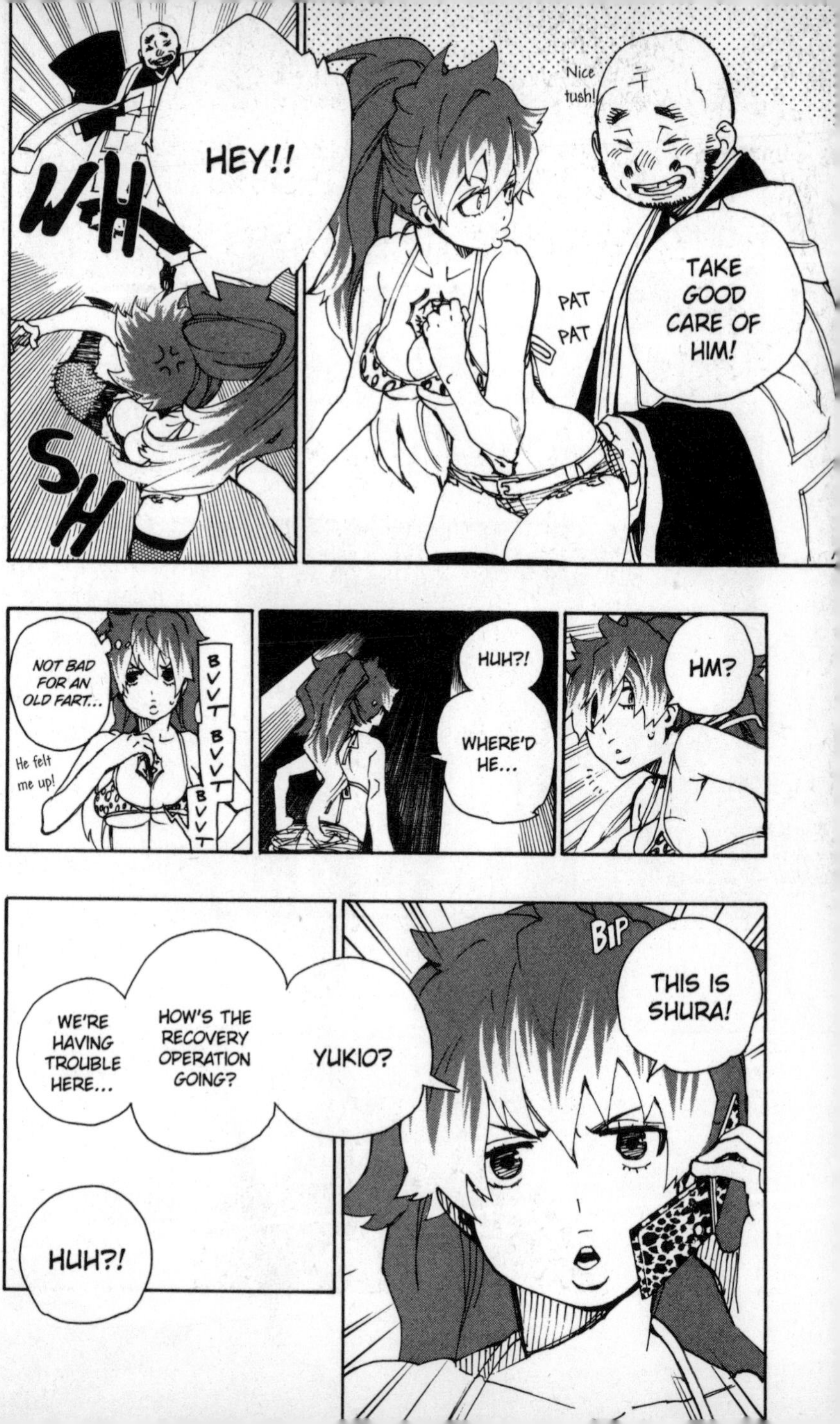
Nice tush!
TAKE GOOD CARE OF HIM!
PAT PAT
HEY!!
WH
SH
HM?
HUH?!
WHERE'D HE...
NOT BAD FOR AN OLD FART...
BVVT BVVT BVVT
He felt me up!
BIP
THIS IS SHURA!
YUKIO?
HOW'S THE RECOVERY OPERATION GOING?
WE'RE HAVING TROUBLE HERE...
HUH?!

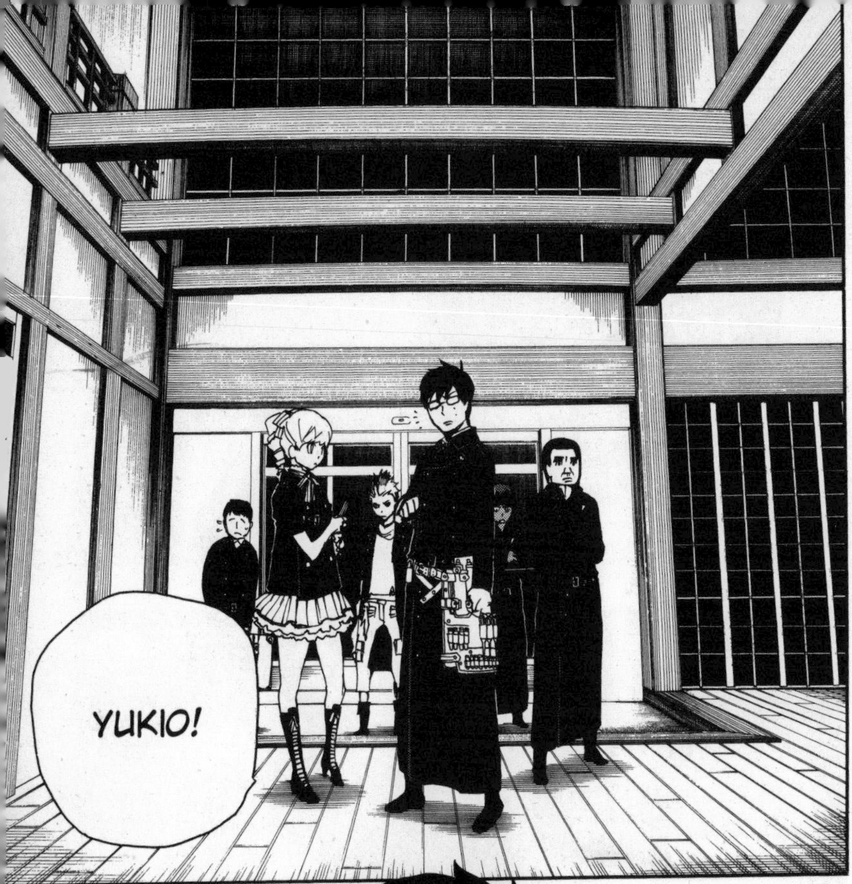
YUKIO!
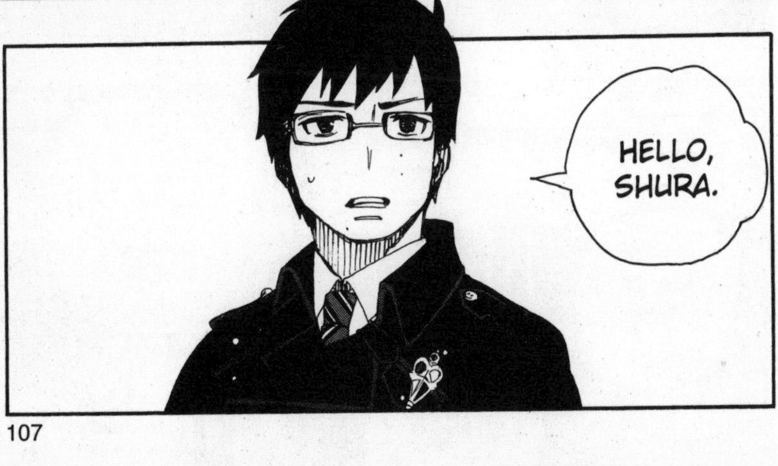
HELLO, SHURA.

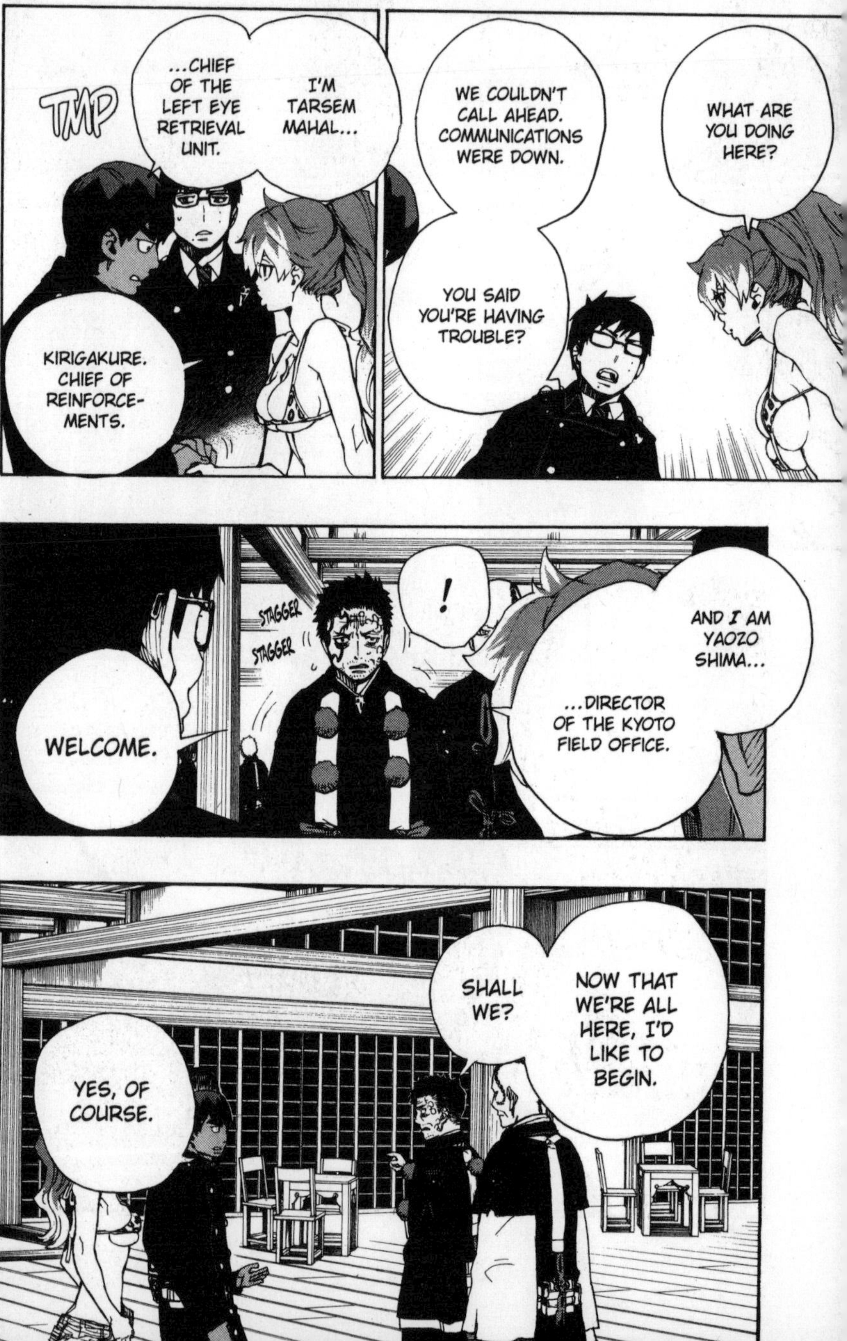
WHAT ARE YOU DOING HERE?
WE COULDN'T CALL AHEAD. COMMUNICATIONS WERE DOWN.
YOU SAID YOU'RE HAVING TROUBLE?
I'M TARSEM MAHAL...
...CHIEF OF THE LEFT EYE RETRIEVAL UNIT.
TMP
KIRIGAKURE. CHIEF OF REINFORCE-MENTS.
AND I AM YAOZO SHIMA...
...DIRECTOR OF THE KYOTO FIELD OFFICE.
!
STAGGER
STAGGER
WELCOME.
NOW THAT WE'RE ALL HERE, I'D LIKE TO BEGIN.
SHALL WE?
YES, OF COURSE.

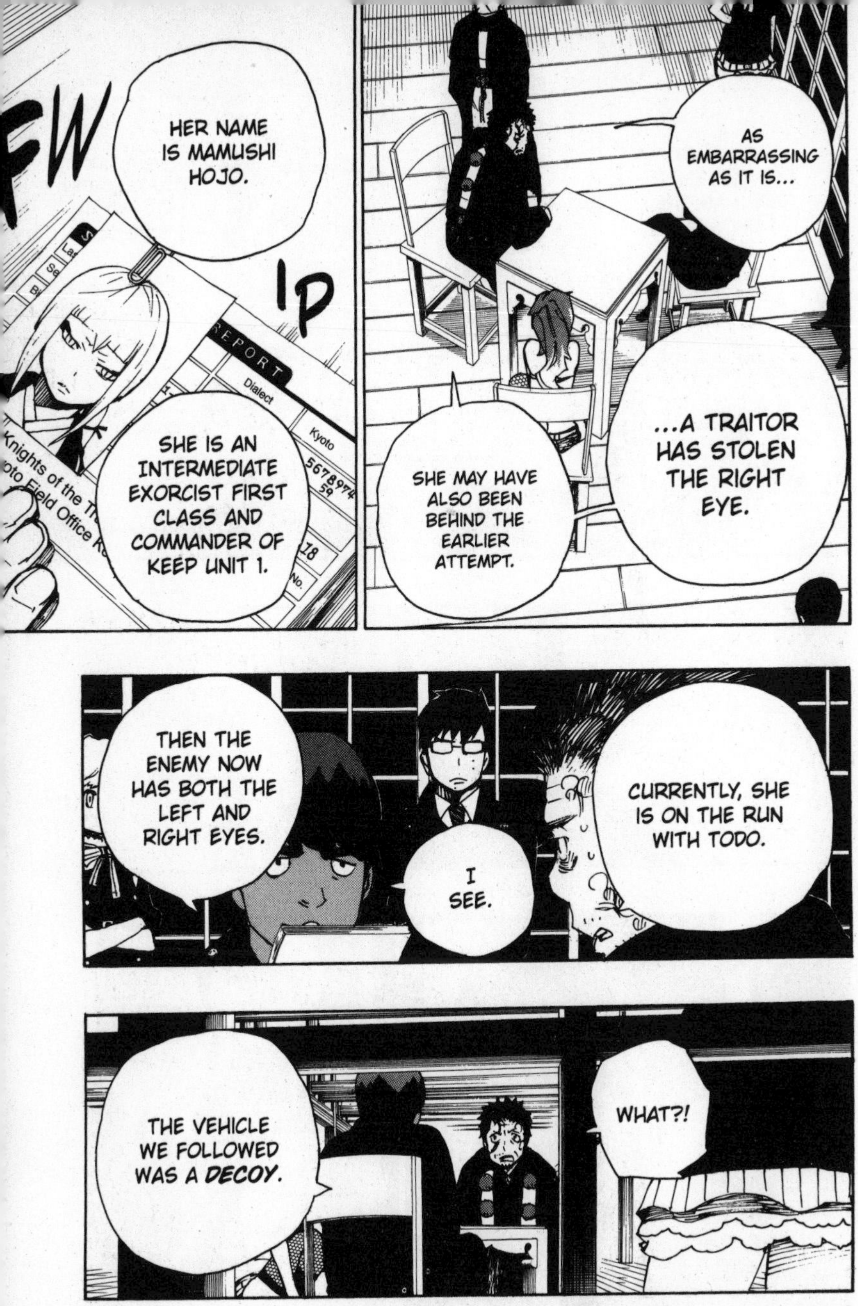
AS EMBARRASSING AS IT IS...
...A TRAITOR HAS STOLEN THE RIGHT EYE.
SHE MAY HAVE ALSO BEEN BEHIND THE EARLIER ATTEMPT.
FWIP
HER NAME IS MAMUSHI HOJO.
REPORT
Dialect
Kyoto
SHE IS AN INTERMEDIATE EXORCIST FIRST CLASS AND COMMANDER OF KEEP UNIT 1.
CURRENTLY, SHE IS ON THE RUN WITH TODO.
I SEE.
THEN THE ENEMY NOW HAS BOTH THE LEFT AND RIGHT EYES.
WHAT?!
THE VEHICLE WE FOLLOWED WAS A *DECOY*.

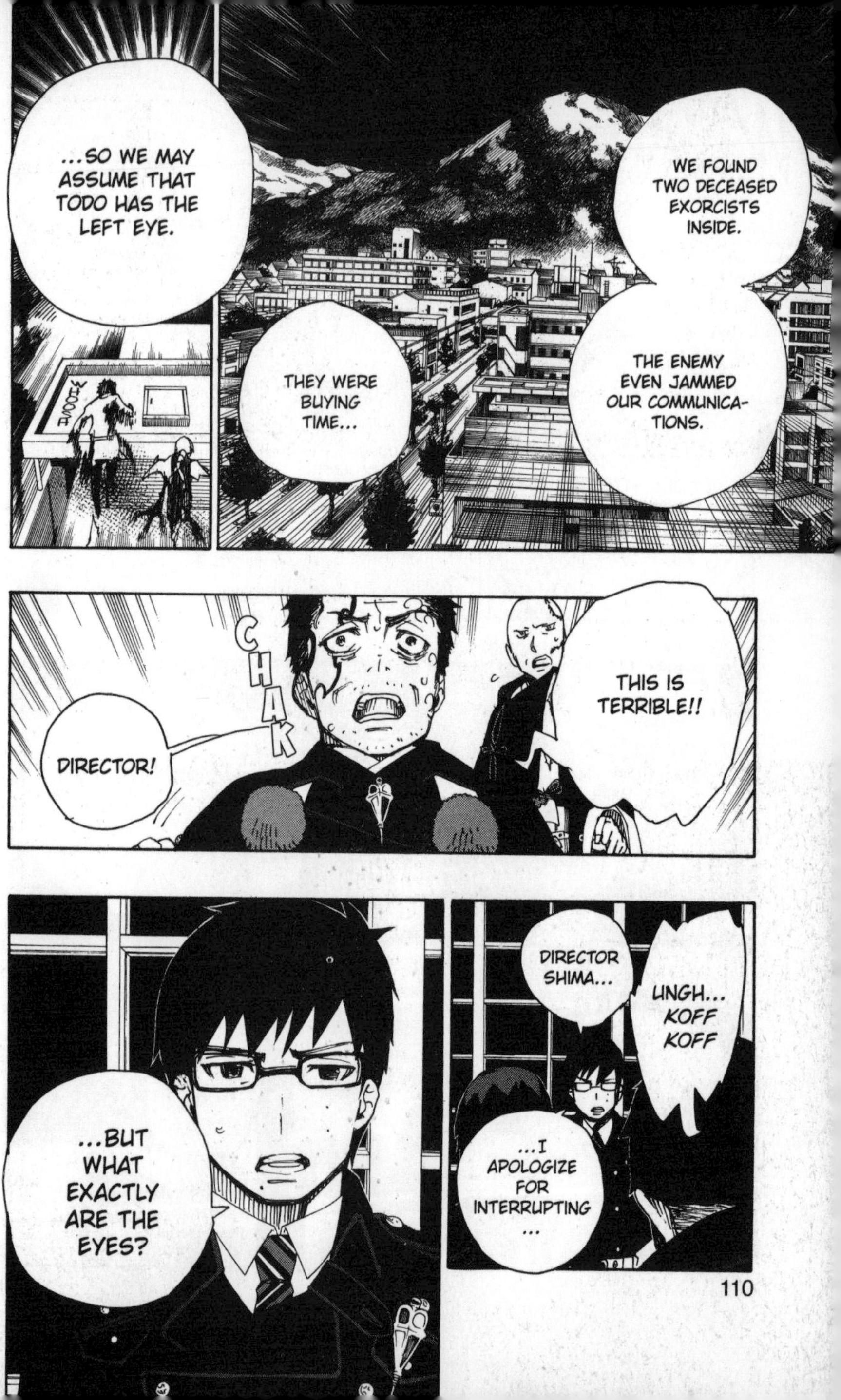
WE FOUND TWO DECEASED EXORCISTS INSIDE.
THE ENEMY EVEN JAMMED OUR COMMUNICATIONS.
THEY WERE BUYING TIME...
...SO WE MAY ASSUME THAT TODO HAS THE LEFT EYE.
WHOOSH
THIS IS TERRIBLE!!
CHAK
DIRECTOR!
UNGH... KOFF KOFF
DIRECTOR SHIMA...
...I APOLOGIZE FOR INTERRUPTING ...
...BUT WHAT EXACTLY ARE THE EYES?

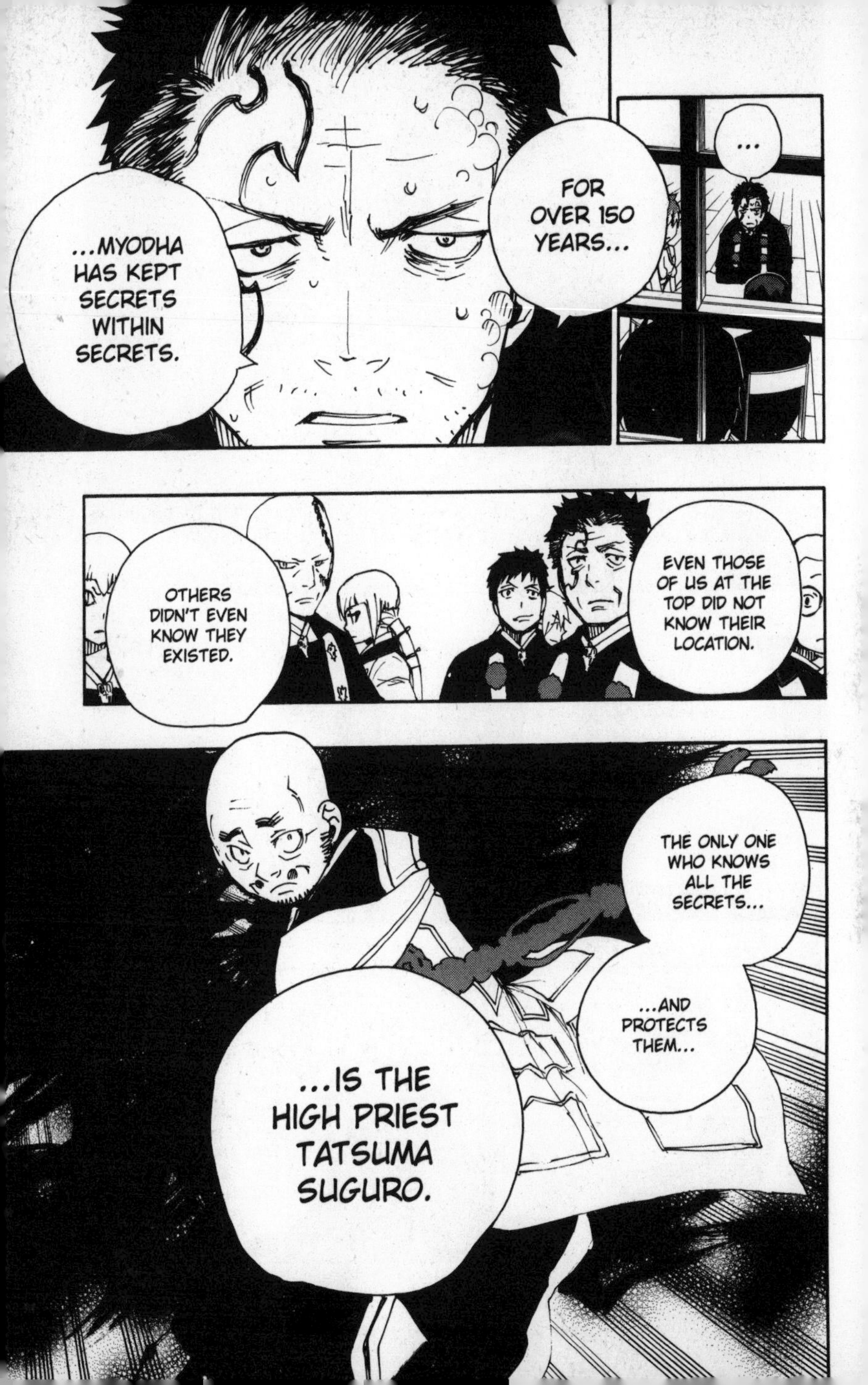
...
FOR OVER 150 YEARS...
...MYODHA HAS KEPT SECRETS WITHIN SECRETS.
EVEN THOSE OF US AT THE TOP DID NOT KNOW THEIR LOCATION.
OTHERS DIDN'T EVEN KNOW THEY EXISTED.
THE ONLY ONE WHO KNOWS ALL THE SECRETS...
...AND PROTECTS THEM...
...IS THE HIGH PRIEST TATSUMA SUGURO.

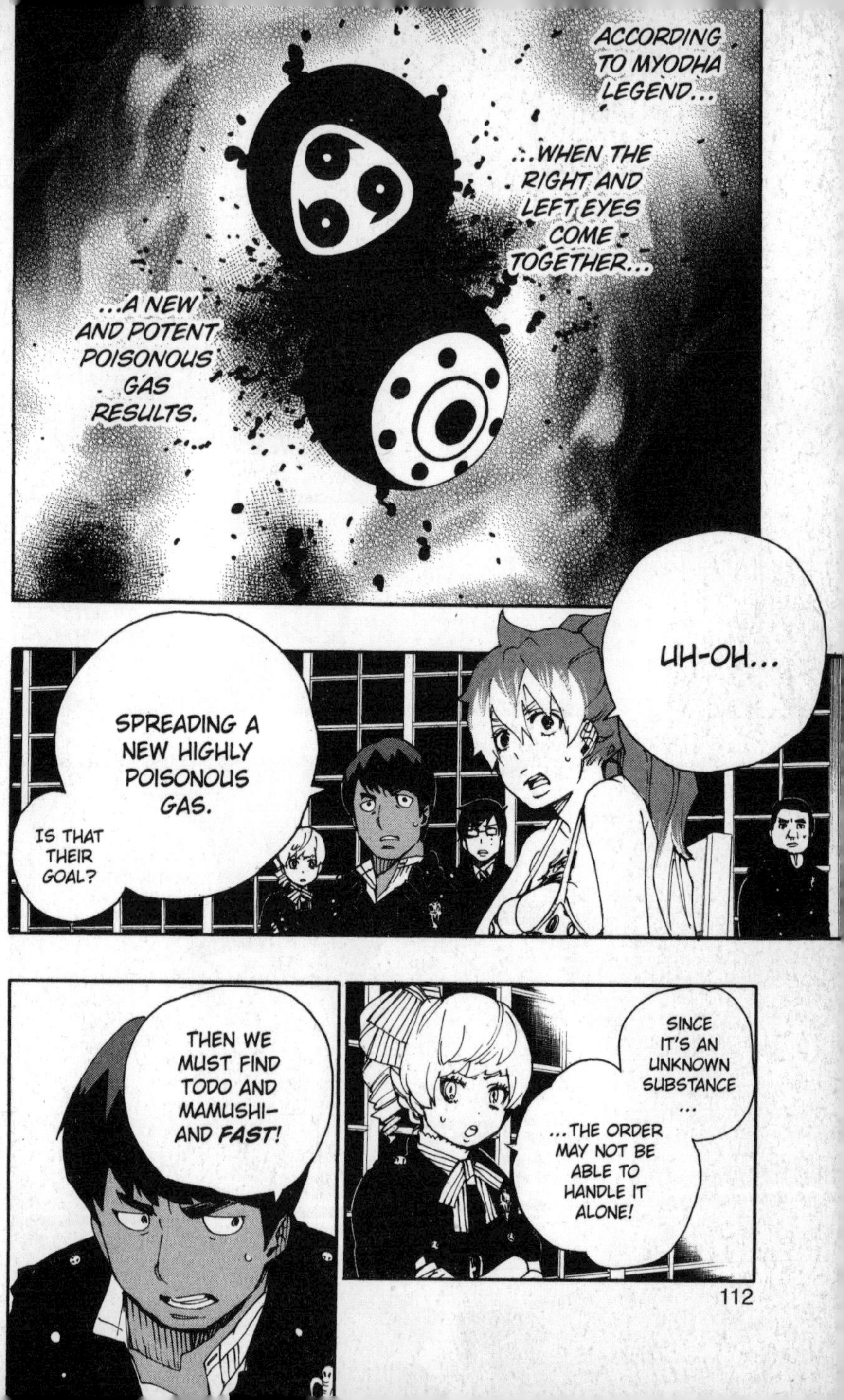
ACCORDING TO MYODHA LEGEND...
...WHEN THE RIGHT AND LEFT EYES COME TOGETHER...
...A NEW AND POTENT POISONOUS GAS RESULTS.
UH-OH...
SPREADING A NEW HIGHLY POISONOUS GAS.
IS THAT THEIR GOAL?
SINCE IT'S AN UNKNOWN SUBSTANCE...
...THE ORDER MAY NOT BE ABLE TO HANDLE IT ALONE!
THEN WE MUST FIND TODO AND MAMUSHI-AND FAST!

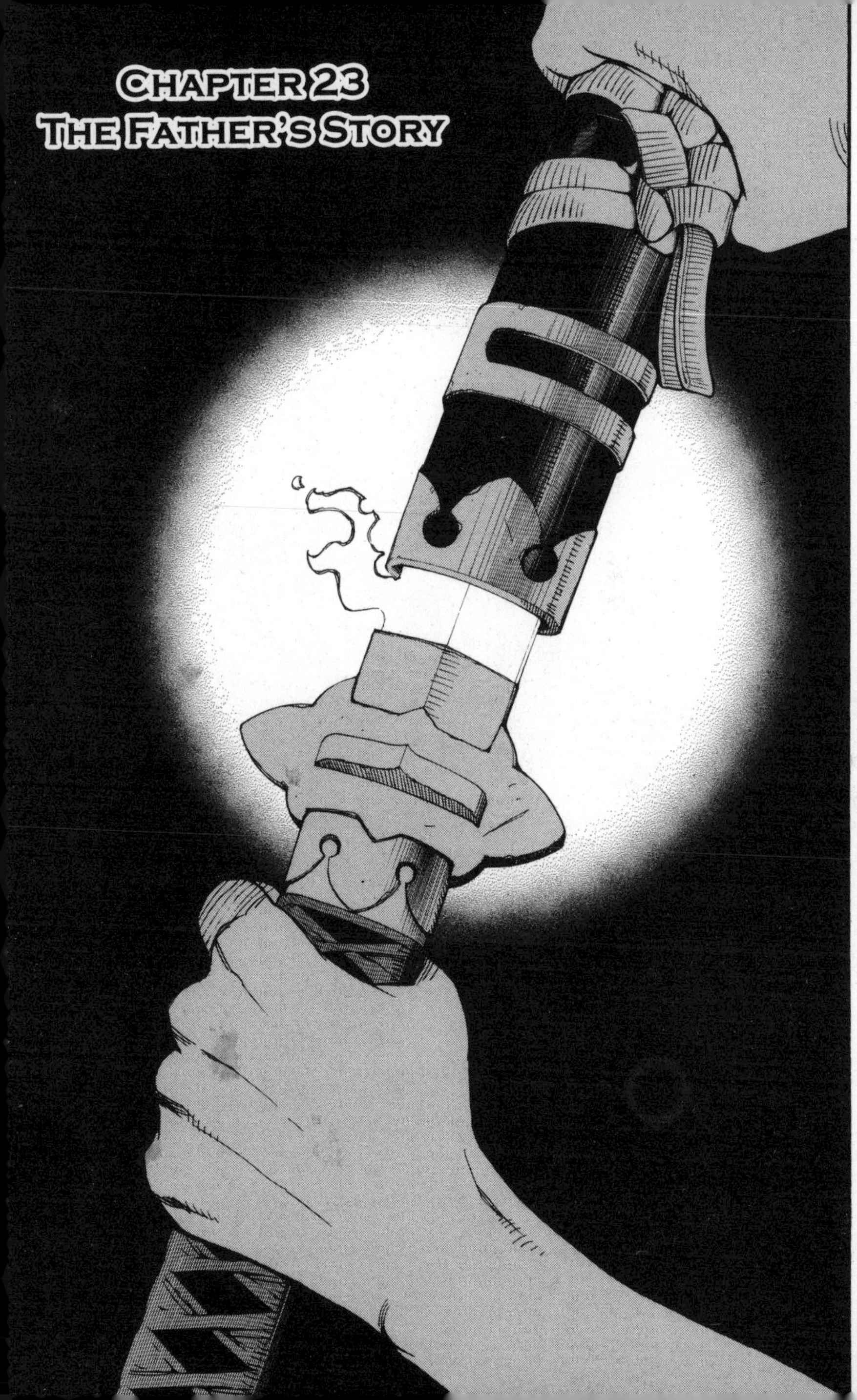
CHAPTER 23
THE FATHER'S STORY

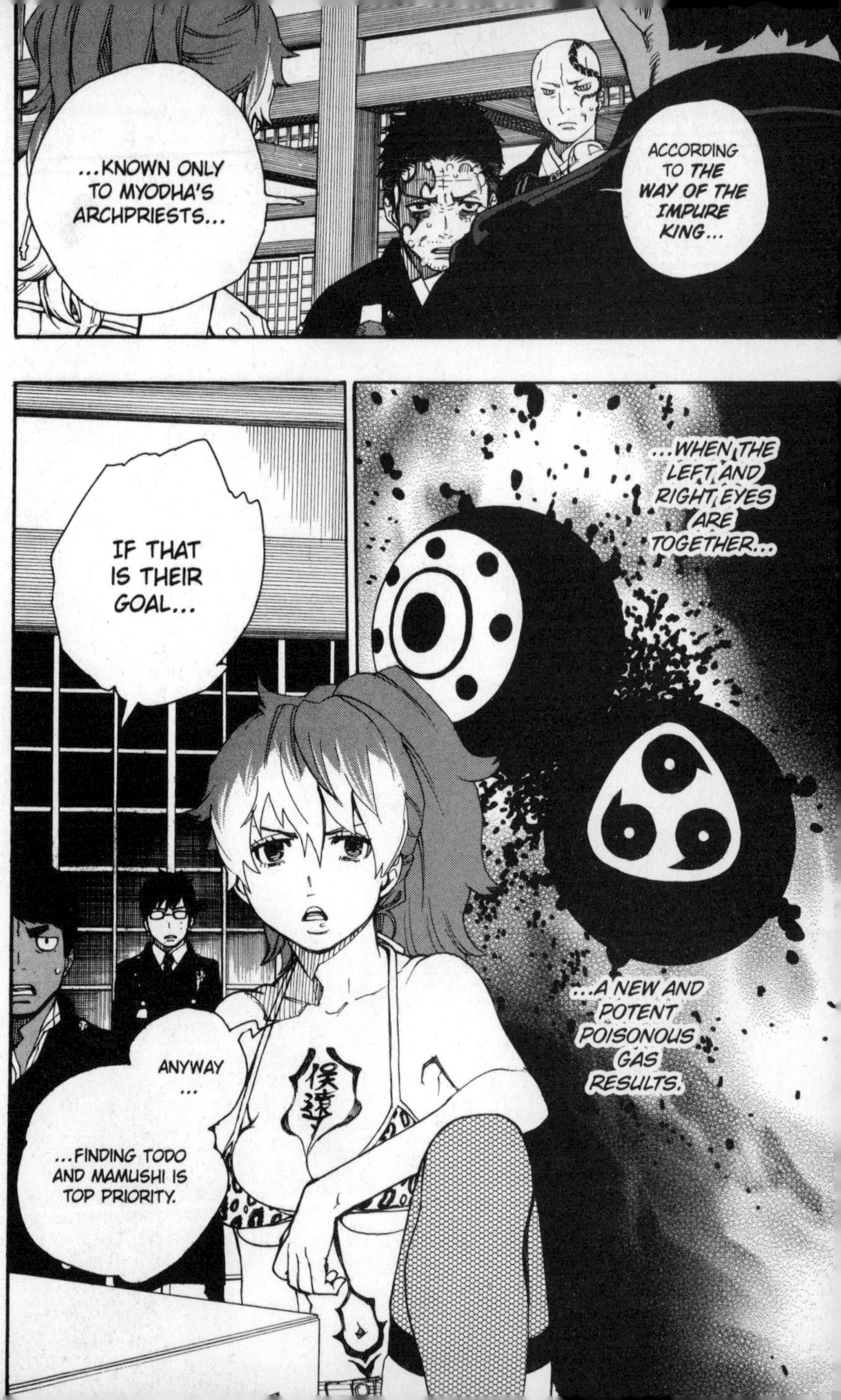
ACCORDING TO THE WAY OF THE IMPURE KING...
...KNOWN ONLY TO MYODHA'S ARCHPRIESTS...
...WHEN THE LEFT AND RIGHT EYES ARE TOGETHER...
...A NEW AND POTENT POISONOUS GAS RESULTS.
IF THAT IS THEIR GOAL...
ANYWAY...
...FINDING TODO AND MAMUSHI IS TOP PRIORITY.

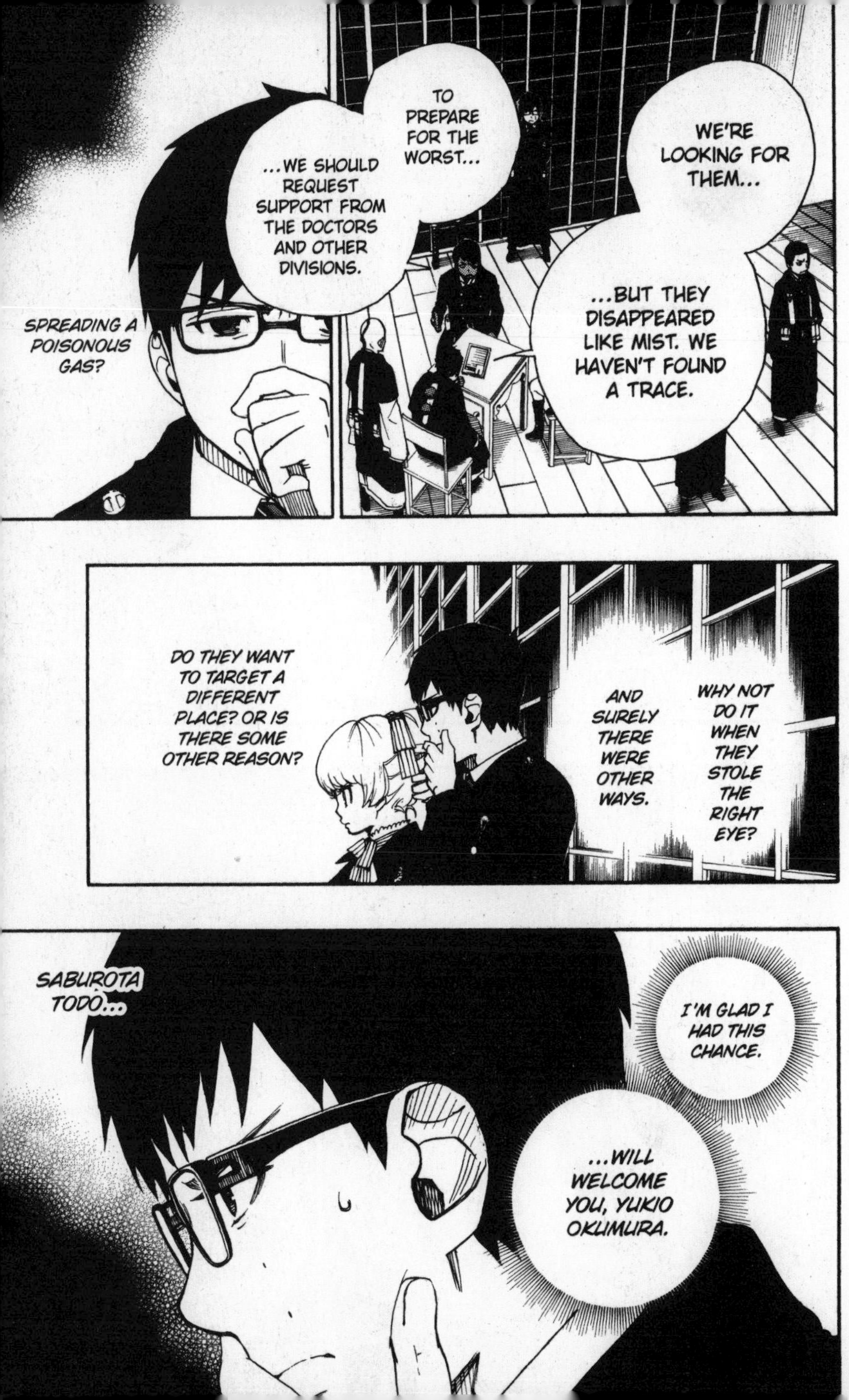
WE'RE LOOKING FOR THEM...
...BUT THEY DISAPPEARED LIKE MIST. WE HAVEN'T FOUND A TRACE.
TO PREPARE FOR THE WORST...
...WE SHOULD REQUEST SUPPORT FROM THE DOCTORS AND OTHER DIVISIONS.
SPREADING A POISONOUS GAS?
WHY NOT DO IT WHEN THEY STOLE THE RIGHT EYE?
AND SURELY THERE WERE OTHER WAYS.
DO THEY WANT TO TARGET A DIFFERENT PLACE? OR IS THERE SOME OTHER REASON?
I'M GLAD I HAD THIS CHANCE.
...WILL WELCOME YOU, YUKIO OKUMURA.
SABUROTA TODO...

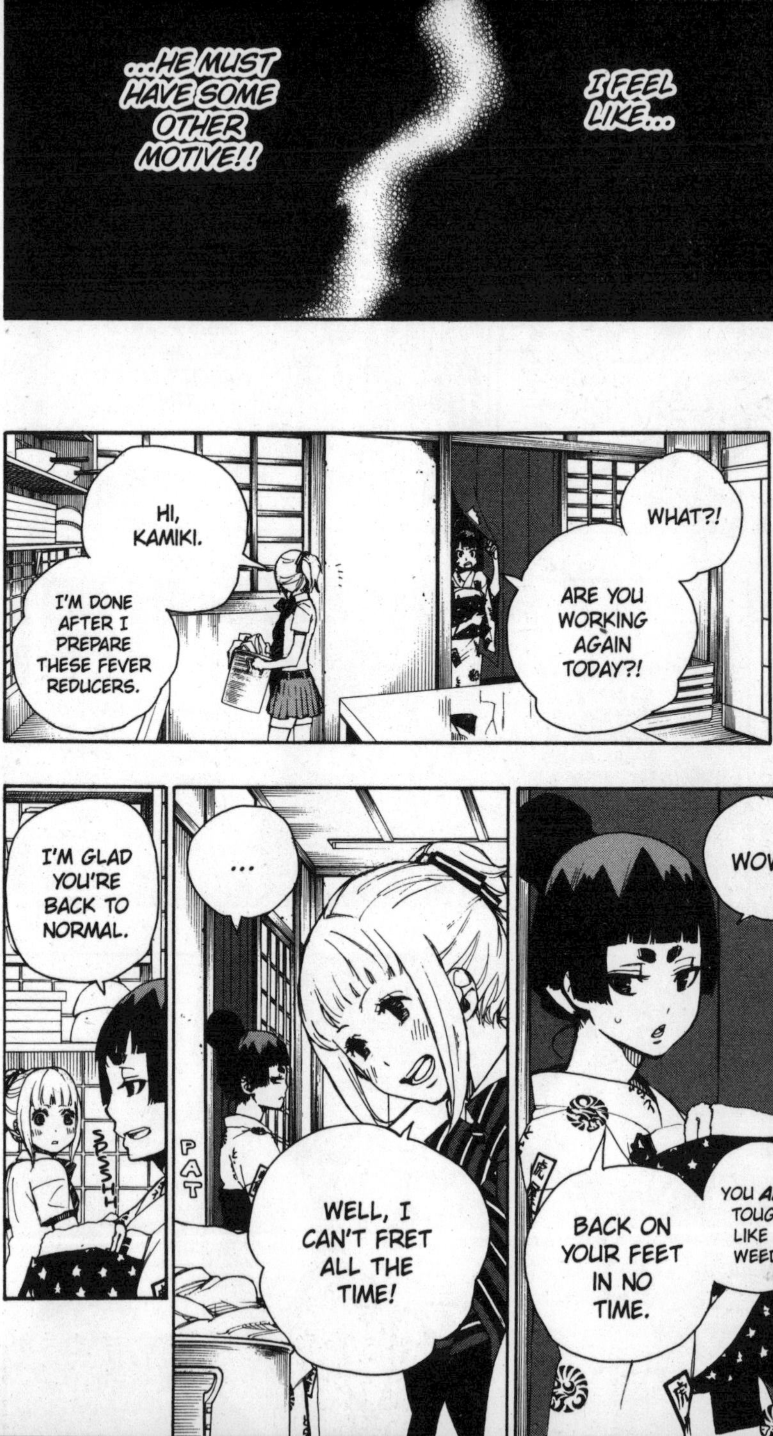
I FEEL LIKE...
...HE MUST HAVE SOME OTHER MOTIVE!!
WHAT?!
ARE YOU WORKING AGAIN TODAY?!
HI, KAMIKI.
I'M DONE AFTER I PREPARE THESE FEVER REDUCERS.
WOW.
YOU *ARE* TOUGH LIKE A WEED.
BACK ON YOUR FEET IN NO TIME.
...
PAT
WELL, I CAN'T FRET ALL THE TIME!
I'M GLAD YOU'RE BACK TO NORMAL.
SPSSHH

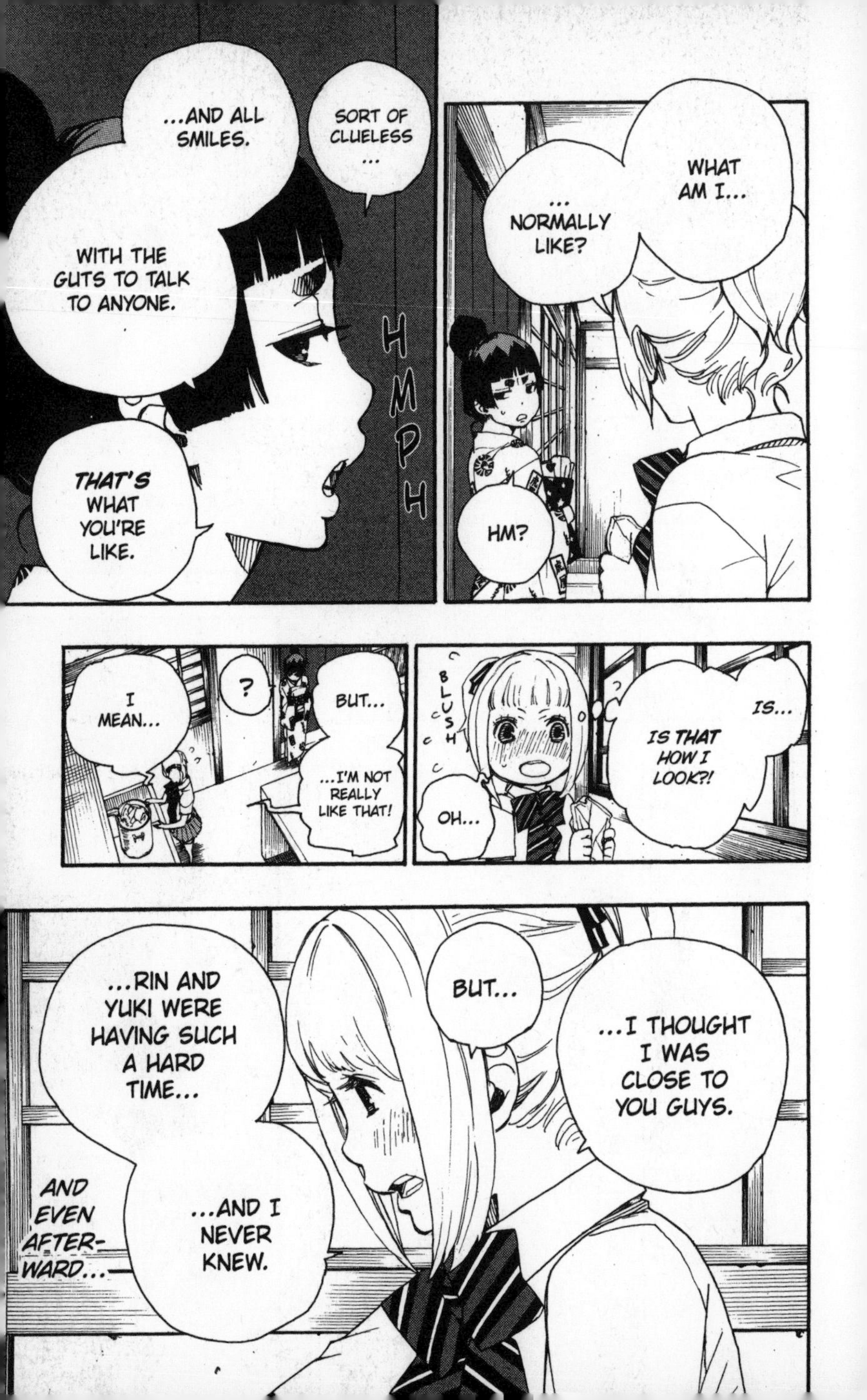
WHAT AM I...
...NORMALLY LIKE?
HM?
SORT OF CLUELESS...
...AND ALL SMILES.
WITH THE GUTS TO TALK TO ANYONE.
HMPH
THAT'S WHAT YOU'RE LIKE.
IS...
IS THAT HOW I LOOK?!
BLUSH
OH...
BUT...
...I'M NOT REALLY LIKE THAT!
?
I MEAN...
BUT...
...I THOUGHT I WAS CLOSE TO YOU GUYS.
...RIN AND YUKI WERE HAVING SUCH A HARD TIME...
...AND I NEVER KNEW.
AND EVEN AFTER-WARD...

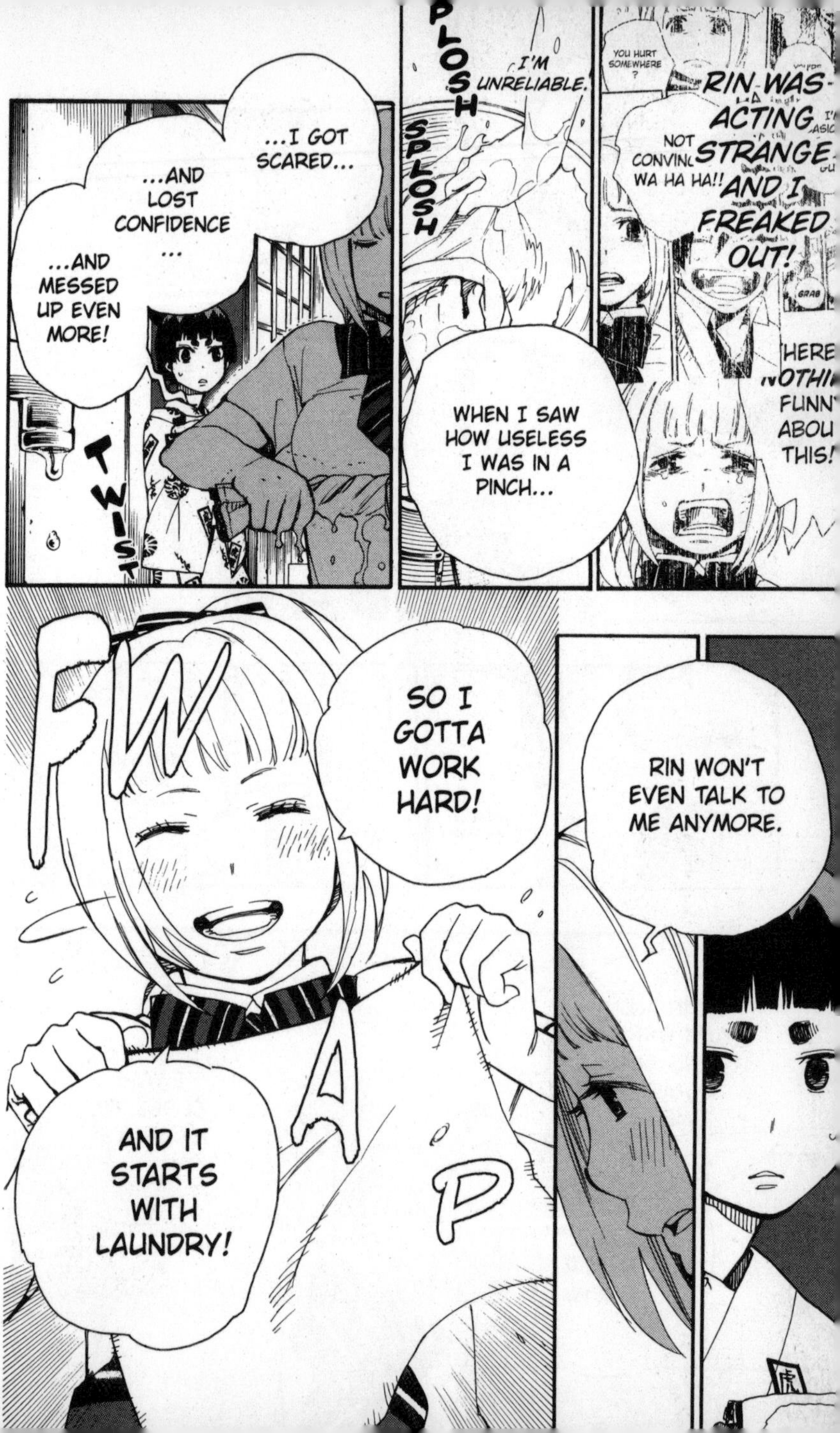
YOU HURT SOMEWHERE ?
RIN WAS ACTING STRANGE AND I FREAKED OUT!
GRAB
SPLOSH
SPLOSH
I'M UNRELIABLE.
WHEN I SAW HOW USELESS I WAS IN A PINCH...
...I GOT SCARED...
...AND LOST CONFIDENCE...
...AND MESSED UP EVEN MORE!
TWIST
RIN WON'T EVEN TALK TO ME ANYMORE.
FWAP
SO I GOTTA WORK HARD!
AND IT STARTS WITH LAUNDRY!

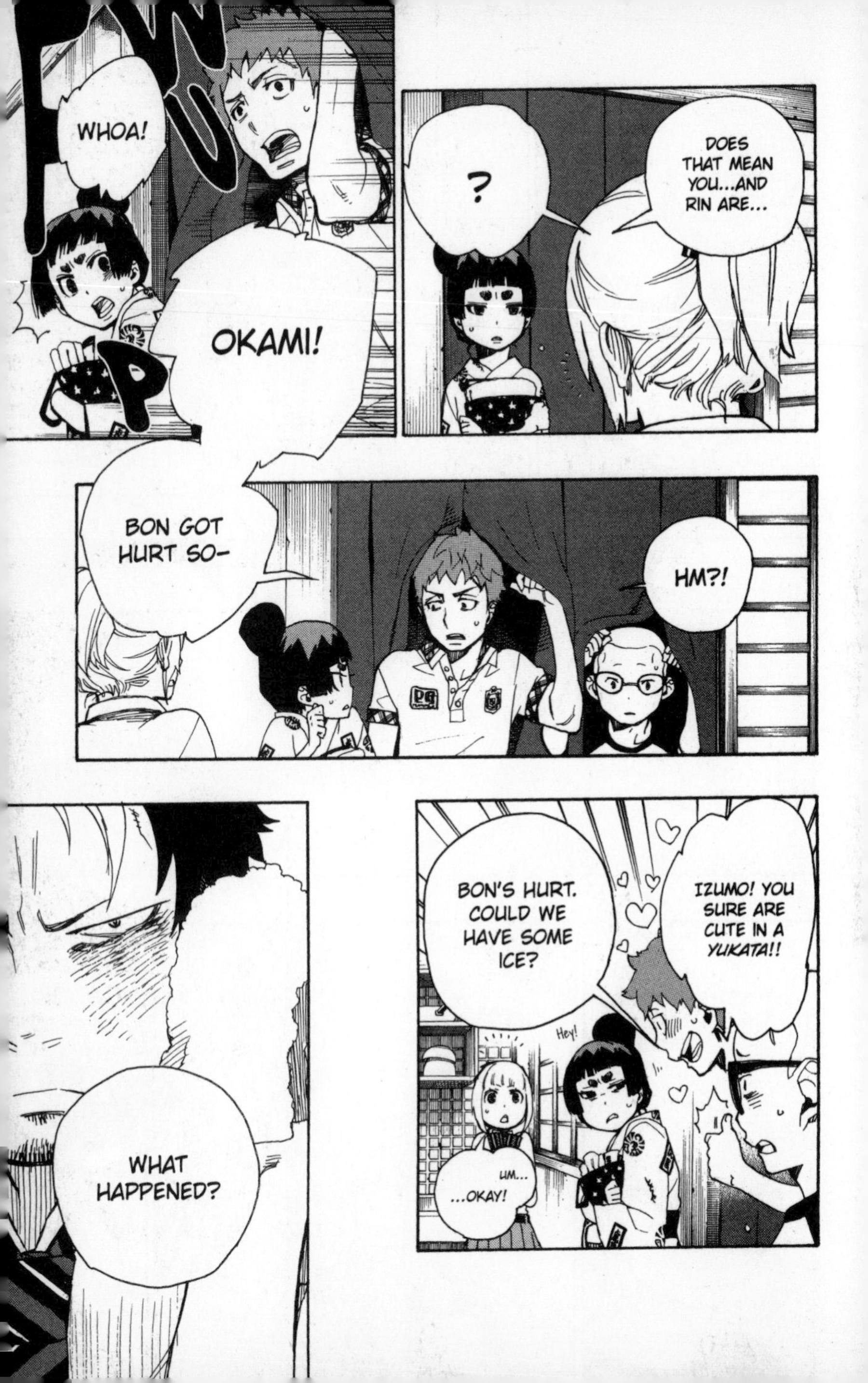
DOES THAT MEAN YOU...AND RIN ARE...
?
WHOA!
OKAMI!
BON GOT HURT SO-
HM?!
IZUMO! YOU SURE ARE CUTE IN A *YUKATA*!!
BON'S HURT. COULD WE HAVE SOME ICE?
Hey!
UM... ...OKAY!
WHAT HAPPENED?

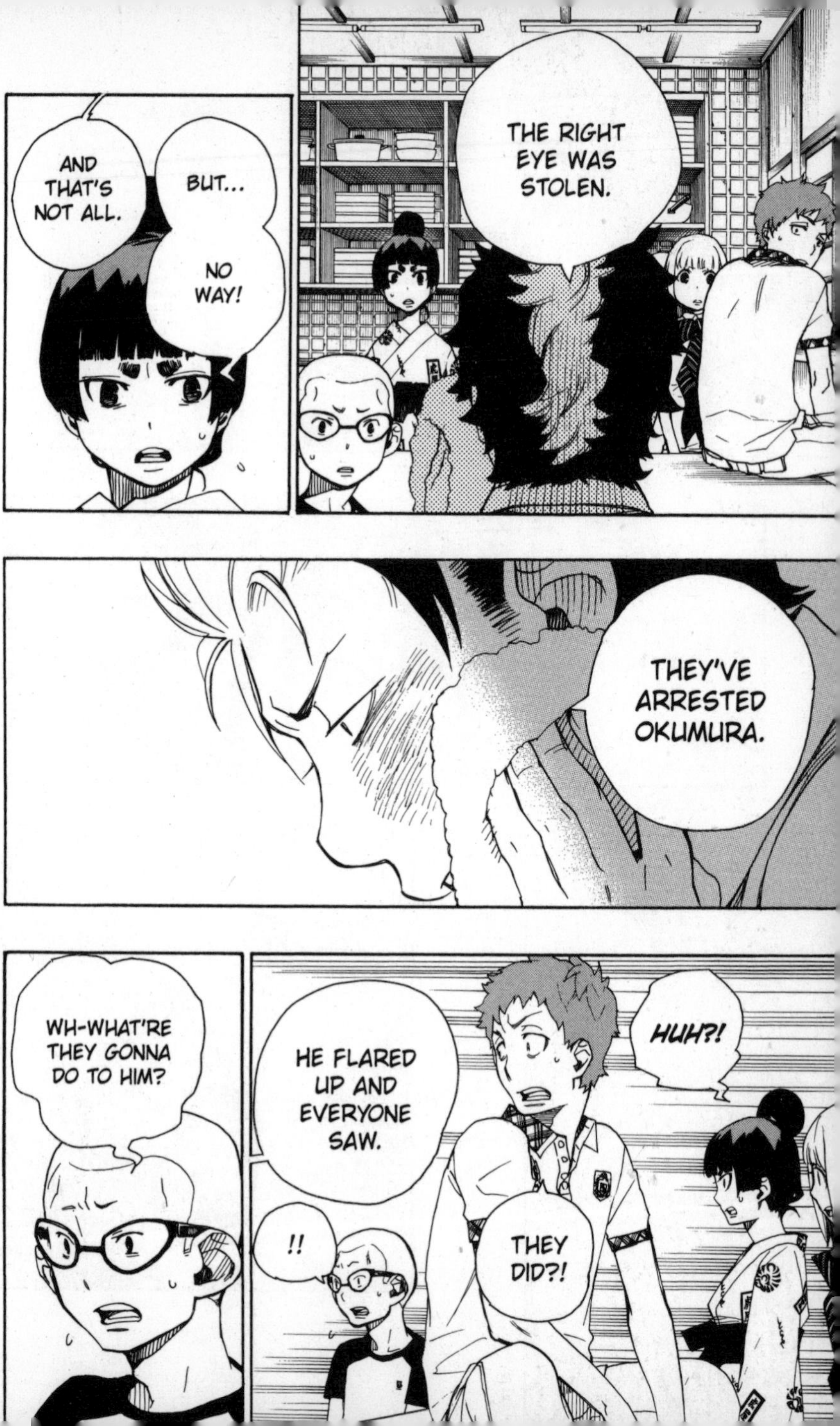
THE RIGHT EYE WAS STOLEN.
BUT...
NO WAY!
AND THAT'S NOT ALL.
THEY'VE ARRESTED OKUMURA.
HUH?!
HE FLARED UP AND EVERYONE SAW.
THEY DID?!
!!
WH-WHAT'RE THEY GONNA DO TO HIM?

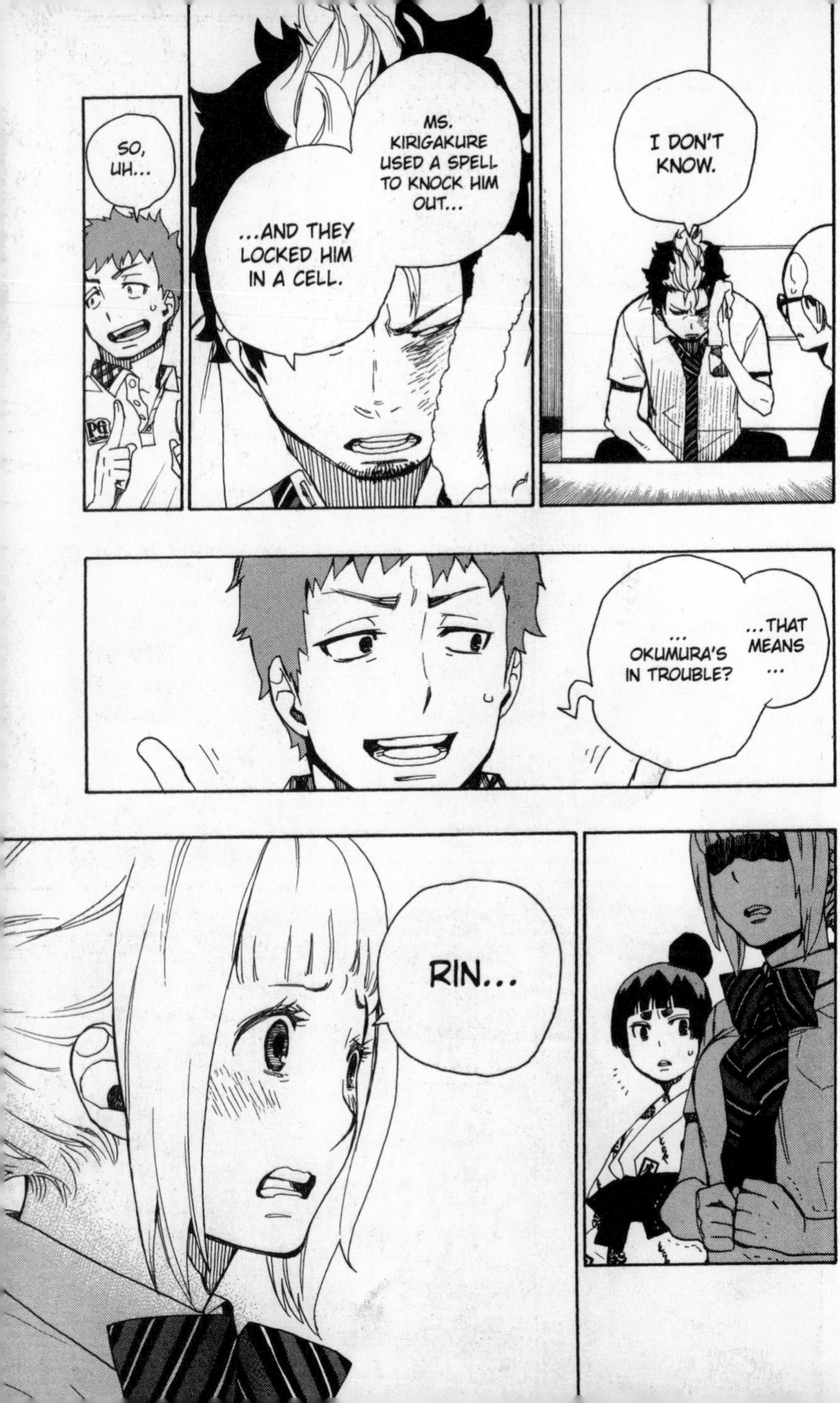
I DON'T KNOW.
MS. KIRIGAKURE USED A SPELL TO KNOCK HIM OUT...
...AND THEY LOCKED HIM IN A CELL.
SO, UH...
...THAT MEANS...
... OKUMURA'S IN TROUBLE?
RIN...

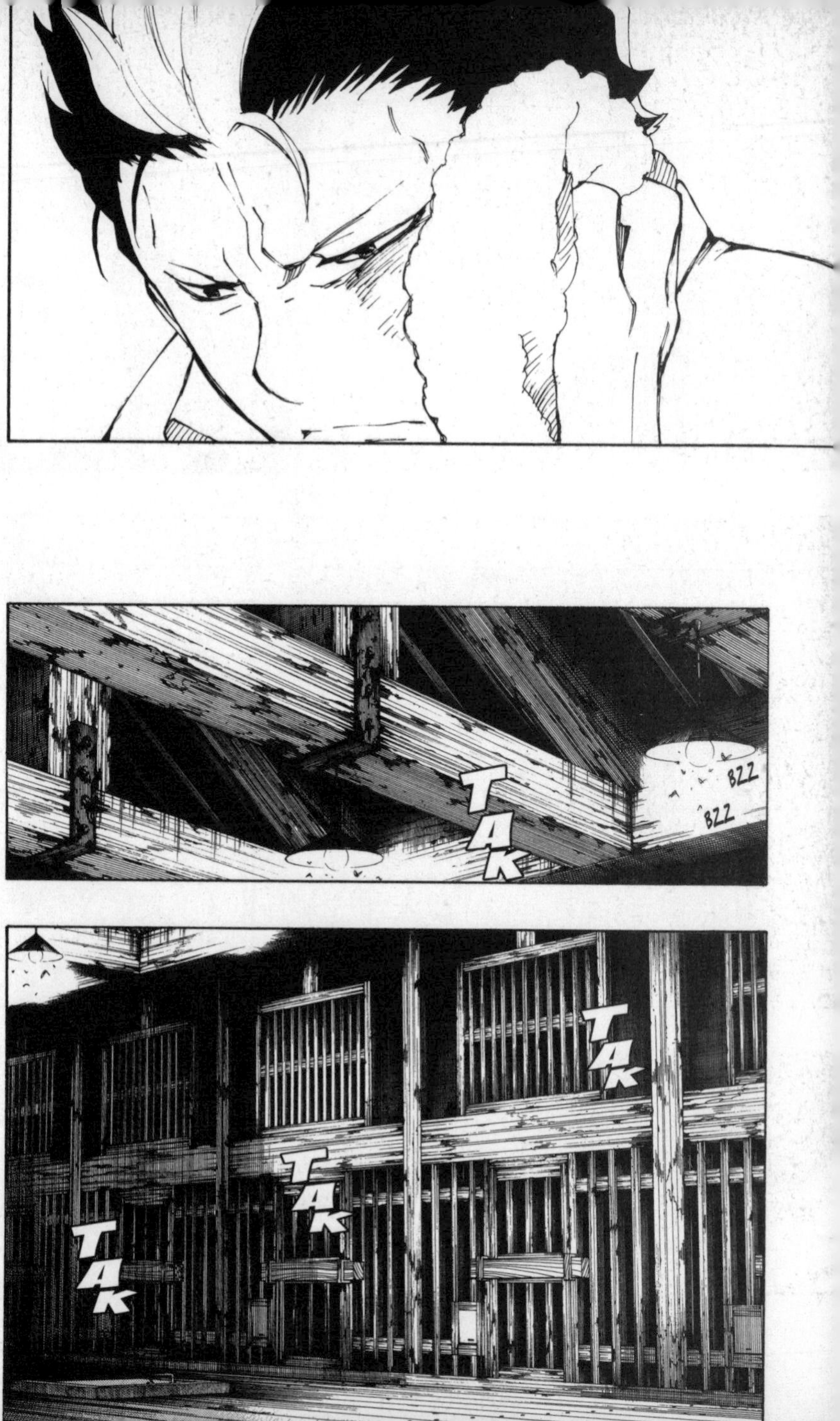
BZZ
BZZ
TAK
TAK
TAK
TAK

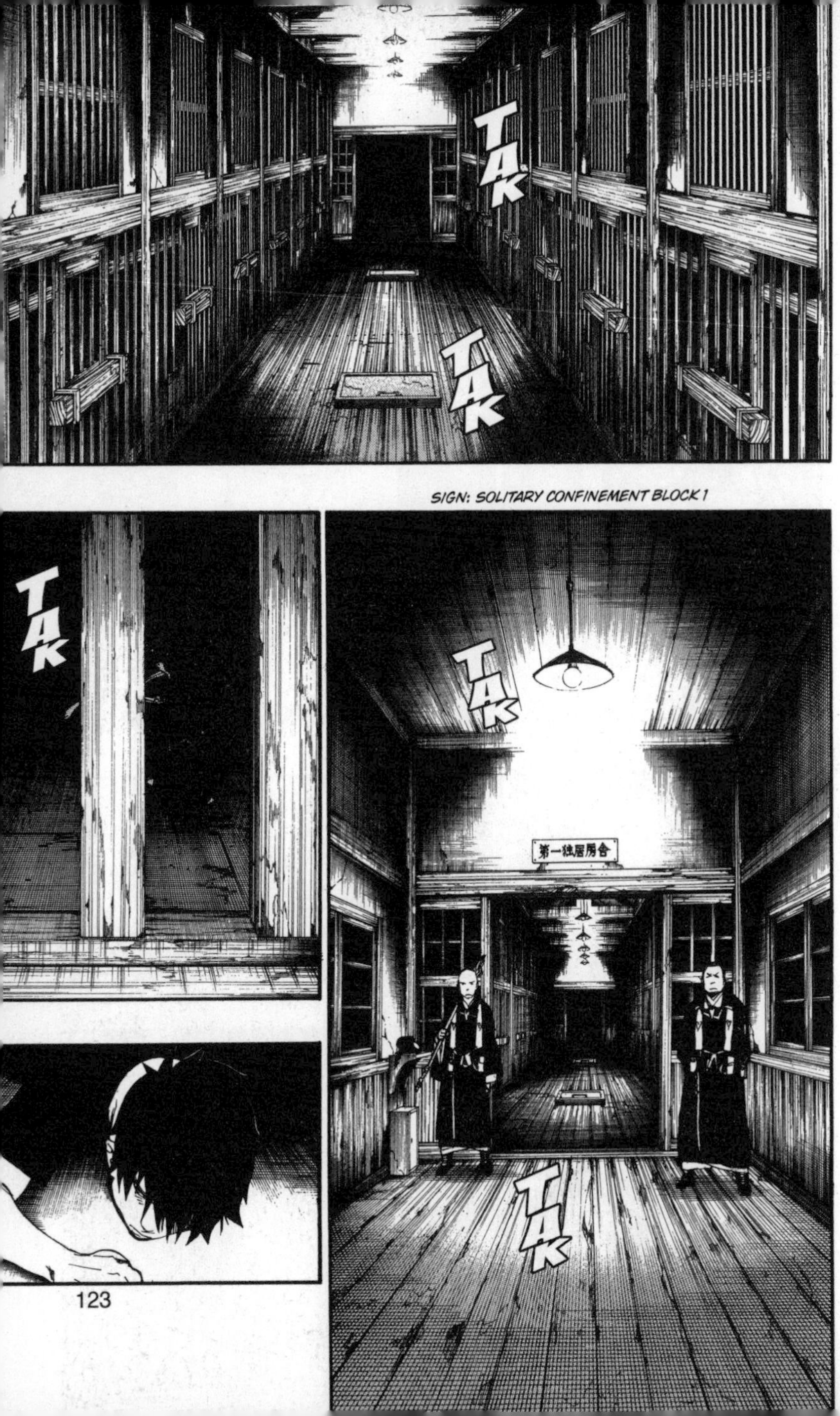
TAK
TAK
SIGN: SOLITARY CONFINEMENT BLOCK 1
第一独居房舎
TAK
TAK
TAK

SHURA...

HAVE YOU COOLED DOWN?

...BUT I CAN MOVE.

I'M STILL WEAK...

UGH

HOW YOU FEELIN'?

A LETTER?

?

THEN READ THIS.

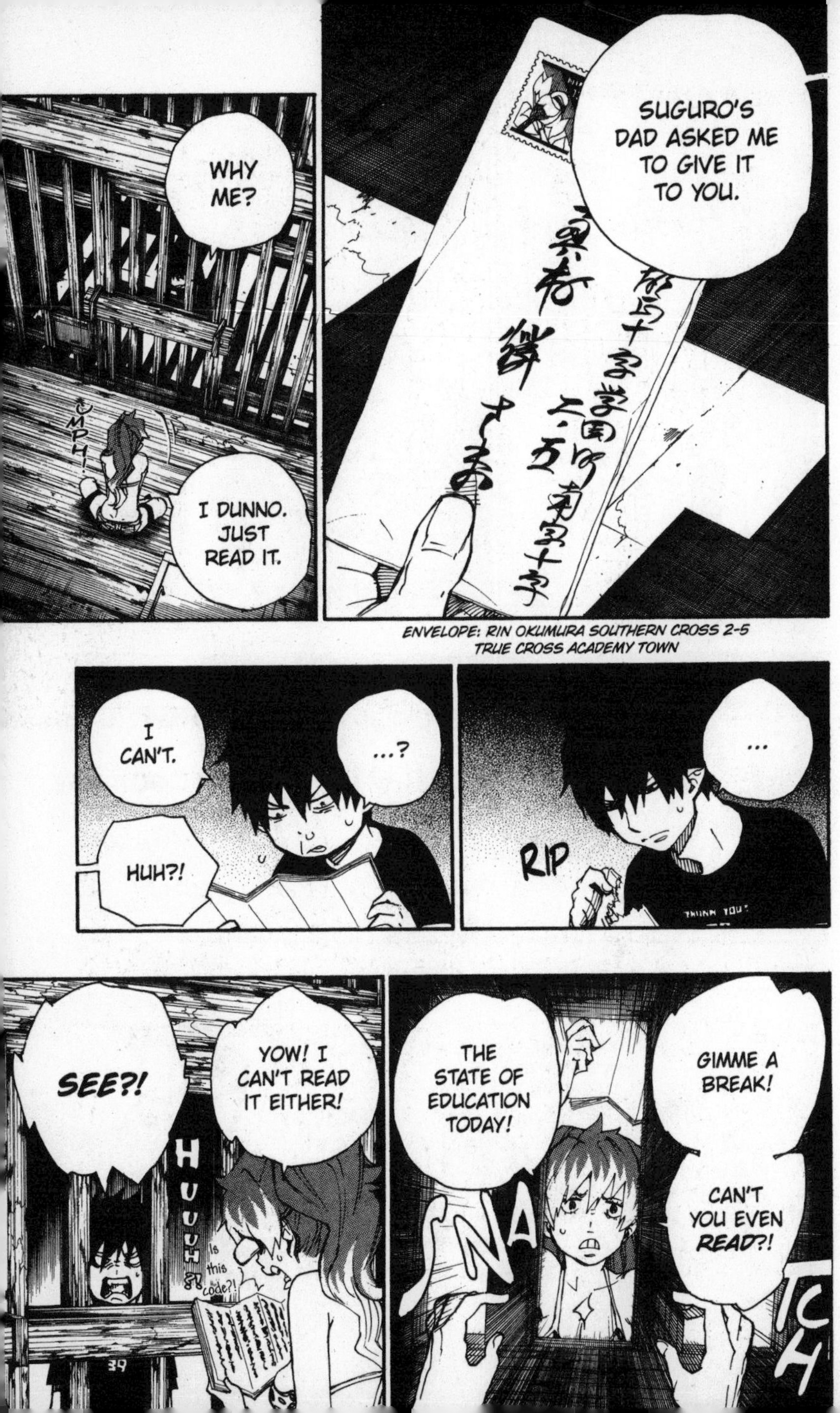
SUGURO'S DAD ASKED ME TO GIVE IT TO YOU.
WHY ME?
UMPH!
I DUNNO. JUST READ IT.
ENVELOPE: RIN OKUMURA SOUTHERN CROSS 2-5 TRUE CROSS ACADEMY TOWN
...
RIP
...?
I CAN'T.
HUH?!
GIMME A BREAK!
CAN'T YOU EVEN READ?!
SNA
TCH
THE STATE OF EDUCATION TODAY!
YOW! I CAN'T READ IT EITHER!
SEE?!
HUUUH?!
Is this code?!

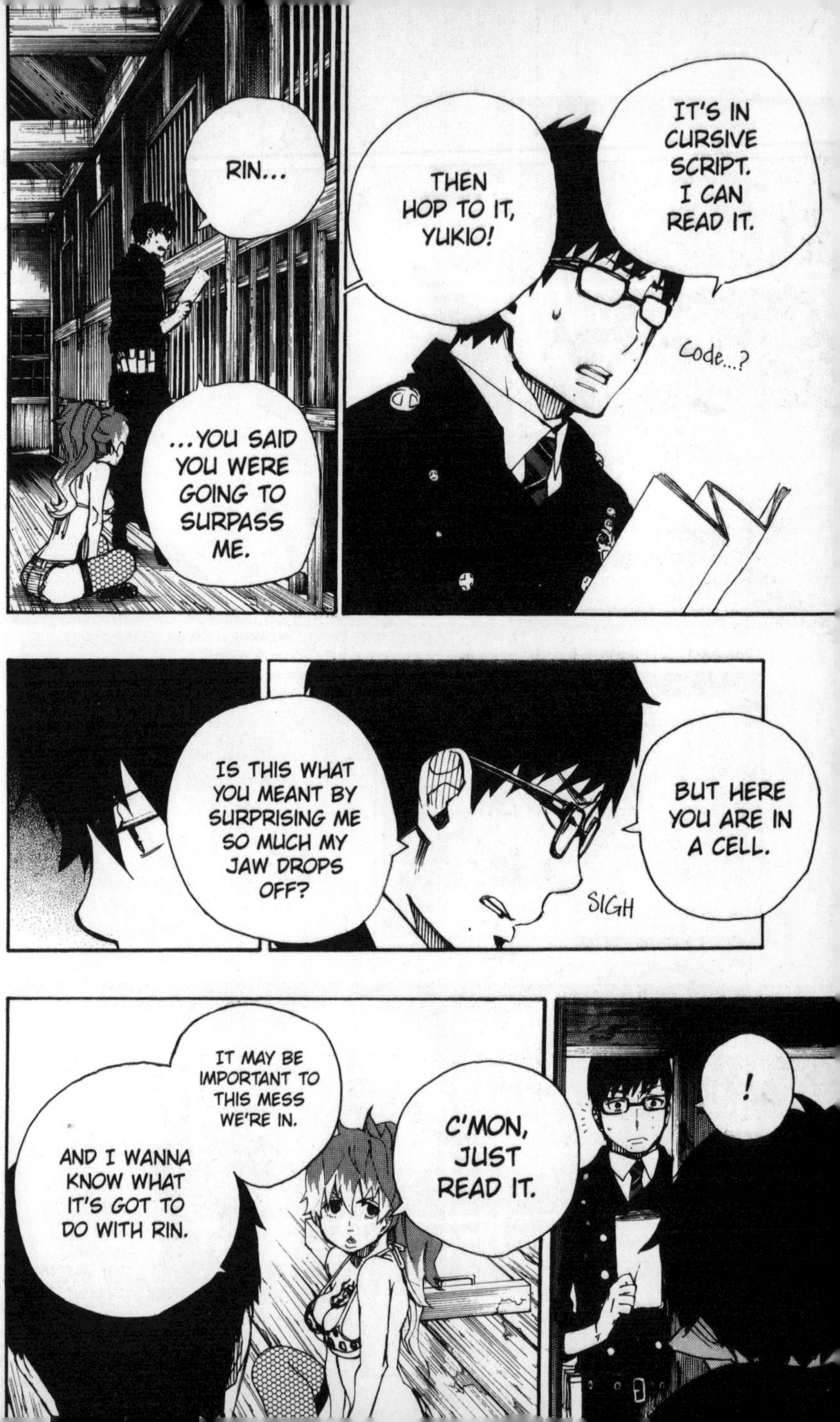
IT'S IN CURSIVE SCRIPT. I CAN READ IT.
THEN HOP TO IT, YUKIO!
Code...?
RIN...
...YOU SAID YOU WERE GOING TO SURPASS ME.
BUT HERE YOU ARE IN A CELL.
SIGH
IS THIS WHAT YOU MEANT BY SURPRISING ME SO MUCH MY JAW DROPS OFF?
!
C'MON, JUST READ IT.
IT MAY BE IMPORTANT TO THIS MESS WE'RE IN.
AND I WANNA KNOW WHAT IT'S GOT TO DO WITH RIN.

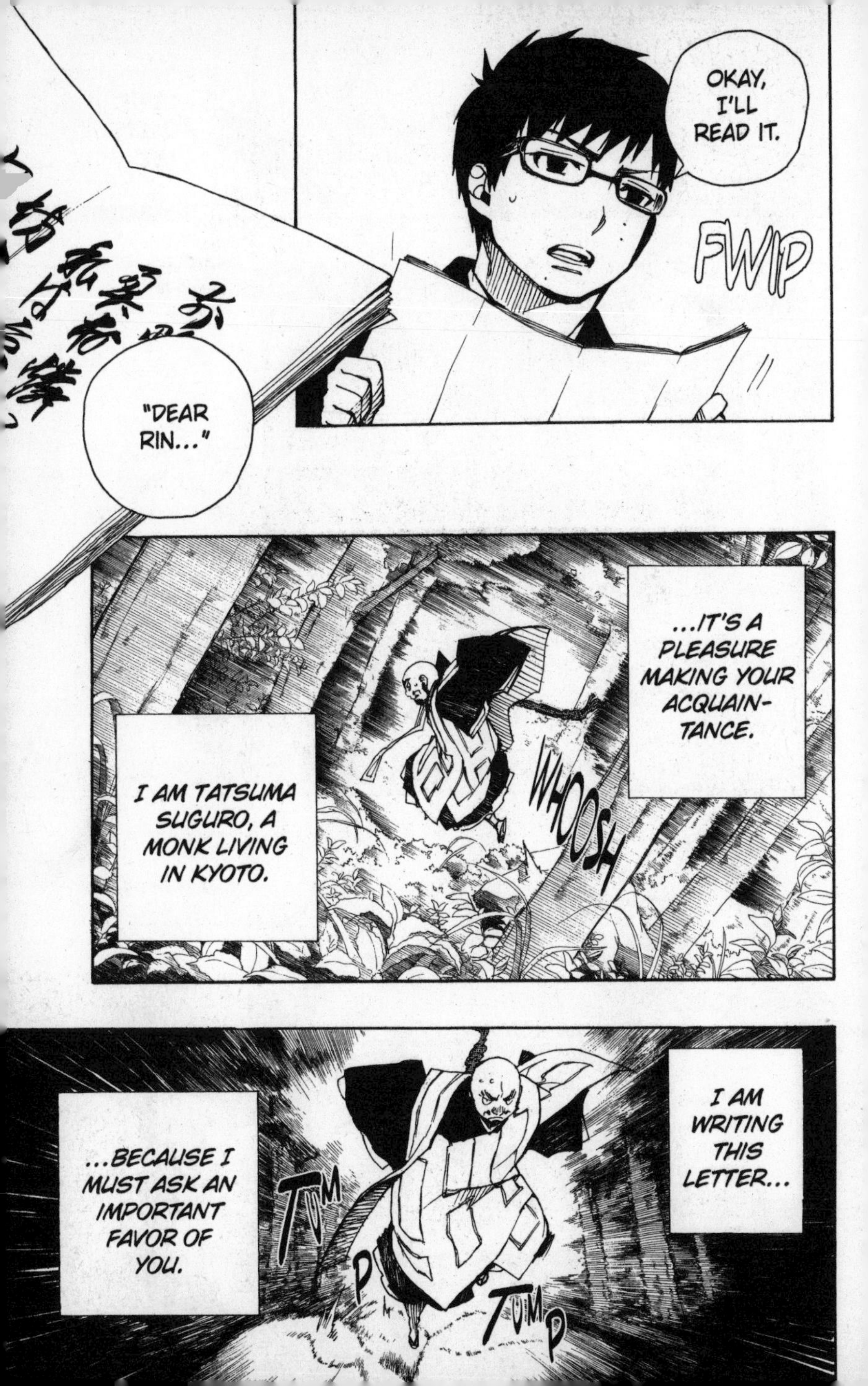
OKAY, I'LL READ IT.
FWIP
"DEAR RIN..."
...IT'S A PLEASURE MAKING YOUR ACQUAIN-TANCE.
I AM TATSUMA SUGURO, A MONK LIVING IN KYOTO.
WHOOSH
I AM WRITING THIS LETTER...
...BECAUSE I MUST ASK AN IMPORTANT FAVOR OF YOU.
TUMP
TUMP

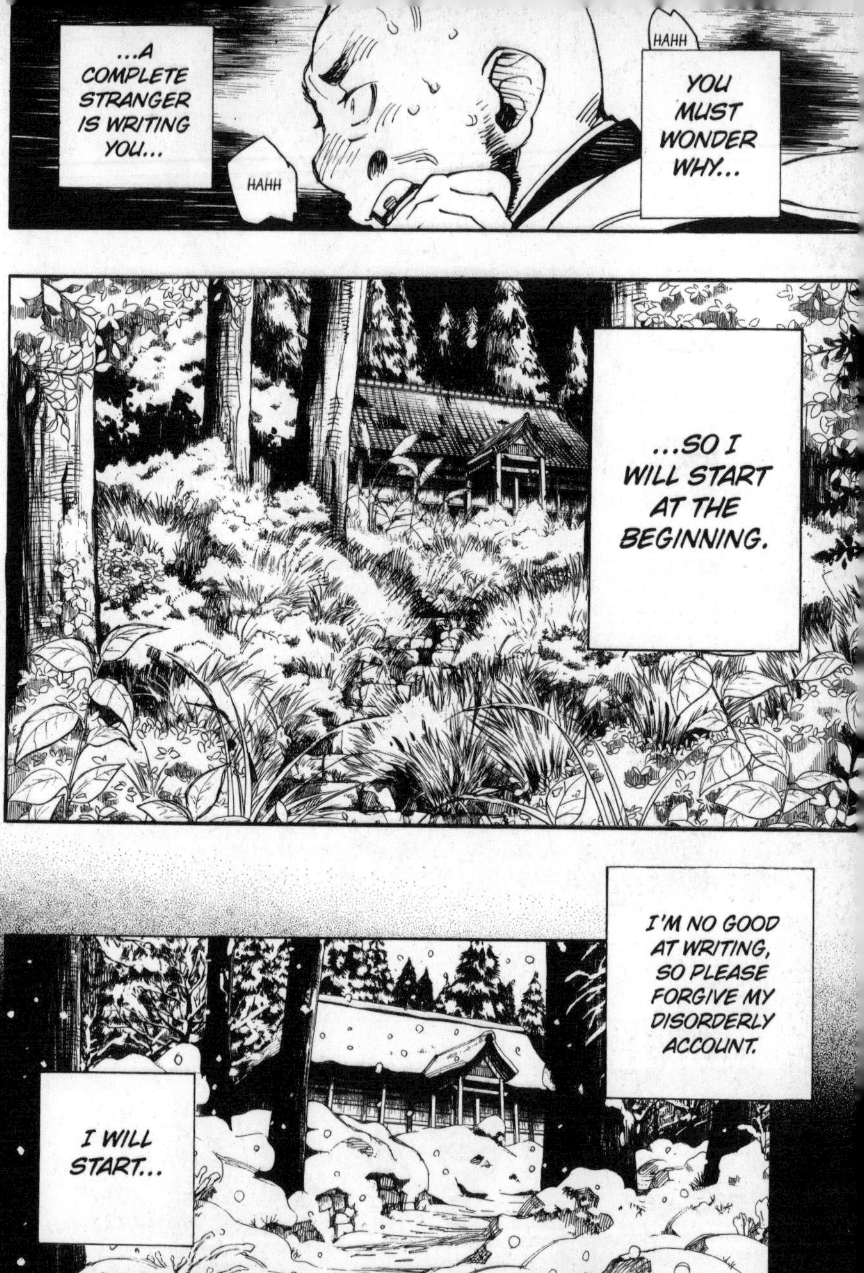
HAHH
YOU MUST WONDER WHY...
...A COMPLETE STRANGER IS WRITING YOU...
HAHH
...SO I WILL START AT THE BEGINNING.
I'M NO GOOD AT WRITING, SO PLEASE FORGIVE MY DISORDERLY ACCOUNT.
I WILL START...

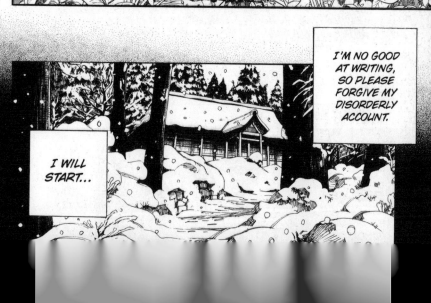

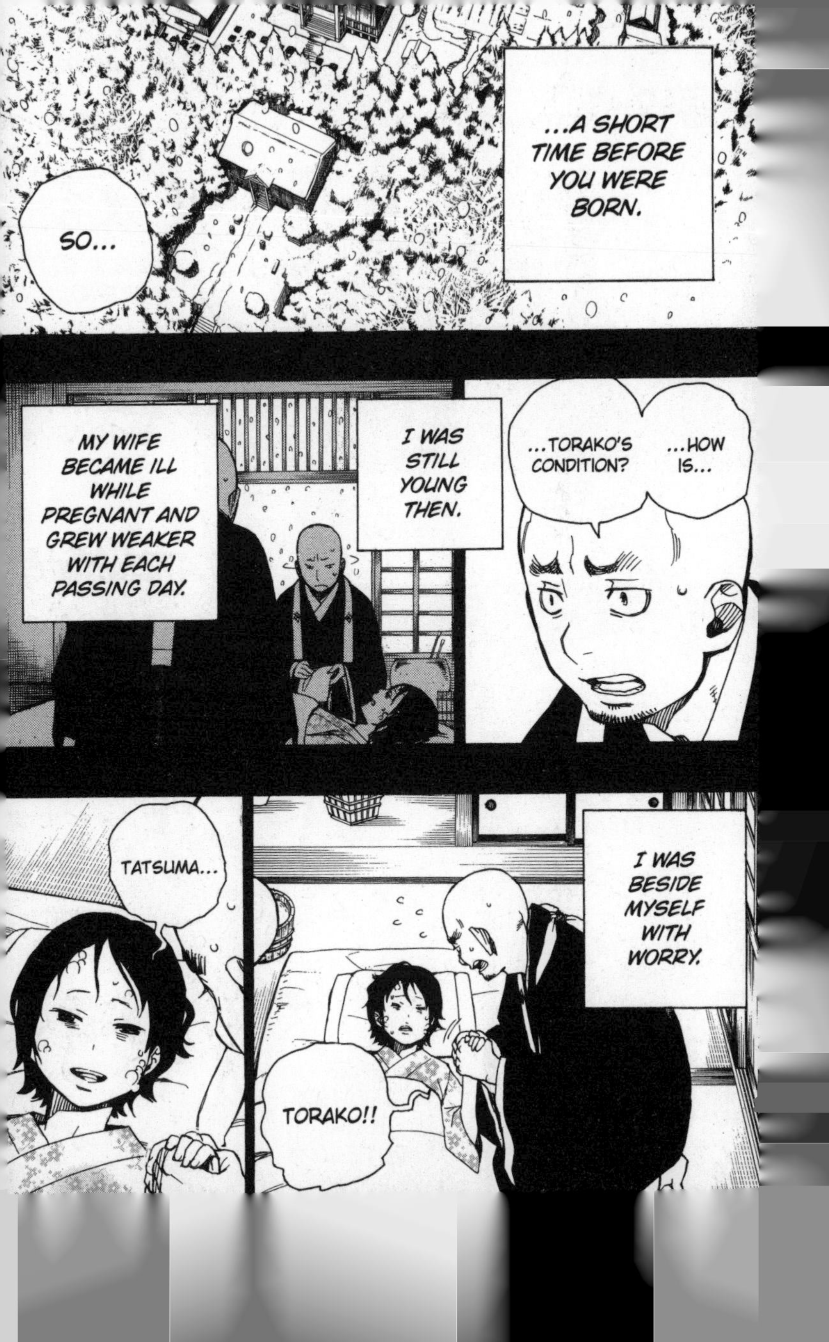
...A SHORT TIME BEFORE YOU WERE BORN.
SO...
...HOW IS...
...TORAKO'S CONDITION?
I WAS STILL YOUNG THEN.
MY WIFE BECAME ILL WHILE PREGNANT AND GREW WEAKER WITH EACH PASSING DAY.
I WAS BESIDE MYSELF WITH WORRY.
TORAKO!!
TATSUMA...

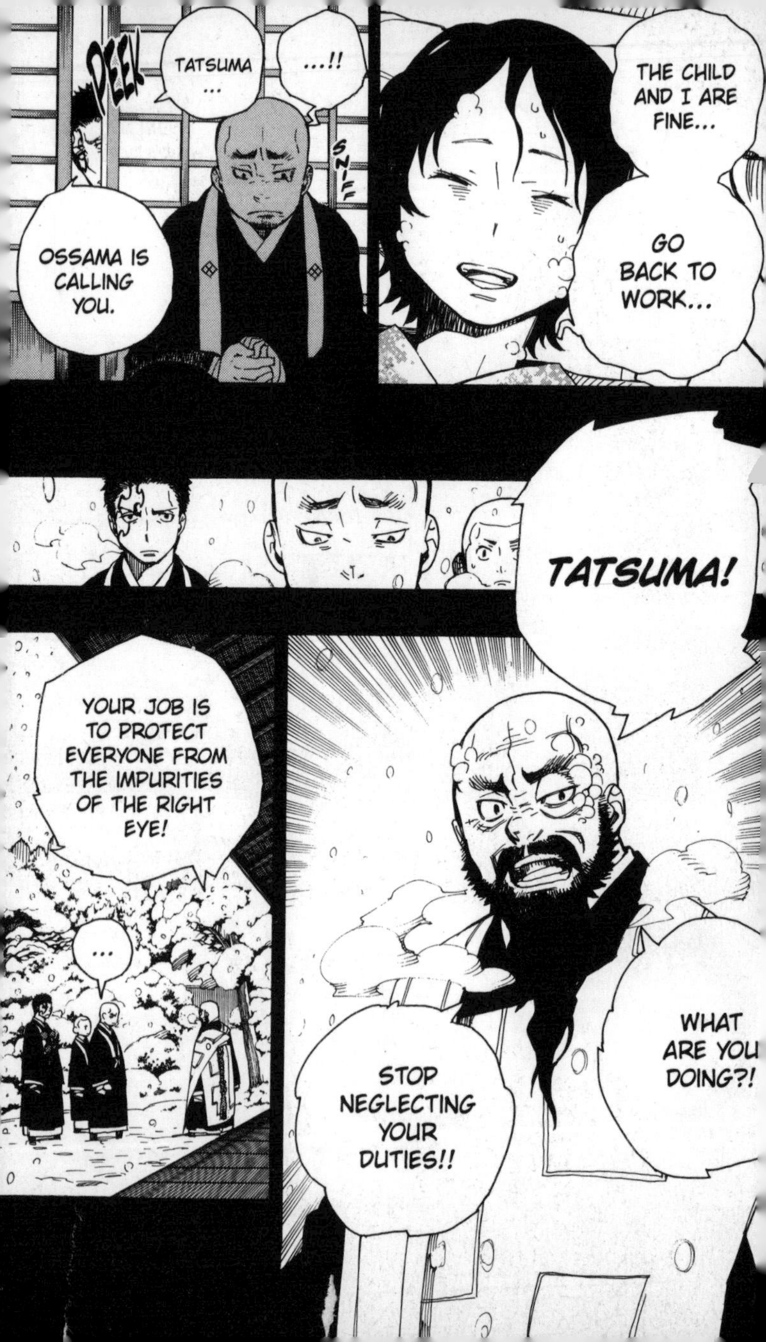
THE CHILD AND I ARE FINE...
GO BACK TO WORK...
PEEK
TATSUMA ...
...!!
SNIFF
OSSAMA IS CALLING YOU.
TATSUMA!
WHAT ARE YOU DOING?!
STOP NEGLECTING YOUR DUTIES!!
YOUR JOB IS TO PROTECT EVERYONE FROM THE IMPURITIES OF THE RIGHT EYE!
...

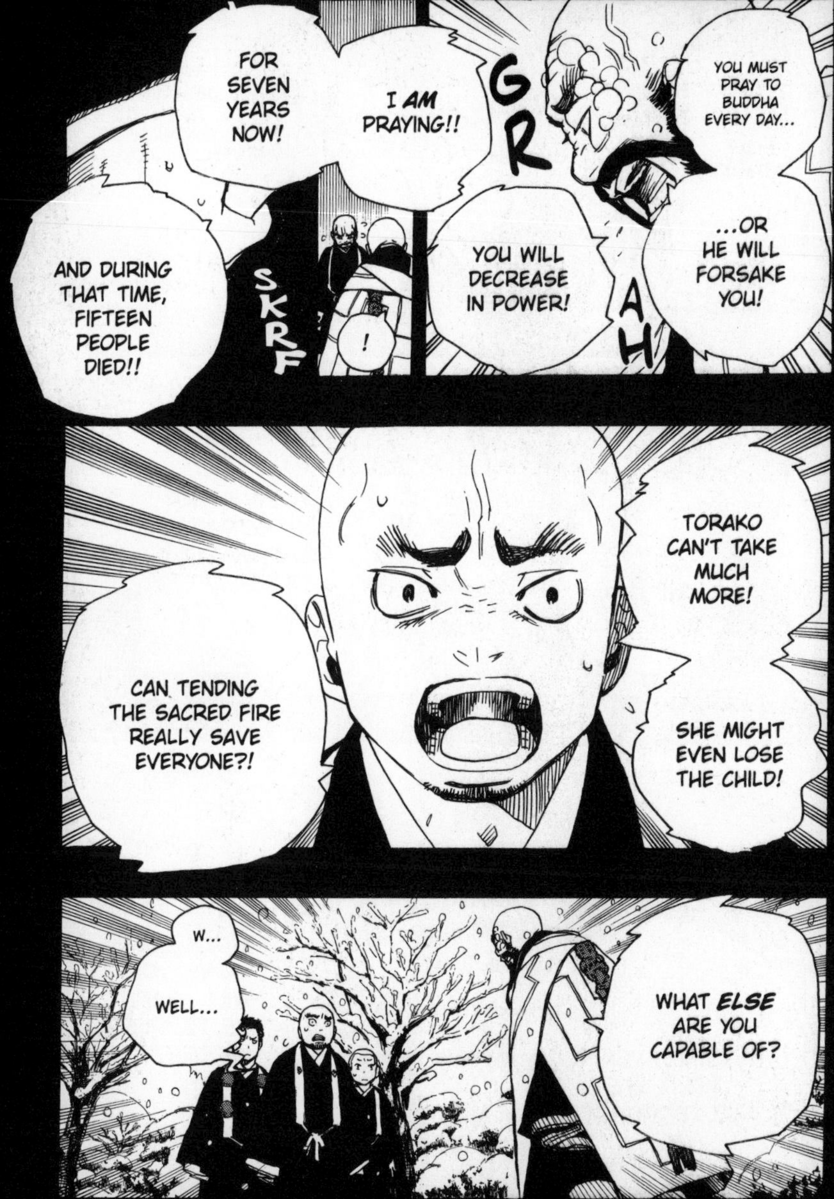
YOU MUST PRAY TO BUDDHA EVERY DAY...
GR
...OR HE WILL FORSAKE YOU!
AH
YOU WILL DECREASE IN POWER!
!
SKRF
I AM PRAYING!!
FOR SEVEN YEARS NOW!
AND DURING THAT TIME, FIFTEEN PEOPLE DIED!!
TORAKO CAN'T TAKE MUCH MORE!
SHE MIGHT EVEN LOSE THE CHILD!
CAN TENDING THE SACRED FIRE REALLY SAVE EVERYONE?!
WHAT ELSE ARE YOU CAPABLE OF?
W...
WELL...

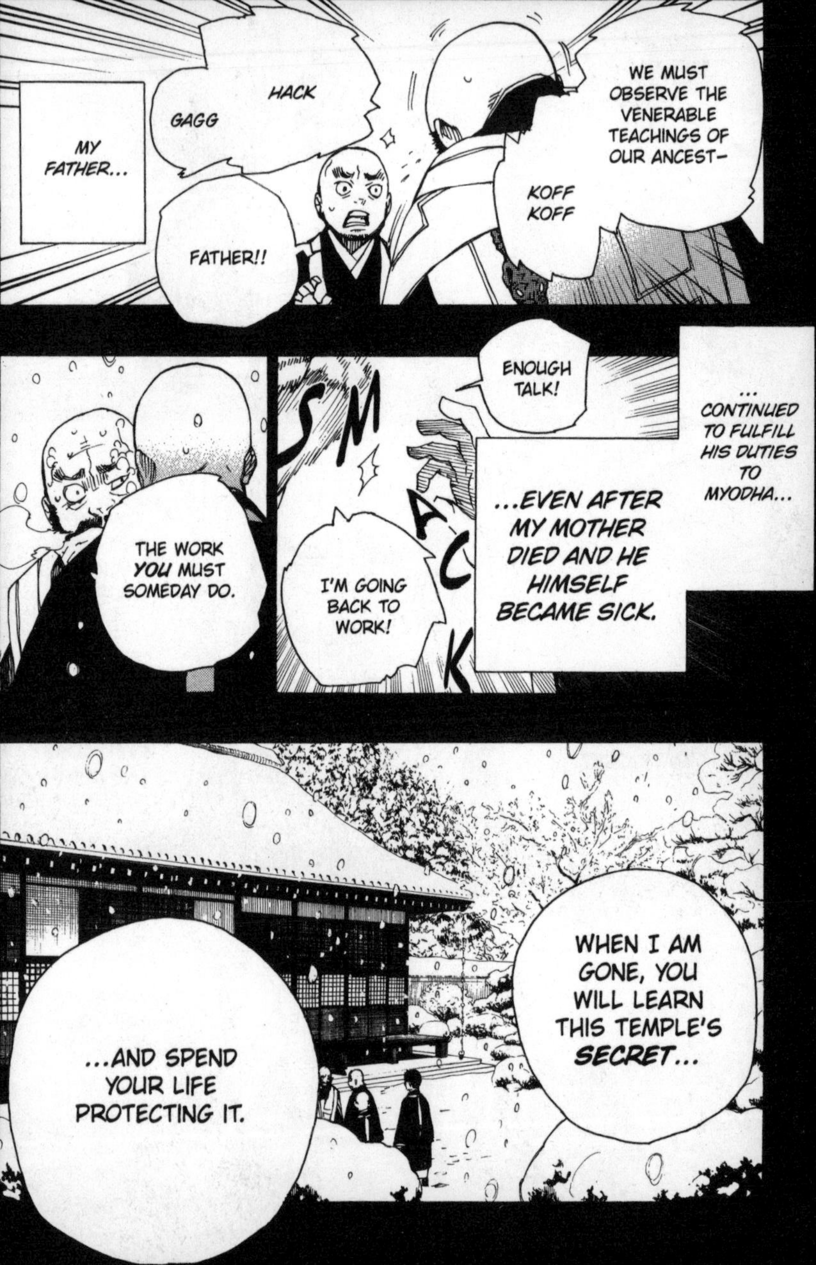
WE MUST OBSERVE THE VENERABLE TEACHINGS OF OUR ANCEST-
KOFF KOFF
HACK
GAGG
FATHER!!
MY FATHER...
...CONTINUED TO FULFILL HIS DUTIES TO MYODHA...
ENOUGH TALK!
...EVEN AFTER MY MOTHER DIED AND HE HIMSELF BECAME SICK.
SMACK
I'M GOING BACK TO WORK!
THE WORK *YOU* MUST SOMEDAY DO.
WHEN I AM GONE, YOU WILL LEARN THIS TEMPLE'S *SECRET*...
...AND SPEND YOUR LIFE PROTECTING IT.

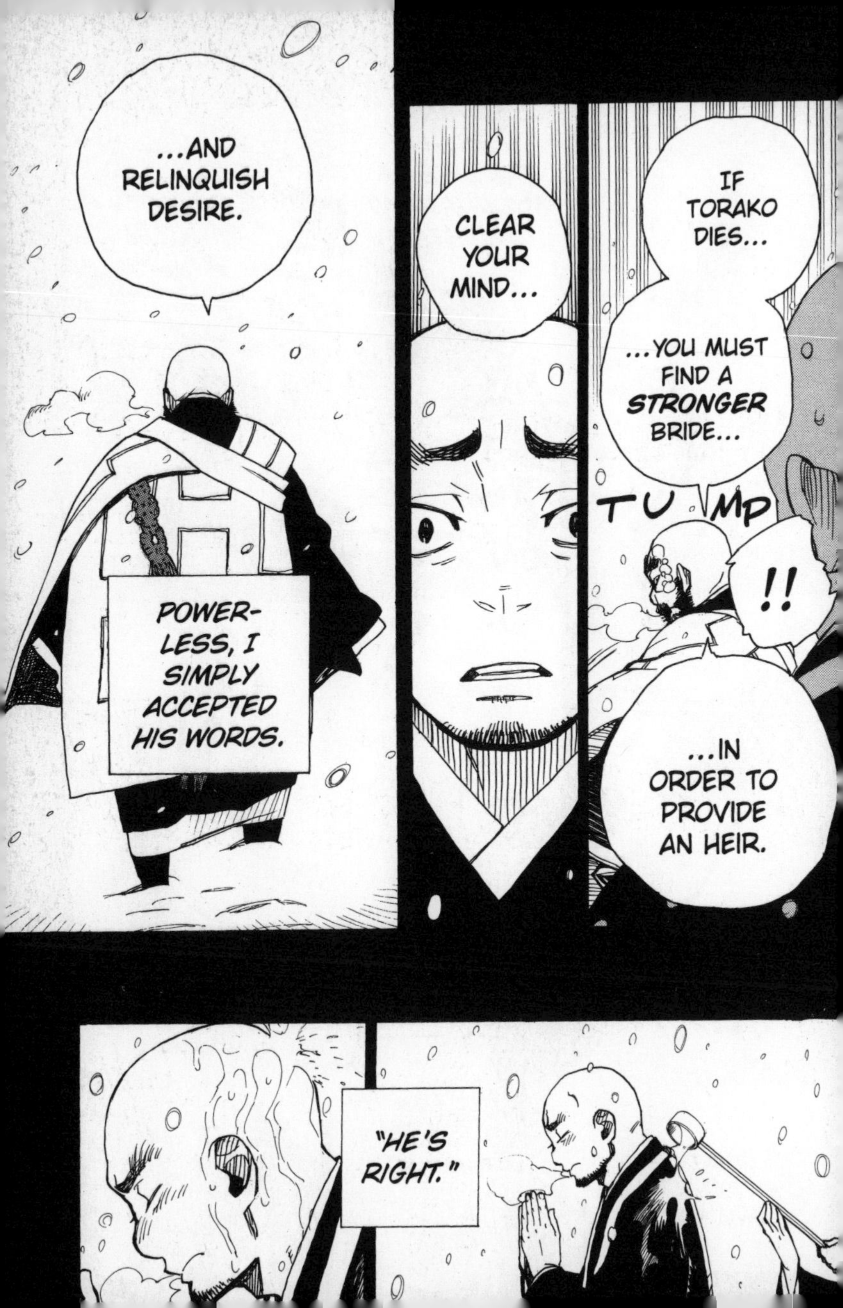
IF TORAKO DIES...
...YOU MUST FIND A STRONGER BRIDE...
TUMP
!!
...IN ORDER TO PROVIDE AN HEIR.
CLEAR YOUR MIND...
...AND RELINQUISH DESIRE.
POWER-LESS, I SIMPLY ACCEPTED HIS WORDS.
"HE'S RIGHT."

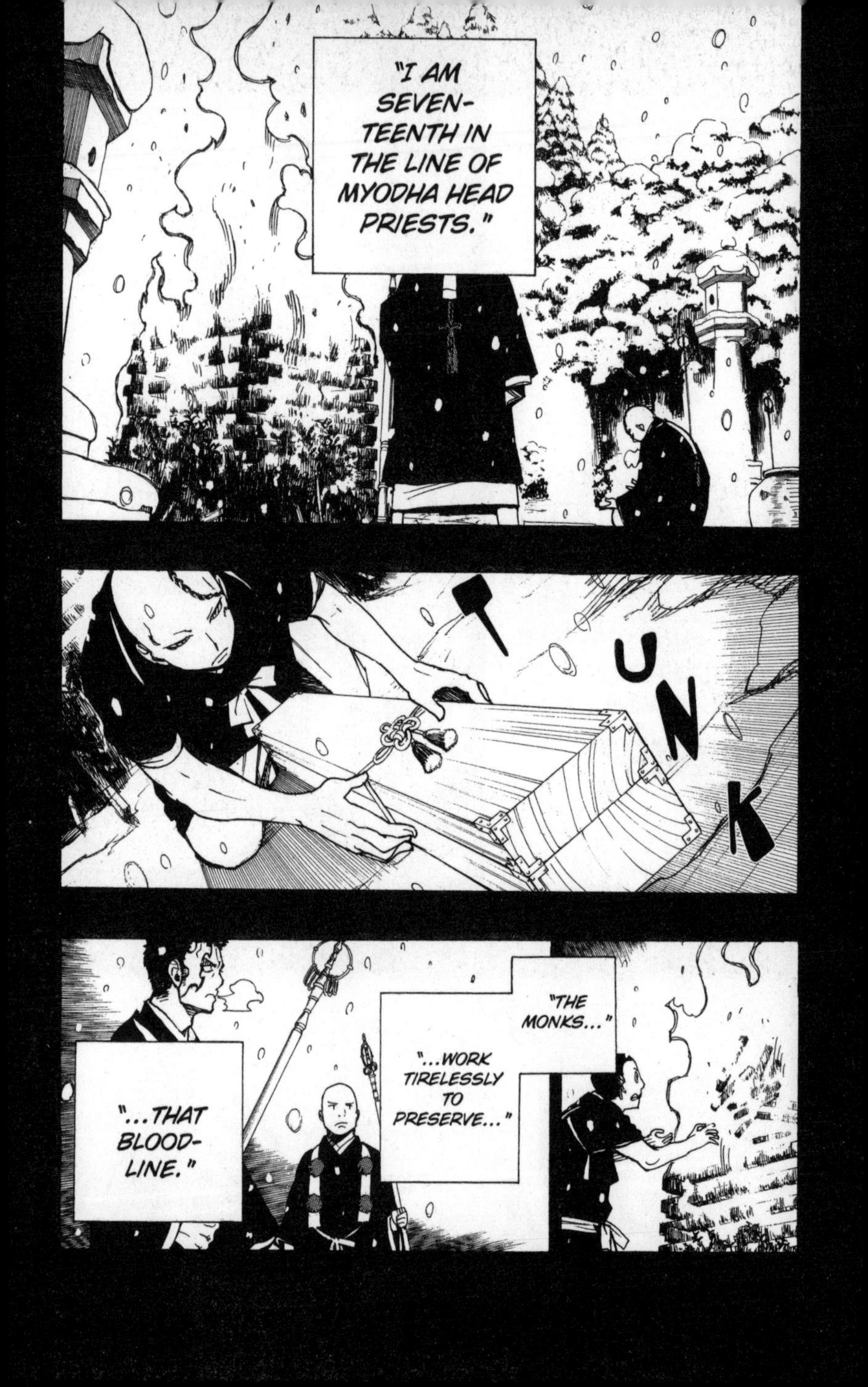
"I AM SEVEN-TEENTH IN THE LINE OF MYODHA HEAD PRIESTS."
TUNK
"THE MONKS..."
"...WORK TIRELESSLY TO PRESERVE..."
"...THAT BLOOD-LINE."

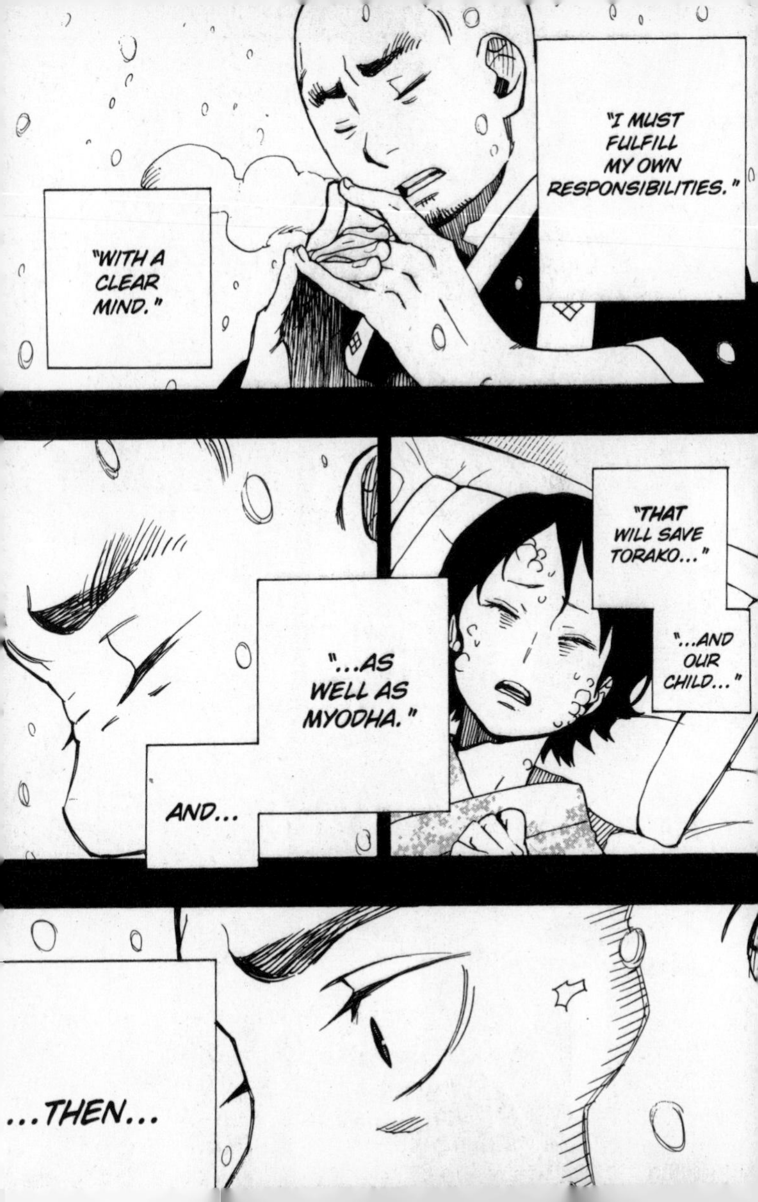
"I MUST FULFILL MY OWN RESPONSIBILITIES."
"WITH A CLEAR MIND."
"THAT WILL SAVE TORAKO..."
"...AND OUR CHILD..."
"...AS WELL AS MYODHA."
AND...
...THEN...

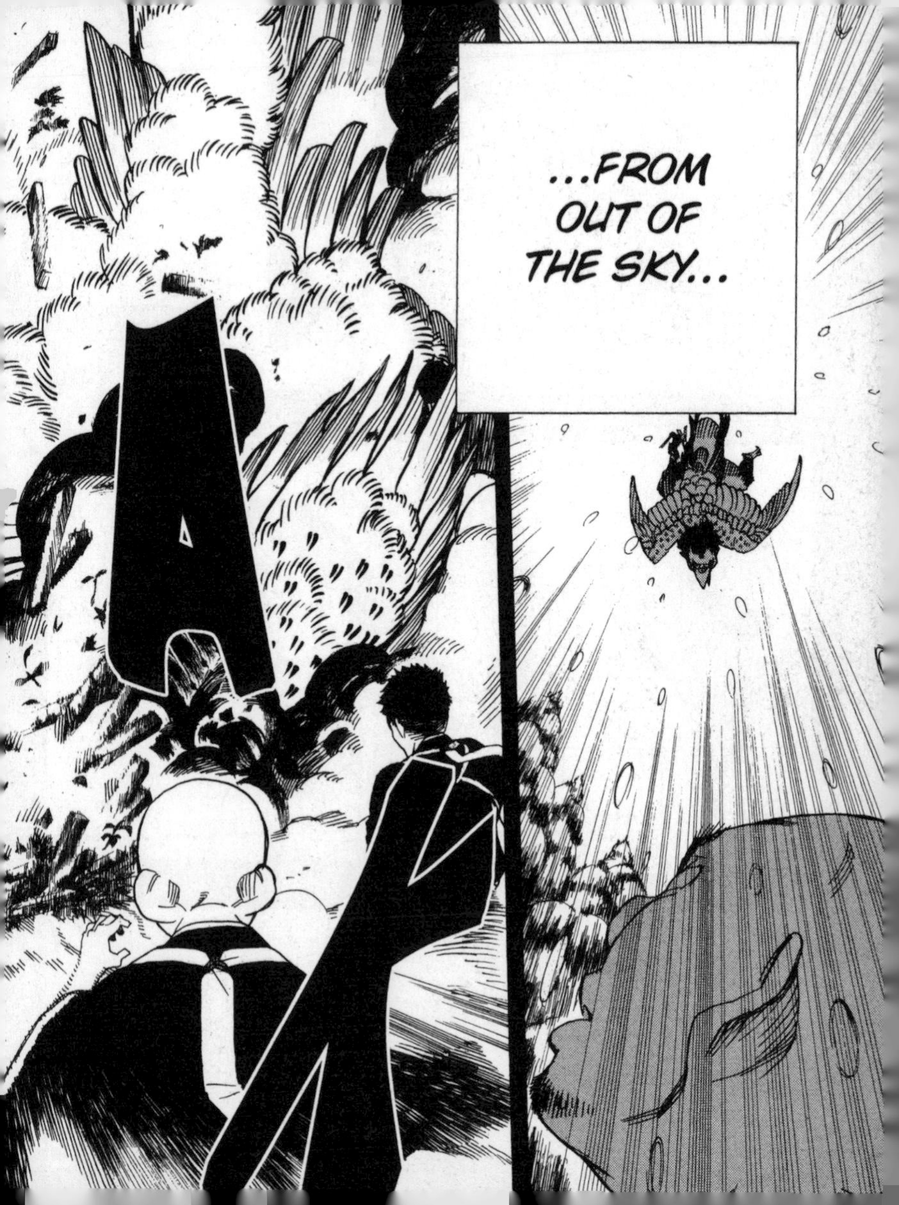
...FROM
OUT OF
THE SKY...

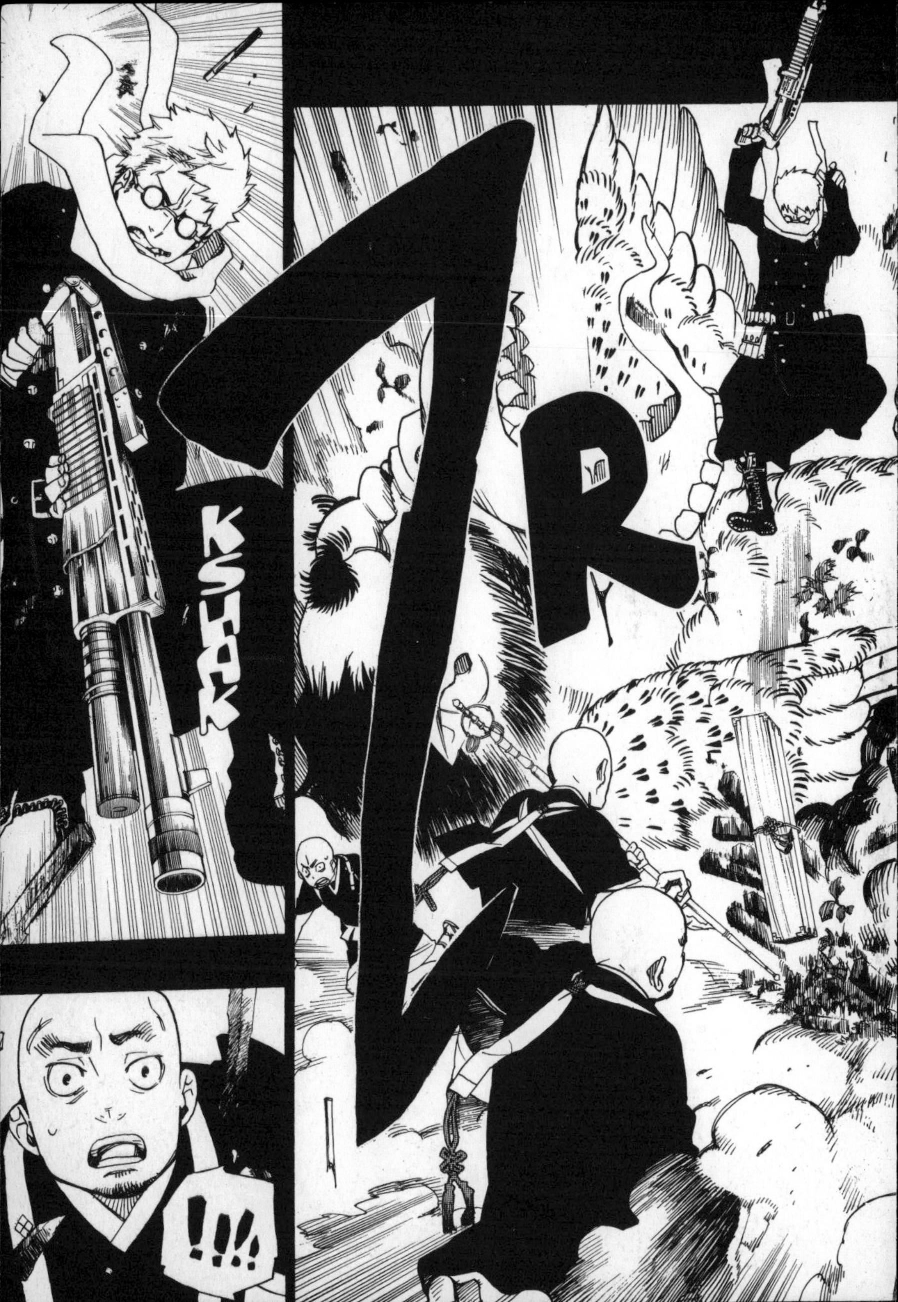
VR
KSHAK
!!!!

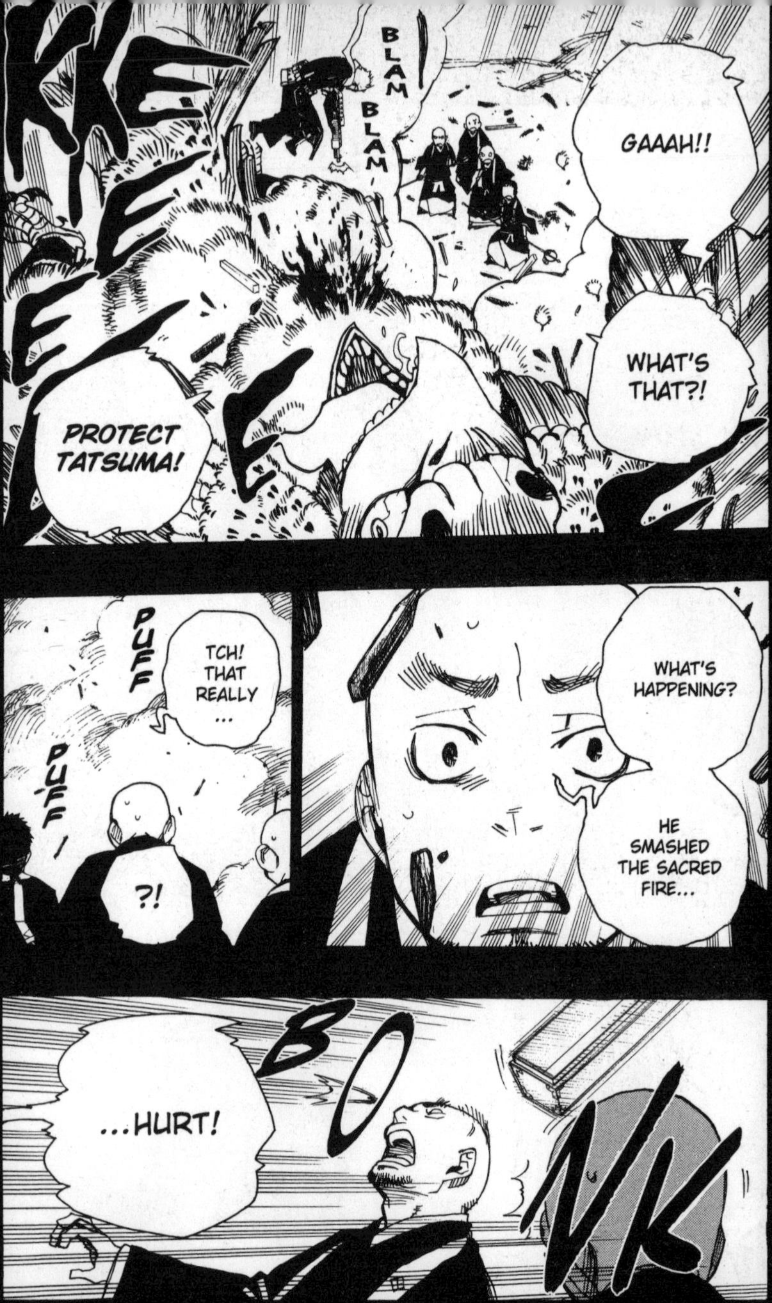
GAAAH!!
BLAM BLAM
WHAT'S THAT?!
PROTECT TATSUMA!
WHAT'S HAPPENING?
HE SMASHED THE SACRED FIRE...
TCH! THAT REALLY ...
PUFF
PUFF
?!
BONK
...HURT!

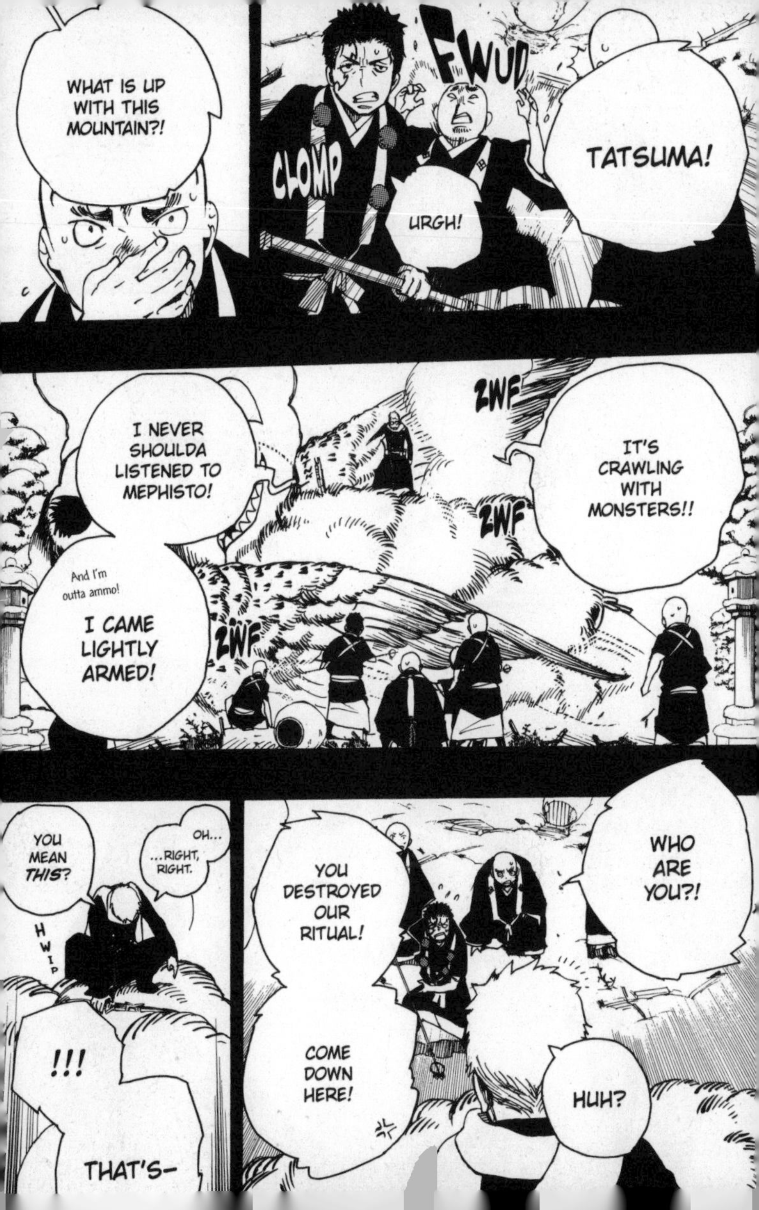
TATSUMA!
FWUD
CLOMP
URGH!
WHAT IS UP WITH THIS MOUNTAIN?!
IT'S CRAWLING WITH MONSTERS!!
ZWF
ZWF
I NEVER SHOULDA LISTENED TO MEPHISTO!
And I'm outta ammo!
I CAME LIGHTLY ARMED!
ZWF
WHO ARE YOU?!
YOU DESTROYED OUR RITUAL!
COME DOWN HERE!
HUH?
OH... ...RIGHT, RIGHT.
YOU MEAN THIS?
HWIP
!!!
THAT'S-

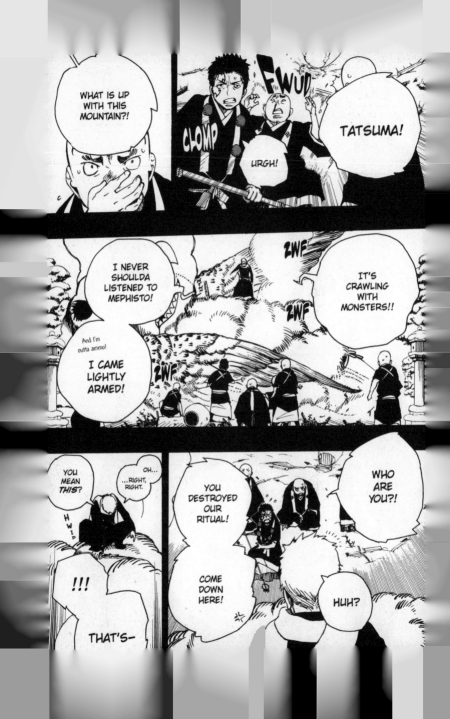

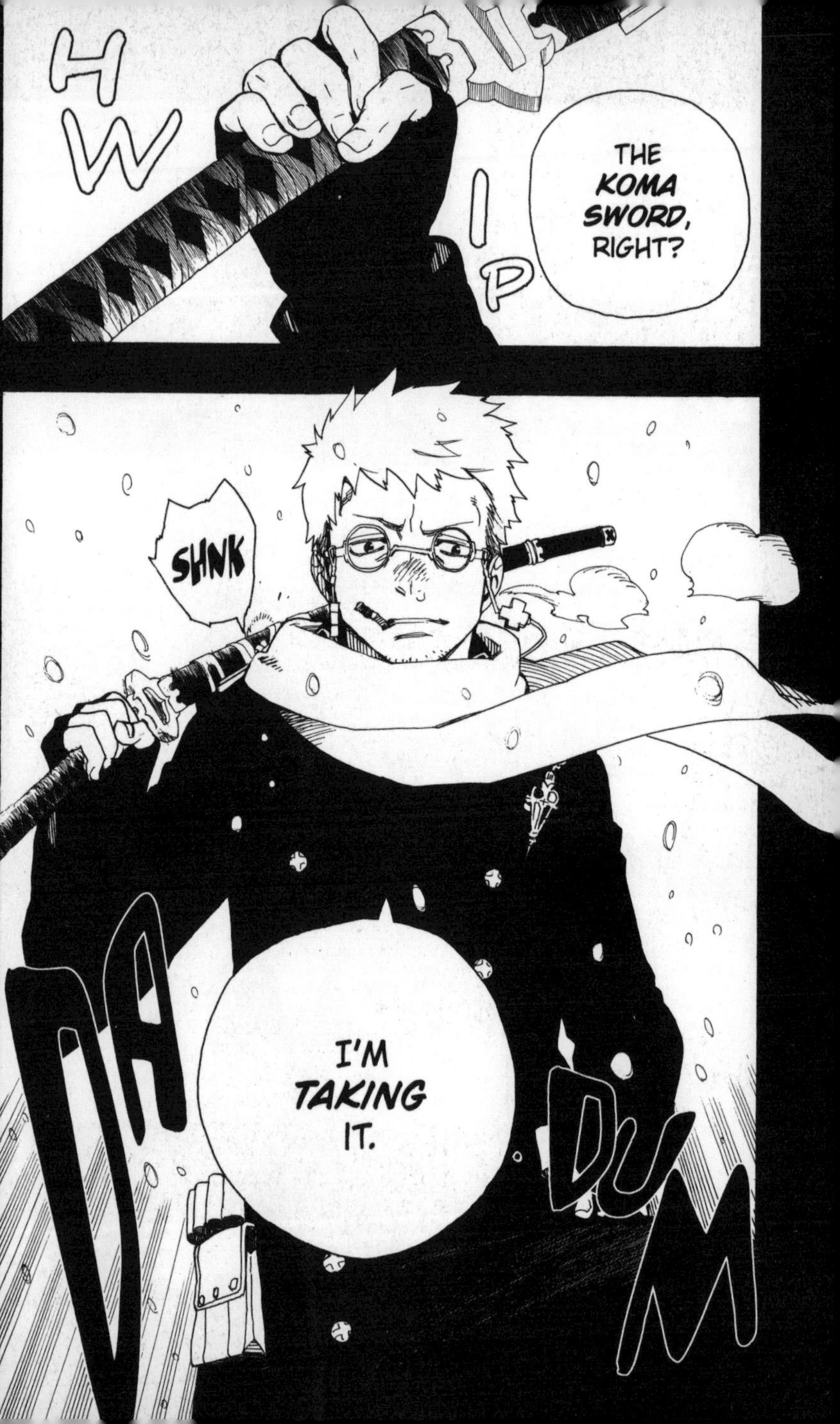
THE KOMA SWORD, RIGHT?
HWIP
SHNK
I'M TAKING IT.
DA DUM

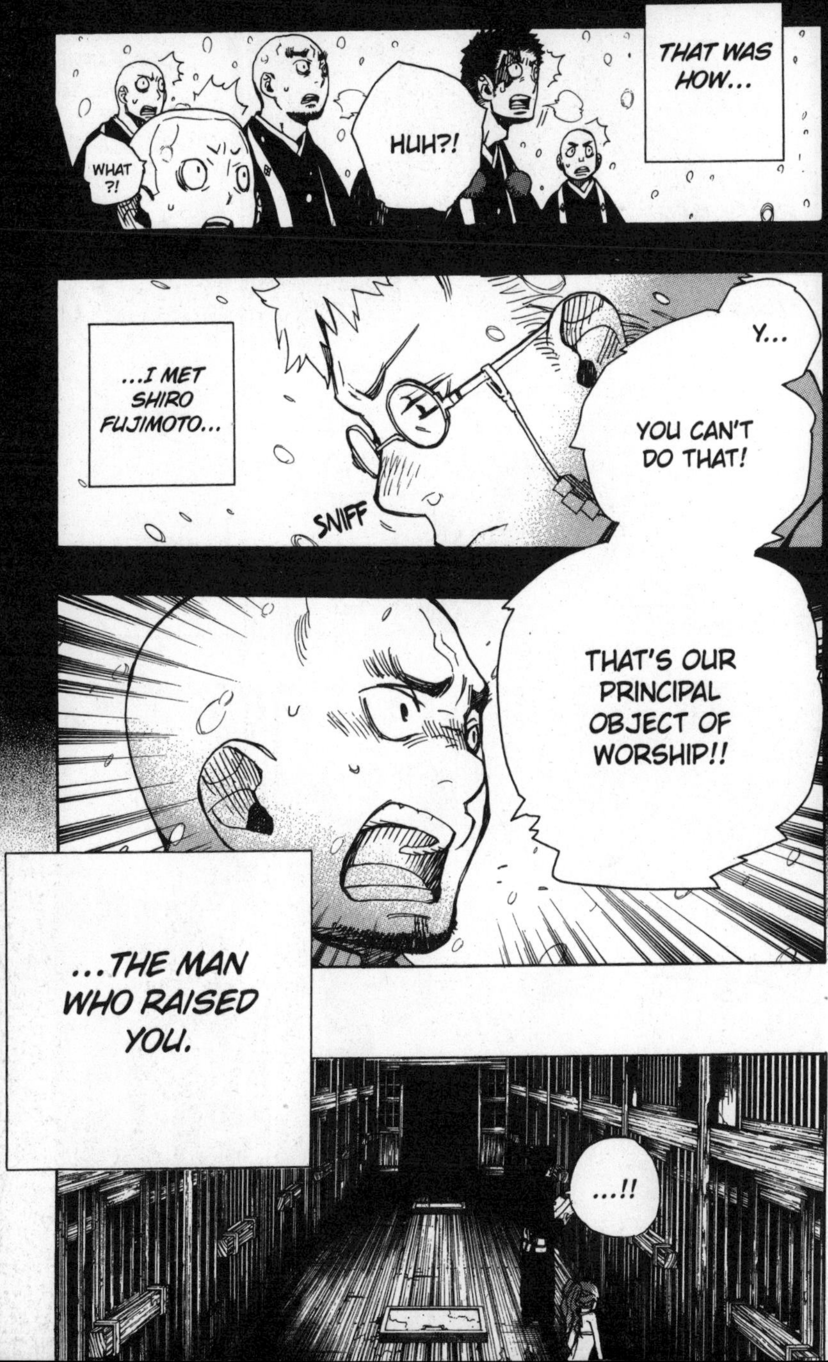
THAT WAS HOW...
HUH?!
WHAT ?!
Y...
YOU CAN'T DO THAT!
...I MET SHIRO FUJIMOTO...
SNIFF
THAT'S OUR PRINCIPAL OBJECT OF WORSHIP!!
...THE MAN WHO RAISED YOU.
...!!

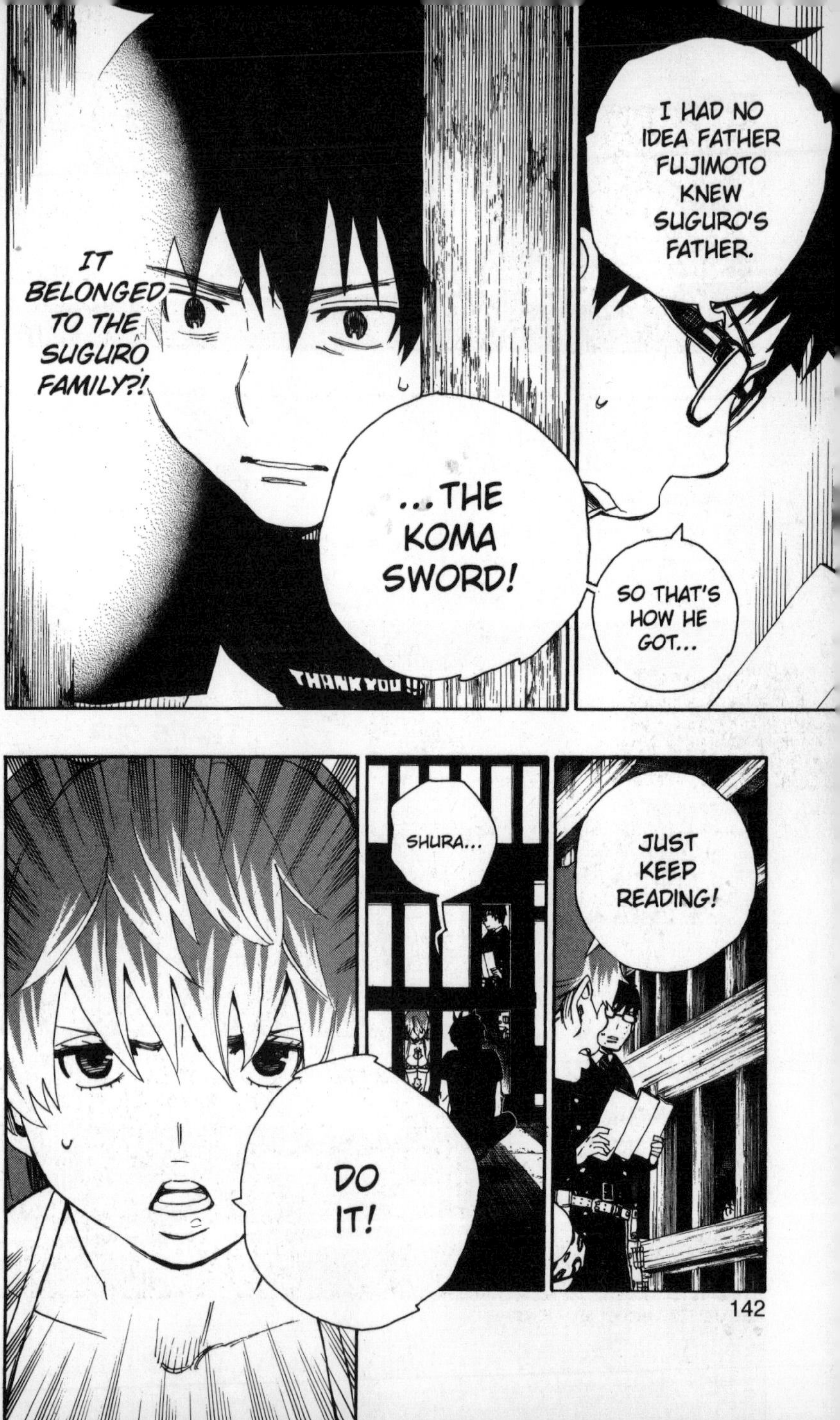
I HAD NO IDEA FATHER FUJIMOTO KNEW SUGURO'S FATHER.
SO THAT'S HOW HE GOT...
...THE KOMA SWORD!
IT BELONGED TO THE SUGURO FAMILY?!
THANK YOU!!
JUST KEEP READING!
SHURA...
DO IT!

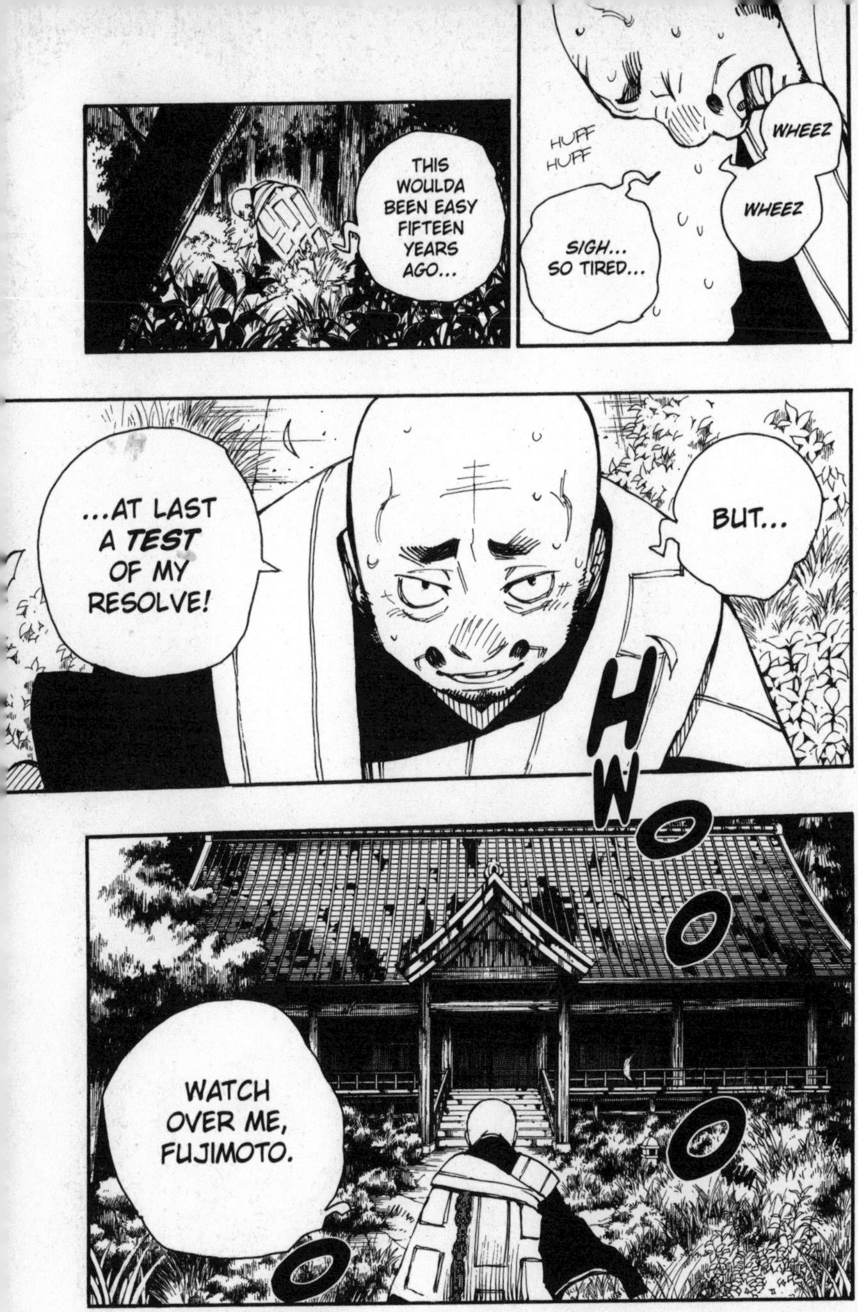
WHEEZ
WHEEZ
HUFF HUFF
SIGH... SO TIRED...
THIS WOULDA BEEN EASY FIFTEEN YEARS AGO...
BUT...
...AT LAST A *TEST* OF MY RESOLVE!
HWOOOOO
WATCH OVER ME, FUJIMOTO.

BLUE EXORCIST 6 – END –

Blue Exorcist Chapter 23 The Father's Story

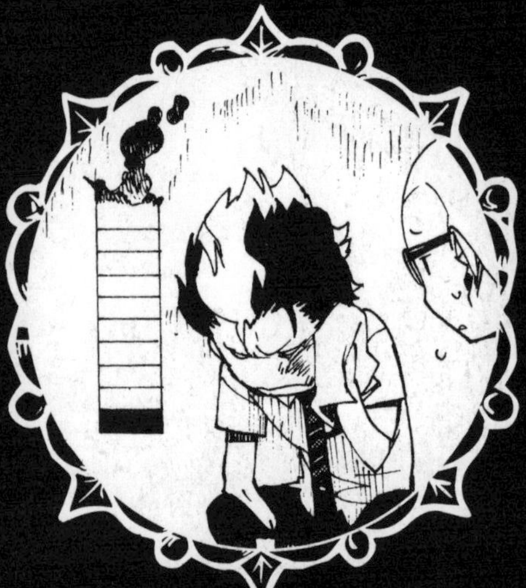

Bonus Story 1 — Phantom Train

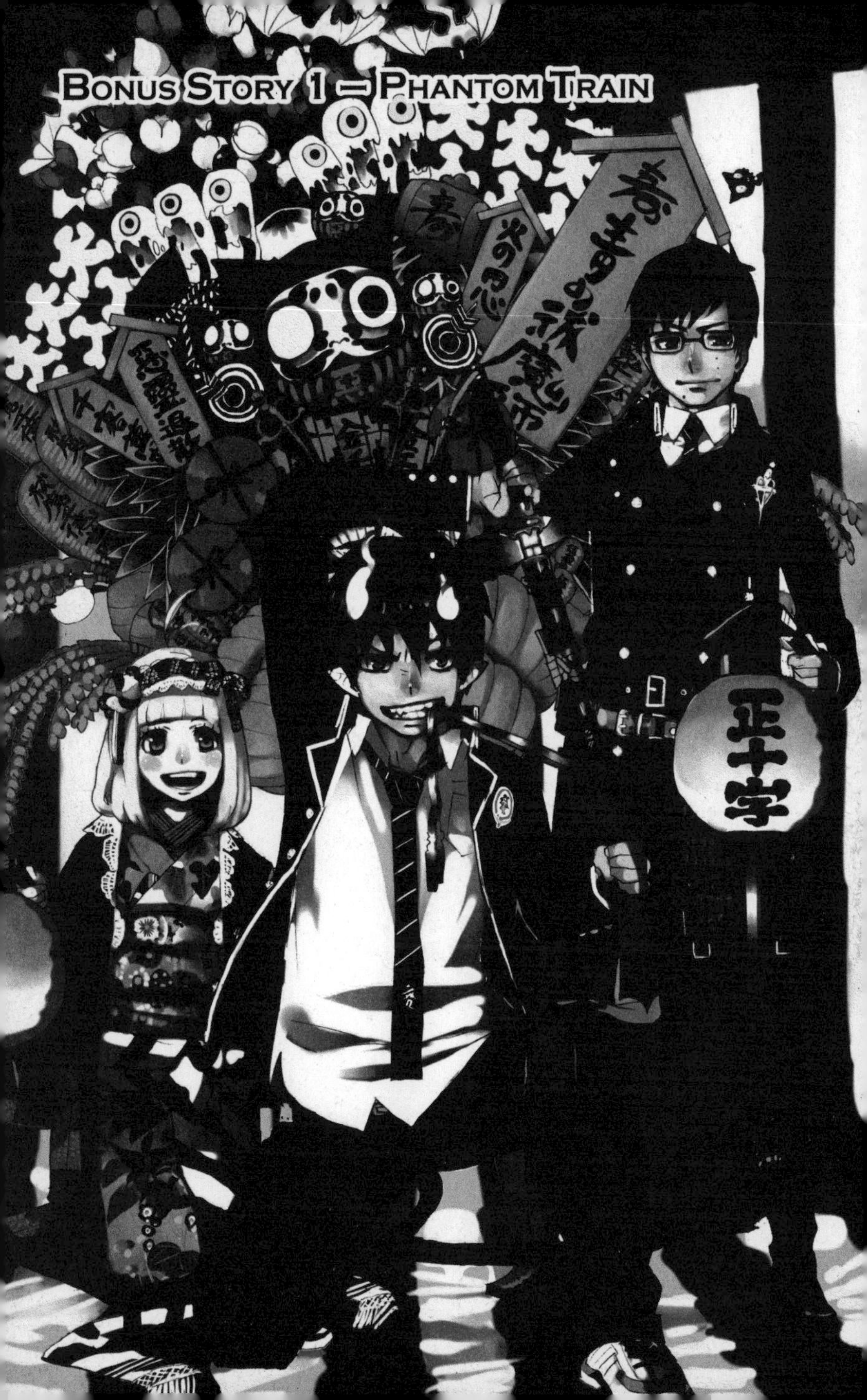
正十字

*Kumade

Urgh!

I can't hold it any longer...

*Kumade: a decorative bamboo rake displayed at New Year's

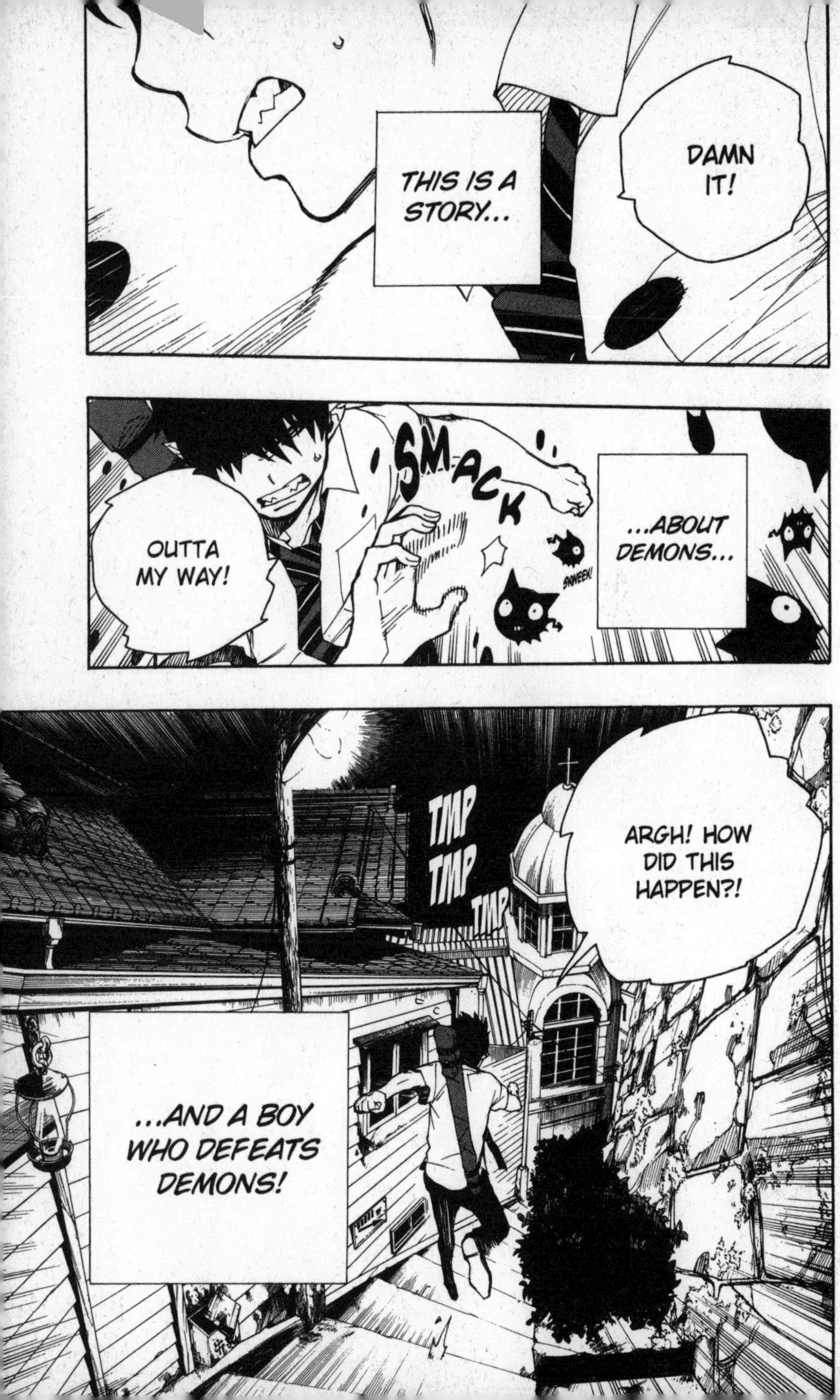
DAMN IT!
THIS IS A STORY...
...ABOUT DEMONS...
SKWEEK!
SMACK
OUTTA MY WAY!
ARGH! HOW DID THIS HAPPEN?!
TMP TMP TMP
...AND A BOY WHO DEFEATS DEMONS!

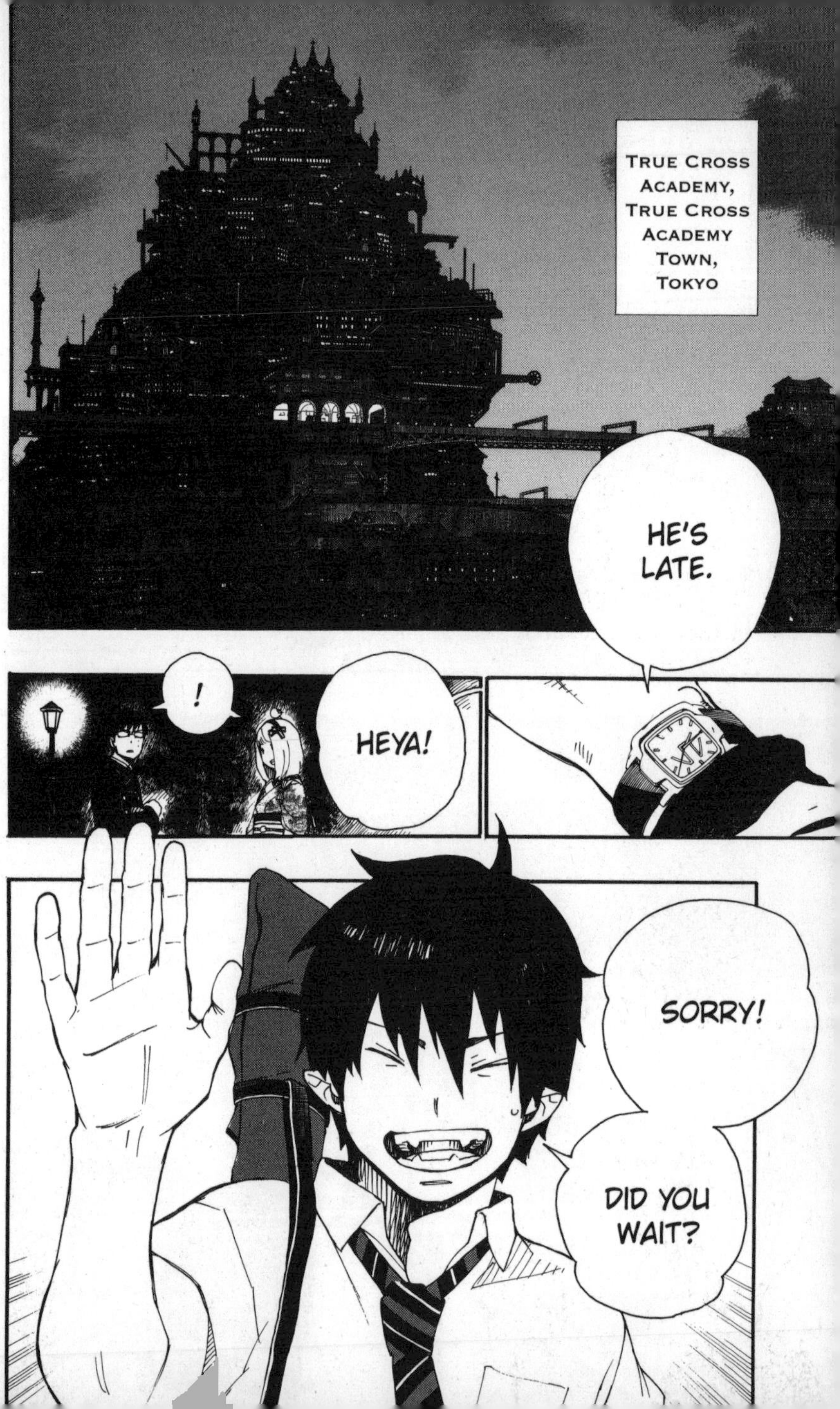
TRUE CROSS ACADEMY, TRUE CROSS ACADEMY TOWN, TOKYO
HE'S LATE.
HEYA!
!
SORRY!
DID YOU WAIT?

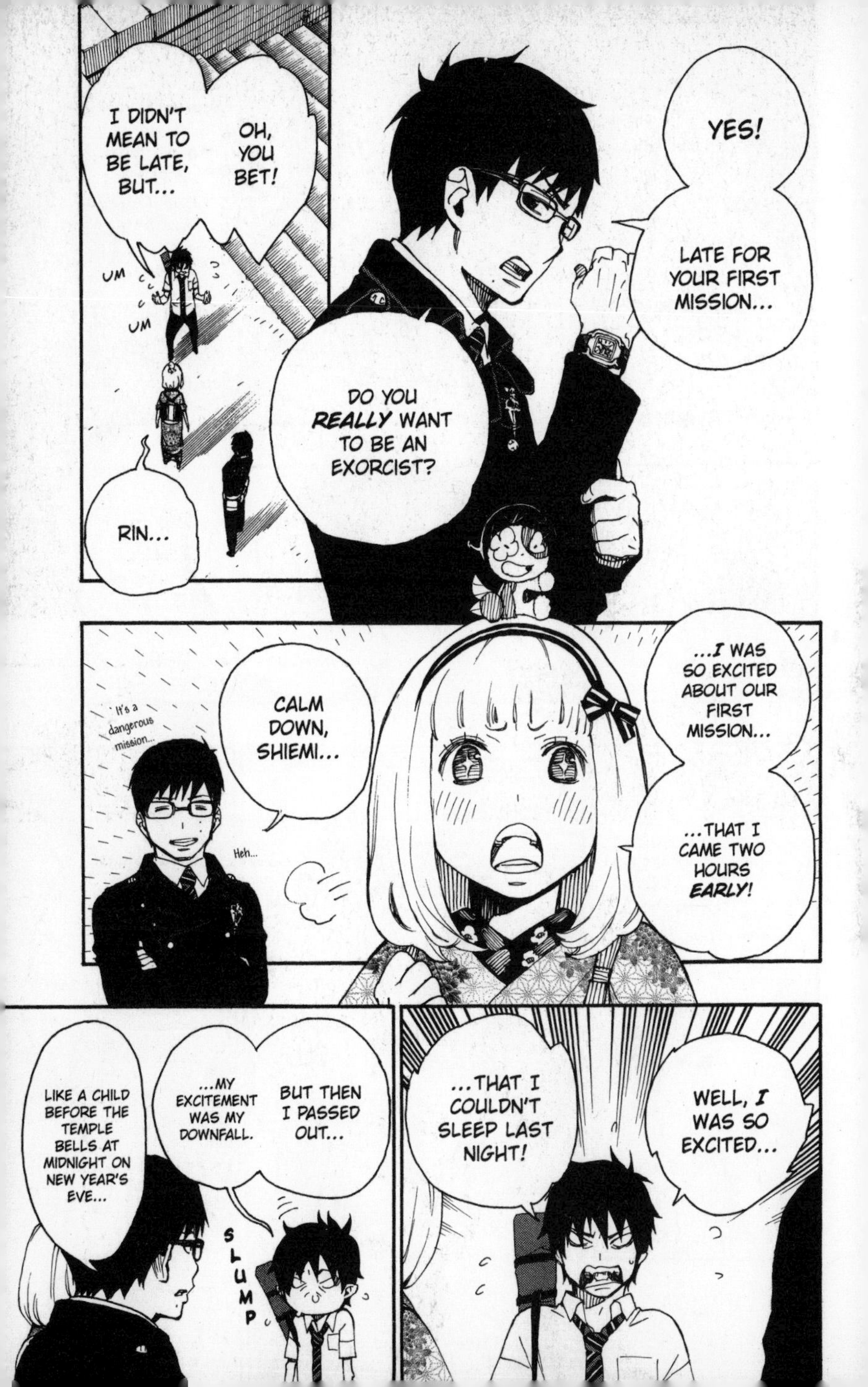
YES!
LATE FOR YOUR FIRST MISSION...
DO YOU REALLY WANT TO BE AN EXORCIST?
OH, YOU BET!
I DIDN'T MEAN TO BE LATE, BUT...
UM
UM
RIN...
...I WAS SO EXCITED ABOUT OUR FIRST MISSION...
...THAT I CAME TWO HOURS EARLY!
CALM DOWN, SHIEMI...
It's a dangerous mission...
Heh...
WELL, I WAS SO EXCITED...
...THAT I COULDN'T SLEEP LAST NIGHT!
BUT THEN I PASSED OUT...
...MY EXCITEMENT WAS MY DOWNFALL.
SLUMP
LIKE A CHILD BEFORE THE TEMPLE BELLS AT MIDNIGHT ON NEW YEAR'S EVE...

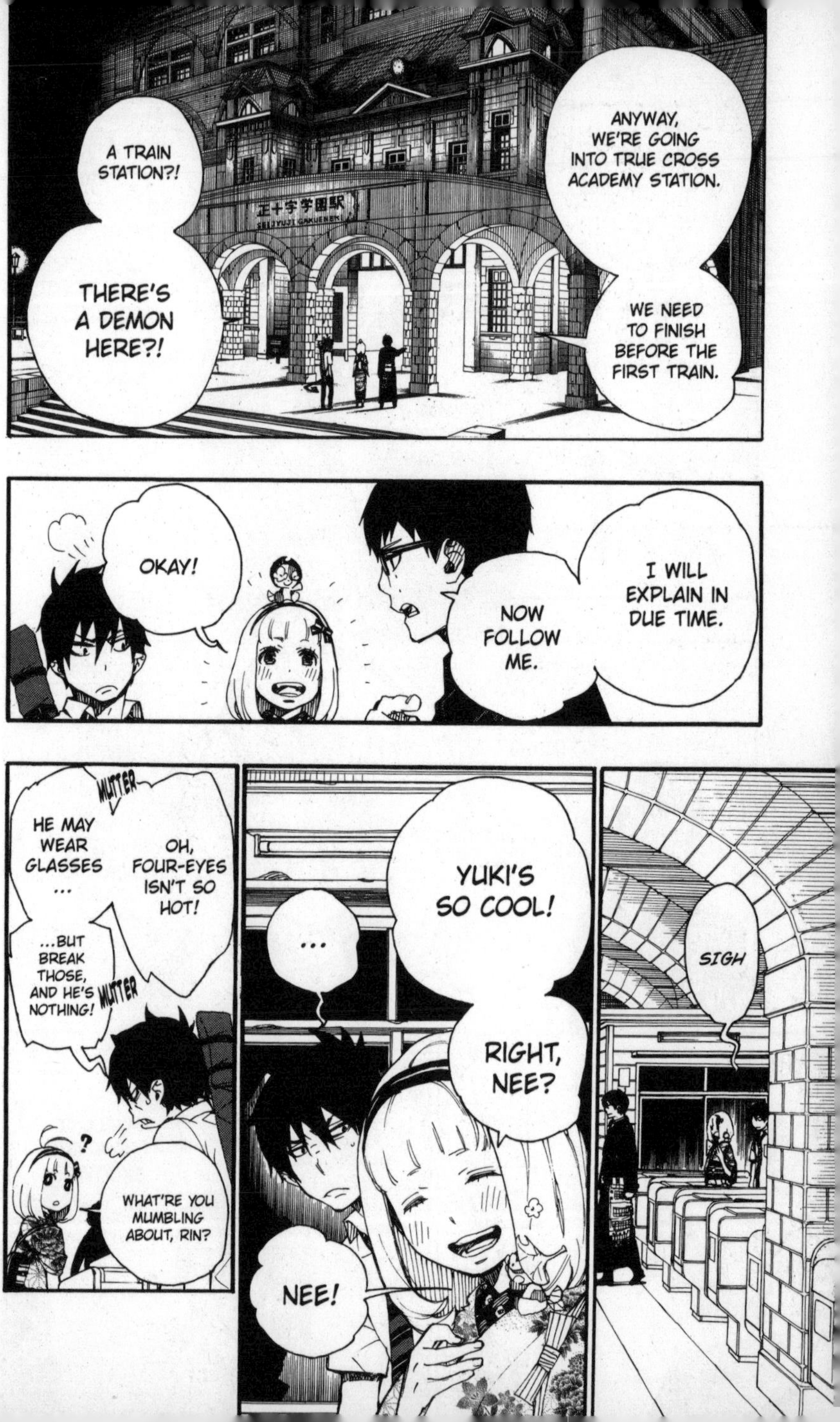
ANYWAY, WE'RE GOING INTO TRUE CROSS ACADEMY STATION.
WE NEED TO FINISH BEFORE THE FIRST TRAIN.
正十字学園駅
A TRAIN STATION?!
THERE'S A DEMON HERE?!
I WILL EXPLAIN IN DUE TIME.
NOW FOLLOW ME.
OKAY!
SIGH
YUKI'S SO COOL!
...
RIGHT, NEE?
NEE!
MUTTER
OH, FOUR-EYES ISN'T SO HOT!
HE MAY WEAR GLASSES ...
...BUT BREAK THOSE, AND HE'S NOTHING!
MUTTER
WHAT'RE YOU MUMBLING ABOUT, RIN?

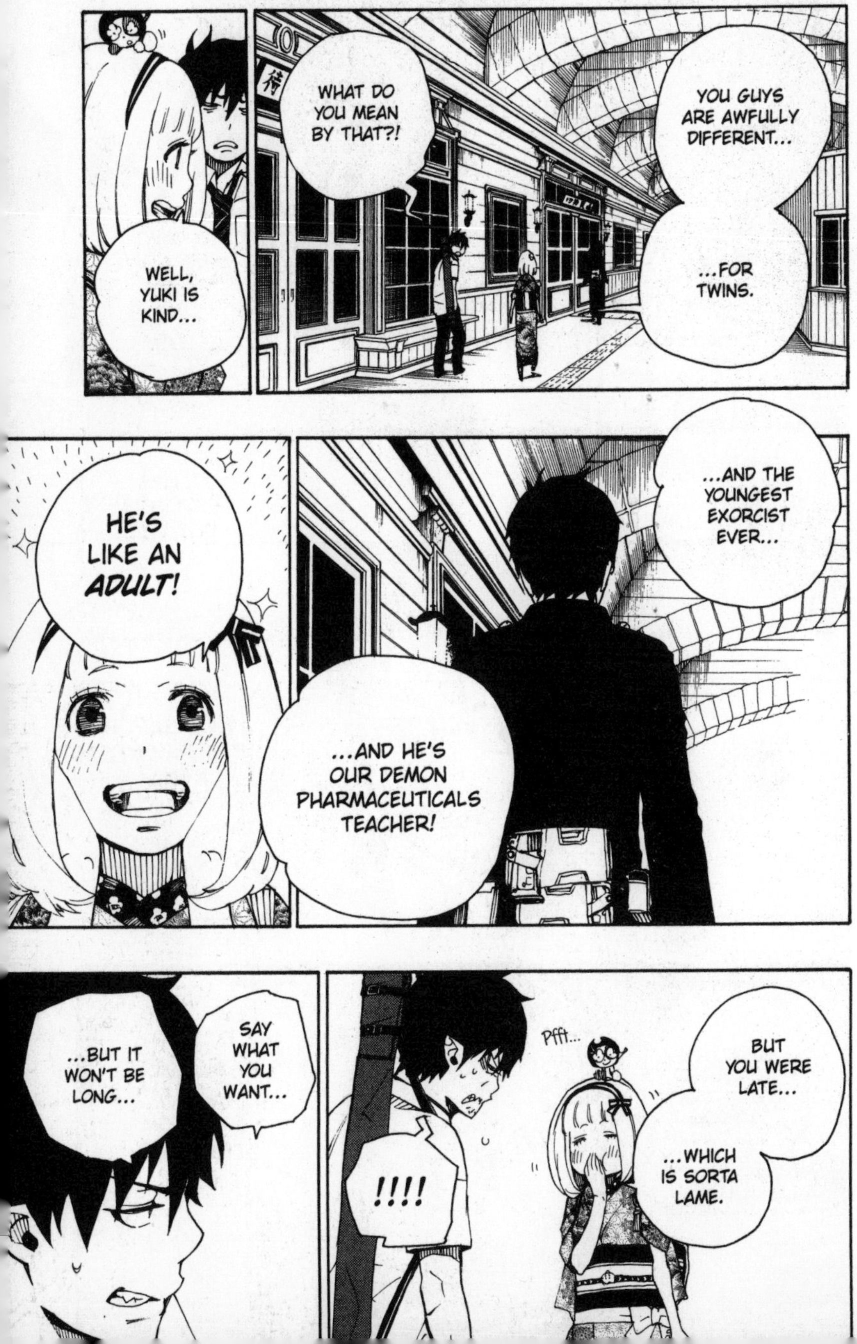
YOU GUYS ARE AWFULLY DIFFERENT...
...FOR TWINS.
WHAT DO YOU MEAN BY THAT?!
WELL, YUKI IS KIND...
...AND THE YOUNGEST EXORCIST EVER...
...AND HE'S OUR DEMON PHARMACEUTICALS TEACHER!
HE'S LIKE AN ADULT!
BUT YOU WERE LATE...
...WHICH IS SORTA LAME.
Pffft...
!!!!
SAY WHAT YOU WANT...
...BUT IT WON'T BE LONG...

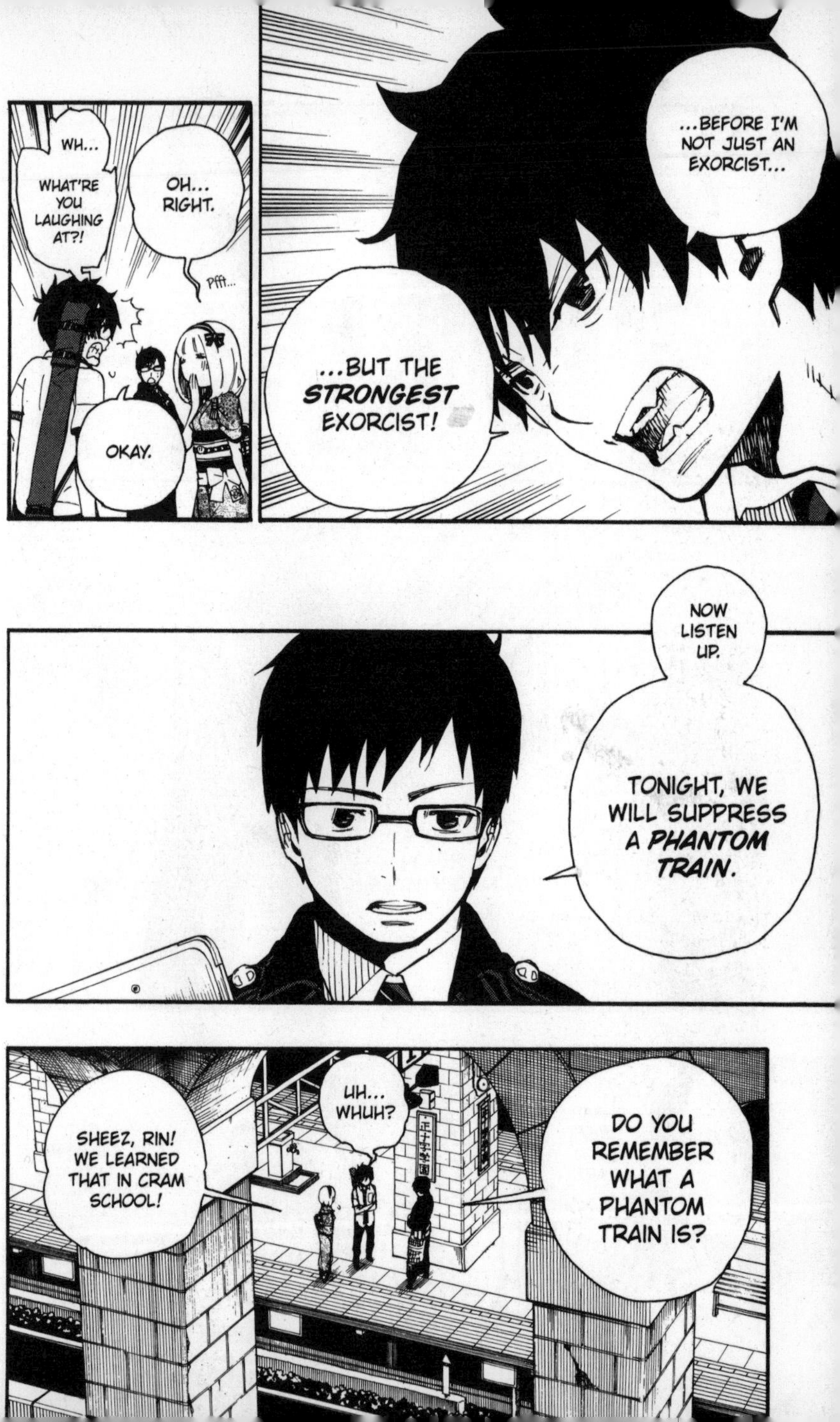
...BEFORE I'M NOT JUST AN EXORCIST...
...BUT THE **STRONGEST** EXORCIST!
OH... RIGHT.
Pfft...
WH... WHAT'RE YOU LAUGHING AT?!
OKAY.
NOW LISTEN UP.
TONIGHT, WE WILL SUPPRESS A **PHANTOM TRAIN**.
DO YOU REMEMBER WHAT A PHANTOM TRAIN IS?
UH... WHUH?
正十字学園
SHEEZ, RIN! WE LEARNED THAT IN CRAM SCHOOL!

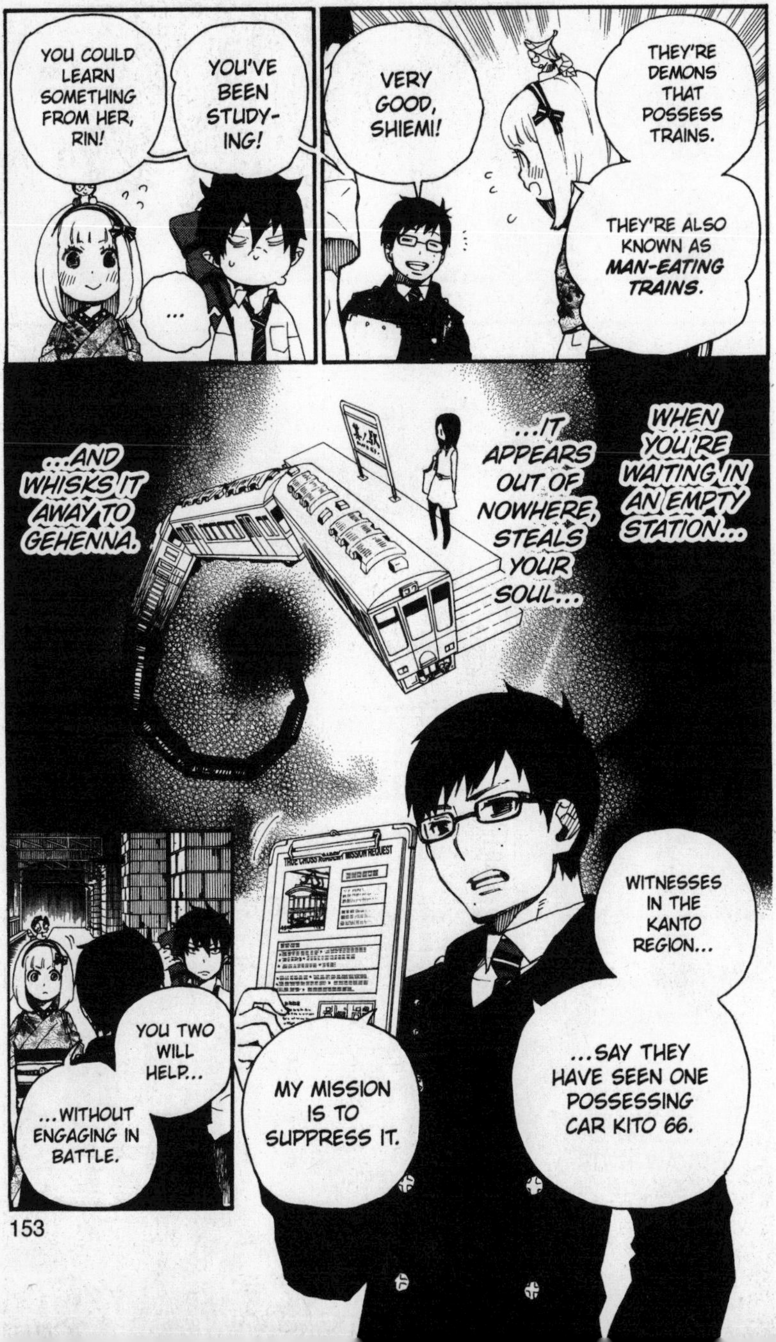
THEY'RE DEMONS THAT POSSESS TRAINS.
THEY'RE ALSO KNOWN AS *MAN-EATING TRAINS.*
VERY GOOD, SHIEMI!
YOU'VE BEEN STUDY-ING!
YOU COULD LEARN SOMETHING FROM HER, RIN!
...
WHEN YOU'RE WAITING IN AN EMPTY STATION...
...IT APPEARS OUT OF NOWHERE, STEALS YOUR SOUL...
...AND WHISKS IT AWAY TO GEHENNA.
WITNESSES IN THE KANTO REGION...
...SAY THEY HAVE SEEN ONE POSSESSING CAR KITO 66.
MY MISSION IS TO SUPPRESS IT.
YOU TWO WILL HELP...
...WITHOUT ENGAGING IN BATTLE.

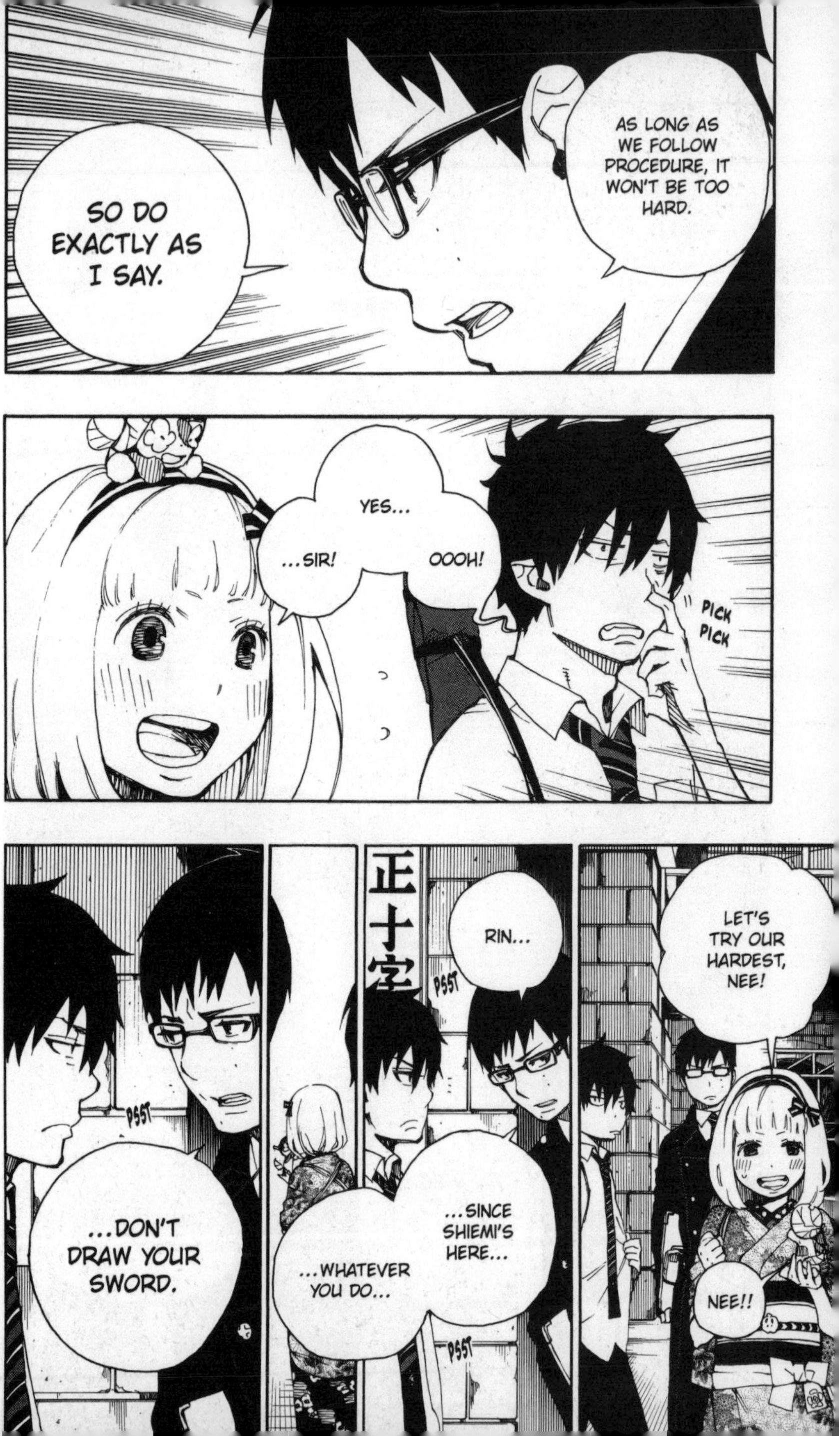
AS LONG AS WE FOLLOW PROCEDURE, IT WON'T BE TOO HARD.
SO DO EXACTLY AS I SAY.
YES...
OOOH!
...SIR!
PICK PICK
LET'S TRY OUR HARDEST, NEE!
NEE!!
正十字
RIN...
PSST
...SINCE SHIEMI'S HERE...
...WHATEVER YOU DO...
PSST
PSST
...DON'T DRAW YOUR SWORD.

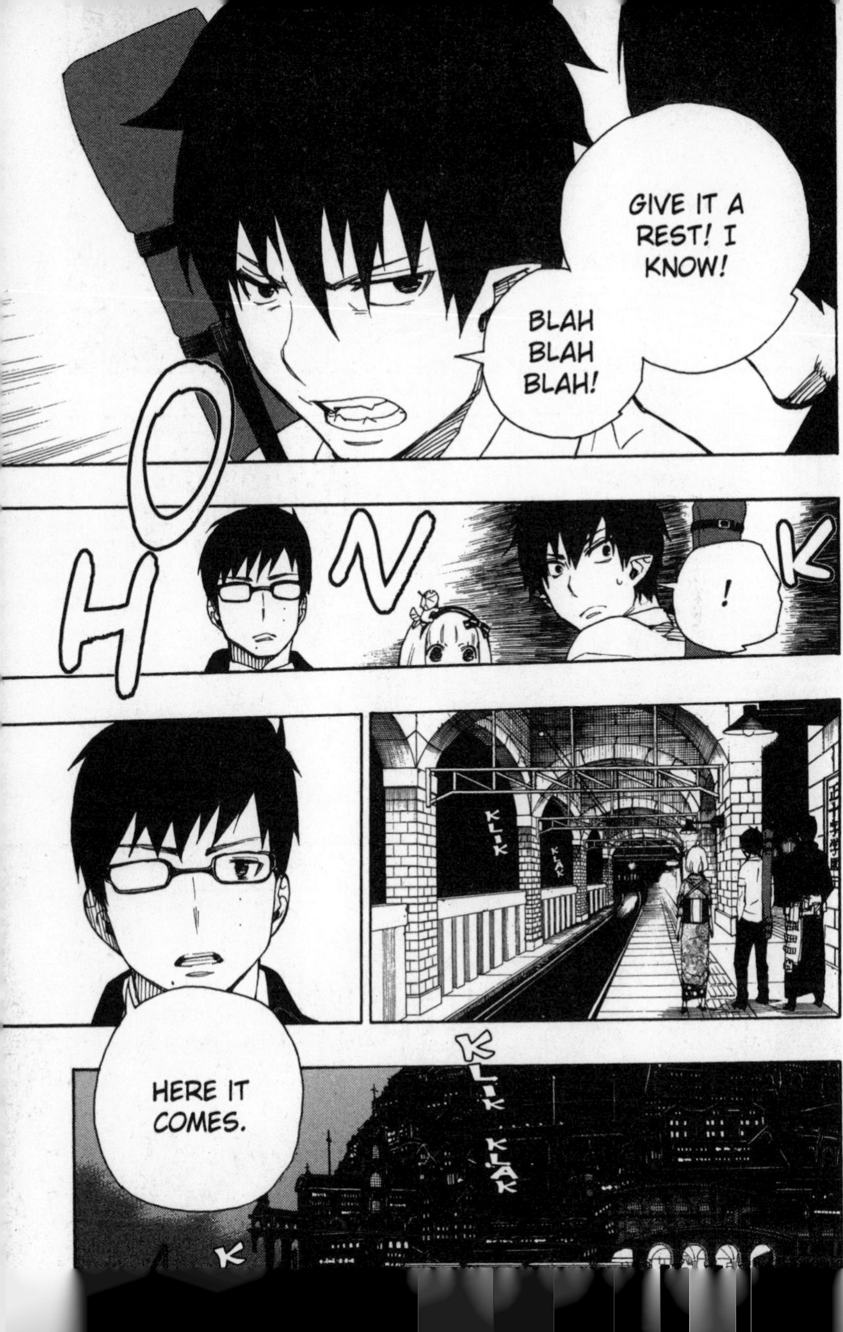
GIVE IT A REST! I KNOW!
BLAH BLAH BLAH!
HONK
!
KLIK
KLAK
KLIK
KLAK
HERE IT COMES.
K

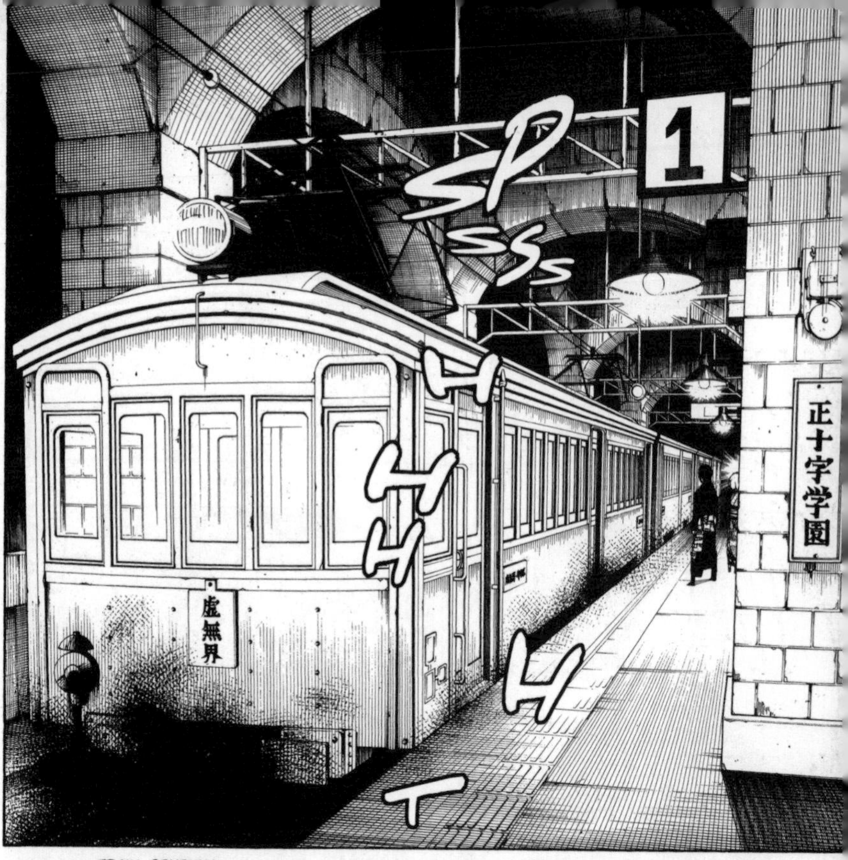
SPSSS
1
正十字学園
HHHHT
虚無界
TRAIN: GEHENNA

SIGN: TRUE CROSS ACADEMY

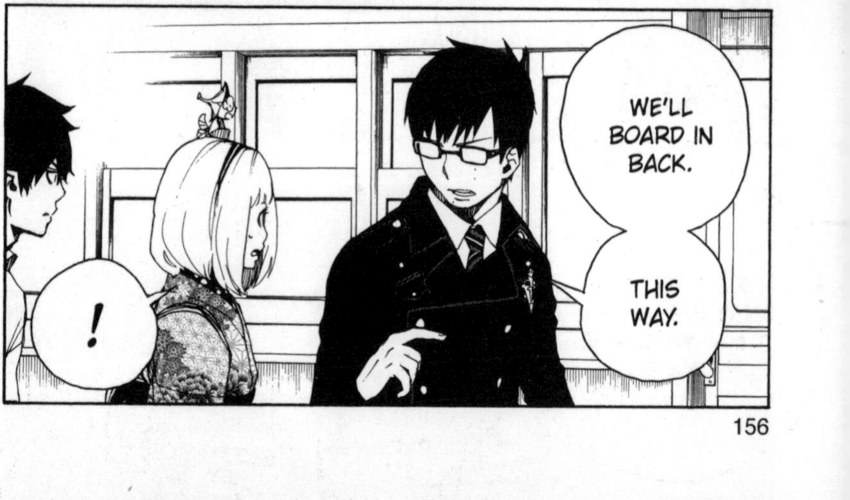
WE'LL BOARD IN BACK.
THIS WAY.
!

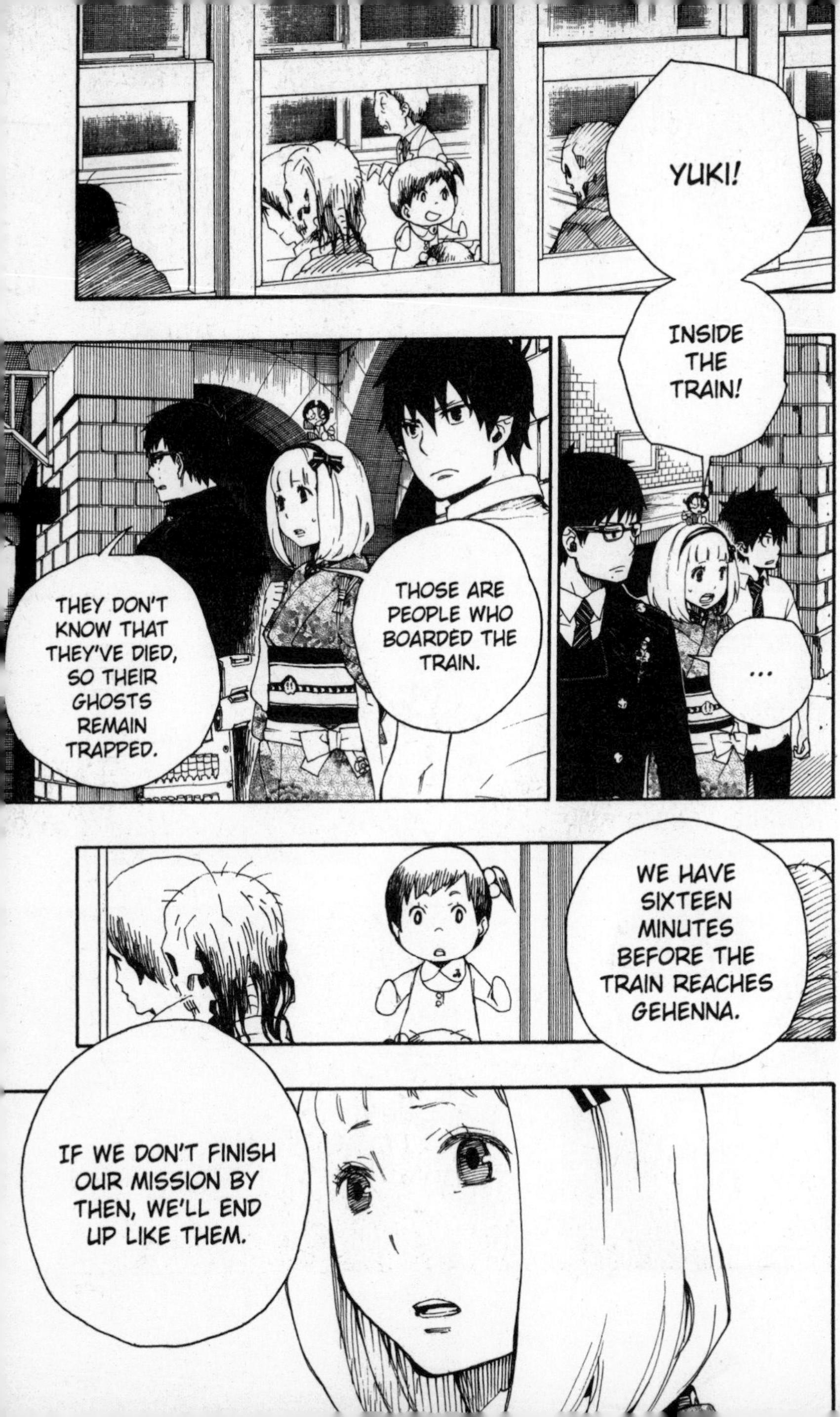
YUKI!
INSIDE THE TRAIN!
...
THOSE ARE PEOPLE WHO BOARDED THE TRAIN.
THEY DON'T KNOW THAT THEY'VE DIED, SO THEIR GHOSTS REMAIN TRAPPED.
WE HAVE SIXTEEN MINUTES BEFORE THE TRAIN REACHES GEHENNA.
IF WE DON'T FINISH OUR MISSION BY THEN, WE'LL END UP LIKE THEM.

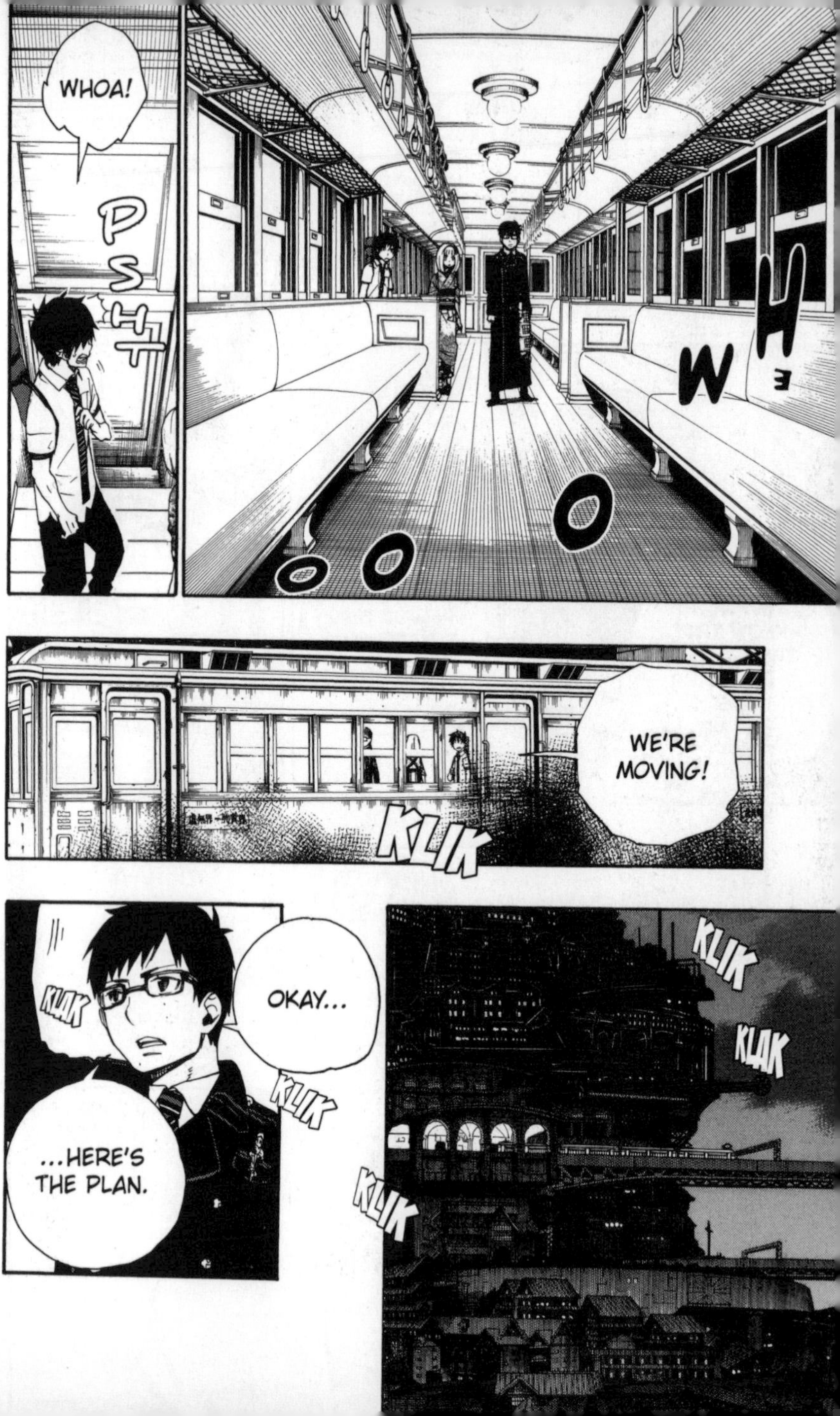
WH
OOO
WHOA!
PSHT
WE'RE MOVING!
KLIK
KLIK
KLAK
KLIK
KLIK
KLAK
OKAY...
...HERE'S THE PLAN.

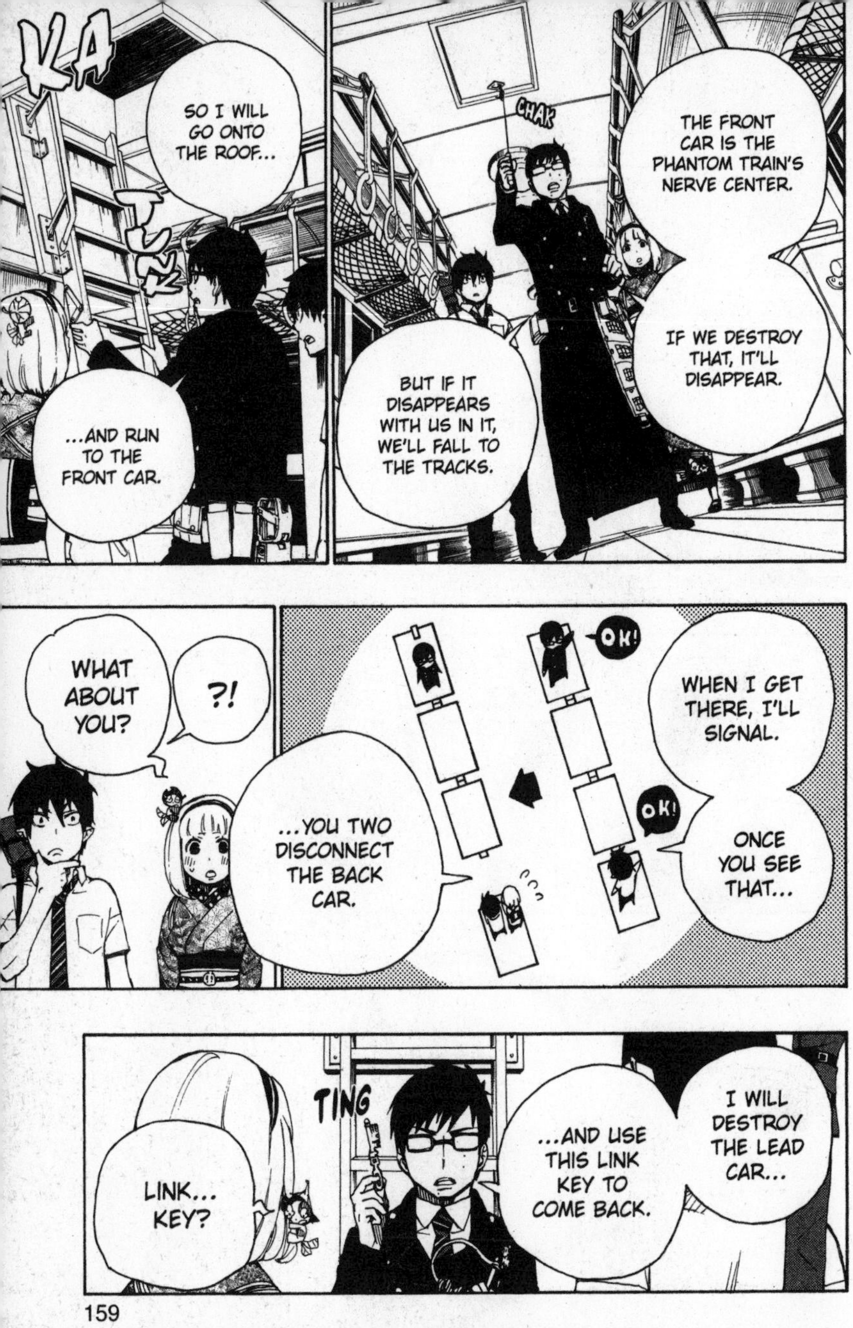
CHAK
THE FRONT CAR IS THE PHANTOM TRAIN'S NERVE CENTER.
IF WE DESTROY THAT, IT'LL DISAPPEAR.
BUT IF IT DISAPPEARS WITH US IN IT, WE'LL FALL TO THE TRACKS.
KA
SO I WILL GO ONTO THE ROOF...
...AND RUN TO THE FRONT CAR.
WHEN I GET THERE, I'LL SIGNAL.
OK!
OK!
ONCE YOU SEE THAT...
...YOU TWO DISCONNECT THE BACK CAR.
?!
WHAT ABOUT YOU?
I WILL DESTROY THE LEAD CAR...
...AND USE THIS LINK KEY TO COME BACK.
TING
LINK... KEY?

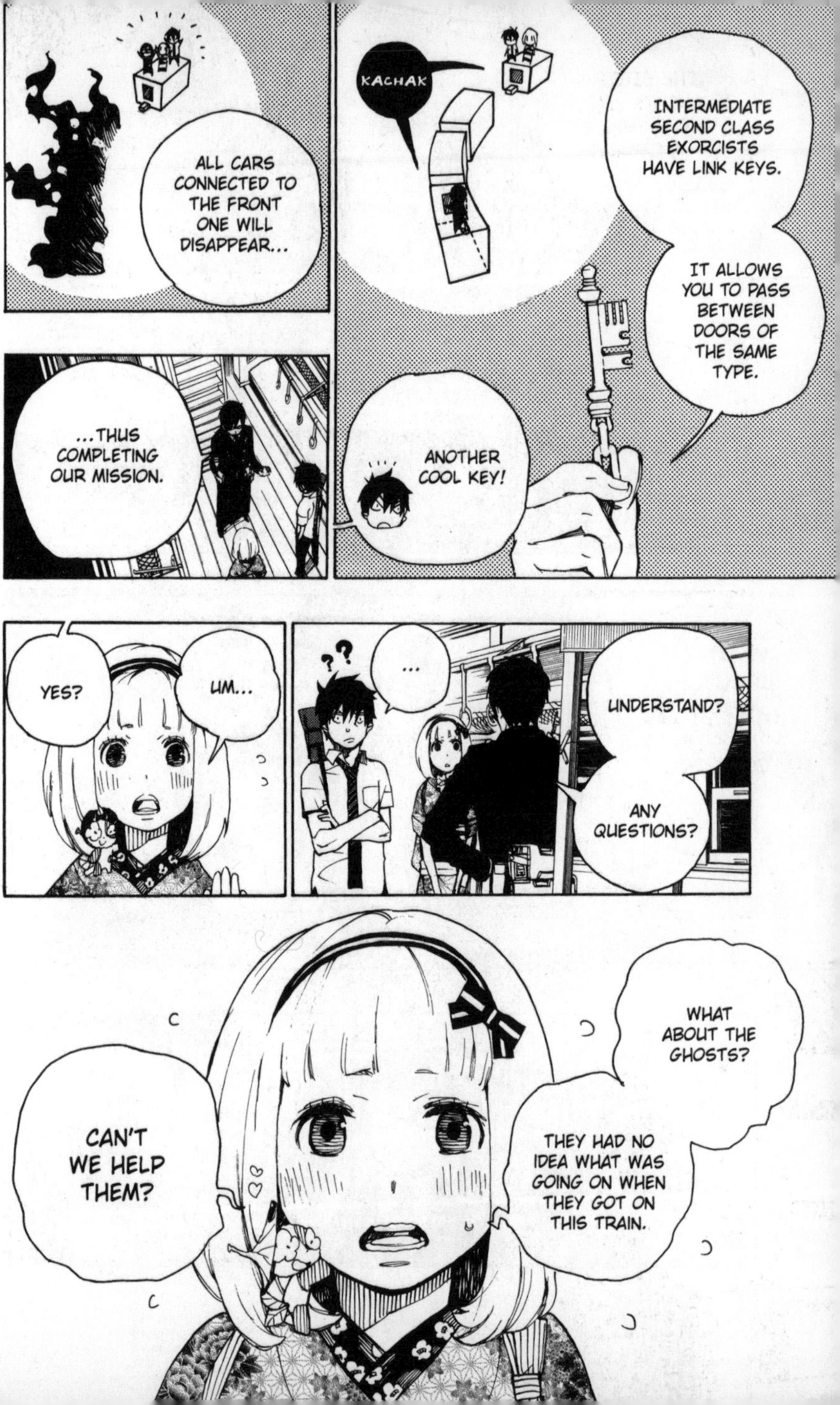
KACHAK
INTERMEDIATE SECOND CLASS EXORCISTS HAVE LINK KEYS.
IT ALLOWS YOU TO PASS BETWEEN DOORS OF THE SAME TYPE.
ANOTHER COOL KEY!
ALL CARS CONNECTED TO THE FRONT ONE WILL DISAPPEAR...
...THUS COMPLETING OUR MISSION.
UNDERSTAND?
ANY QUESTIONS?
...
UM...
YES?
WHAT ABOUT THE GHOSTS?
THEY HAD NO IDEA WHAT WAS GOING ON WHEN THEY GOT ON THIS TRAIN.
CAN'T WE HELP THEM?

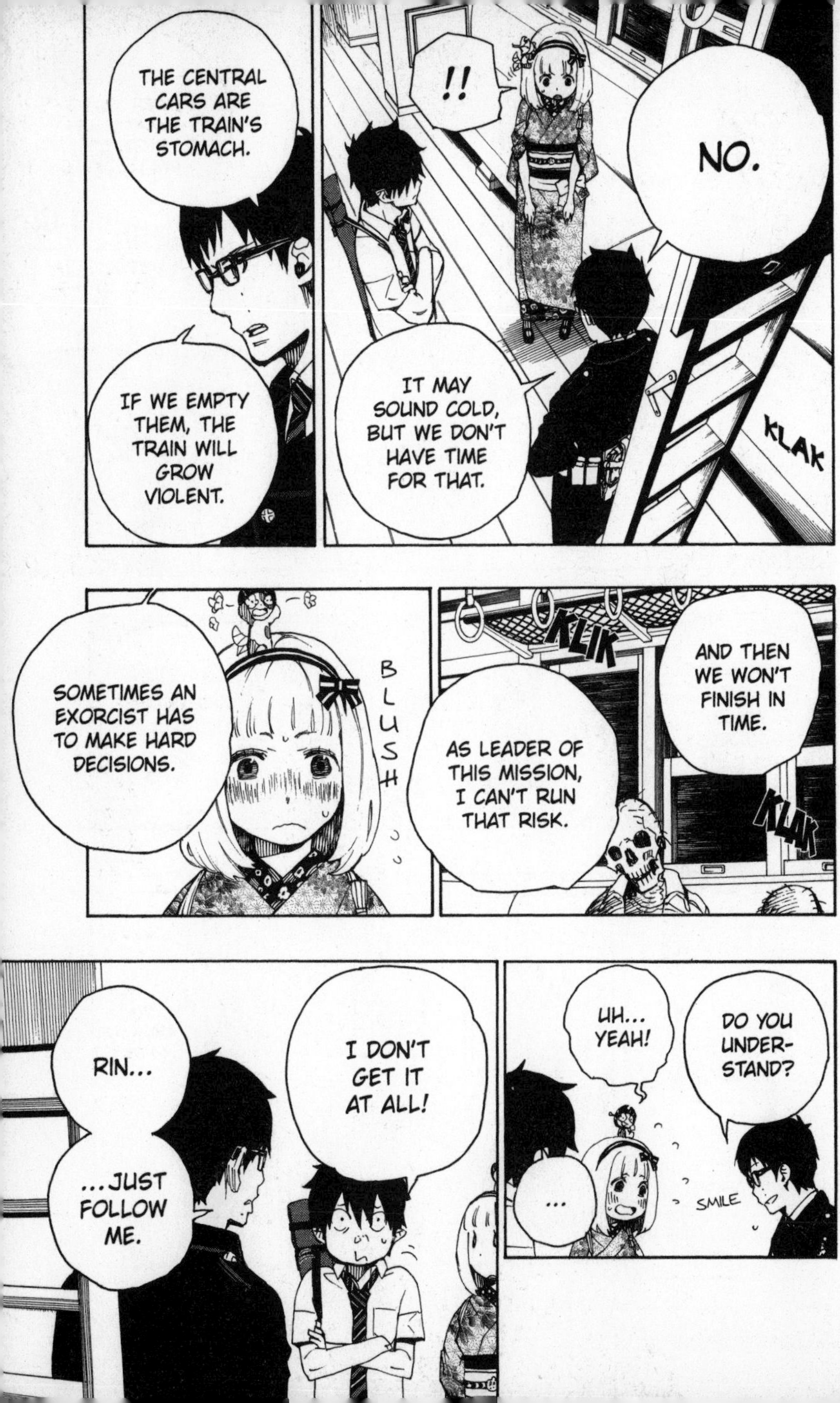
NO.
!!
KLAK
IT MAY SOUND COLD, BUT WE DON'T HAVE TIME FOR THAT.
THE CENTRAL CARS ARE THE TRAIN'S STOMACH.
IF WE EMPTY THEM, THE TRAIN WILL GROW VIOLENT.
AND THEN WE WON'T FINISH IN TIME.
KLIK
AS LEADER OF THIS MISSION, I CAN'T RUN THAT RISK.
KLAK
BLUSH
SOMETIMES AN EXORCIST HAS TO MAKE HARD DECISIONS.
DO YOU UNDER-STAND?
UH... YEAH!
SMILE
...
I DON'T GET IT AT ALL!
RIN...
...JUST FOLLOW ME.

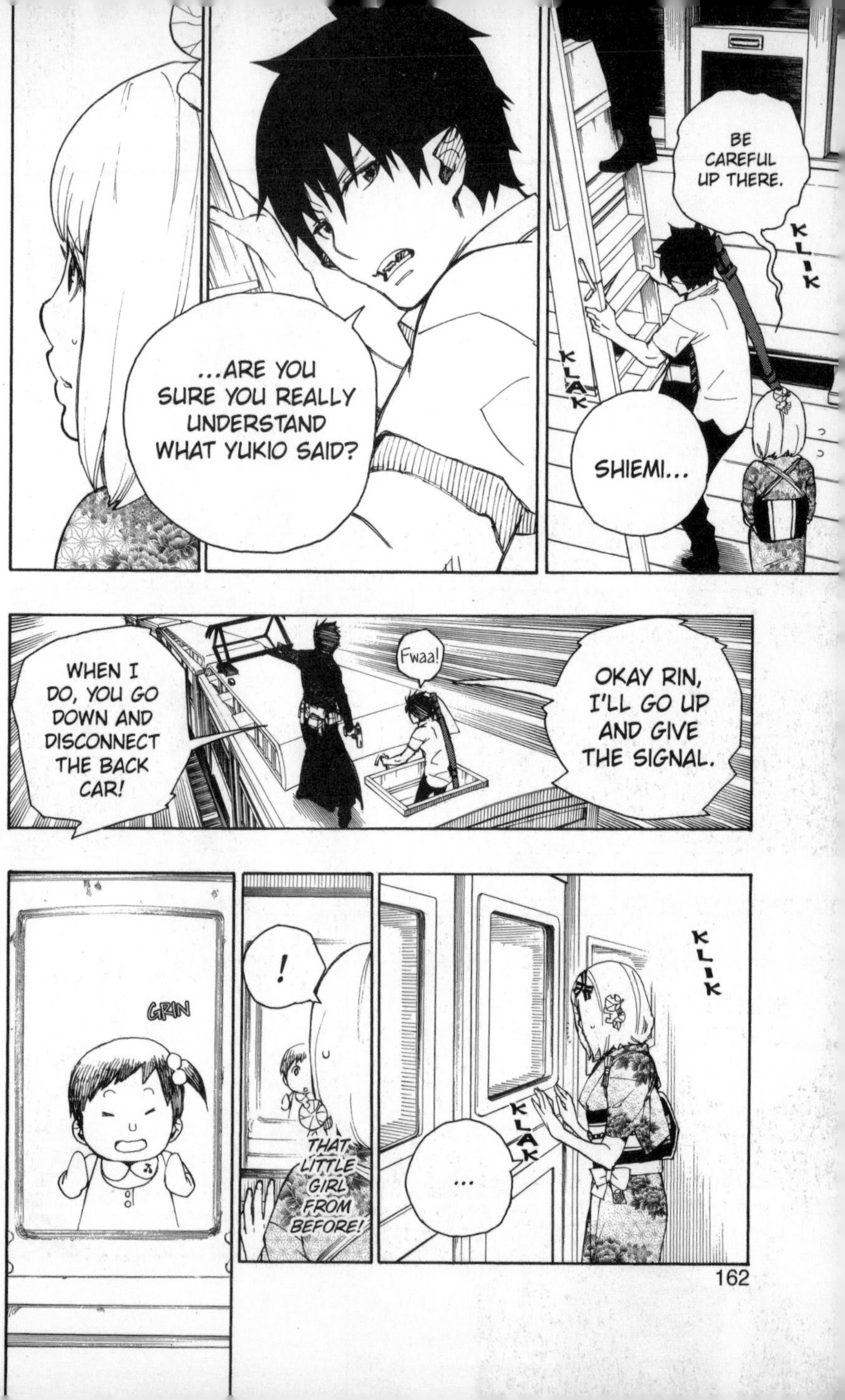
BE CAREFUL UP THERE.
KLIK
KLAK
SHIEMI...
...ARE YOU SURE YOU REALLY UNDERSTAND WHAT YUKIO SAID?
OKAY RIN, I'LL GO UP AND GIVE THE SIGNAL.
Fwaa!
WHEN I DO, YOU GO DOWN AND DISCONNECT THE BACK CAR!
KLIK
KLAK
...
!
THAT LITTLE GIRL FROM BEFORE!
GRIN

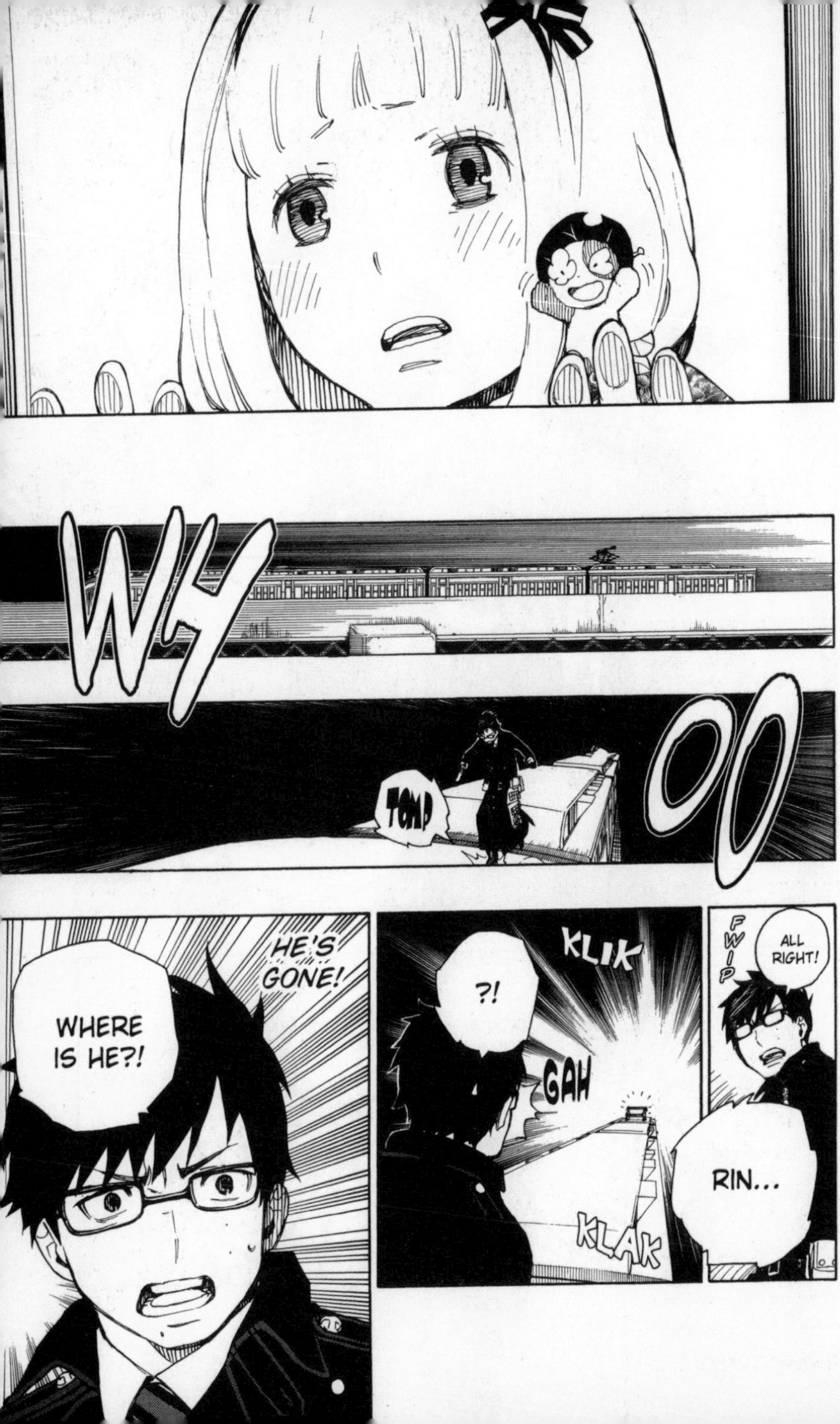
WHOO
TOMP
FWIP
ALL RIGHT!
RIN...
KLIK
?!
GAH
KLAK
HE'S GONE!
WHERE IS HE?!

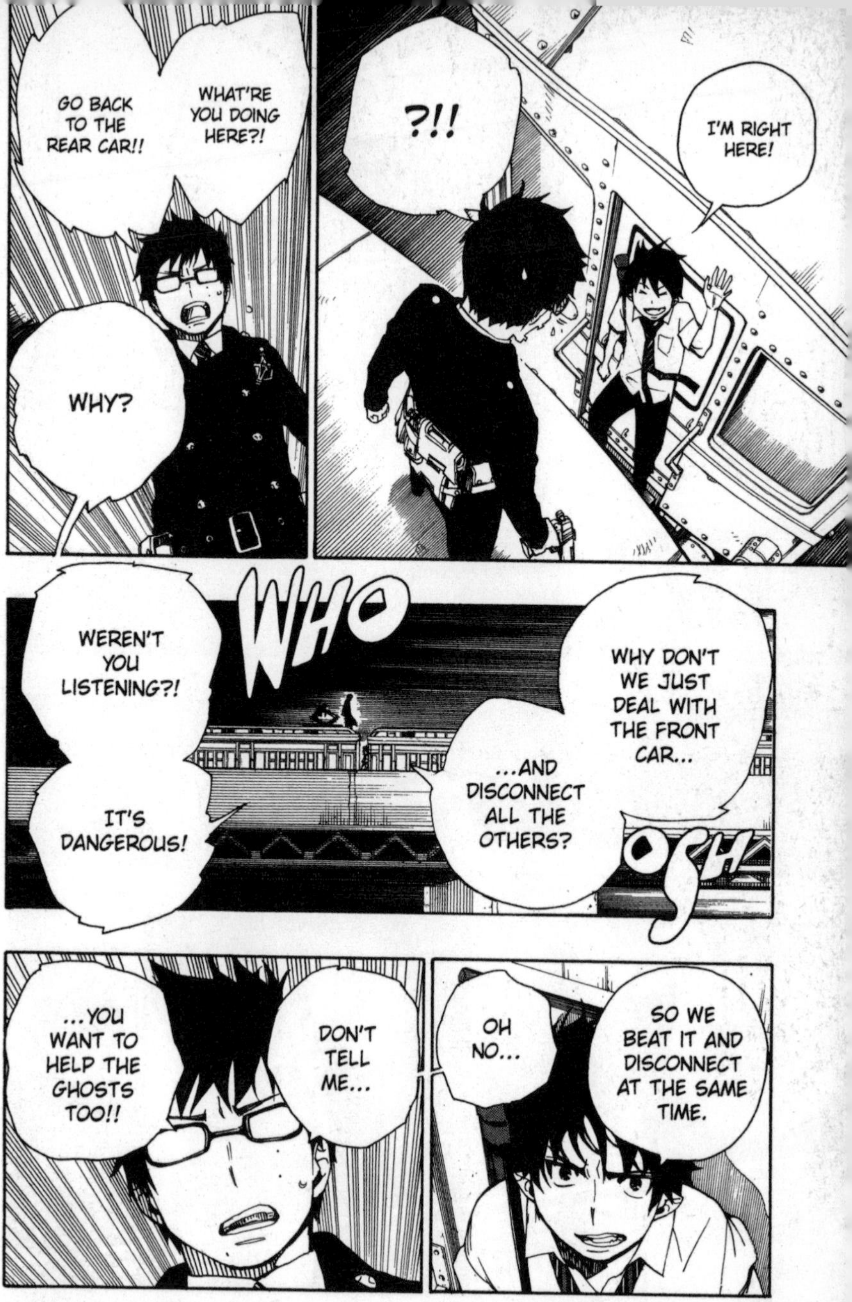
I'M RIGHT HERE!
?!!
WHAT'RE YOU DOING HERE?!
GO BACK TO THE REAR CAR!!
WHY?
WHY DON'T WE JUST DEAL WITH THE FRONT CAR...
...AND DISCONNECT ALL THE OTHERS?
WHOOSH
WEREN'T YOU LISTENING?!
IT'S DANGEROUS!
SO WE BEAT IT AND DISCONNECT AT THE SAME TIME.
OH NO...
DON'T TELL ME...
...YOU WANT TO HELP THE GHOSTS TOO!!

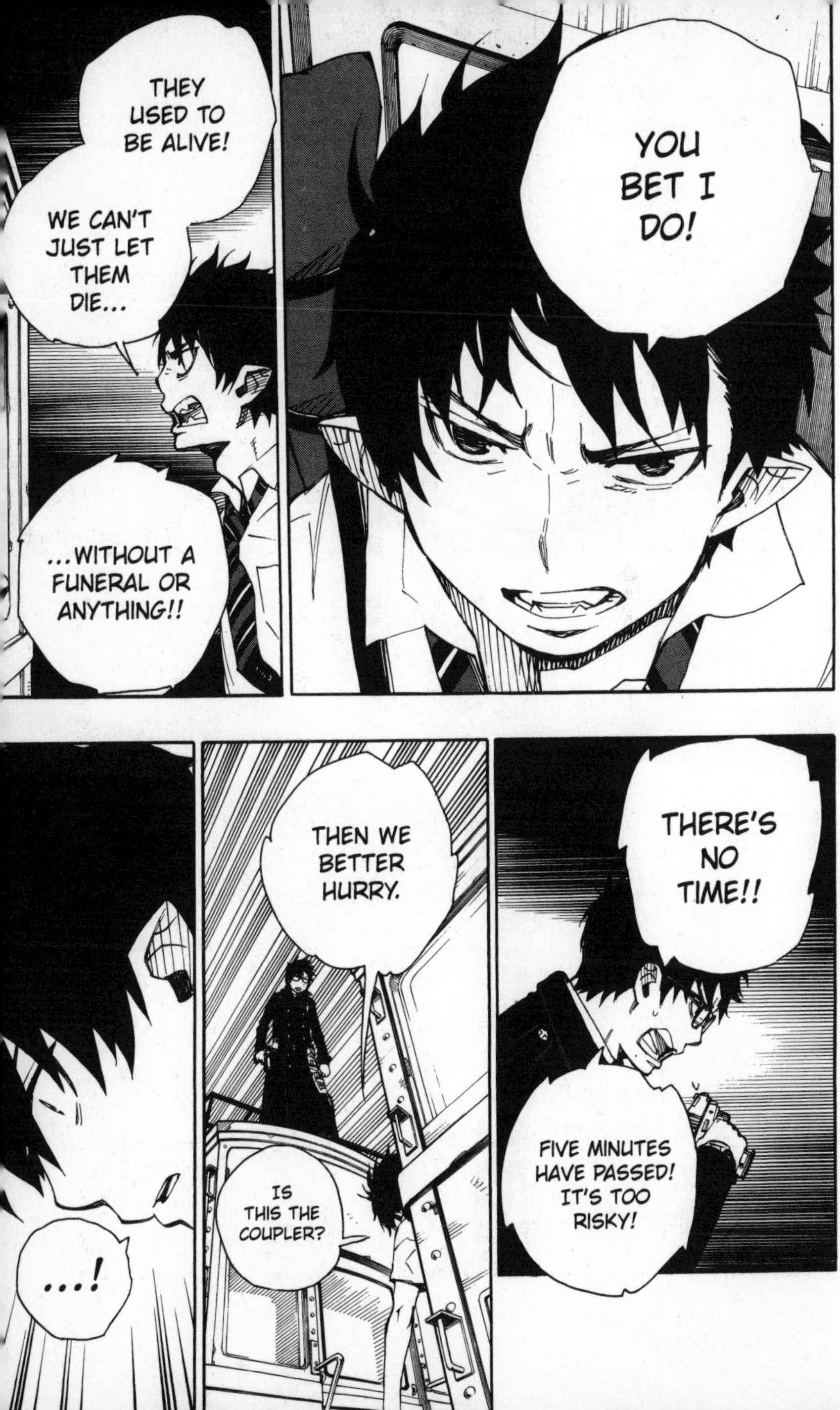
YOU BET I DO!
THEY USED TO BE ALIVE!
WE CAN'T JUST LET THEM DIE...
...WITHOUT A FUNERAL OR ANYTHING!!
THERE'S NO TIME!!
FIVE MINUTES HAVE PASSED! IT'S TOO RISKY!
THEN WE BETTER HURRY.
IS THIS THE COUPLER?
...!

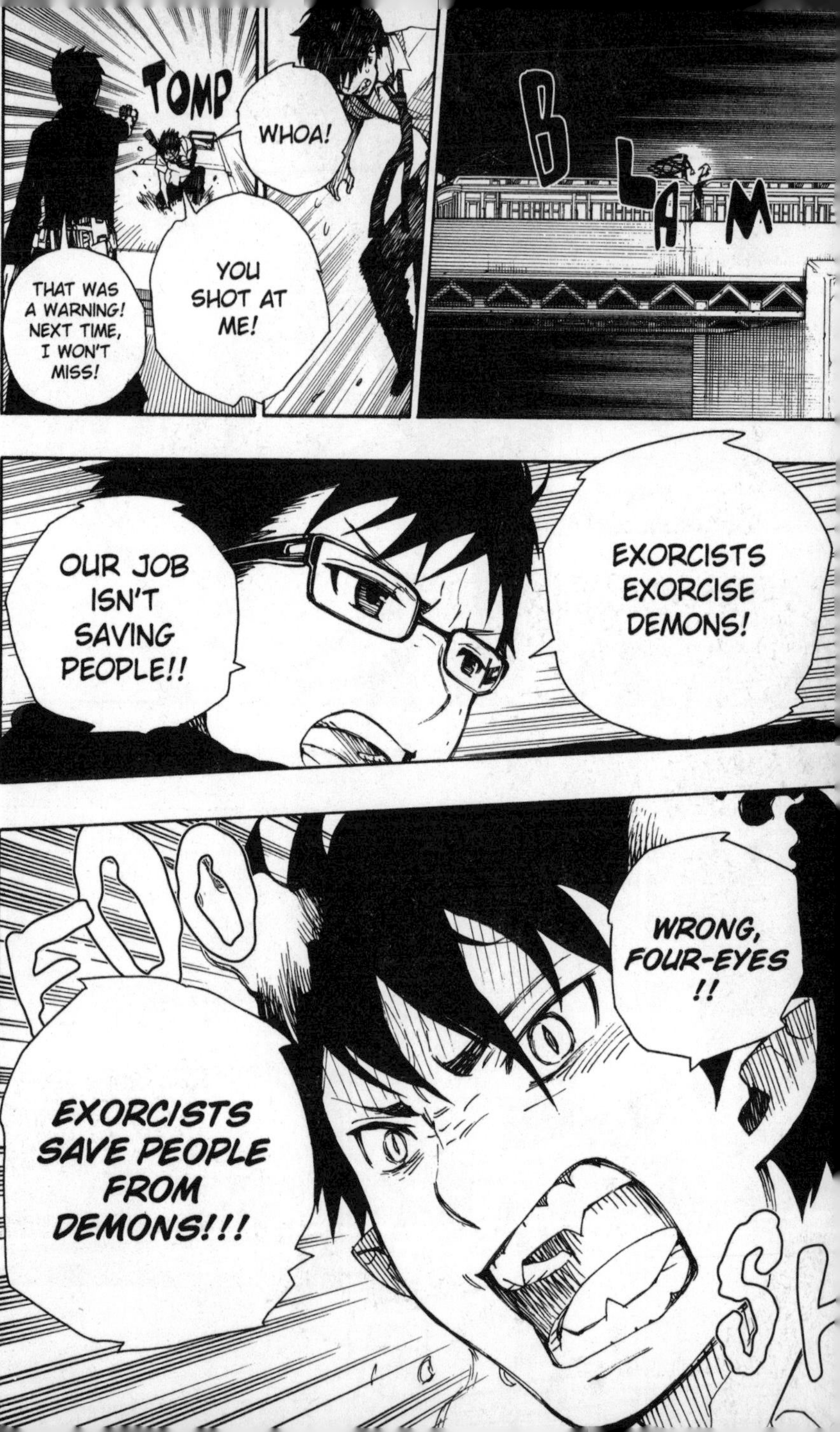
BLAM
WHOA!
TOMP
YOU SHOT AT ME!
THAT WAS A WARNING! NEXT TIME, I WON'T MISS!
EXORCISTS EXORCISE DEMONS!
OUR JOB ISN'T SAVING PEOPLE!!
WRONG, FOUR-EYES!!
EXORCISTS SAVE PEOPLE FROM DEMONS!!!

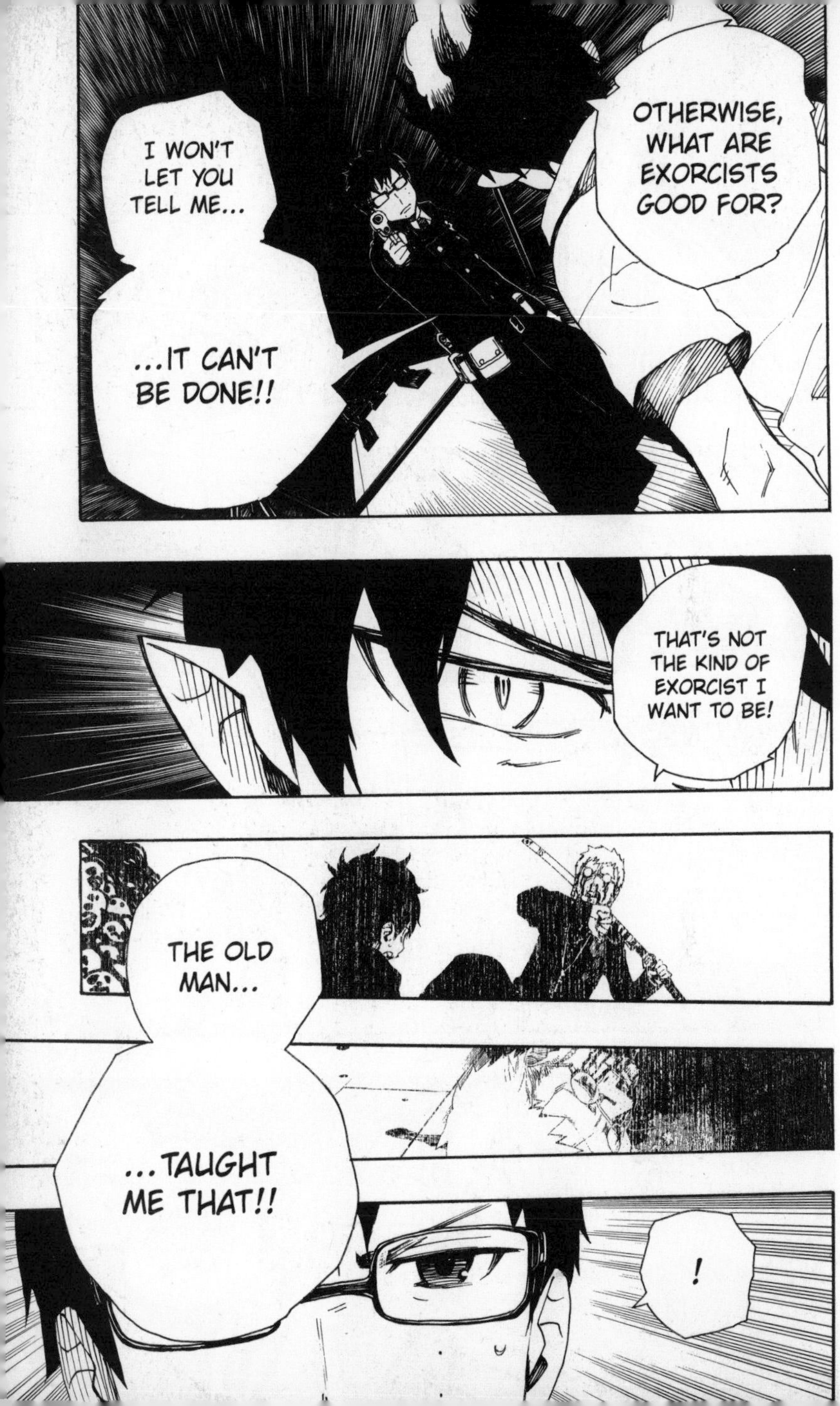
OTHERWISE, WHAT ARE EXORCISTS GOOD FOR?
I WON'T LET YOU TELL ME...
...IT CAN'T BE DONE!!
THAT'S NOT THE KIND OF EXORCIST I WANT TO BE!
THE OLD MAN...
...TAUGHT ME THAT!!
!

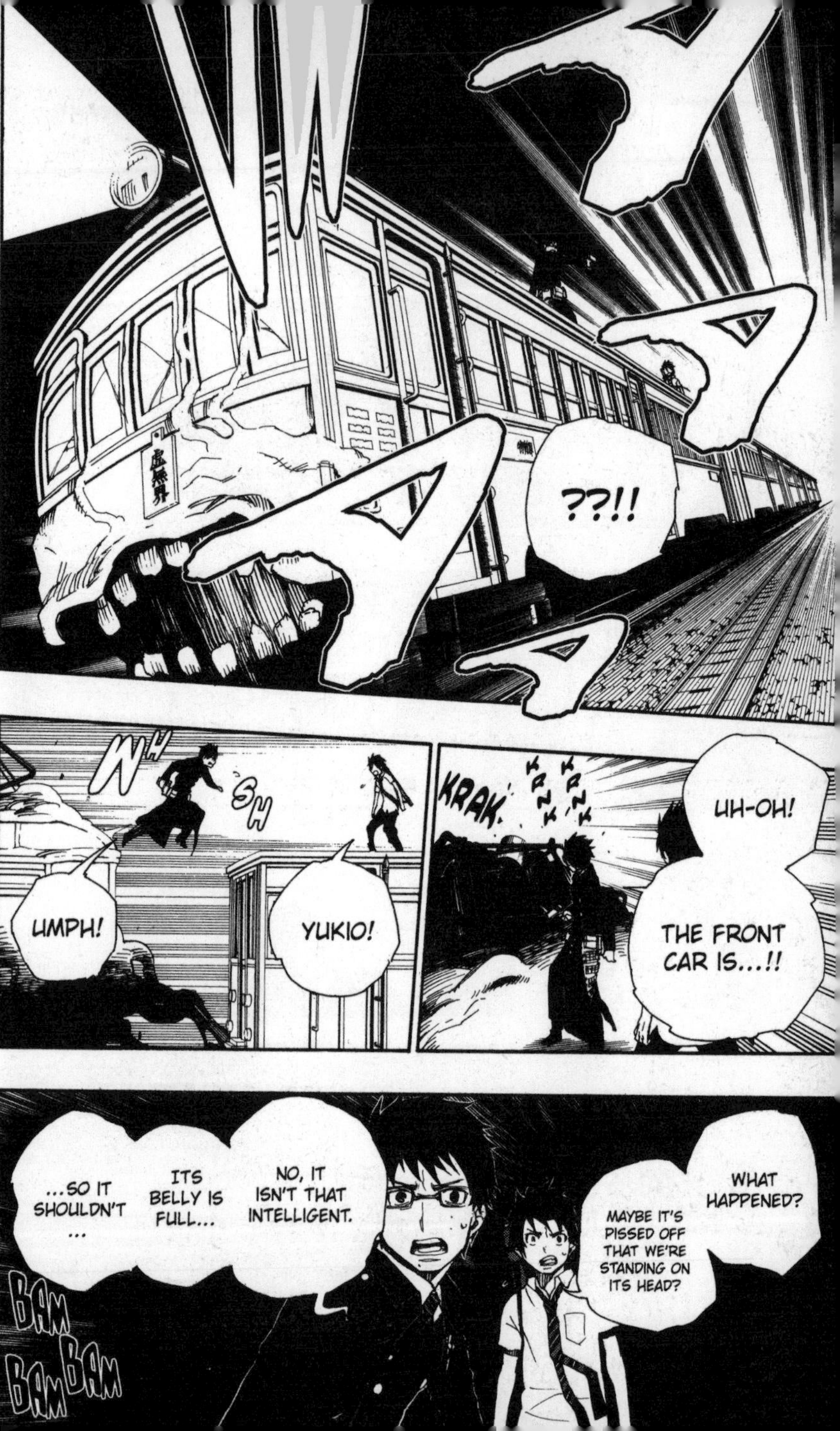
VWAAAA
??!!
UH-OH!
THE FRONT CAR IS...!!
KRAK
KRNK KRNK
YUKIO!
WHSH
UMPH!
WHAT HAPPENED?
MAYBE IT'S PISSED OFF THAT WE'RE STANDING ON ITS HEAD?
NO, IT ISN'T THAT INTELLIGENT.
ITS BELLY IS FULL...
...SO IT SHOULDN'T ...
BAM BAM BAM

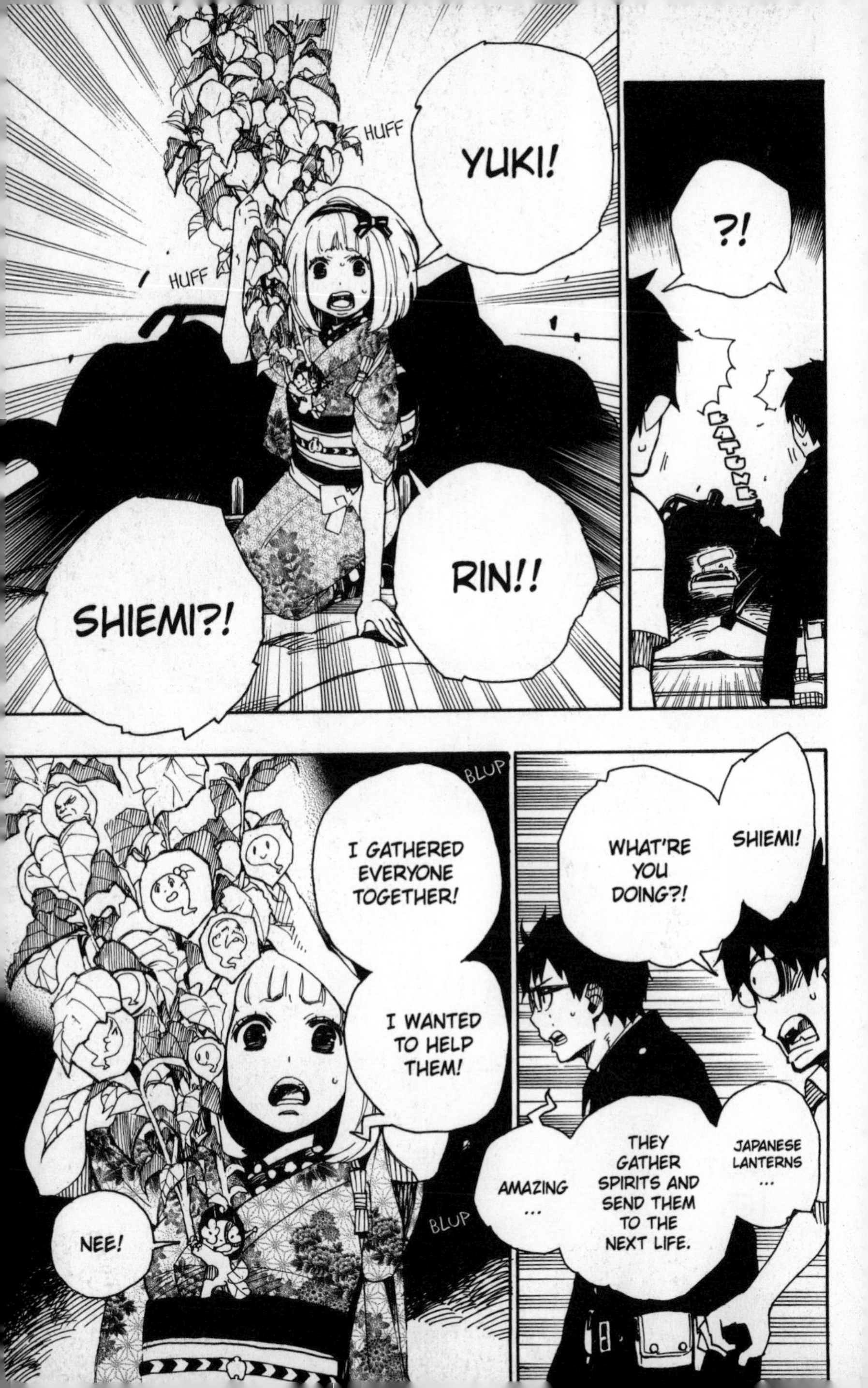
?!
KATUNK
YUKI!
HUFF
HUFF
RIN!!
SHIEMI?!
SHIEMI!
WHAT'RE YOU DOING?!
JAPANESE LANTERNS...
THEY GATHER SPIRITS AND SEND THEM TO THE NEXT LIFE.
AMAZING...
BLUP
I GATHERED EVERYONE TOGETHER!
I WANTED TO HELP THEM!
BLUP
NEE!

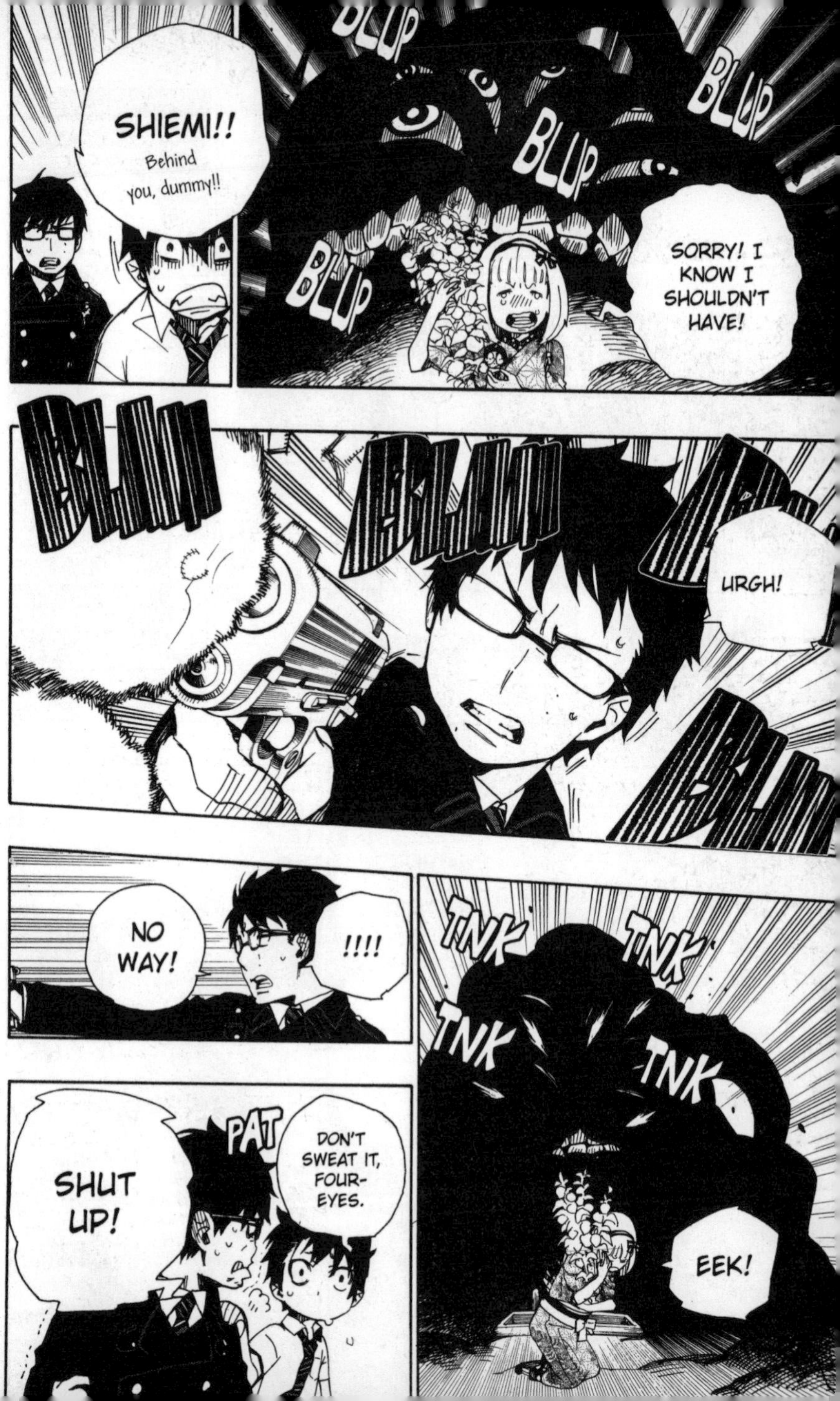
BLUP
BLUP
BLUP
BLUP
SORRY! I KNOW I SHOULDN'T HAVE!
SHIEMI!! Behind you, dummy!!
BLAM
URGH!
BLAM
BLAM
BLAM
TNK
TNK
TNK
TNK
EEK!
!!!!
NO WAY!
DON'T SWEAT IT, FOUR-EYES.
PAT
SHUT UP!

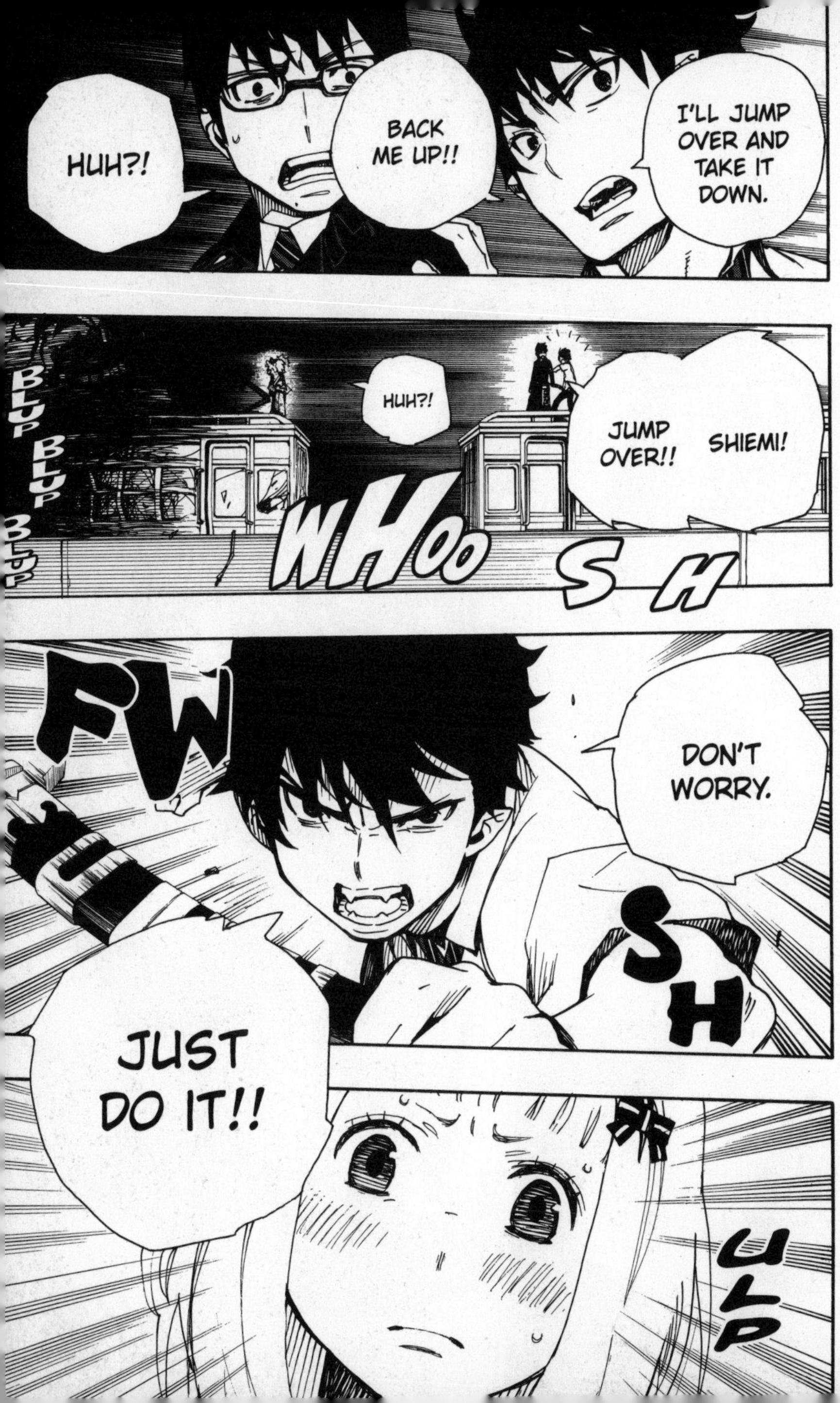
I'LL JUMP OVER AND TAKE IT DOWN.
BACK ME UP!!
HUH?!
SHIEMI!
JUMP OVER!!
HUH?!
WHOOSH
BLUP BLUP BLUP
DON'T WORRY.
FWSH
JUST DO IT!!
ULP

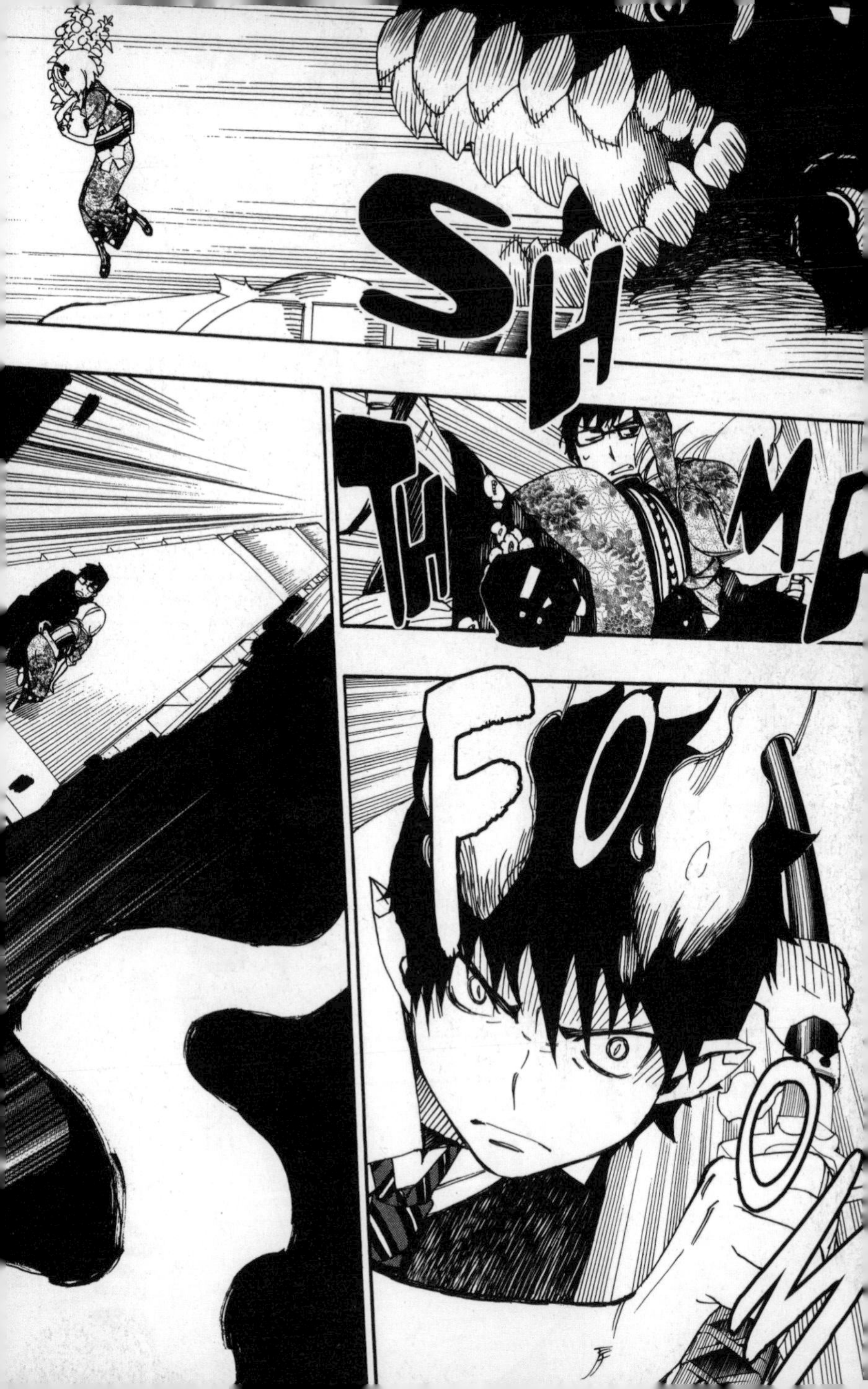
SH
TH
!
M
FOOM

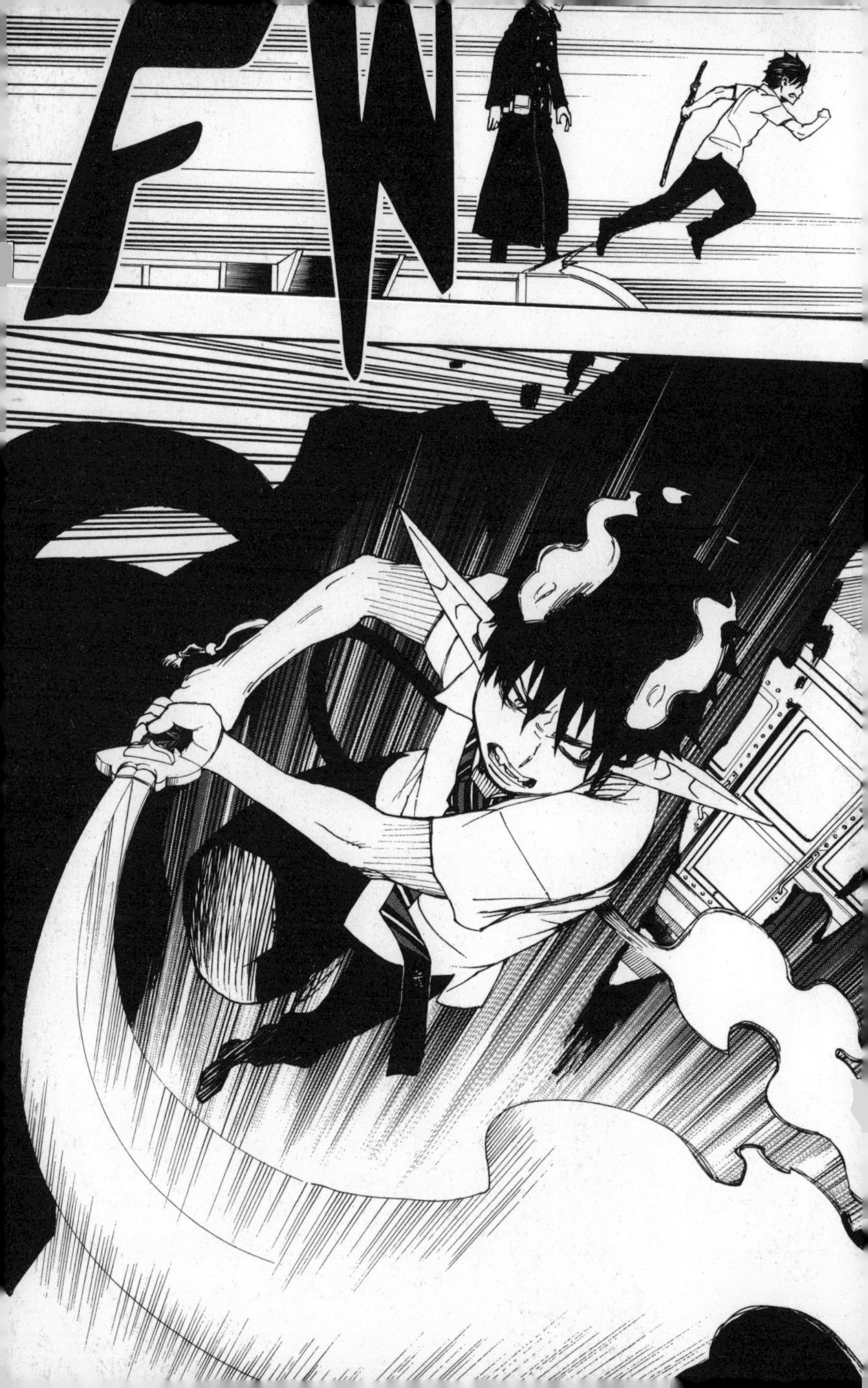
FW

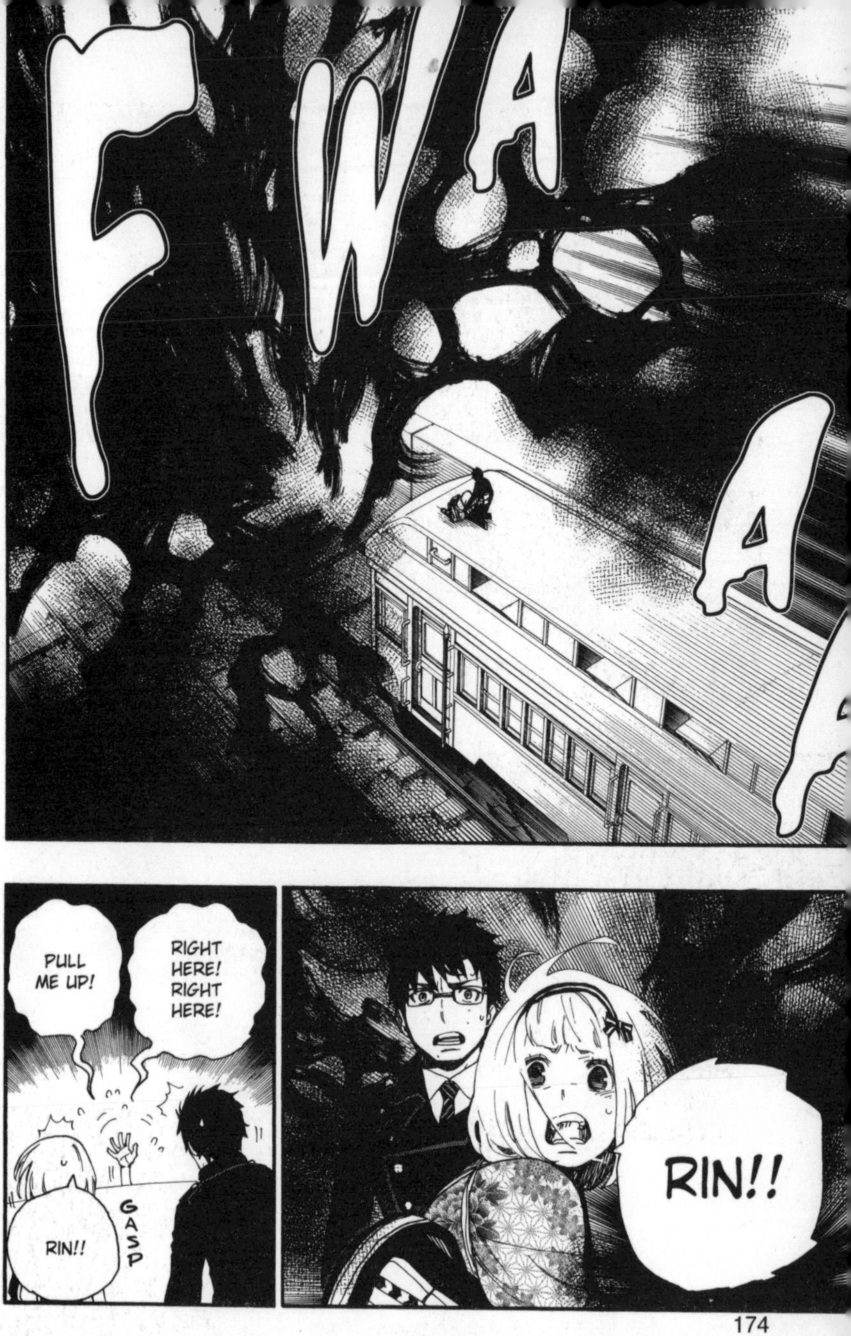
FWAAA
RIN!!
RIGHT HERE! RIGHT HERE!
PULL ME UP!
GASP
RIN!!

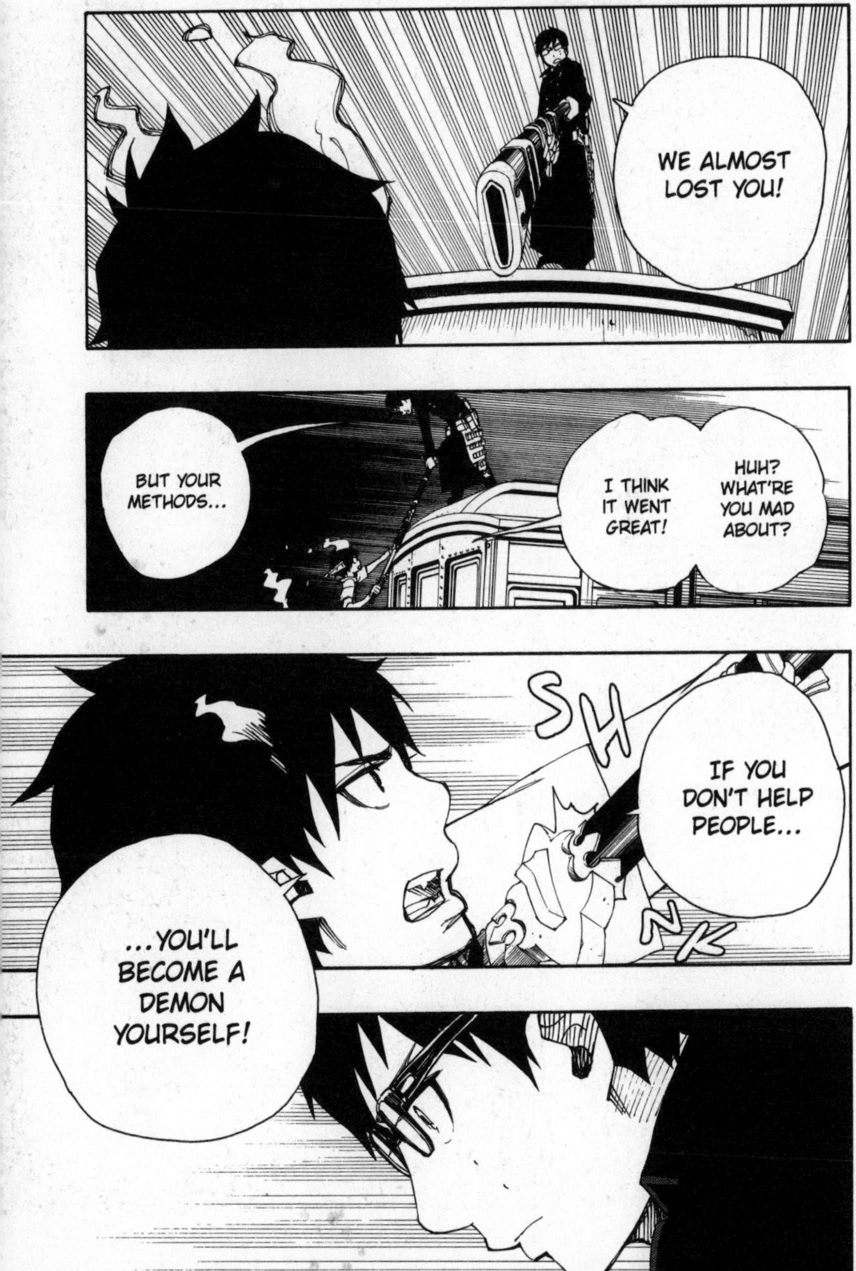
WE ALMOST LOST YOU!
HUH? WHAT'RE YOU MAD ABOUT?
I THINK IT WENT GREAT!
BUT YOUR METHODS...
SHNK
IF YOU DON'T HELP PEOPLE...
...YOU'LL BECOME A DEMON YOURSELF!

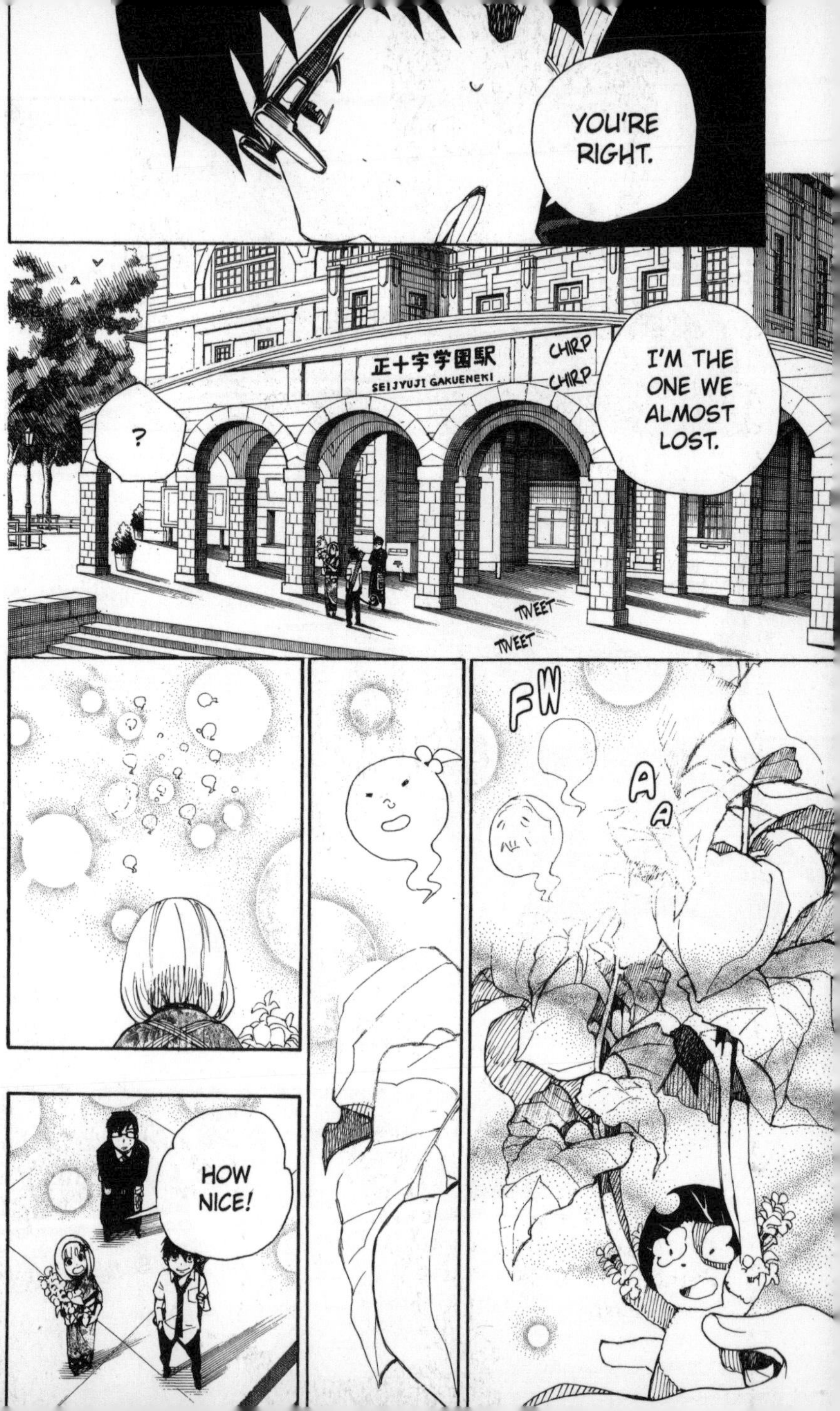
YOU'RE RIGHT.
I'M THE ONE WE ALMOST LOST.
CHIRP CHIRP
正十字学園駅
SEIJYUJI GAKUENEKI
?
TWEET TWEET
FW
A A
HOW NICE!

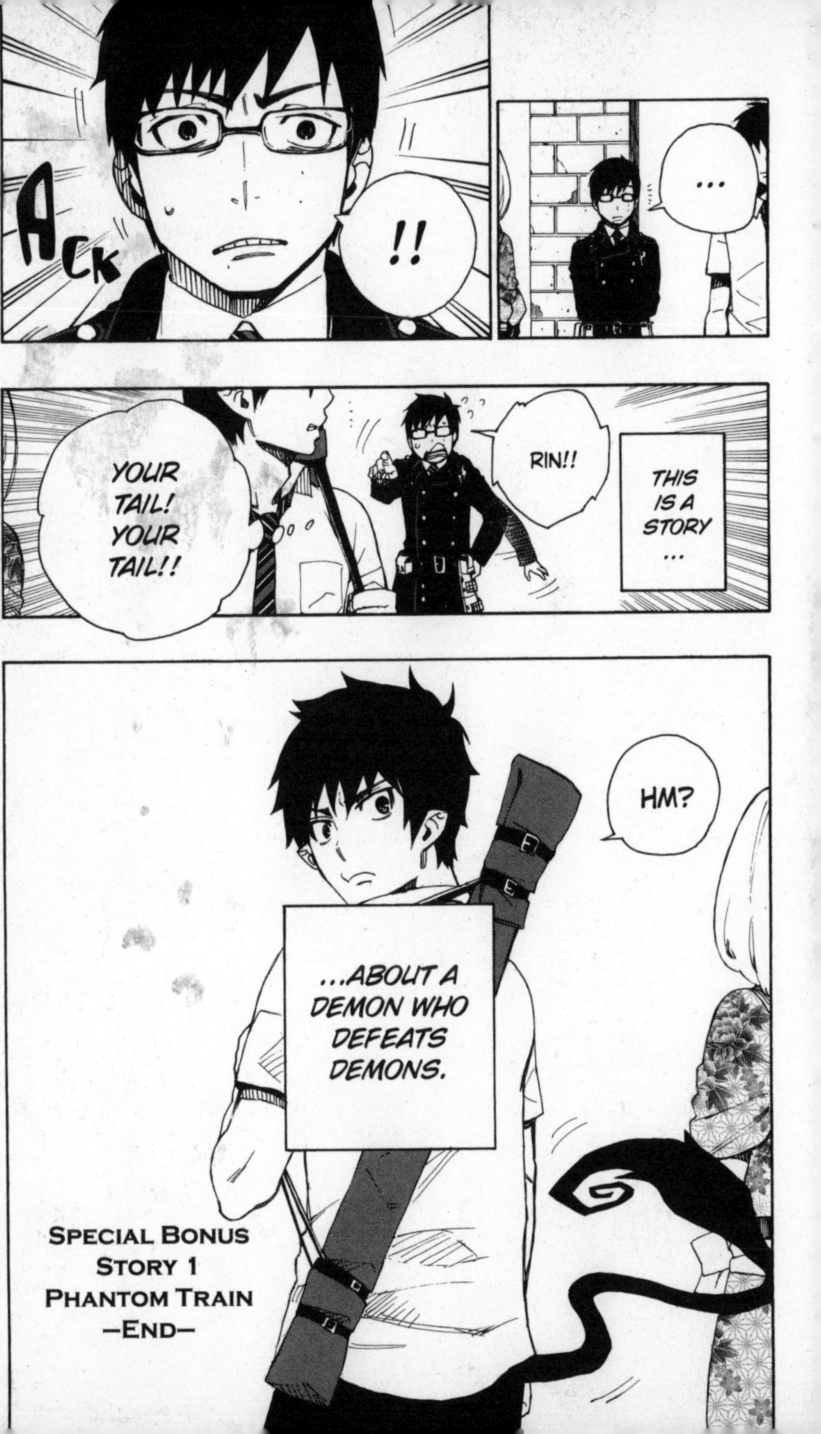
...
ACK
!!
THIS IS A STORY ...
RIN!!
YOUR TAIL! YOUR TAIL!!
HM?
...ABOUT A DEMON WHO DEFEATS DEMONS.
SPECIAL BONUS STORY 1 PHANTOM TRAIN —END—

Blue Exorcist Special Bonus Story 1 Phantom Train

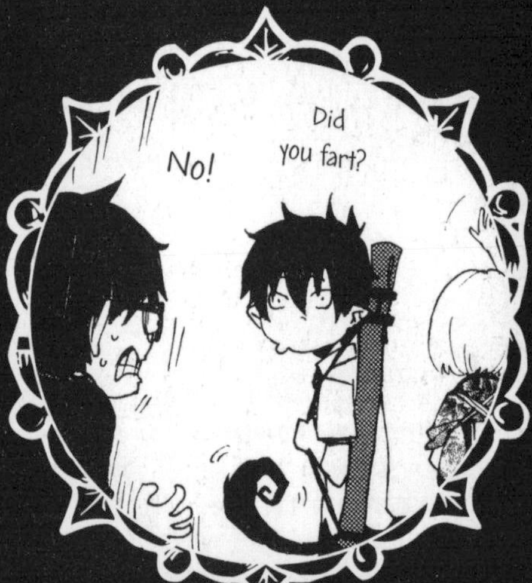
Did you fart?
No!

Special Bonus Story 2
Kuro Runs Away

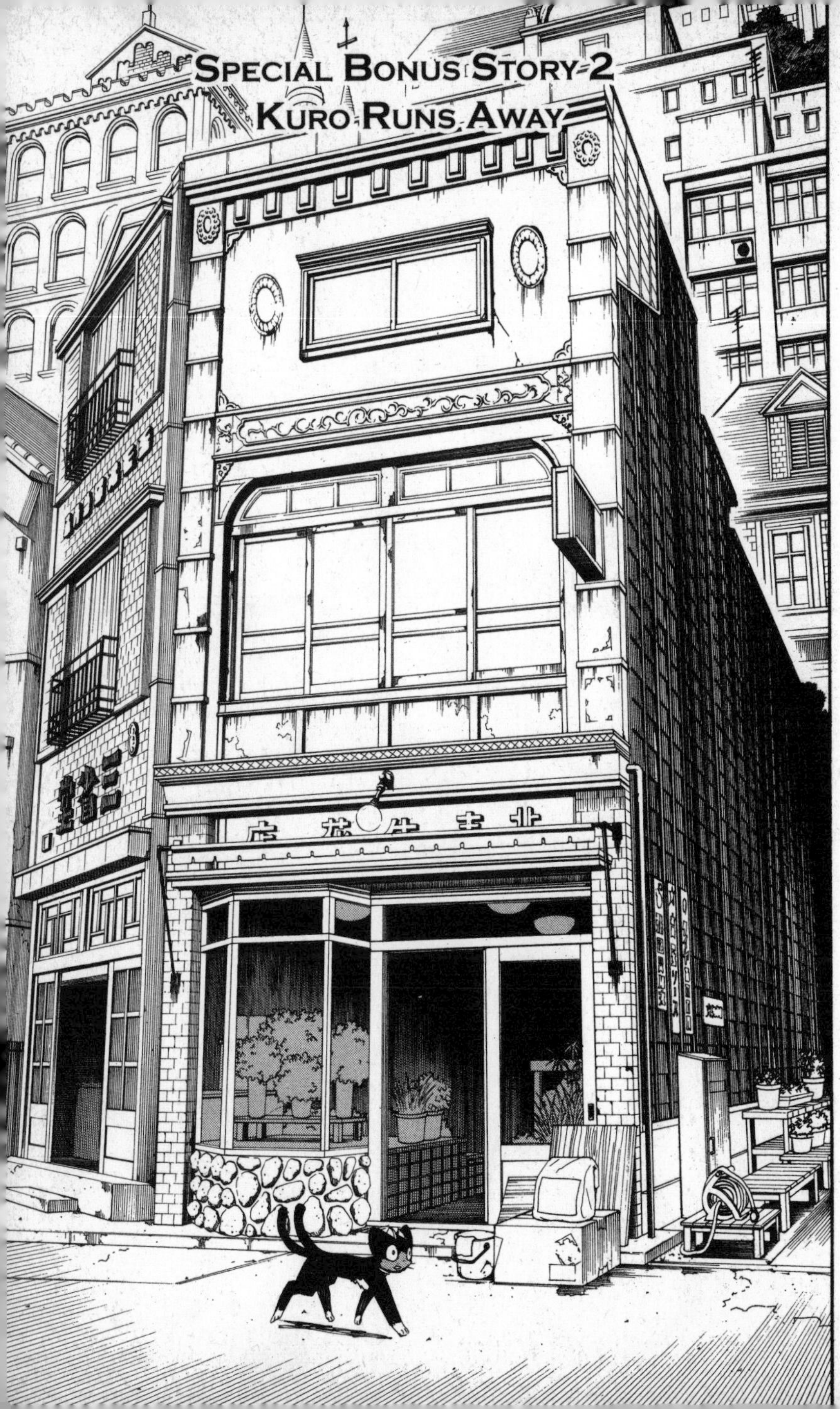

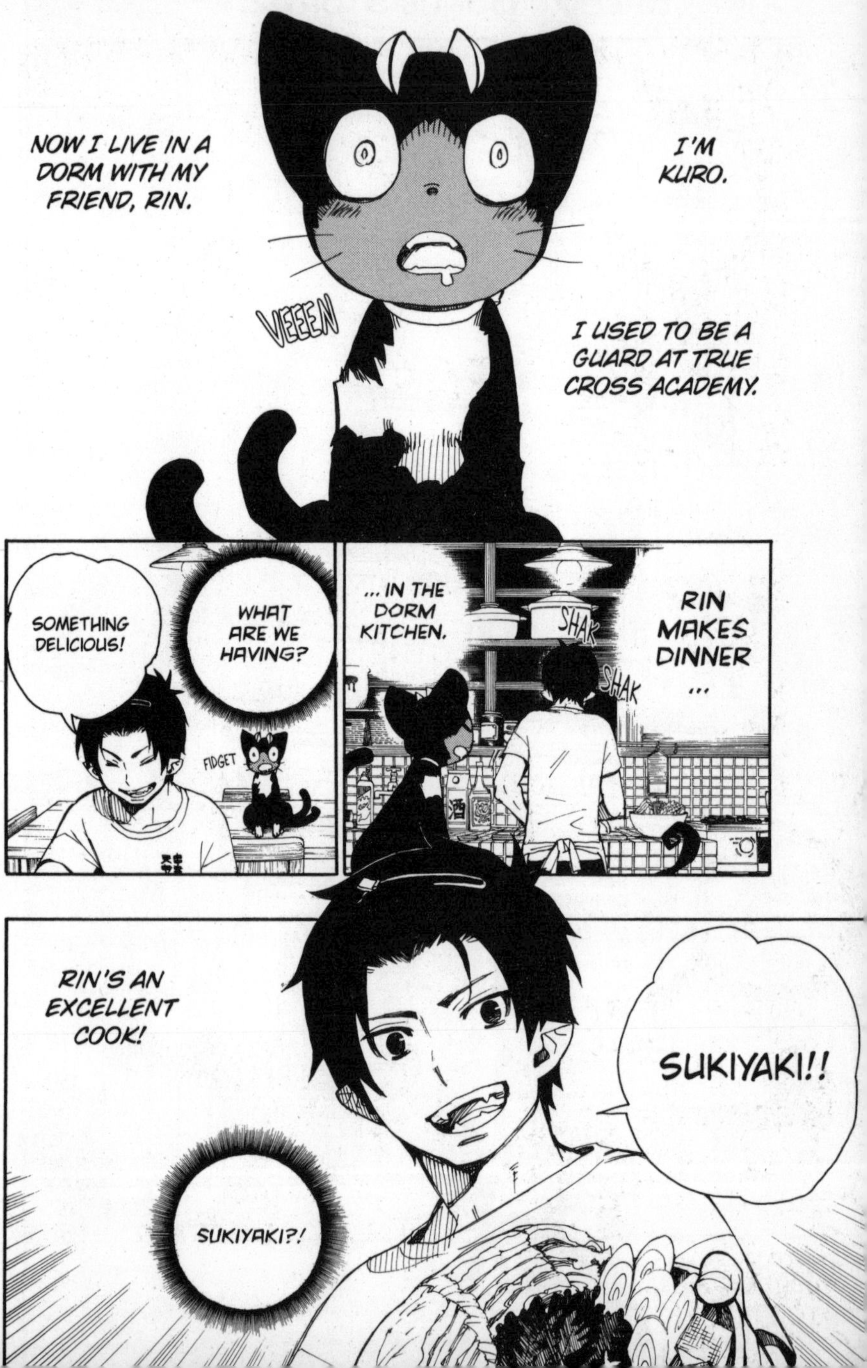
I'M KURO.
I USED TO BE A GUARD AT TRUE CROSS ACADEMY.
NOW I LIVE IN A DORM WITH MY FRIEND, RIN.
VEEEN
RIN MAKES DINNER ...
SHAK
SHAK
... IN THE DORM KITCHEN.
WHAT ARE WE HAVING?
FIDGET
SOMETHING DELICIOUS!
SUKIYAKI!!
RIN'S AN EXCELLENT COOK!
SUKIYAKI?!

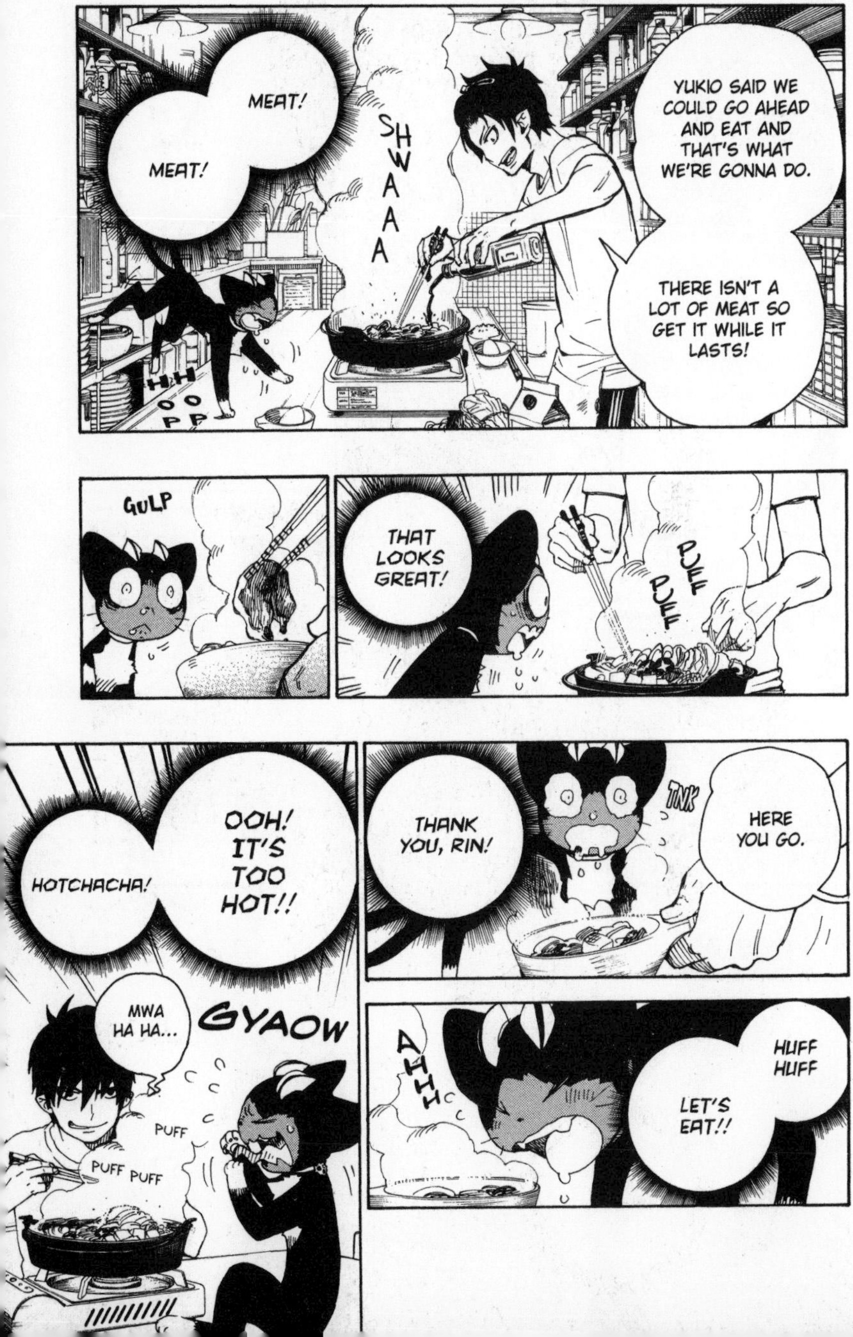
YUKIO SAID WE COULD GO AHEAD AND EAT AND THAT'S WHAT WE'RE GONNA DO.
THERE ISN'T A LOT OF MEAT SO GET IT WHILE IT LASTS!
SHWAAAA
MEAT!
MEAT!
HOOP
PUFF PUFF
THAT LOOKS GREAT!
GULP
HERE YOU GO.
TNK
THANK YOU, RIN!
HUFF HUFF
LET'S EAT!!
AHHH
OOH! IT'S TOO HOT!!
HOTCHACHA!
GYAOW
MWA HA HA...
PUFF
PUFF PUFF

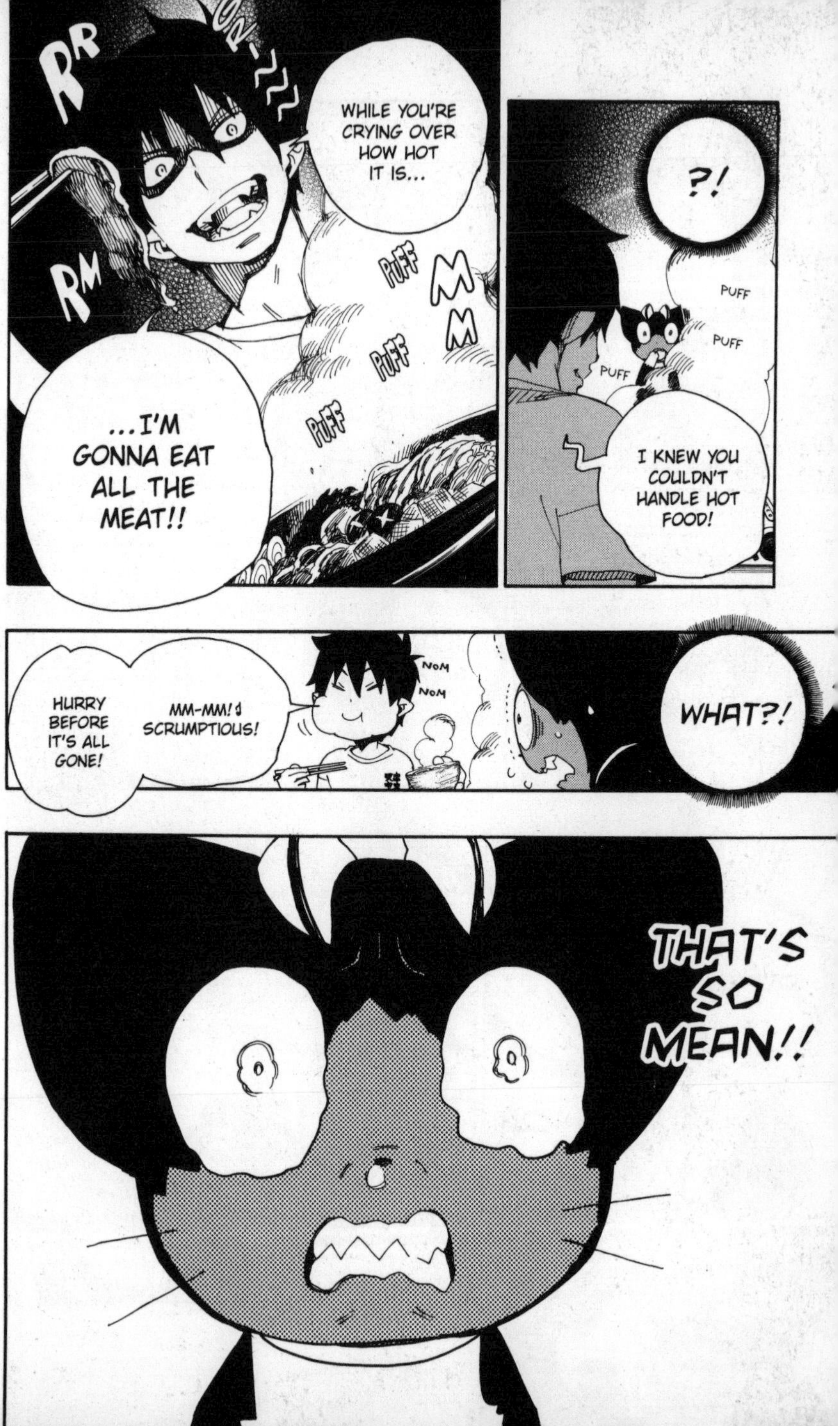
?!
PUFF
PUFF
PUFF
I KNEW YOU COULDN'T HANDLE HOT FOOD!
RR
WHILE YOU'RE CRYING OVER HOW HOT IT IS...
RM
PUFF
MM
MM
PUFF
PUFF
...I'M GONNA EAT ALL THE MEAT!!
WHAT?!
NOM
NOM
MM-MM! ♪ SCRUMPTIOUS!
HURRY BEFORE IT'S ALL GONE!
THAT'S SO MEAN!!

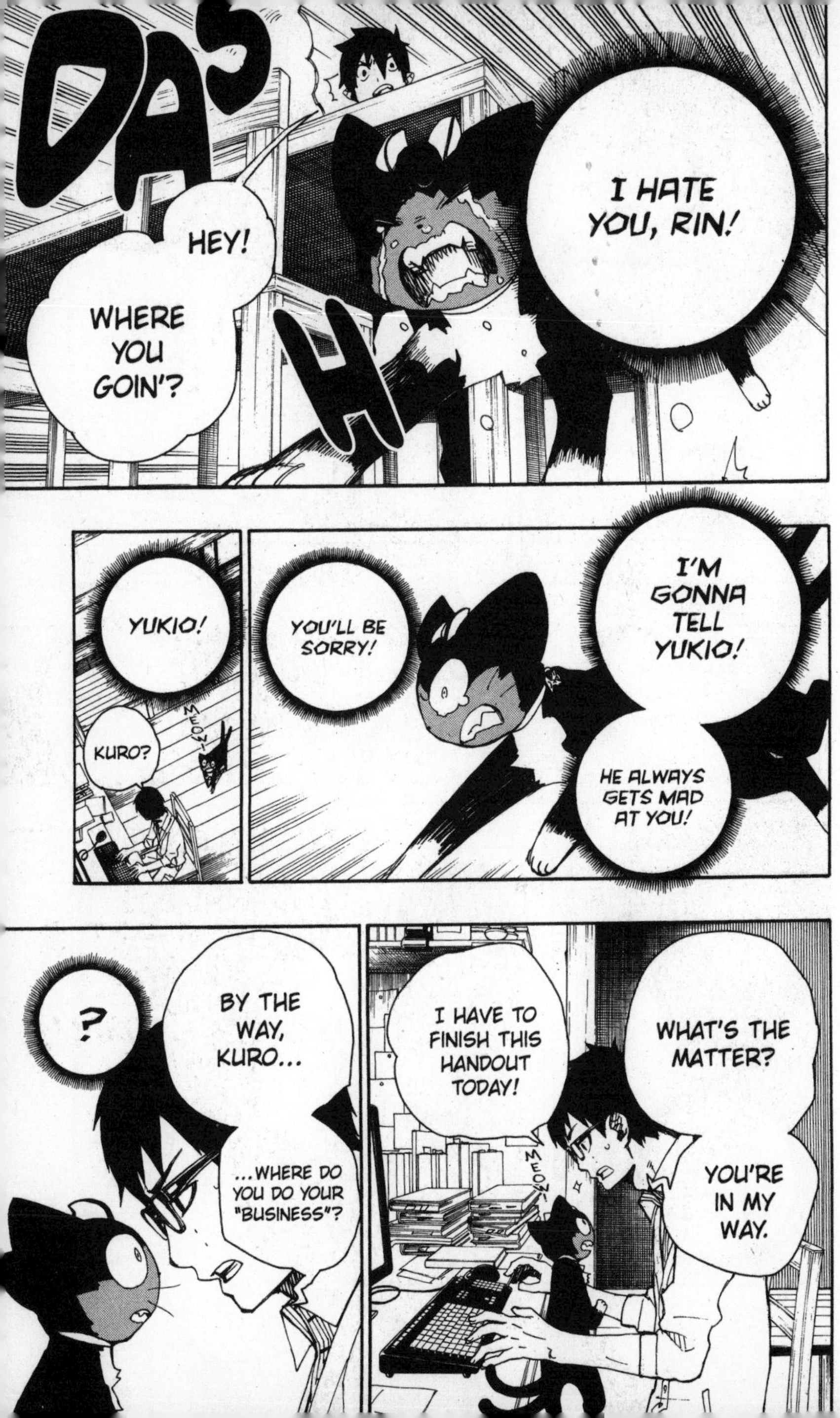
I HATE YOU, RIN!
DASH
HEY!
WHERE YOU GOIN'?
I'M GONNA TELL YUKIO!
HE ALWAYS GETS MAD AT YOU!
YOU'LL BE SORRY!
YUKIO!
MEOW!
KURO?
WHAT'S THE MATTER?
YOU'RE IN MY WAY.
I HAVE TO FINISH THIS HANDOUT TODAY!
MEOW!
?
BY THE WAY, KURO...
...WHERE DO YOU DO YOUR "BUSINESS"?

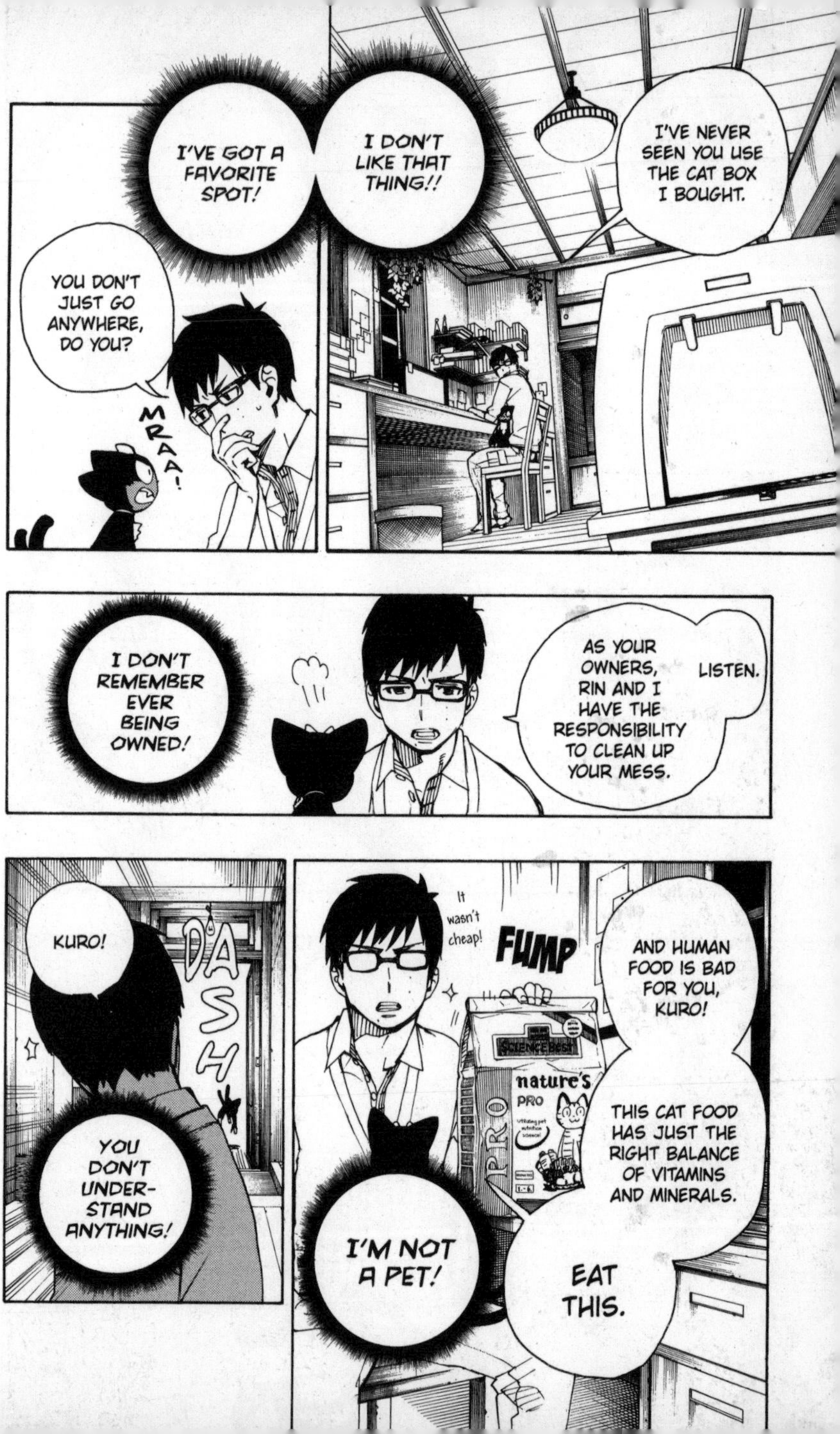
I'VE NEVER SEEN YOU USE THE CAT BOX I BOUGHT.
I DON'T LIKE THAT THING!!
I'VE GOT A FAVORITE SPOT!
YOU DON'T JUST GO ANYWHERE, DO YOU?
MRAAA!
LISTEN.
AS YOUR OWNERS, RIN AND I HAVE THE RESPONSIBILITY TO CLEAN UP YOUR MESS.
I DON'T REMEMBER EVER BEING OWNED!
AND HUMAN FOOD IS BAD FOR YOU, KURO!
It wasn't cheap!
FUMP
SCIENCE BEST
nature's
PRO
THIS CAT FOOD HAS JUST THE RIGHT BALANCE OF VITAMINS AND MINERALS.
EAT THIS.
I'M NOT A PET!
KURO!
DASH
YOU DON'T UNDERSTAND ANYTHING!

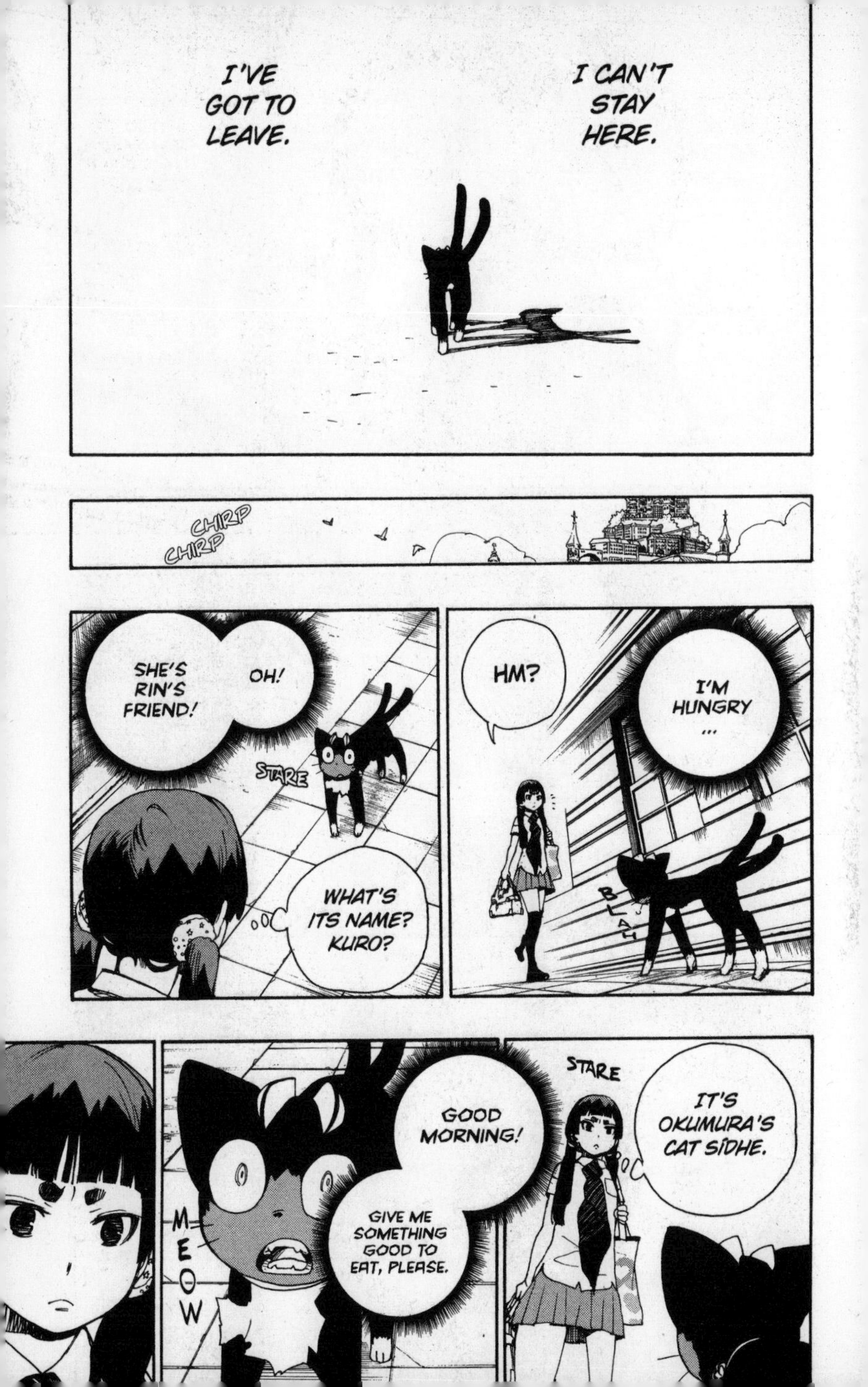
I CAN'T STAY HERE.
I'VE GOT TO LEAVE.
CHIRP
CHIRP
I'M HUNGRY ...
HM?
BLAH
OH!
SHE'S RIN'S FRIEND!
STARE
WHAT'S ITS NAME? KURO?
IT'S OKUMURA'S CAT SÍDHE.
STARE
GOOD MORNING!
GIVE ME SOMETHING GOOD TO EAT, PLEASE.
MEOW

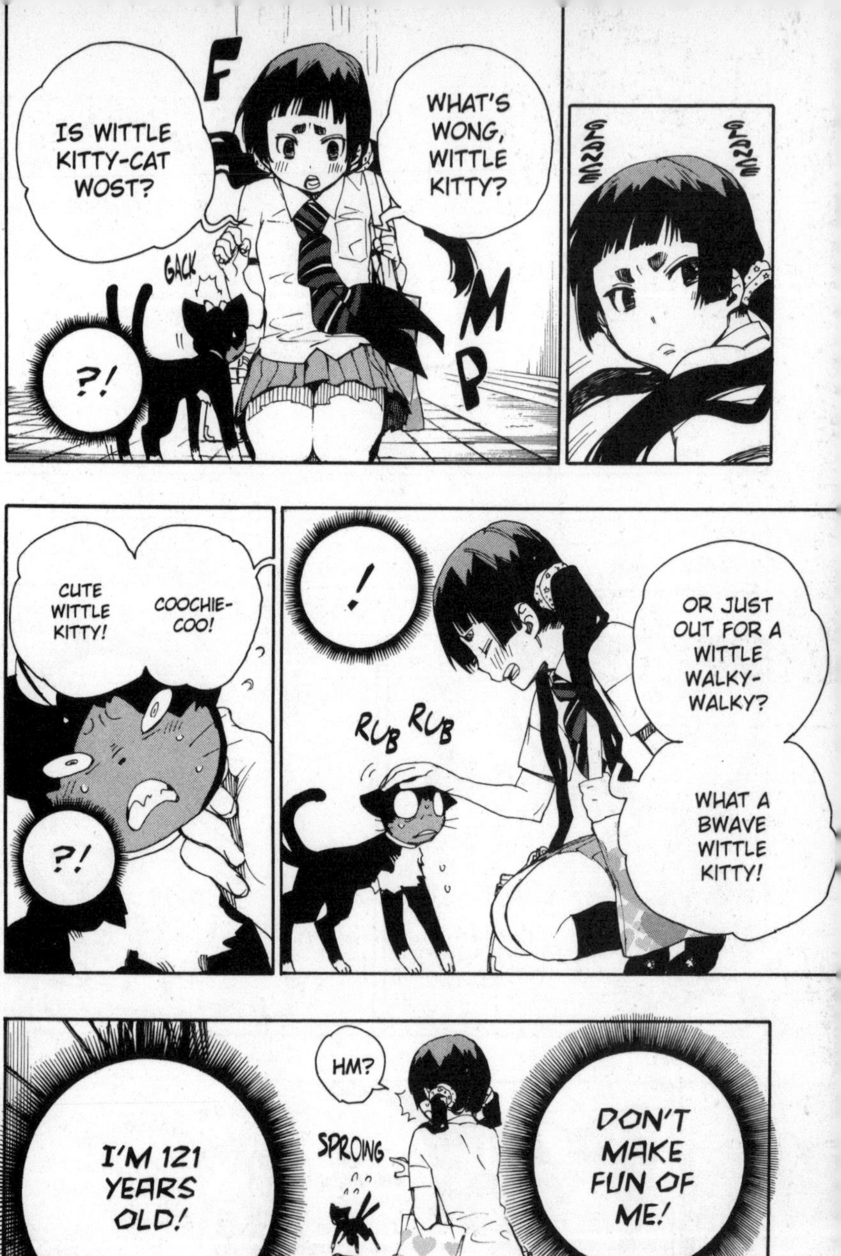
GLANCE
GLANCE
FMP
WHAT'S WONG, WITTLE KITTY?
IS WITTLE KITTY-CAT WOST?
GACK
?!
OR JUST OUT FOR A WITTLE WALKY-WALKY?
!
RUB RUB
WHAT A BWAVE WITTLE KITTY!
COOCHIE-COO!
CUTE WITTLE KITTY!
?!
DON'T MAKE FUN OF ME!
HM?
SPROING
I'M 121 YEARS OLD!

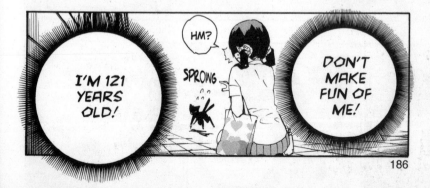

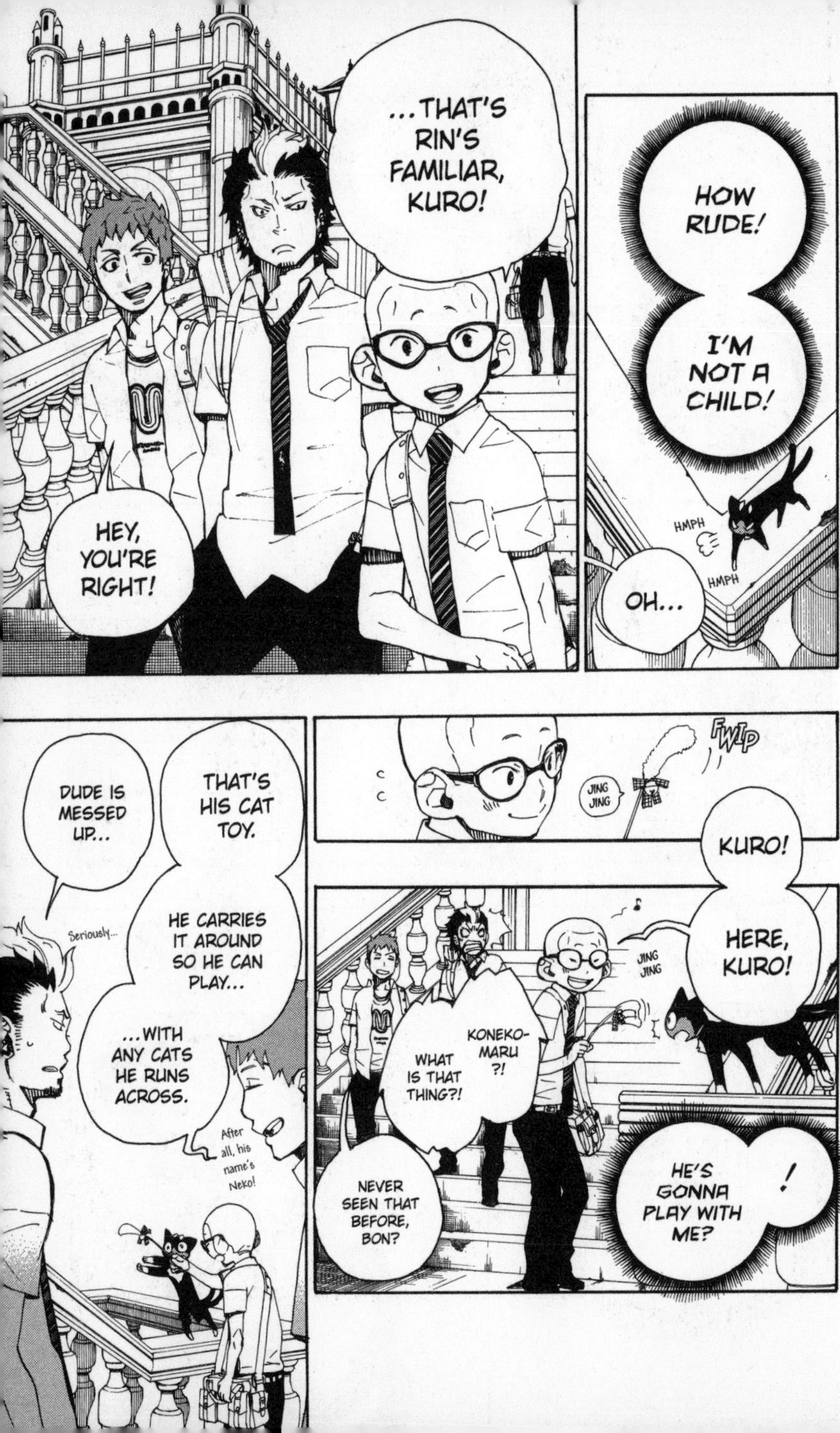
HOW RUDE!
I'M NOT A CHILD!
HMPH
HMPH
OH...
...THAT'S RIN'S FAMILIAR, KURO!
HEY, YOU'RE RIGHT!
FWIP
JING JING
KURO!
HERE, KURO!
JING JING
KONEKO-MARU?!
WHAT IS THAT THING?!
!
HE'S GONNA PLAY WITH ME?
NEVER SEEN THAT BEFORE, BON?
THAT'S HIS CAT TOY.
HE CARRIES IT AROUND SO HE CAN PLAY...
...WITH ANY CATS HE RUNS ACROSS.
DUDE IS MESSED UP...
Seriously...
After all, his name's Neko!

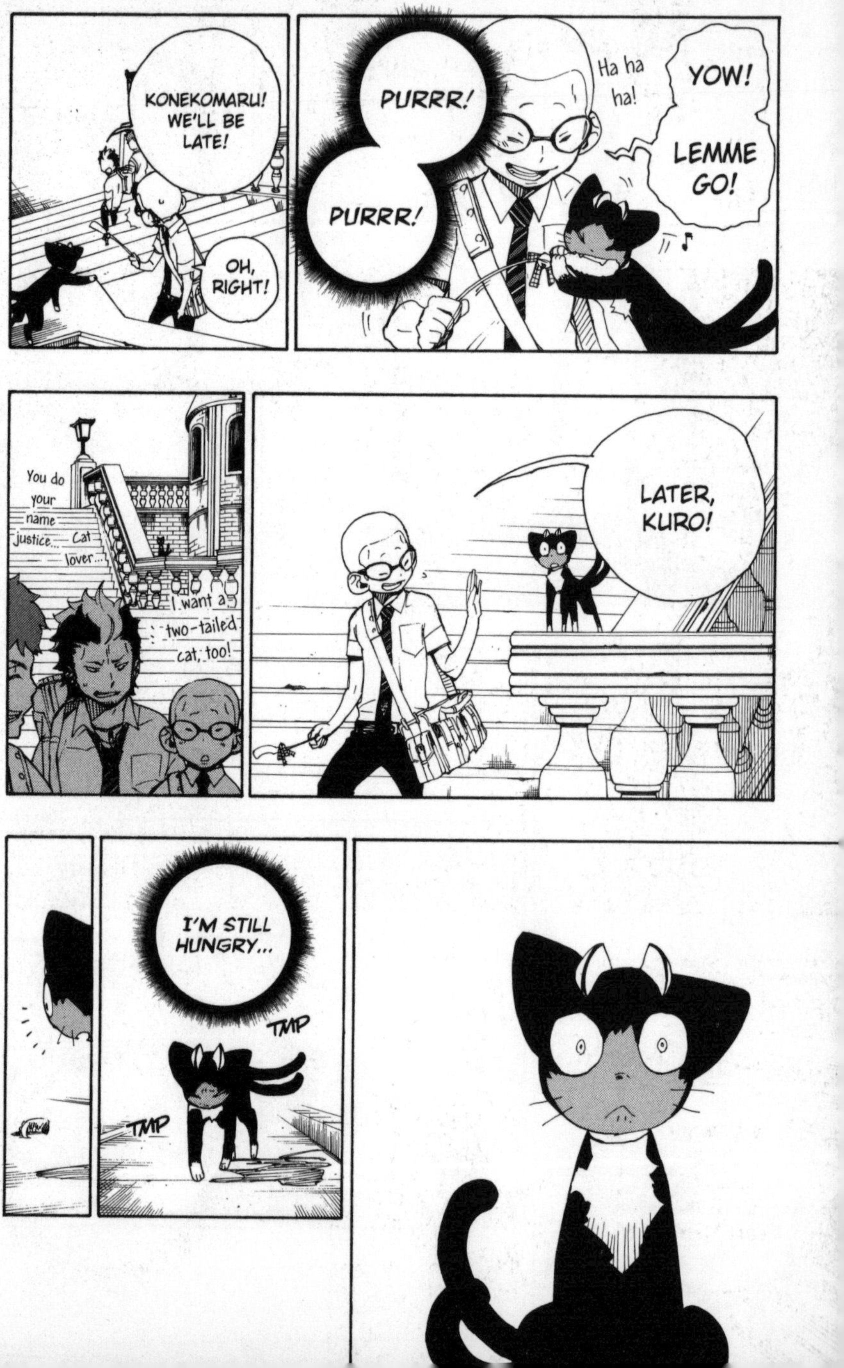
YOW!
LEMME GO!
Ha ha ha!
PURRR!
PURRR!
KONEKOMARU! WE'LL BE LATE!
OH, RIGHT!
LATER, KURO!
You do your name justice... Cat lover...
I want a two-tailed cat, too!
I'M STILL HUNGRY...
TMP
TMP

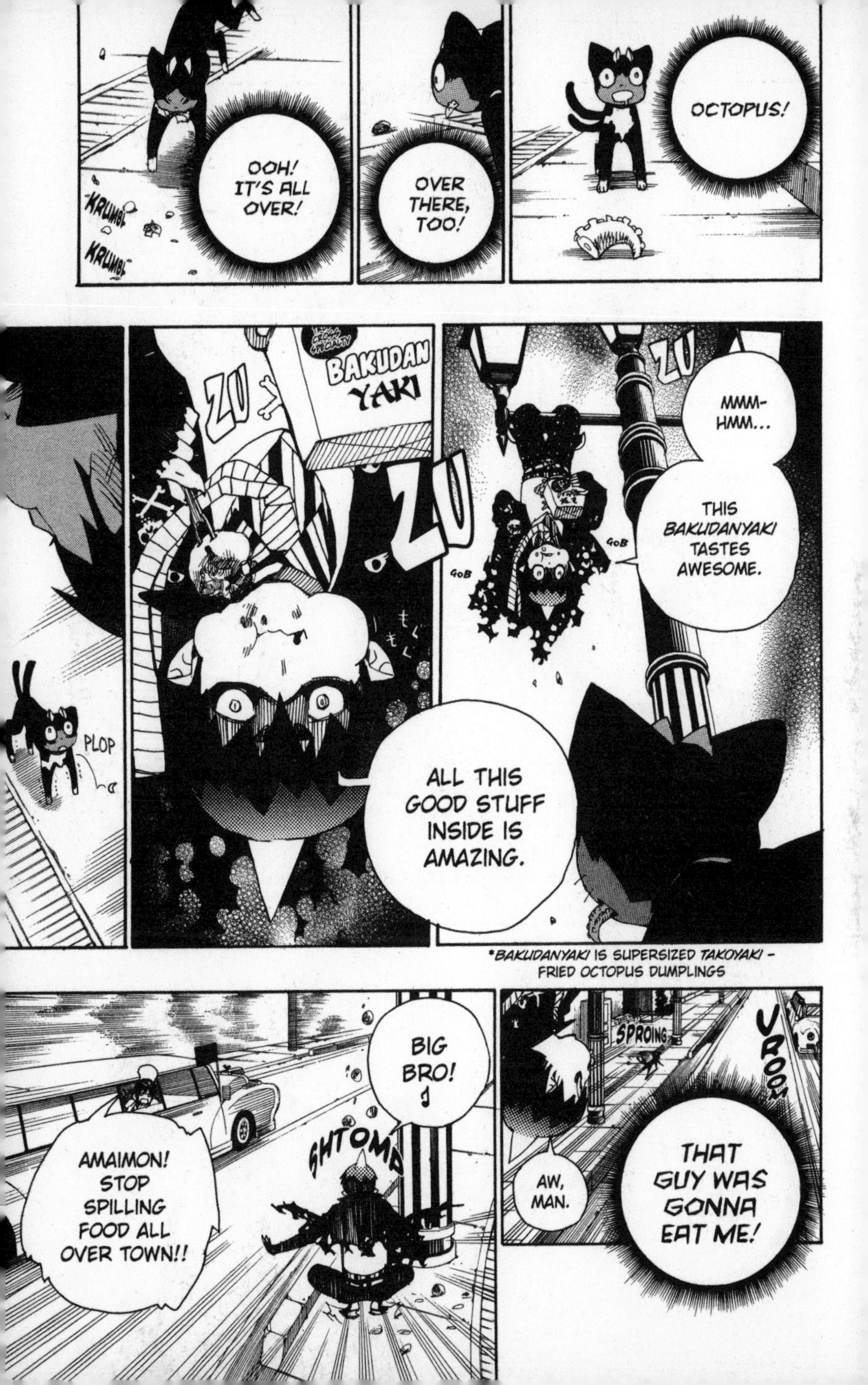
OCTOPUS!
OVER THERE, TOO!
OOH! IT'S ALL OVER!
KRUMB!
KRUMB!
MMM-HMM...
THIS BAKUDANYAKI TASTES AWESOME.
GOB
GOB
ZU
BAKUDAN YAKI
ZU
ZU
ALL THIS GOOD STUFF INSIDE IS AMAZING.
PLOP
VROOM
SPROING
THAT GUY WAS GONNA EAT ME!
AW, MAN.
BIG BRO! ♪
SHTOMP
AMAIMON! STOP SPILLING FOOD ALL OVER TOWN!!

**BAKUDANYAKI* IS SUPERSIZED *TAKOYAKI* – FRIED OCTOPUS DUMPLINGS

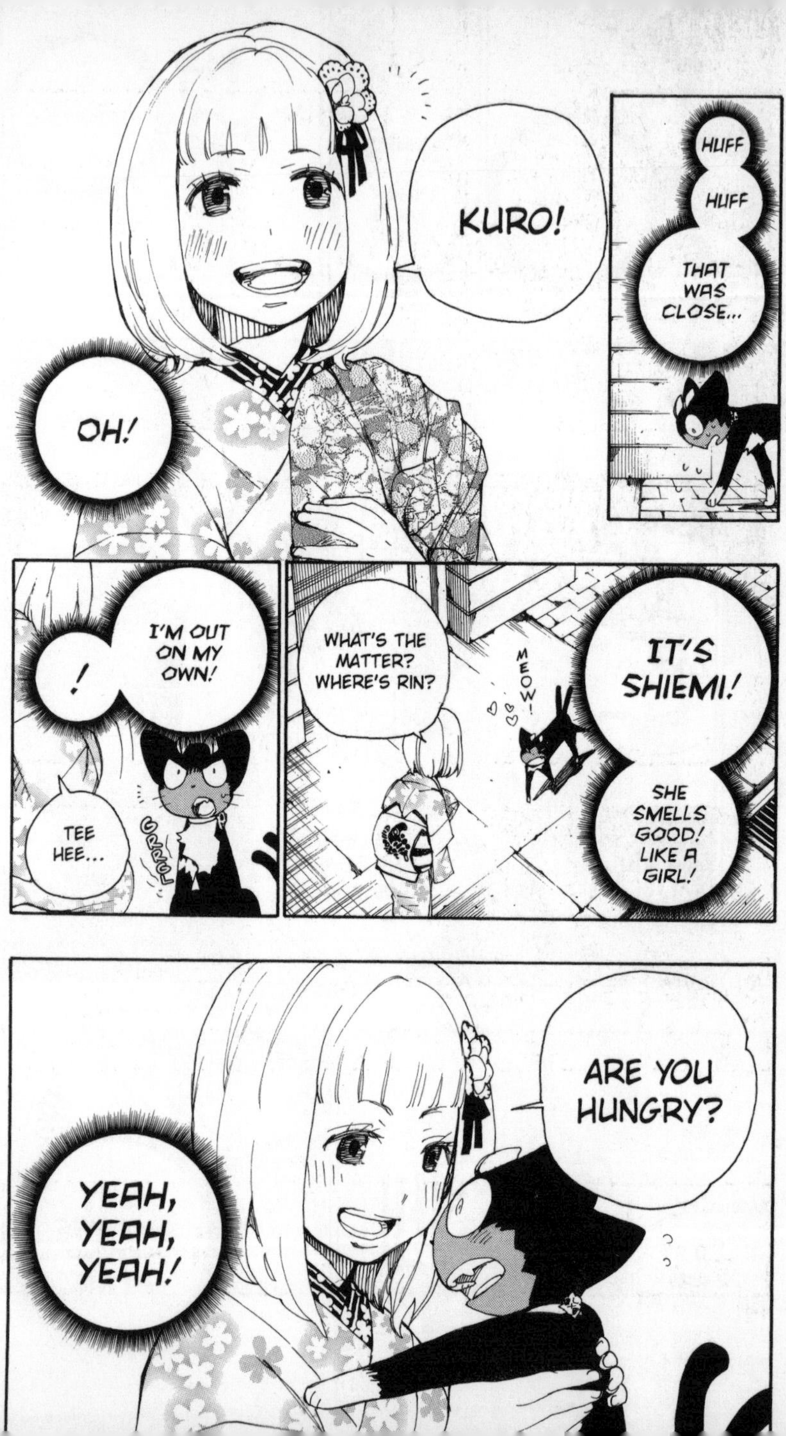
HUFF
HUFF
THAT WAS CLOSE...
KURO!
OH!
IT'S SHIEMI!
SHE SMELLS GOOD! LIKE A GIRL!
MEOW!
WHAT'S THE MATTER? WHERE'S RIN?
I'M OUT ON MY OWN!
!
TEE HEE...
GRRGL
ARE YOU HUNGRY?
YEAH, YEAH, YEAH!

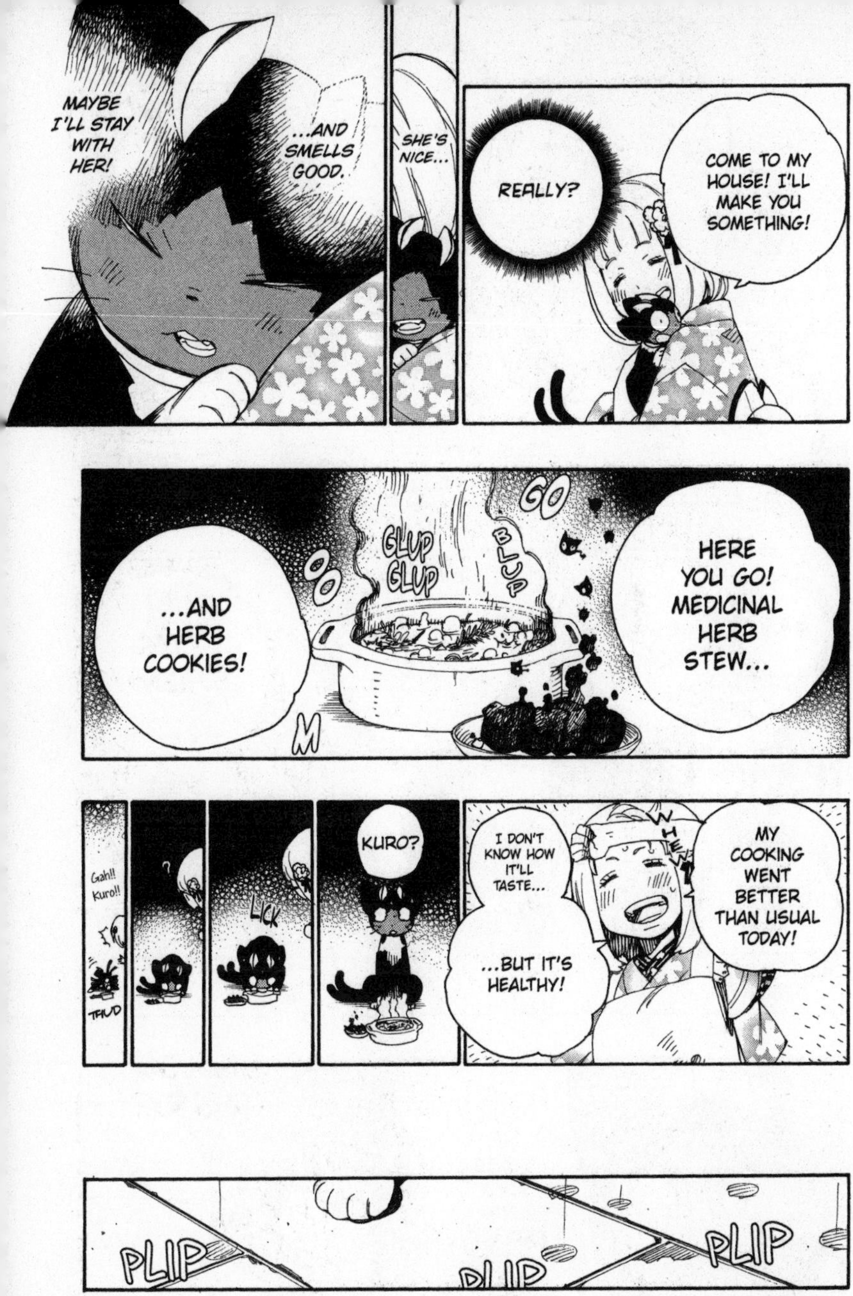

COME TO MY HOUSE! I'LL MAKE YOU SOMETHING!
REALLY?
SHE'S NICE...
...AND SMELLS GOOD.
MAYBE I'LL STAY WITH HER!
HERE YOU GO! MEDICINAL HERB STEW...
GO
BLUP
GLUP GLUP
OO
M
...AND HERB COOKIES!
MY COOKING WENT BETTER THAN USUAL TODAY!
I DON'T KNOW HOW IT'LL TASTE...
...BUT IT'S HEALTHY!
KURO?
LICK
Gah!! Kuro!!
THUD
PLIP
PLIP
PLIP

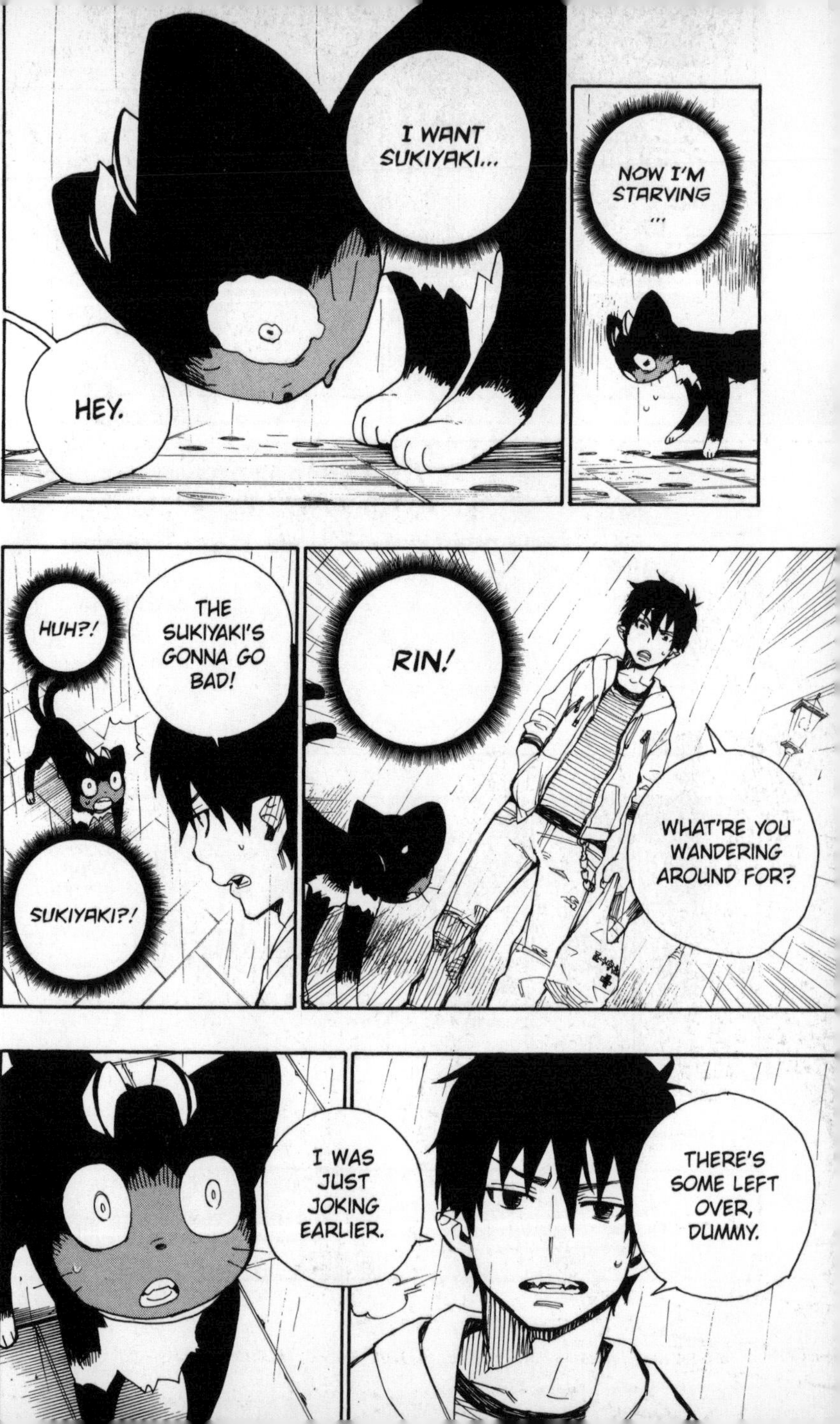
NOW I'M STARVING ...
I WANT SUKIYAKI...
HEY.
RIN!
WHAT'RE YOU WANDERING AROUND FOR?
THE SUKIYAKI'S GONNA GO BAD!
HUH?!
SUKIYAKI?!
THERE'S SOME LEFT OVER, DUMMY.
I WAS JUST JOKING EARLIER.

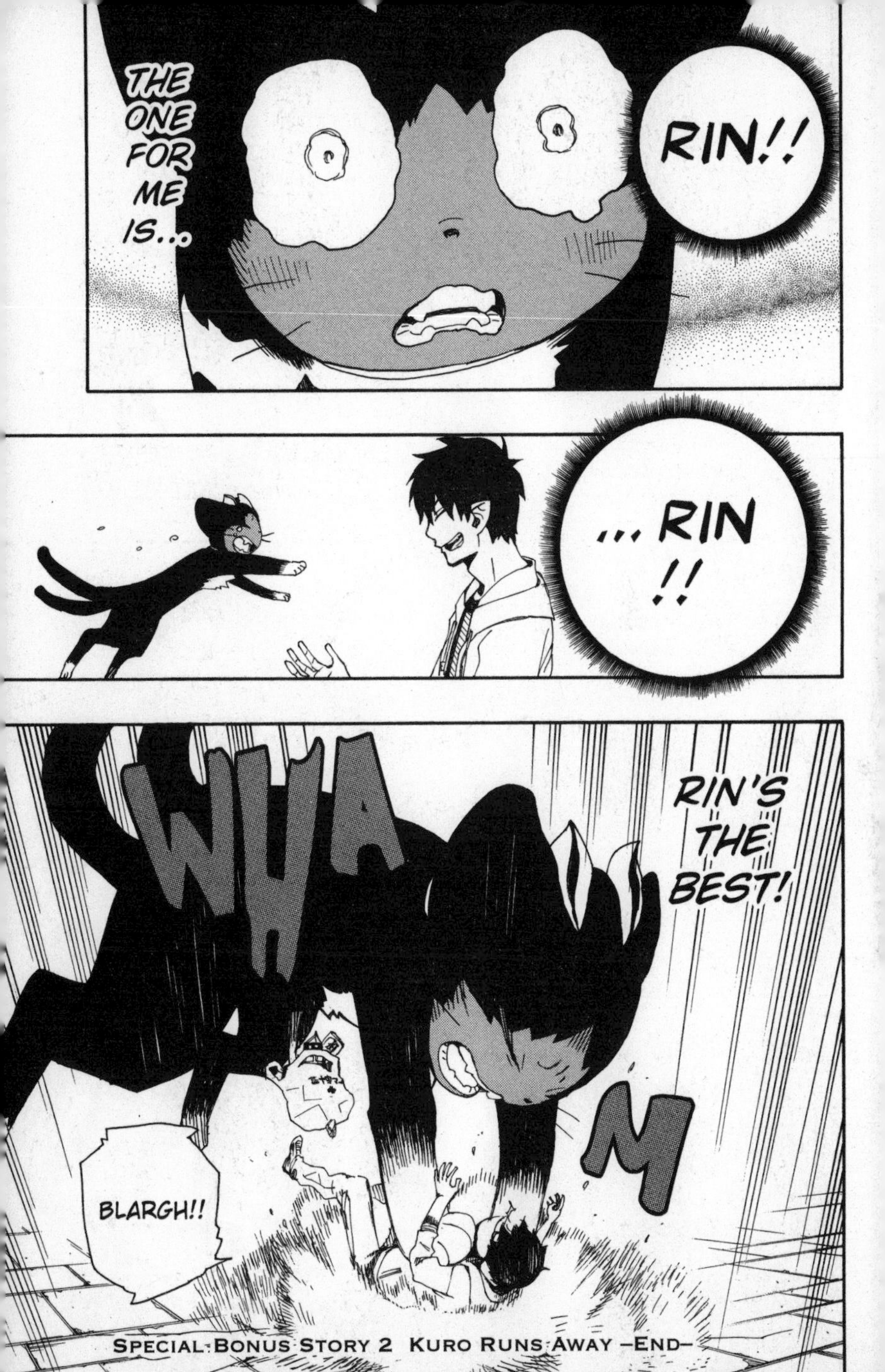
THE ONE FOR ME IS...
RIN!!
...RIN !!
RIN'S THE BEST!
WHAM
BLARGH!!
SPECIAL BONUS STORY 2 KURO RUNS AWAY –END–

Blue Exorcist Special Bonus Story 2 Kuro Runs Away

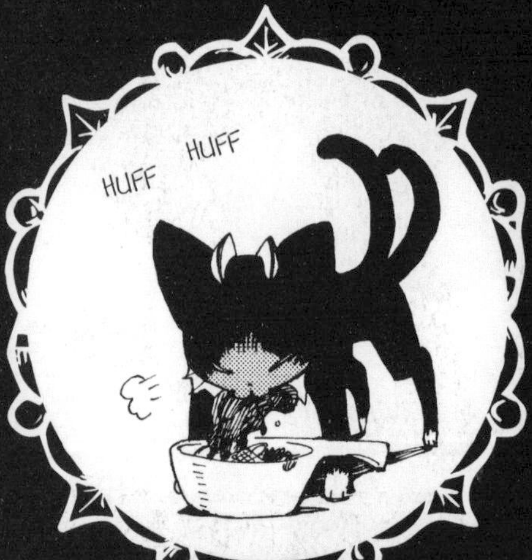
HUFF
HUFF

BONUS

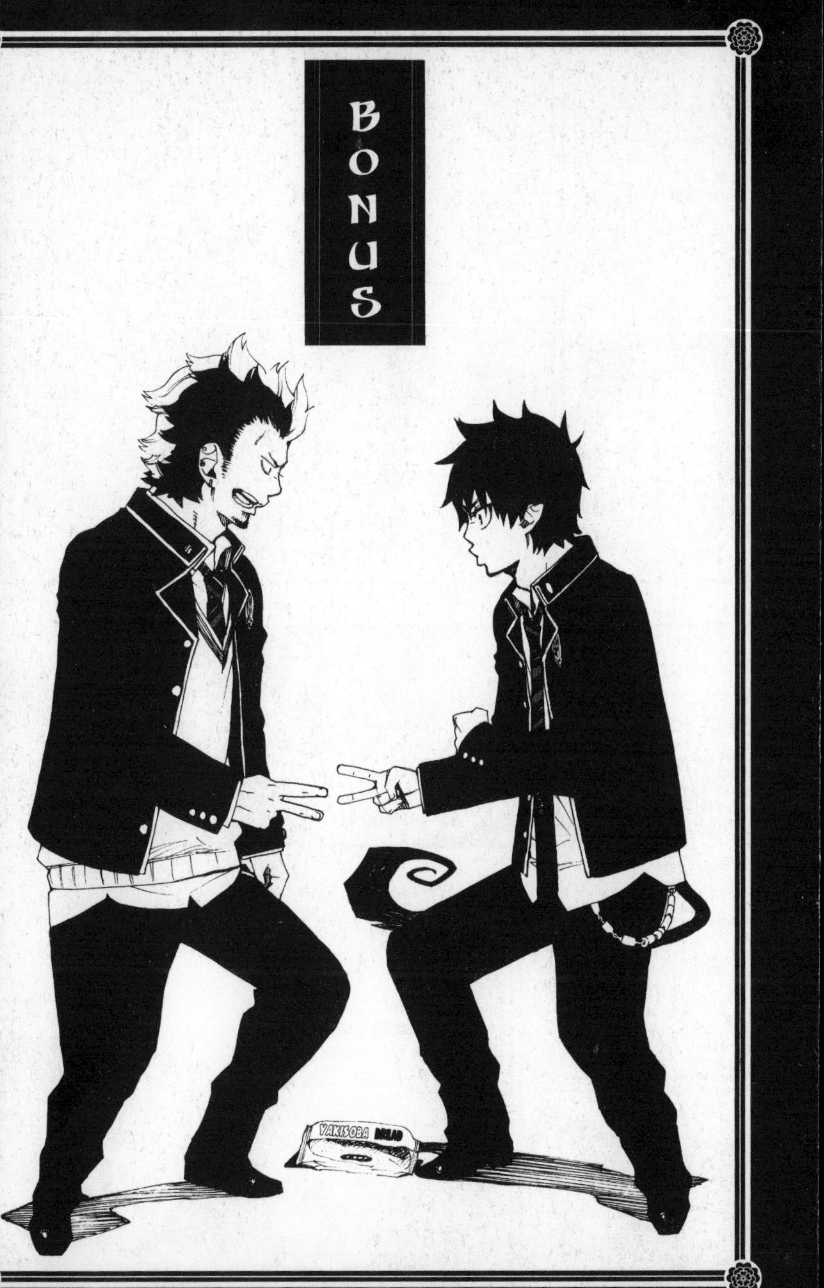
YAKISOBA BREAD

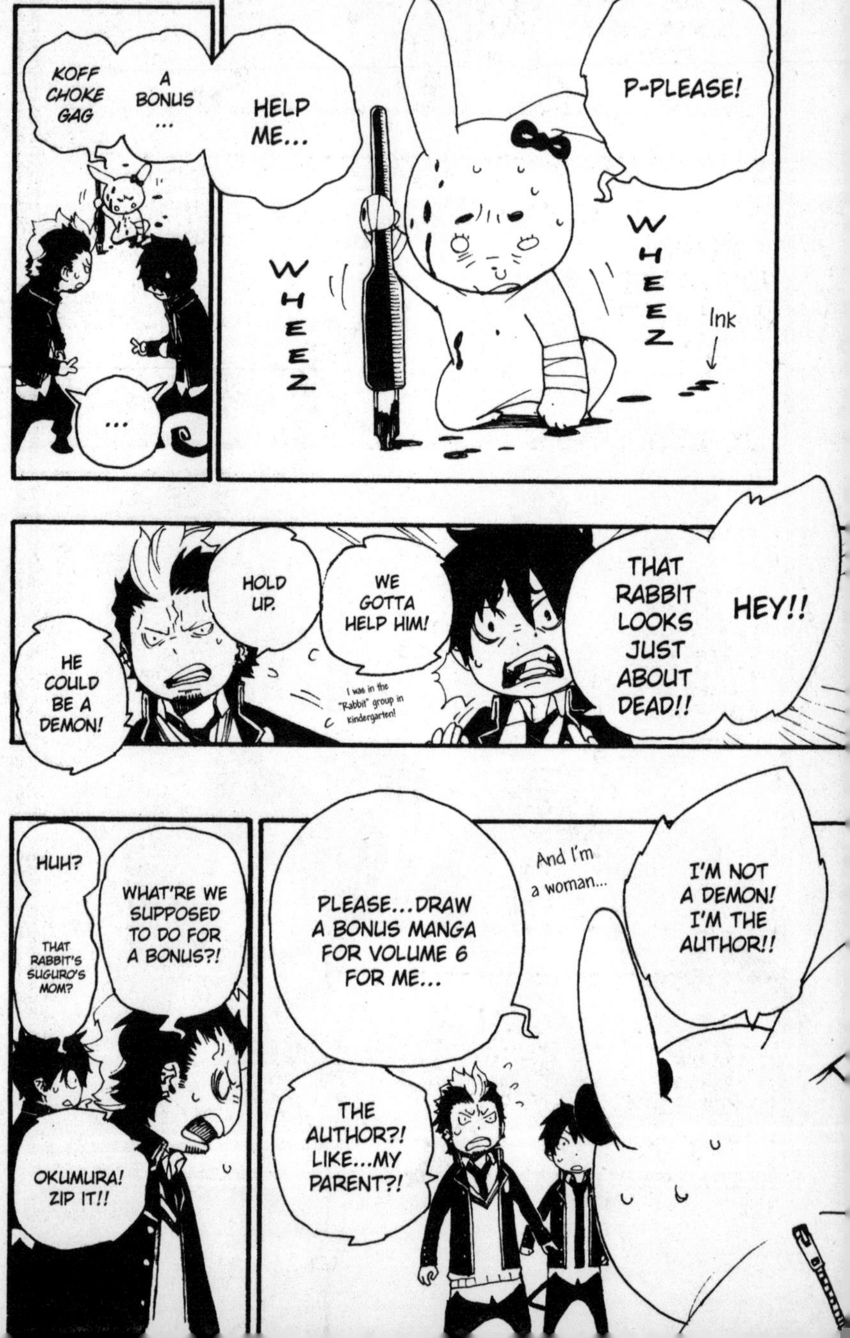
P-PLEASE!
WHEEZ
Ink
HELP ME...
WHEEZ
A BONUS ...
KOFF CHOKE GAG
...
HEY!!
THAT RABBIT LOOKS JUST ABOUT DEAD!!
WE GOTTA HELP HIM!
I was in the "Rabbit" group in kindergarten!
HOLD UP.
HE COULD BE A DEMON!
I'M NOT A DEMON! I'M THE AUTHOR!!
And I'm a woman...
PLEASE...DRAW A BONUS MANGA FOR VOLUME 6 FOR ME...
THE AUTHOR?! LIKE...MY PARENT?!
HUH?
WHAT'RE WE SUPPOSED TO DO FOR A BONUS?!
THAT RABBIT'S SUGURO'S MOM?
OKUMURA! ZIP IT!!

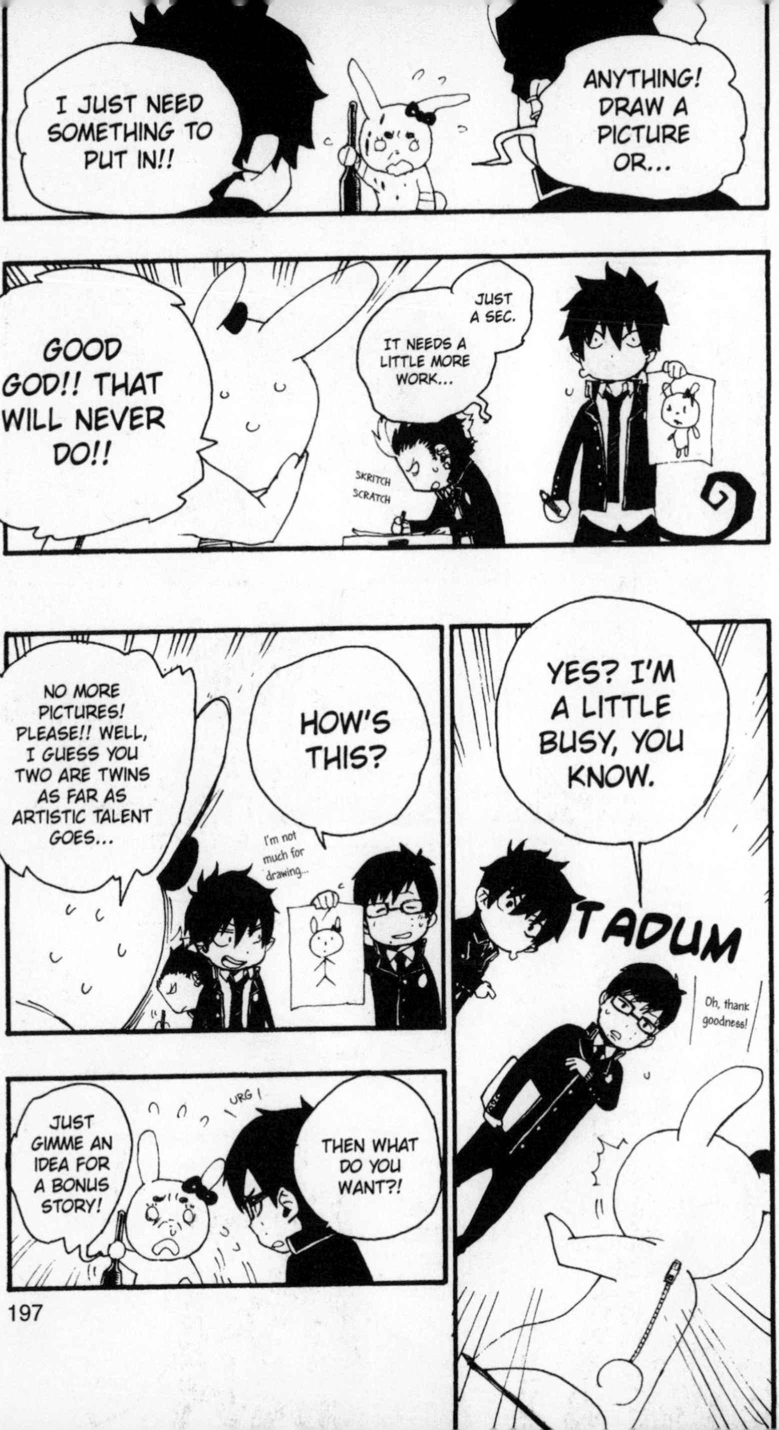
ANYTHING! DRAW A PICTURE OR...
I JUST NEED SOMETHING TO PUT IN!!
JUST A SEC.
IT NEEDS A LITTLE MORE WORK...
SKRITCH SCRATCH
GOOD GOD!! THAT WILL NEVER DO!!
YES? I'M A LITTLE BUSY, YOU KNOW.
TADUM
Oh, thank goodness!
HOW'S THIS?
I'm not much for drawing...
NO MORE PICTURES! PLEASE!! WELL, I GUESS YOU TWO ARE TWINS AS FAR AS ARTISTIC TALENT GOES...
THEN WHAT DO YOU WANT?!
URG!
JUST GIMME AN IDEA FOR A BONUS STORY!

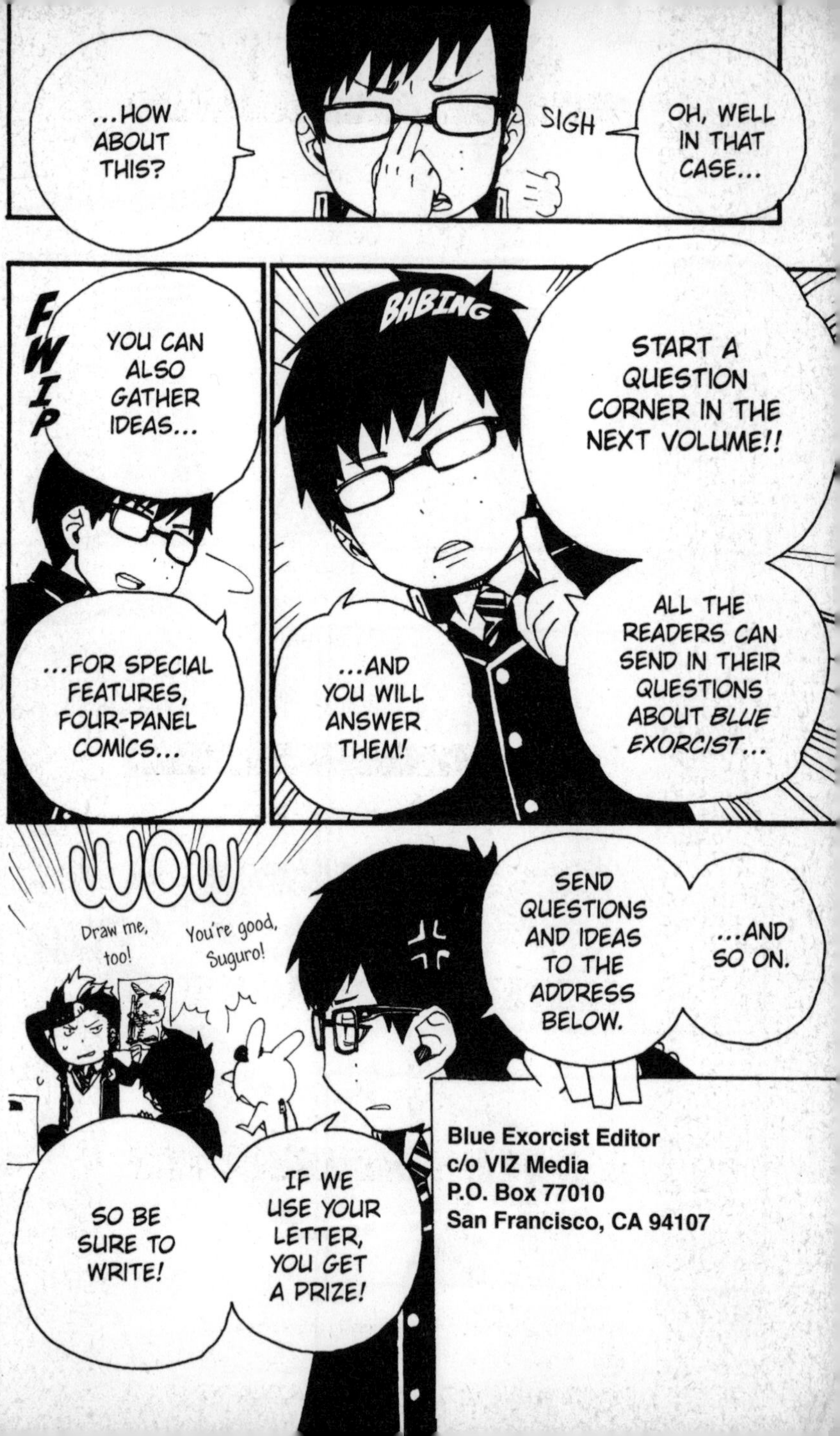
OH, WELL IN THAT CASE...
SIGH
...HOW ABOUT THIS?
BABING
START A QUESTION CORNER IN THE NEXT VOLUME!!
ALL THE READERS CAN SEND IN THEIR QUESTIONS ABOUT *BLUE EXORCIST*...
...AND YOU WILL ANSWER THEM!
FWIP
YOU CAN ALSO GATHER IDEAS...
...FOR SPECIAL FEATURES, FOUR-PANEL COMICS...
...AND SO ON.
SEND QUESTIONS AND IDEAS TO THE ADDRESS BELOW.
WOW
You're good, Suguro!
Draw me, too!
Blue Exorcist Editor
c/o VIZ Media
P.O. Box 77010
San Francisco, CA 94107
IF WE USE YOUR LETTER, YOU GET A PRIZE!
SO BE SURE TO WRITE!

BLUE EXORCIST 6

Art Assistants:

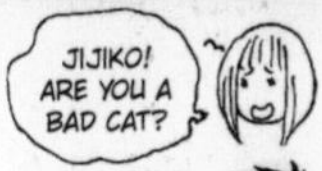
JIJIKO! ARE YOU A BAD CAT?

Shibu-tama

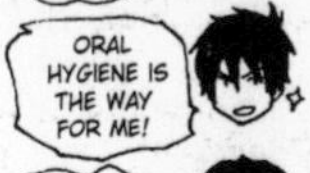
ORAL HYGIENE IS THE WAY FOR ME!

Uemura-san

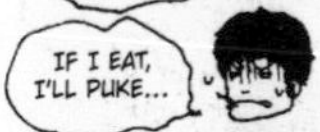
IF I EAT, I'LL PUKE...

Kimura-kun

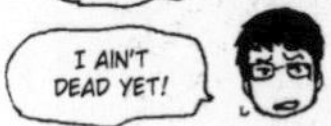
I AIN'T DEAD YET!

Hayashi-kun

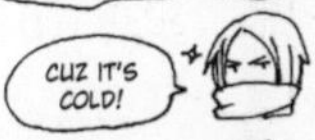
CUZ IT'S COLD!

Kawamura-san

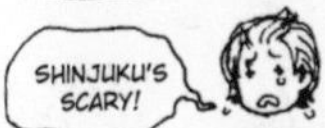
SHINJUKU'S SCARY!

Fukushi-san

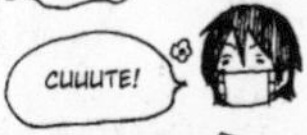
CUUUTE!

Yamanaka-san

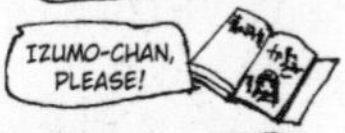
IZUMO-CHAN, PLEASE!

Araki-san

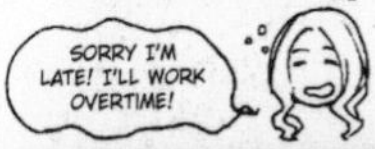
SORRY I'M LATE! I'LL WORK OVERTIME!

Mintia

Editor:

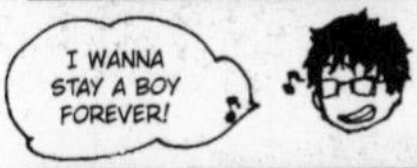
I WANNA STAY A BOY FOREVER!

Shihei Rin

Graphic Novel Editor:

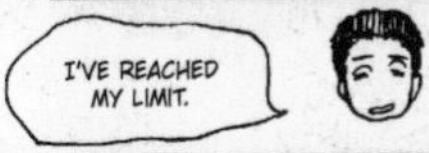
I'VE REACHED MY LIMIT.

Ryusuke Kuroki

Graphic Novel Design:

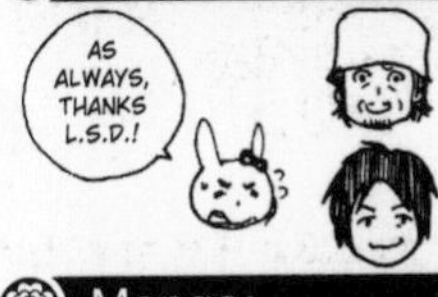
AS ALWAYS, THANKS L.S.D.!

Hideaki Shimada

Masaaki Tsunoda (L.S.D.)

Manga:

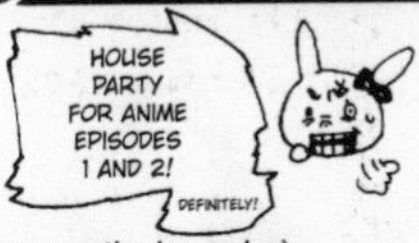
HOUSE PARTY FOR ANIME EPISODES 1 AND 2!
DEFINITELY!

Kazue Kato

(in no particular order)
(Note: The caricatures and statements are from memory!)

Continued in Volume 7! Please, keep reading!

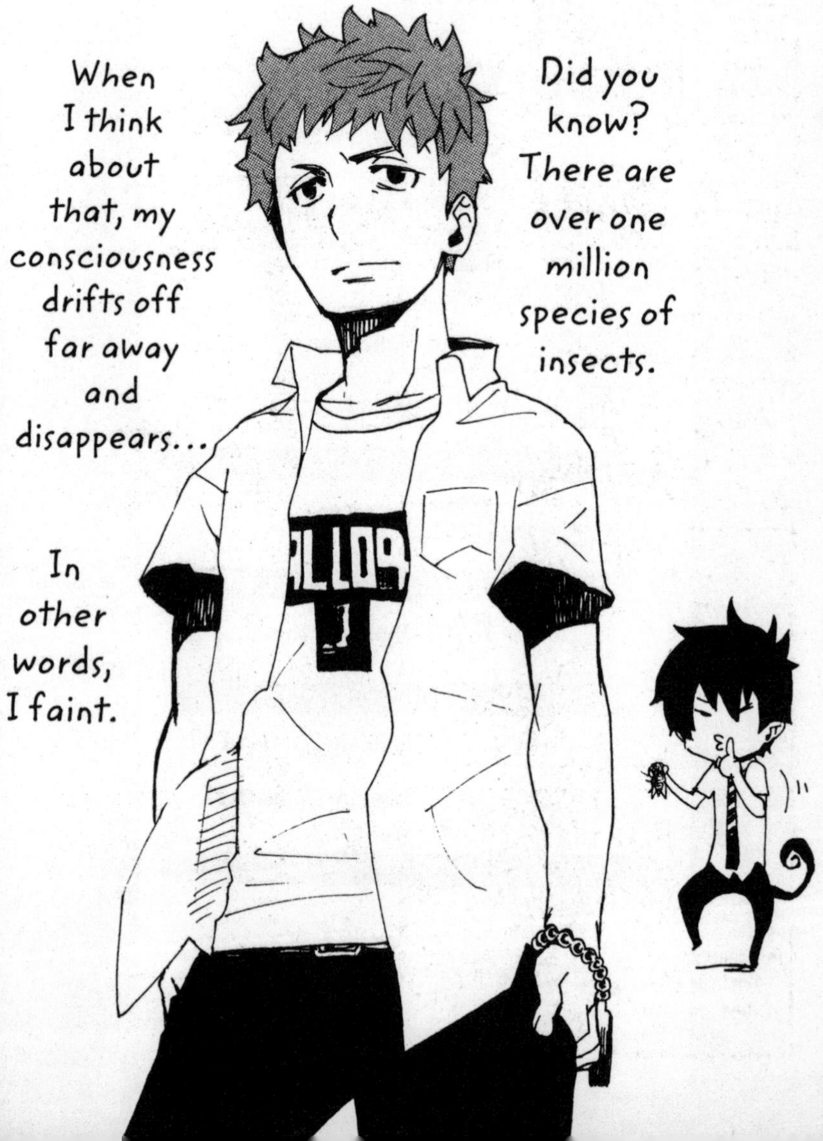
Did you know? There are over one million species of insects.
When I think about that, my consciousness drifts off far away and disappears...
In other words, I faint.

This Is What True Fear Is

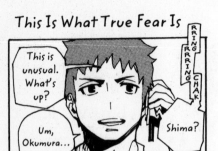

RRRING
RRRING
CHAK
Shima?
Um, Okumura...
This is unusual. What's up?
I'm facing my biggest crisis this year.
Huh?!
Bon and Koneko turned their backs on me. You're the only one I can count on!
TWITCH
TWITCH
What've I gotta do?
Don't hang up, okay?
I need to hear your voice until I overcome this. Easy, right?
FLK
FLK
Huh? No way!
Just be brave, man!
KLIK
BEEEP
BEEEP
GASP
I don't remember how I got into my room that day.

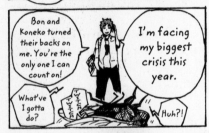

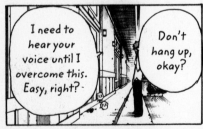

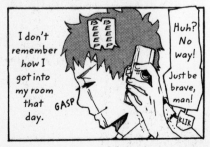

Gyaiiee!!!

It's g-gonna be an anime?!

KAZUE KATO

WE'VE REACHED THE MIDDLE OF THIS LONG STORY ARC. IT GOES ON FOR JUST A BIT LONGER!

AND SOMETHING AMAZING HAPPENED. BLUE EXORCIST *IS GOING TO BE AN ANIME!* I CAN'T WAIT!

NOW ENJOY VOLUME 6!

BLUE EXORCIST

BLUE EXORCIST VOL. 6
SHONEN JUMP ADVANCED Manga Edition

STORY & ART BY KAZUE KATO

Translation & English Adaptation/John Werry
Touch-up Art & Lettering/John Hunt, Primary Graphix
Cover & Interior Design/Sam Elzway
Editor/Mike Montesa

AO NO EXORCIST © 2009 by Kazue Kato
All rights reserved.
First published in Japan in 2009 by SHUEISHA Inc., Tokyo.
English translation rights arranged by SHUEISHA Inc.

Printed in the U.S.A.

Published by VIZ Media, LLC
P.O. Box 77010
San Francisco, CA 94107

10 9 8 7 6 5 4 3 2 1
First printing, February 2012

In the next volume...

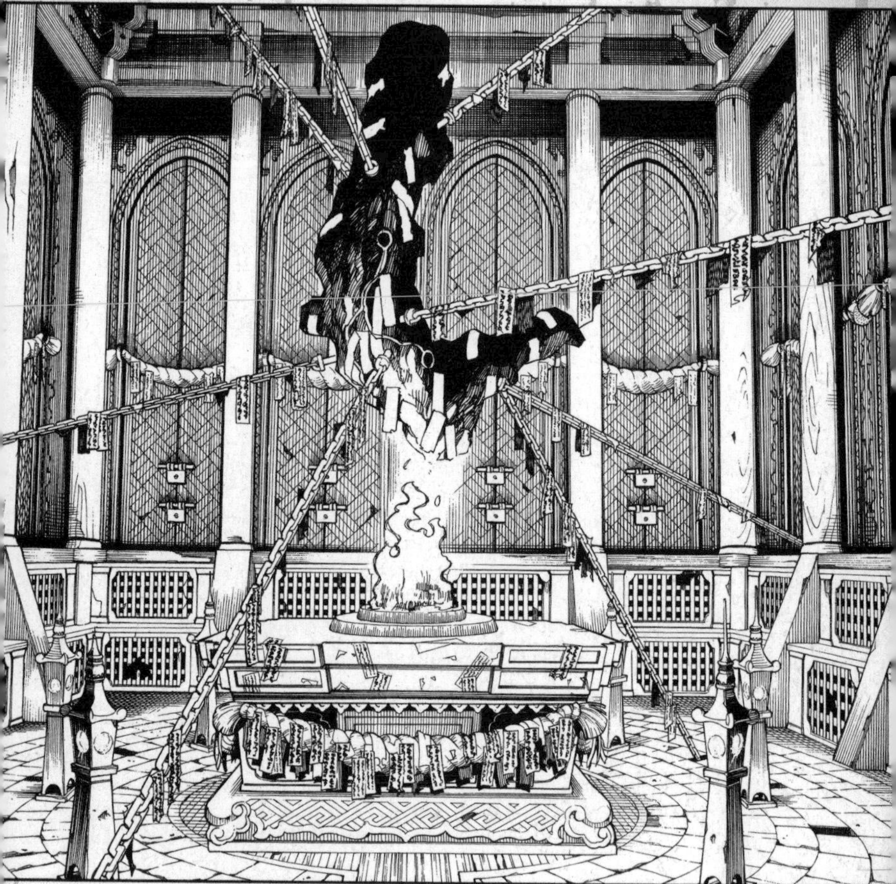

Mamushi and Todo now have both eyes of the Impure King and are headed for the temple that was once the center of the Myodha sect. Mamushi wants to seal the eyes away, but may be too late to realize Todo's true purpose—the awakening of the Impure King! Meanwhile, Rin learns more about Father Fujimoto's connection to Tatsuma and the origin of the Koma Sword. Rin will need the weapon and all of his strength to face the terrible power of the Impure King!

Coming April 2012!

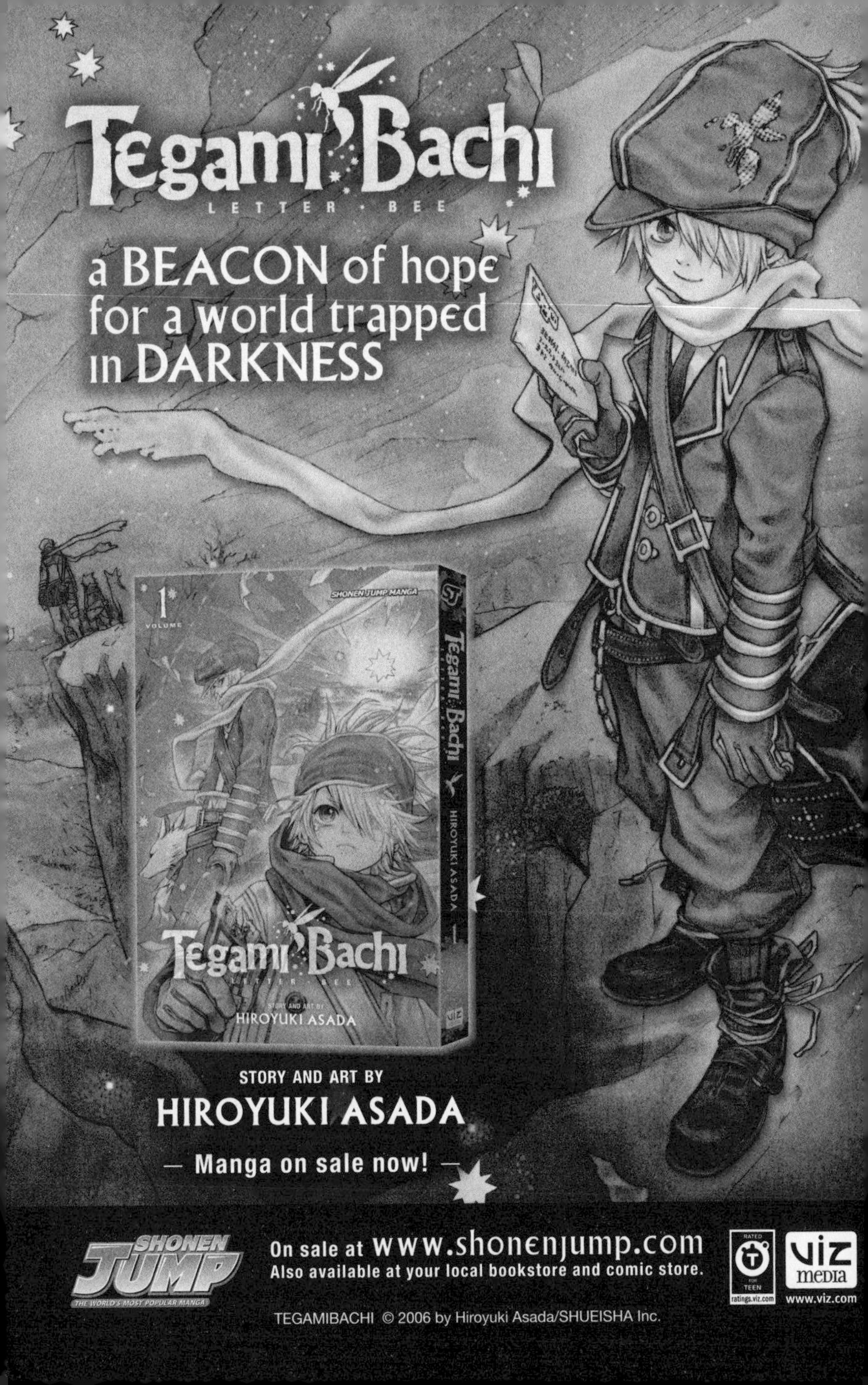
Tegami Bachi
LETTER · BEE
a BEACON of hope for a world trapped in DARKNESS
SHONEN JUMP MANGA
1 VOLUME
Tegami Bachi
LETTER BEE
STORY AND ART BY
HIROYUKI ASADA
STORY AND ART BY
HIROYUKI ASADA
— Manga on sale now! —
SHONEN JUMP
THE WORLD'S MOST POPULAR MANGA
On sale at www.shonenjump.com
Also available at your local bookstore and comic store.
RATED T FOR TEEN
ratings.viz.com
VIZ MEDIA
www.viz.com
TEGAMIBACHI © 2006 by Hiroyuki Asada/SHUEISHA Inc.

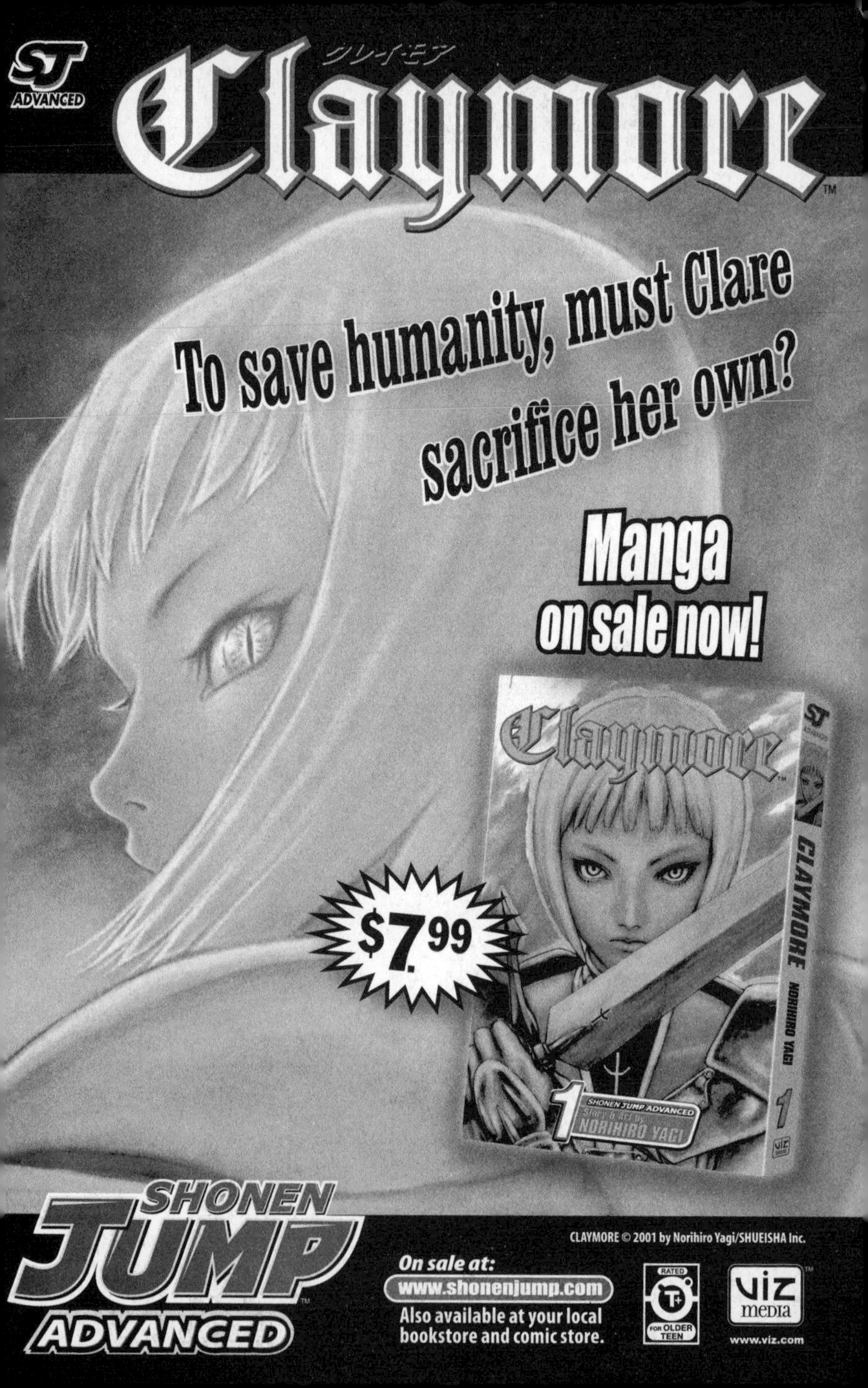
SJ ADVANCED
Claymore™
To save humanity, must Clare sacrifice her own?
Manga on sale now!
$7.99
Claymore
CLAYMORE
NORIHIRO YAGI
1 SHONEN JUMP ADVANCED Story & Art by NORIHIRO YAGI
SHONEN JUMP ADVANCED
CLAYMORE © 2001 by Norihiro Yagi/SHUEISHA Inc.
On sale at:
www.shonenjump.com
Also available at your local bookstore and comic store.
RATED T+ FOR OLDER TEEN
viz media
www.viz.com

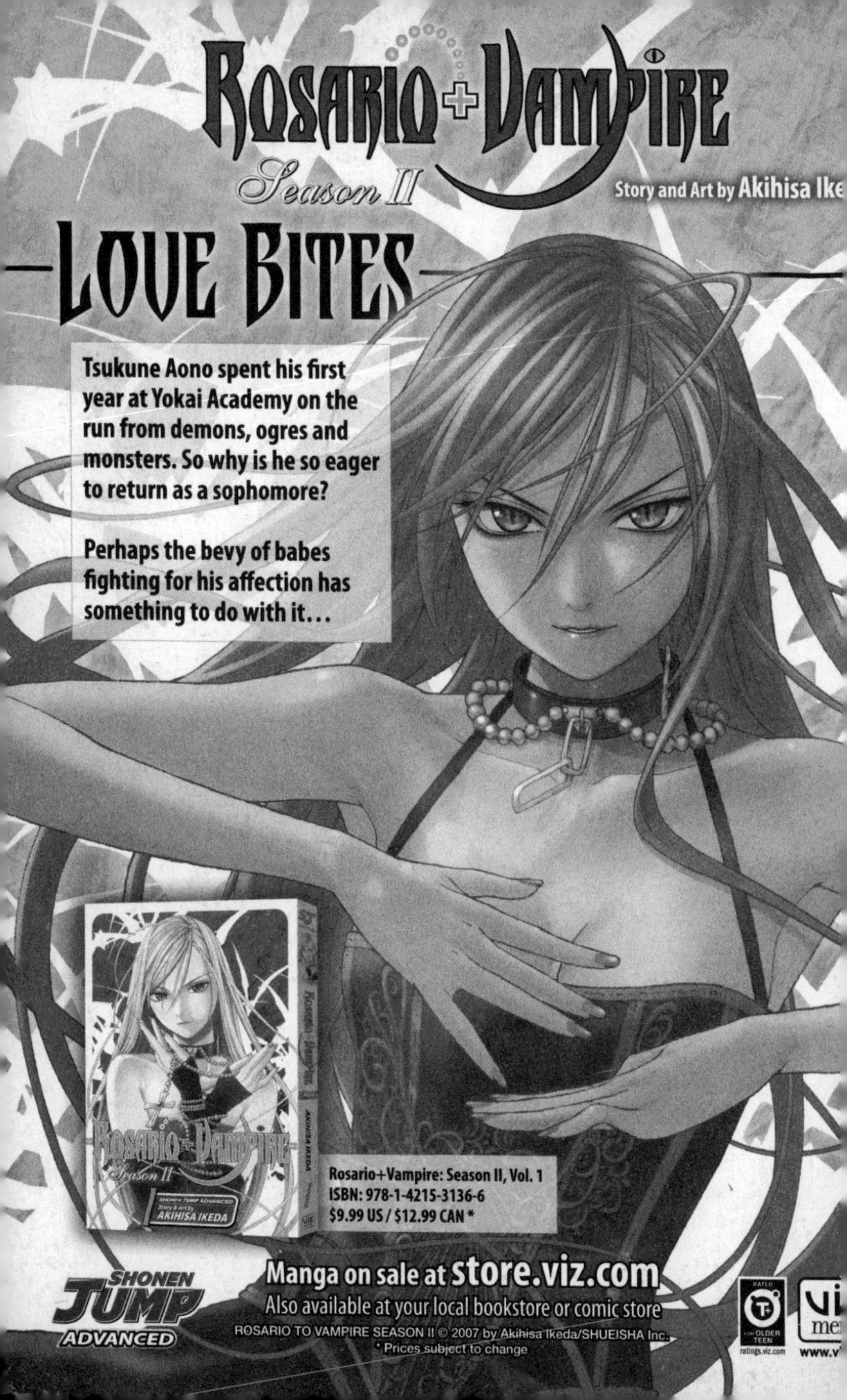
ROSARIO+VAMPIRE
Season II
Story and Art by Akihisa Ike
LOVE BITES
Tsukune Aono spent his first year at Yokai Academy on the run from demons, ogres and monsters. So why is he so eager to return as a sophomore?
Perhaps the bevy of babes fighting for his affection has something to do with it…
ROSARIO+VAMPIRE Season II
SHONEN JUMP ADVANCED
Story & Art by AKIHISA IKEDA
Rosario+Vampire: Season II, Vol. 1
ISBN: 978-1-4215-3136-6
$9.99 US / $12.99 CAN *
SHONEN JUMP ADVANCED
Manga on sale at store.viz.com
Also available at your local bookstore or comic store
ROSARIO TO VAMPIRE SEASON II © 2007 by Akihisa Ikeda/SHUEISHA Inc.
* Prices subject to change
RATED T+ FOR OLDER TEEN
ratings.viz.com

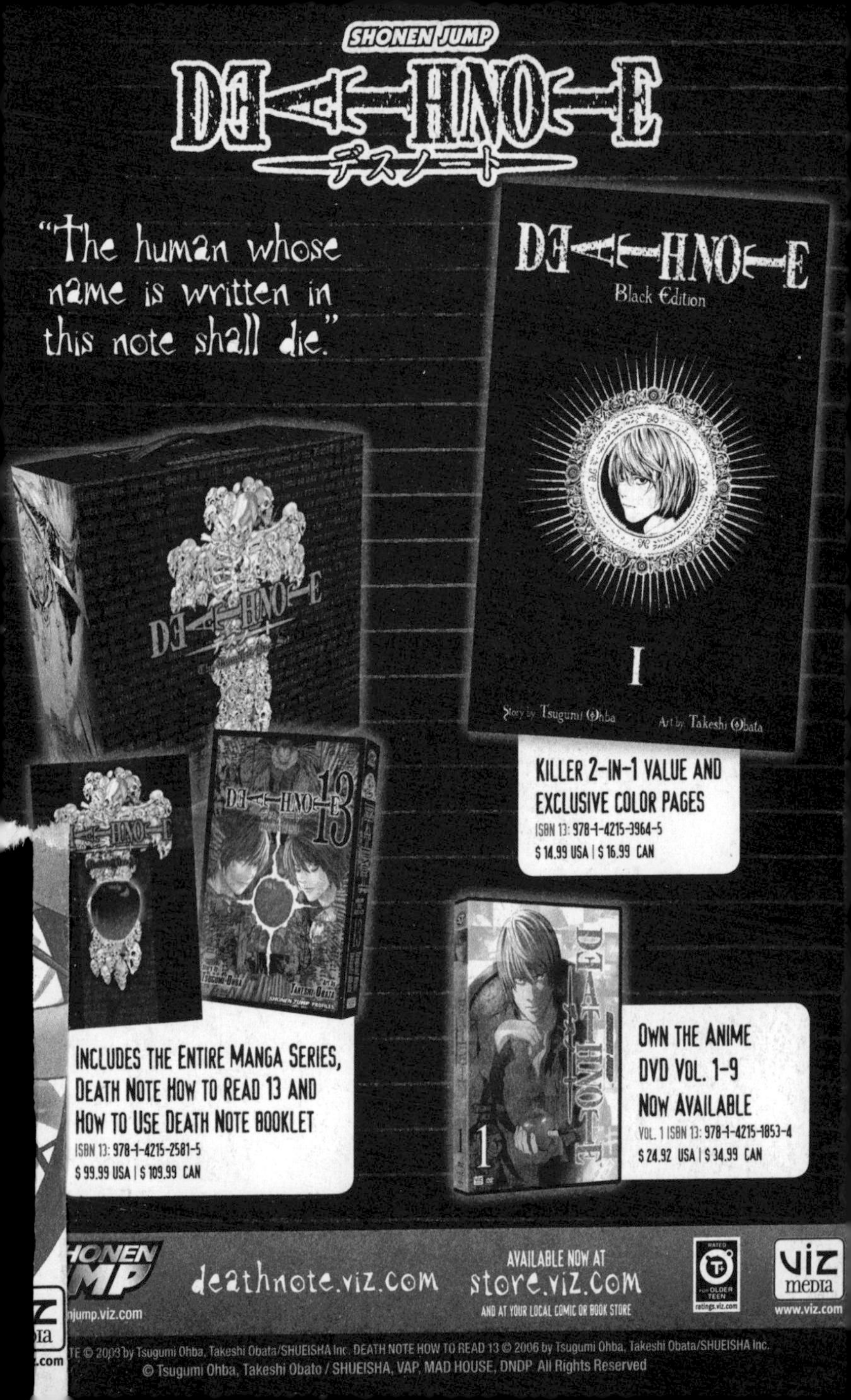
SHONEN JUMP
DEATH NOTE
デスノート
"The human whose name is written in this note shall die."
DEATH NOTE
Black Edition
I
Story by Tsugumi Ohba
Art by Takeshi Obata
KILLER 2-IN-1 VALUE AND EXCLUSIVE COLOR PAGES
ISBN 13: 978-1-4215-3964-5
$ 14.99 USA | $ 16.99 CAN
INCLUDES THE ENTIRE MANGA SERIES, DEATH NOTE HOW TO READ 13 AND HOW TO USE DEATH NOTE BOOKLET
ISBN 13: 978-1-4215-2581-5
$ 99.99 USA | $ 109.99 CAN
OWN THE ANIME DVD VOL. 1-9 NOW AVAILABLE
VOL. 1 ISBN 13: 978-1-4215-1853-4
$ 24.92 USA | $ 34.99 CAN
HONEN JUMP
njump.viz.com
deathnote.viz.com
AVAILABLE NOW AT
store.viz.com
AND AT YOUR LOCAL COMIC OR BOOK STORE
RATED T+ FOR OLDER TEEN
ratings.viz.com
VIZ media
www.viz.com
TE © 2003 by Tsugumi Ohba, Takeshi Obata/SHUEISHA Inc. DEATH NOTE HOW TO READ 13 © 2006 by Tsugumi Ohba, Takeshi Obata/SHUEISHA Inc.
© Tsugumi Ohba, Takeshi Obato / SHUEISHA, VAP, MAD HOUSE, DNDP All Rights Reserved